THE
TECHNOLOGICAL
ARSENAL

EMERGING DEFENSE
CAPABILITIES

EDITED BY WILLIAM C. MARTEL

SMITHSONIAN INSTITUTION PRESS
WASHINGTON AND LONDON

To my children, William and Catherine

© 2001 by Smithsonian Institution
All rights reserved

Copy editor: Terry Belanger
Production editor: Robert A. Poarch
Design by Janice Wheeler

Library of Congress Cataloging-in-Publication Data

The technological arsenal : emerging defense capabilities / edited by William C. Martel
 p. cm.
Includes bibliographical references and index.
ISBN 1-56098-961-0 (alk. paper)
 1. Weapons systems—United States—Forecasting. 2. Military art and science—Technological innovations—United States. 3. Directed-energy weapons. 4. Target acquisition. 5. Command and control systems—United States. I. Martel, William C.
UF503.T43 2001
355.8'0973—dc21   00-047099

British Library Cataloguing-in-Publication Data is available

Manufactured in the United States of America
06 05 04 03 02 01   5 4 3 2 1

The paper used in this book meets the requirements of American National Standard for Information Sciences—Permanence of Paper for Printed Library Materials, ANSI Z39.48-1984. Binding materials were selected for strength and durability.

Contents

Acknowledgments   v
List of Abbreviations   vii
Introduction   xi
William C. Martel

PART ONE:
Directed Energy
 1.   **Lasers in Space: Technological Options for Warfare**   3
       Mark E. Rogers
 2.   **Lasers and Missile Defense**   20
       William H. Possel
 3.   **Airborne and Space-Based Lasers**   38
       Kenneth W. Barker
 4.   **Directed-Energy and Fleet Defense**   55
       William J. McCarthy
 5.   **High-Power Microwaves and Modern Warfare**   90
       Eileen M. Walling

PART TWO:
Military Targeting and Its Effects
 6.   **Cruise Missiles and War**   107
       David J. Nicholls
 7.   **Nonlethal Technologies and Military Strategy**   129
       Joseph W. Siniscalchi

8. Space Operations Vehicles: Commercial and Military Applications 153

John E. Ward Jr.

9. Unmanned Aerial Vehicles 173

David B. Glade II

PART THREE:
Command and Control

10. Directing War from Home 199

Scott M. Britten

11. Computers and Controlling War 220

William B. McClure

12. Information Warfare and Deterrence 241

Richard J. Harknett

Conclusion: Technological Foundations of Military Power 257

William C. Martel

Contributors **269**

Index **277**

Acknowledgments

As with all books, this work is the product of the efforts of many individuals. I am indebted to the anonymous outside reviewers for their many insightful comments and suggestions. My deepest thanks go two people. The first is Ted Hailes at the Center for Strategy and Technology at the Air War College, without whose superb intellectual contributions this work could not have been written. The second is my editor at Smithsonian, Mark Gatlin, who envisioned this project from the beginning, and whose insight and perseverance were a constant source of inspiration and support.

In addition, I would like to express my gratitude and appreciation to Nicole Sloan, Robert A. Poarch, and Annette Windhorn and the marketing staff at Smithsonian for their unflagging dedication and support during the production of this book. Finally, I want to thank my copyeditor, Terry Belanger, for her hard work on the manuscript. It has been a pleasure working with all of these individuals.

All of the contributors to this work are united in their view that we could not have completed this project without the dedication and support of our colleagues in the defense establishment who work so diligently to protect the national interest.

Abbreviations

ABL	airborne laser
ABM	antiballistic missile
ACO	airspace control order
AFSPC	Air Force Space Command
AGOS	Air Ground Operations School
ALL	Airborne Laser Laboratory
ANSI	American National Standards Institute
AOA	Airborne Optical Adjunct
ARG	amphibious ready group
ARPANET	Advanced Research Projects Agency Network
ASAT	antisatellite
ASCI	Accelerated Strategic Computing Initiative
ATO	air tasking order
ATP/FC	acquisition, tracking, pointing, and fire control
AWACS	Airborne Warning and Control System
BDA	battle damage assessment
BMDO	Ballistic Missile Defense Organization
BW	biological warfare
CAP	combat air patrol
CCWC	Certain Conventional Weapons Convention
C4I	command, control, communications, computers, and intelligence
CINC	commander in chief
COIL	chemical oxygen iodine laser

CONOPS	concept of operations
CONUS	continental United States
CTAPS	Contingency Theater Automated Planning System
CVN	designation for aircraft carrier, nuclear
CW	chemical warfare; also, continuous wave
CWIS	close-in weapon system
DAOC	Distributed Air Operations Center
DARPA	Defense Advanced Research Projects Agency
DCS	Deputy Chief of Staff
DE ATAC	Directed-Energy Applications for Tactical Airborne Contact
D4	deny, disrupt, damage, and destroy
D5	deny, disrupt, damage, destroy, and defend
DIAL	differential absorption laser radar
DO	Directorate of Operations
DOD	Department of Defense
DOMN	Directorate of Operations, Nuclear Operations, and Future Concepts Branch
DRS	Director of Requirements (Space and Support)
EELV	evolved expendable launch vehicle
EMP	electromagnetic pulse
ENIAC	electronic numerical integrator and computer
EO	electro-optical
FSU	former Soviet Union
GBL	ground-based laser
GCCS	Global Command and Control System
GPS	Global Positioning System
HABE	high-altitude balloon experiment
HEL	high-energy laser
HPM	high-power microwave
HQ	headquarters
HQ AFSPC/ DOMN	Headquarters, Air Force Space Command, Directorate of Operations, Nuclear Operations, and Future Concepts Branch
ICBM	intercontinental ballistic missile
IFF	identify friend or foe
IFX	Integrated Flight Experiment
IRBM	intermediate range ballistic missile
IRCM	infrared countermeasure
ISO	Information Systems Office
ISR	intelligence, surveillance, and reconnaissance
IW	information warfare

JAOC	Joint Air Operations Center
JASSM	Joint Air to Surface Standoff Missile
JFACC	Joint Air Force Component Commander
JFC	Joint Force Commander
JIPTL	joint integrated prioritized target list
JSTARS	Joint Surveillance and Target Attack Reconnaissance System
LANTIRN	low-altitude navigation and targeting infrared for night
LODE	Large Optics Demonstration Experiment
MAAP	master air attack plan
MASINT	measurement and signature intelligence
MCG	magneto-cumulative generator
MEF	Marine Expeditionary Forces
MILO	magnetically insulated linear oscillator
MIRACL	mid-infrared advanced chemical laser
MOP	memorandum of policy
MTCR	Missile Technology Control Regime
NASA	National Aeronautics and Space Administration
NATO	North Atlantic Treaty Organization
NGST	next-generation space telescope
NMD	national missile defense
NPT	Nuclear Proliferation Treaty
NSSMS	NATO Seasparrow missile system
NVD	night-vision device
NPT	Nuclear Proliferation Treaty
OODA	observe, orient, decide, act
PE	program element
PRF	pulse repetition frequency
RAM	rolling airframe missile
RCS	radar cross section
RF	radio frequency
RLV	reusable launch vehicle
RPV	remotely piloted vehicle
SAB	Scientific Advisory Board
SBL	space-based laser
SB-LTD	space-based laser target designator
SMV	space maneuver vehicle
SOV	space operations vehicle
SOV CONOPS	Space Operations Vehicle Concepts of Operation
SPINS	special instructions
SRBM	short-range ballistic missile

SSN	Space Surveillance Network
TSSAM	Tri-Service Standoff Attack Missile
UAV	unmanned aerial vehicle
UCAV	unmanned combat air vehicle
USAF	U.S. Air Force
USCINCSPACE	U.S. Commander in Chief, Space Command
USSPACECOM	U.S. Space Command
UWB	ultra-wideband
WMD	weapons of mass destruction
XOIR	Headquarters, U.S. Air Force, Director of Operations, Intelligence/Requirements

Introduction

William C. Martel

The late twentieth century was a time of extraordinary technological progress in virtually all facets of human endeavor. This is no more apparent than in the case of how technologies are used for the conduct of war. The Persian Gulf War in 1991 and the emergence of "information war" in the 1990s highlight the new technologies that are changing how states fight wars. During the 1990s, the defense and foreign policy establishment coined the phrase "revolution in military affairs" to express the ideas that the rapid pace of technological innovation is altering the ways in which states conduct military operations and, even more fundamentally, that technology could change the nature of war and the basic foundation of security.[1] This revolution could be as profound as the development of nuclear weapons in 1945, which heralded an era when governments and societies understood that the new technology would reduce the chance of war because the destruction it could bring would vastly exceed any possible gains.

During the twenty-first century, with the development of numerous technologies in which computers will play a central role, states will have vastly more lethal and effective instruments for war. Although there are still doubts about the effectiveness of the North Atlantic Treaty Organization (NATO) air campaign against Serbia in the spring of 1999, this use of military force highlights the role of modern technology in war.[2] During the air campaign, the United States used cruise missiles to attack air defense missile sites, communication centers, and other critical targets.[3] The air campaign commenced with cruise missile strikes because military planners believed that Serbian air defenses were so advanced that U.S. and allied aircraft were vulnerable. As if to prove the point, Serbian air defenses shot down an F-117 Stealth fighter on the fourth day of the air campaign.[4]

During the air campaign, the United States used the B-2 bomber, which cost at least $1 billion per plane, as well as B-1 and B-52 bombers, to launch cruise missiles, global position system (GPS)–aided bombs, and laser-guided bombs, whose accuracies are measured in feet. The United States also used a virtual armada of sophisticated satellites and reconnaissance aircraft for locating, identifying, and tracking military targets and government facilities in Serbia and Kosovo. Although the political outcome of the war is subject to debate, militarily, the United States and NATO effectively dismantled Serbia's military forces, communications system, and power facilities. There are reports that President Slobodan Milosevic was most concerned when NATO shut off power and thus crippled the Serbian government and society.

As this recent case suggests, the devastation imposed on Serbia was possible because of the development of late twentieth-century defense technologies. It is imperative that we remember the fact that an exceptionally sophisticated array of defense technologies were brought to bear against Serbia, which, by all accounts, is a small and relatively weak state. Although these technologies are impressive, they are essentially decades old and thus pale in comparison with the directed energy, targeting, and command and control technologies in which the United States is investing billions of dollars during the early years of the twenty-first century. When these technologies mature, their integration into the U.S. military arsenal during the first decades of the twenty-first century can produce capabilities that reach far beyond what we now consider state of the art.

With the extraordinary pace of technological innovation in both the military and commercial worlds, advances in directed energy, cruise missiles, nonlethal technologies, computers, and microwaves, among other innovations, could redefine how military force is used. The pace of innovation, which is the foundation for revolutionary advances in defense technologies, is not accidental. Political and military authorities in the executive and legislative branches of the U.S. government on both sides of the political aisle are deliberately investing tens of billions of dollars in advanced technologies. For example, within a decade, the United States could destroy ballistic missiles; radically limit the number of casualties; disrupt modern electronic weapons, telecommunications, power, and banking systems; and wage wars from the relative safety of the homeland. Although these are admittedly radical ideas, the United States is investing in technologies that could make such options quite achievable.

Each chapter focuses on a specific defense technology and uses nontechnical terms to describe the technology and how it could be used in war. These discussions are aimed at readers who seek to understand military technologies but who are not themselves specialists. It is taken for granted in each of the chapters that these technologies are likely to produce significantly new capabilities for the American defense establishment. Because the United States is investing in an extraordinarily comprehensive range of defense technologies, it is not possible to describe all areas of defense research. Nor are these technologies confined to the United States. Many states are developing these and related technologies, but the United States has such a dominant position that it likely would acquire these technologies before other states.

This book is organized into three functional sections: (1) directed energy, (2) military targeting and its effects, and (3) command and control. The chapters in Part I are devoted to understanding how directed-energy technologies, such as lasers and microwaves, can influence the conduct of war and international security in the twenty-first century. These chapters address the wide range of ways in which lasers can be used in military operations, such as sensing, communications, and destruction.

In Chapter 1, Mark E. Rogers examines the wide range of ways in which lasers could be used by the military, from sensing and communications to destructive effects. The United States is investing in technologies that could use lasers to destroy missiles; to sense remotely vast areas of the earth from space; to identify and illuminate targets from space; to build constellations of satellites that use lasers to communicate; and to assess the effects of military attacks, as well as weather conditions, from orbit. This chapter reviews the ability of lasers to perform a vast array of military functions and discusses how technological innovation is expanding the role of lasers in military operations.

Iraq, Iran, and North Korea, among other rogue states (now known as "states of concern"),[5] are developing ballistic missiles and weapons of mass destruction. Given concerns about these states, the United States is accelerating the development of technologies for intercepting missiles, known as national missile defense. William H. Possel in Chapter 2 focuses on using high-energy lasers to defend the United States against ballistic missiles. As a result of investments in high-energy lasers and optics since the 1980s, the Department of Defense and commercial firms have dramatically advanced the state of technology in ground-based and space-based lasers. Because national missile defense has strong support in Washington, this technology is a realistic possibility within a decade. This chapter evaluates the technological risks and economic costs associated with developing and deploying directed energy weapons for destroying ballistic missiles.

Not all directed energy research for destroying missiles is decades in the future. The United States is investing billions of dollars in the development of the airborne laser (ABL). This is a 747 aircraft armed with a high-energy laser projected to be deployed in 2005 or 2006 that is designed to shoot down theater ballistic missiles. Kenneth W. Barker in Chapter 3 examines the technologies and military doctrines that could determine how lasers are used for national missile defense. Technological and military communities in the United States are proceeding on the assumption that the strengths of airborne and space-based lasers provide a better way to defeat missiles. The dominant belief is that the Airborne Laser is the precursor, both technologically and operationally, to the space-based laser (SBL). The SBL is a constellation of twenty satellites at an altitude of 780 miles (1,300 km) that are designed to attack missiles in their boost phase (because the engine plume creates a distinctive target). A weapon that autonomously destroys ballistic missiles at distances of about 2,400 miles (4,000 km) could instantaneously protect any spot on the earth against ballistic missile attack. This chapter discusses technological and operational compatibility and risk as they relate to developing laser weapons for missile defense.

The development of directed-energy weapons is not confined to space and national missile defense. As a result of advances in directed-energy technologies, the United States could develop high-energy lasers and high-power microwaves that could reshape naval warfare during the twenty-first century. In Chapter 4, William J. McCarthy investigates how integrating microwave devices, high-energy lasers, and surface-to-air missiles could redefine the conduct of maritime operations. For technological and operational reasons, the United States could initially use a *Nimitz*-class nuclear-powered aircraft carrier to deploy directed-energy technologies. Used for defending against antiship cruise missiles, aircraft, and fast patrol boats, directed-energy weapons could fundamentally shift battle group operations for aircraft carriers from attrition-based defense to dispersed offensive operations.

In Chapter 5, Eileen M. Walling explores how one form of directed energy, known as high-power microwaves, could be used in military operations. The military has a long history of exploiting electromagnetic frequencies that began with "wireless" communications during the late 1800s and radar during the 1930s. Military research laboratories have demonstrated that high-power microwave technologies have matured to the point where they can disrupt and destroy military and commercial electronics. They could become the next generation of weapons on the electronic battlefield, which is highly vulnerable to microwave weapons, and spur a technological revolution in warfare much sooner than is commonly thought.

Part II shifts the reader's attention to how new technologies could change the nature of military targeting. The United States is developing and refining technologies that influence what targets are chosen and the effects that are desired.

These effects might not always involve killing people or destroying weapons. In some cases, the United States is investing in technologies that involve entirely new military options, such as developing nonlethal weapons and refining existing technologies, such as cruise missiles, to create more effective military operations. These chapters examine the critical technologies that could strengthen the ability of the United States to attack military forces more decisively.

In Chapter 6, David J. Nicholls examines how technological progress has improved cruise missiles. Although, historically, their military value has been limited, cruise missiles are now a cost-effective and militarily effective alternative to manned aircraft and ballistic missiles. For example, the United States used cruise missiles in many military operations during the 1990s, notably in attacks on Iraq, Serbia, Afghanistan, and Sudan. As cruise missile technology continues to spread to other states, however, it might be more difficult for the United States to defend itself against cruise missiles. The forces of technological progress could transform these weapons into a significant instrument of military power.

In Chapter 7, Joseph W. Siniscalchi investigates the development of nonlethal technologies as a step toward a radically new generation of military options. Although, historically, states have made their weapons more lethal, the end of the Cold War and the outbreak of humanitarian crises have persuaded states to limit casualties in military operations. Simply making weapons more lethal no longer might be the most rational way to defend U.S. vital interests in peacekeeping and peace enforcement operations. This chapter examines how employing nonlethal weapons could rewrite the basic rules that govern the use of military force.

In Chapter 8, John E. Ward Jr., discusses the development of reusable space vehicles for commercial and military purposes. Because the U.S. military is heavily involved in space, the natural assumption is that reusable space vehicles might be used for military operations. These vehicles could be used for reconnaissance and targeting, but the fundamental reason for developing reusable vehicles is to place satellites in orbit. Amid questions about the efficiency or cost-effectiveness of the U.S. military placing satellites in orbit, commercial firms are investing billions of dollars in technologies and might dominate the space launch business, which could reshape how space is used for commercial and military purposes.

As a result of technological progress, the United States can develop aircraft that do not require human pilots (known as unmanned or uninhabited air or space vehicles), which might be less expensive to operate and also keep humans out of harm's way. In Chapter 9, David B. Glade discusses the technologies that could permit the United States to use uninhabited air vehicles in many types of military operations. Although the military is only beginning to explore such possibilities, these vehicles could eventually replace many of the piloted vehicles that dominated the twentieth century. This chapter discusses the technologies that could contribute to unmanned vehicles and examines how they might best be used in military operations. The development of this technology raises important questions about using uninhabited vehicles, rather than humans, to deliver lethal force and whether technology should diminish the role of humans in future military operations.

The focus in Part III shifts to a consideration of how technological innovation could alter the ability to control military forces, which is known in military parlance as "command and control." These chapters examine the role of technology in how states plan, direct, and control military operations from the homeland, the use of computers to make crucial decisions in war, and whether information warfare could reshape how states deter one another from war.

In Chapter 10, Scott M. Britten addresses the technological developments that could permit the United States to plan and execute an air war from the relative safety of its homeland. This chapter discusses "reachback operations," which is the military term for campaigns that are planned and directed from the homeland. Planning wars is an extraordinarily complex task, and developments in computer and communications technologies could make it possible to fight wars from the American homeland. Ideally, military commanders could manage wars from secure locations, control military forces that are thousands of miles away, and limit the risk to military forces as they decisively defeat an enemy.

A recurring theme in these chapters is that technology could create new options for using military force. William B. McClure, in Chapter 11, addresses whether technological innovation could endow computers with the ability and authority to make the life-and-death decisions in war historically reserved for humans. This technology would reverse the tradition in which humans make the fundamental decisions about life and death in war. Because technology is accelerating the pace of military operations, commanders are required to make decisions more quickly and to operate at a faster pace, or "operational tempo." Although computers could make wartime decisions more quickly and arguably more efficiently than humans, there are reservations about giving computers this power. Nonetheless, computers are increasingly making decisions in military operations. For example, U.S. Navy Aegis-guided missile cruisers rely on computers to decide when to attack cruise missiles or aircraft approaching the ships. Although this technology represents a radical departure from the American military tradition that machines cannot replace humans, technological innovation might lead to a machine commander that can make decisions in combat.

With the advance of computers and communications technologies, states can now attack computers and communications networks in modern societies. This is known as information warfare. In Chapter 12, Richard J. Harknett addresses the implications of an era when telecommunications, banking, and power systems are vulnerable to electronic attack. This chapter considers whether these technologies could alter the ability to deter war in the information age.

In the Conclusion, William C. Martel investigates how fundamental trends in technology are reshaping both how the United States makes choices about the technologies that it should develop and how it uses military force in the twenty-first century.

This book proceeds from the proposition that investments in technology could have revolutionary effects on strategy and security, even at a time when the United States and other nations' military forces are conducting peacekeeping and humanitarian operations rather than classic wars. Technological progress is reshaping national security in the twenty-first century, even as other states develop technologies that could disrupt or destroy the overwhelming military superiority of the United States.

Neither the editor nor the contributors of this book are advocates for the position that the United States should or should not be developing these or any other technologies. As a matter of analytic rigor, this work evaluates how specific technologies might influence national security and does so without any advocacy for these defense programs or the firms that are developing them. This perspective applies equally to whether the technologies discussed in this book are technologically mature or decades away from fruition. For reference, because these technologies will influence U.S. national security and foreign policy on different time scales, the preface to each chapter describes whether the specific technology under discussion will be relevant during the short term (within five years), medium term (within ten years), or long term (fifteen to twenty years). These time periods are meant to illustrate how mature these technologies are and how soon they could affect U.S. military capabilities.

The fundamental point is that the technologies discussed in this book are funded, and thus legally authorized, by the Congress of the United States. In fact, the contributors do not make specific recommendations about which technologies should be developed or debate whether there is a political need for specific weapons. Rather, they focus on how these technologies and programs could influence national security. This work also seeks to help the American people to understand the effect of each type of technology on U.S. military capabilities and national security.

Obviously, this book could not discuss all of the technologies that are under development because of the sheer volume and because many are classified. The subjects discussed in this book, however, address the more critical technological programs in which the U.S. Department of Defense and commercial firms are currently investing billions of dollars. Because these technologies are likely to be introduced into military forces over the next couple of decades, the ideas discussed in this book should be relevant for the foreseeable future. To cite just one example, it will take the United States several decades to deploy directed-energy technologies for missile defense, which will influence U.S. security throughout the twenty-first century.

This book is designed to help readers who are interested in the effects of technology on public affairs and national security. The unifying theme in these chapters is the exploration of the relationship between technology and security and their influence on each other. An inescapable question for American society is whether technologies originate because of a military need or a technological opportunity, although, in reality, all defense technologies share a lineage that is a product of both. The Conclusion discusses this issue in greater depth. Conceived for the purpose of furthering our understanding of the relationship between national security and technology, this book was written by some of the individuals in the defense establishment who actively shape how the United States develops critical defense technologies and who influence how the military spends the nation's treasure.[6] Its authors were motivated by the desire to advance the compact between the American people and those technological, political, and military guardians who protect their society.

Notes

1. For a discussion of the revolution in military affairs, see Andrew Bacevich, "Preserving the Well-Bred Horse," *The National Interest* (fall 1994), 43; Andrew F. Krepinevich, "Cavalry to Computer: The Pattern of Military Revolutions," *The National Interest* (fall 1994), 37; Philip Ritcheson, "The Future of Military Affairs: Revolution or Evolution?" *Strategic Review* 24, no. 2 (1996), 31; Eric Sterner, "You Say You Want a Revolution (in Military Affairs)?" *Comparative Strategy* 18, no. 4 (1999), 297.
2. "The Kosovo Cover-Up," *Newsweek,* May 15, 2000, 23–26.
3. See "'We Are Attacked for Nothing;' Belgrade Residents Express Bewilderment as Explosions Light Up the City," *The Washington Post,* Mar. 25, 1999, A1; "Missiles Destroy Key Facilities in Belgrade," *The Washington Post,* Apr. 3, 1999, A1; "Flames Gut Belgrade Buildings; Yugoslav Crowds Denounce First Downtown Attacks," *The Washington Post,* Apr. 3, 1999, A11.
4. "U.S. Rescues Pilot as NATO Widens Attack; Stealth Fighter Down in Serbia; Reports of Atrocities Mounting," *The Washington Post,* Mar. 28, 1999, A1; "U.S. Confirms Yugoslavs Downed Stealth Fighter," *The Washington Post,* Nov. 25, 1999, A18.

5. "What's in a Name? U.S. Drops Term 'Rogue State,'" *The Washington Post,* June 20, 2000, 16.
6. Most of the research in these chapters was originally conducted under the auspices of the Center for Strategy and Technology at the Air War College during the late 1990s when, as the center's director, the book's editor supervised these studies.

PART ONE
Directed Energy

1.   Lasers in Space
Technological Options for Warfare

Mark E. Rogers

Space is a vital arena for military and commercial reasons, and its importance is bound to grow in future decades. To maintain its technological edge, the U.S. military and the technological communities have invested billions of dollars over several decades in developing laser technologies for destructive and nonlethal military purposes. As a military technology, lasers hold great promise, especially if used from space. Lasers could be used for a wide variety of purposes, from remote sensing, designation and illumination of targets on the battlefield, and communications to remote sensing of battle damage and weather and destruction of ballistic missiles. Lasers could assume a critical role in virtually all types of military operations in the short, medium, and long terms by giving political authorities and military commanders the ability to watch events anywhere on earth and to intervene with deadly force. This chapter examines the broad areas in which lasers in space might well reshape how states use military force in the future. The author also provides a framework for the directed energy technologies that are the focus of the first part of this book.

Definition of Laser Technology

Laser technology has matured so substantially in recent decades that the United States now has the capability to use lasers from space-based platforms to change radically the conduct of war. Laser light, which is uniquely suited to the vacuum of space, gives the military the means to communicate, illuminate, and designate targets; to conduct remote sensing; and to destroy targets in space or on the ground. The vacuum of space enhances the military utility of lasers because there is no atmosphere to attenuate (or diffuse) the beam and lasers in space can cover the entire surface of the earth. Lasers also provide highly reliable, cost-

effective, and energy-efficient systems for military operations. As military organizations use lasers for remote sensing, active imaging, optical communication, power beaming, and high-energy weapons, a reasonable assumption is that,
together, lasers and space can have revolutionary implications for warfare.

Exploitable Characteristics

By their nature, lasers have several characteristics that can be exploited by the
military. As a unique source of optical radiation, lasers use the phenomenon of
stimulated emission to generate a very narrow beam of light that is highly coherent when compared with the sun or ordinary light bulbs. As a result of co-
herence, laser beams can travel for great distances with little spreading of the
beam, which means that the beam can be tightly focused. Thus, lasers generate
coherent radiation in the form of highly directional, pencil-like beams of light
that can accurately place energy on targets that are thousands of kilometers
away.[1] A further advantage, which has benefits for covert applications, is that
laser beams are difficult to detect.

Lasers are described in terms of their wavelength, which ranges from the infrared to the visible and ultraviolet regions of the electromagnetic spectrum.
Many lasers generate light in a very narrow band, which is critical for remotely
sensing specific chemicals as well as distortion-free communications. Although
most lasers operate at one wavelength, tuning lasers to operate on several wavelengths gives them considerable agility. An example is their capability of remote sensing of materials in the atmosphere from satellites in low-earth orbit.[2]

The output from lasers can be pulsed or continuous (termed *continuous
wave*).[3] For example, laser designators for laser-guided bombs rely on pulsed
lasers. The military has substantial interest in continuous wave (CW) lasers for
high-energy weapons. For example, the U.S. Air Force is developing the Airborne Laser (ABL), which places a laser on a 747 aircraft for the purpose of
shooting down missiles.

The amount of power generated by a laser depends on the application. Although communication systems use sensitive detectors for low-energy lasers,
laser weapons require megawatts of power to damage targets thousands of kilometers away. If the laser carries an adequate fuel supply or uses energy from the
sun to power the laser directly or indirectly, high-energy lasers can be fired so
many times that one can speak of virtually unlimited "magazines"—a capability
totally unlike that of conventional weapons.

Another exploitable characteristic of lasers is the ability to adjust the energy
output.[4] Ideally, a properly designed system could be used passively (with the
laser turned off) for surveillance or actively (with the laser activated) for illuminating or destroying targets. At low power, a laser could actively illuminate

or designate targets for guiding precision-guided munitions, and, at high power, it could destroy targets.[5] Although another unique feature of lasers is the complete absence of recoil when the weapon is fired, a high-energy chemical laser can generate thrust from the exhaust gases that create the laser beam.

Because lasers travel at about 186,000 miles (300,000 km) per second, targets that are thousands of miles away can be attacked almost instantaneously.[6] If the target can be tracked visually, the laser beam can be placed on the target and held there until enough energy is delivered to produce the desired effect. This feature is particularly important when attacking time-critical targets or engaging targets at great distances.

Finally, lasers are reliable, easy to maintain, relatively affordable, and have long service lives. A good example is the semiconductor diode laser, which can operate for tens of thousands of hours, is quite rugged and reliable, and can generate substantial power. This feature is critically important for space systems that are not easily repaired in orbit.[7] For these reasons, the semiconductor laser is a leading candidate for many space-based applications, including communication, target designation, and remote sensing.

Laser Challenges
Although the above characteristics make lasers attractive for military operations, this technology faces significant challenges. One technical challenge, for example, is to produce lasers that can generate enough power to destroy missiles. Another is to point, track, and "fire" the laser beam through the atmosphere for communications purposes. Yet another challenge in using laser systems is gathering sufficient scattered light from the target to generate useful information, such as measuring winds or remotely sensing chemicals. Finally, the target might limit the energy that it reflects and absorbs. Lasers also have other fundamental limitations.

Inefficiency
Generating highly coherent laser beams can be a very inefficient process. Lasers often transform only a small percentage of input energy into laser light, and the rest of the energy becomes waste heat. The most efficient lasers are semiconductor lasers, which are 20–50 percent efficient, but they do not generate enough power for weapons. The laser in the Airborne Laser Laboratory (ALL) that shot down five Sidewinder missiles and three Navy drones during tests in 1983 was only 20–30 percent efficient.[8] The hydrogen fluoride laser, which is a leading candidate for space-based laser weapons, is only 20 percent efficient.[9] The remaining technological challenges are to make lasers operate more efficiently and to manage the waste heat more effectively.

Refueling
Some lasers consume fuel to generate the beam. For example, hydrogen fluoride lasers consume hydrogen, fluorine, and helium. Lasers that use consumable fuels, however, might be less desirable than lasers powered from electricity or directly from the sun because of the need to replenish the consumable fuels. In the case of lasers that orbit the earth, it would be necessary to use rockets to refuel them while they are in orbit.

Acquiring Targets
It is difficult to point laser beams with great precision. The highly collimated (that is, parallel) nature of lasers complicates pointing the beam accurately at a target, which could be a communications satellite or a missile warhead that carries a nuclear weapon. Cooperative targets, such as communications satellites that are stationary or that move in a predictable fashion could be designed to reflect the laser light directly back to the source. For example, a laser floodlight could scan a wide region of space until it senses a reflection and points a narrow beam at the target. For uncooperative targets, which can maneuver to evade attack, other methods of acquiring the target, including passive optical sensors and radars, may be needed. With the Global Positioning System (GPS) of satellites that defines precisely the location of a satellite, airplane, or automobile, space-based lasers could point at targets on the surface of the earth with extraordinary accuracy. Other technological developments could make it possible to track fast-moving targets, such as missiles or satellites.

Penetration of Atmosphere
For many promising applications for space-based lasers, including remote sensing of chemical effluents, measurement of wind speeds, and destruction of targets on the ground, on the sea, or in the air, the laser must be aimed through the atmosphere. The atmosphere, however, reduces the total laser energy placed on the target. This effect can be used in interesting ways. For example, the hydrogen fluoride laser is the leading candidate for a space-based laser weapon. Because its wavelength is strongly absorbed by water vapor, the laser could not attack targets that are below 30,000 feet (10 km), which would prevent accidentally blinding people or attacking targets on the ground.[10]

Deposition of Energy on Target
It is difficult to deposit laser energy on a target that is sufficient to cause destructive effects, particularly because some targets reflect much of the laser radiation. The laser beam must be absorbed by the target to cause structural dam-

age. Although this is relatively easy for "soft" targets, such as solar panels and optical systems on satellites, it is quite difficult to burn through the outer skin of a reentry vehicle.

Human Vulnerability

Laser beams will cause injury if a person looks directly into a visible or near infrared laser beam.[11] Even a small amount of laser energy entering the cornea causes a catastrophic hemorrhage of the retina because the eye's optics magnify the laser's intensity 100,000 times as the light travels from the cornea to the retina. Retinal injuries are permanent and can lead to some loss of sight. This is particularly worrisome if space-based lasers are pointed toward the earth, but these risks are manageable if one controls where the laser is pointing before it is activated. In addition, international agreements prohibit the intentional use of lasers to cause blindness, which means that this risk must receive serious consideration even for space-based lasers that are not designed as weapons.

Military Uses

Since their invention, lasers have been touted as a "solution in search of a problem." During the past twenty years, lasers have revolutionized medicine, telecommunications, industrial welding and cutting, and data processing. The ubiquitous laser bar code scanners in stores and compact disc players provide daily examples of how people use lasers. Beyond these commercial uses, scientists and military personnel understood in the 1960s that lasers could perform many military functions. Although the United States has yet to deploy a high-energy laser weapon, this technology is maturing so rapidly that the Air Force will deploy the ABL aircraft that can destroy theater ballistic missiles early in this century.[12]

Lasers have been used for years, beginning in the Vietnam War and more recently as seen on television during the Persian Gulf War, to guide bombs precisely to their targets.[13] Precision-guided laser bombs were used during the Vietnam and the Persian Gulf Wars. Other military laser applications include highly accurate range finders, secure communication systems, and laser spotlights that improve the performance of night vision devices.

Despite their widespread and successful uses in military operations, lasers have not been used much in space. Space is an ideal place for using lasers in military operations, however, for four reasons.

First, space systems can be pre-positioned in orbits to provide optimal support for specific military purposes. Space systems can be maintained in a state of wartime readiness as long as there are sufficient satellites in orbit and proper ground support. Given the difficulty and expense of deploying systems in space, defense planners carefully decide where to place these systems to maximize their value in military contingencies.

Second, space-based systems are present over land, sea, and air targets.[14] Positioning surveillance systems in space reduces the risk that the United States will be surprised if an adversary conducts military operations or if it attempts to hide equipment or facilities. Systems in low earth orbit move at approximately 4 miles (7 km) per second and complete an orbit every one to two hours, depending on the altitude. This orbit provides the best coverage of the earth, but it requires many satellites to maintain continuous coverage. Systems in middle earth orbit have longer orbital periods, such as the twelve-hour period for GPS satellites. This orbit reduces the required number of satellites, so only twenty-four satellites are needed for the GPS constellation to provide global navigation. Satellites in geosynchronous orbit circle the earth once every twenty-four hours and remain over the same point on the earth's surface. Although only three satellites in geosynchronous orbit can cover almost the entire surface of the earth, it is difficult to achieve high-resolution images from an altitude of 22,300 miles (35,000 km) above the earth.

Third, the orbit affects the ability of space systems to cover nearly every point on the earth. Known as *timeliness,* a sufficient number of satellites could permit the near–real-time transfer of high-bandwidth information that military forces need to attack targets rapidly.[15] High-speed orbiting satellites that are frequently overhead would give military commanders more opportunities to attack targets.

Fourth, the vacuum of space is perfect for lasers because there is no atmosphere to weaken the beam, which increases the energy that is delivered to distant targets.[16]

Use of Lasers in Space
For military planners and strategists, lasers can support the military objectives of gathering and relaying information, as well as delivering energy on targets. Lasers can guide missiles toward targets, illuminate targets for optical sensors, and provide information about targets that enhance the effectiveness of weapon systems. For example, a laser target designator could illuminate a target to guide conventional bombs more accurately toward that target.

Optical sensing systems gather information by collecting optical energy, which can be emitted by the infrared emissions from an aircraft engine or scattered or reflected when a laser is aimed at a target. The common procedure is to photograph a target after it has been attacked in order to evaluate the damage.

This is termed *battle damage assessment* (BDA). Current optical systems, such as reconnaissance satellites, infrared missile tracking sensors, and weather satellites, are passive, which means that they do not emit any radiation. Lasers, however, can illuminate a target to produce new information about its condition. Some information-gathering systems use active illumination to image the target with optical systems, whereas others use lasers to gather "non-image" information. An example of the former is the U.S. Air Force's Starfire Optical Range at Kirtland Air Force Base, New Mexico, where laser beams are used to illuminate space objects and form images.[17] Another example is remote sensing with differential absorption laser radar (DIAL) technology, which measures the chemical signatures of targets. This latter technology is especially important for targets that manufacture chemical or biological weapons.

Military and commercial satellites that relay data, voice, television, and other information are well-known examples of communications and data-relay satellites. Although most systems use microwaves to transmit data through the atmosphere, laser communication systems can carry much more information than microwave beams. Lasers also can be used to deliver power, as in beaming power to recharge satellite batteries or delivering energy to remote locations on the earth. Another example is using high-energy laser pulses to vaporize material on spacecraft to generate thrust for maneuvering. Finally, lasers can deliver destructive energy. One example is the use of high-energy laser weapons to damage or blind sensors that detect heat or light.

Use of Lasers in Military Operations

This section discusses how lasers could be used in military operations during the twenty-first century.

Laser Targeting

Lasers have been used for years for targeting in ground-based operations. Similarly, a space-based laser target designator (SB-LTD) can project a laser beam onto a target to aim a weapon. This can be accomplished with a high-resolution imaging system and video data link operated from a command center in the United States, from an aircraft, or in the theater of combat operations. A laser on a satellite has a clear view of most targets as the satellite passes over the target. By moving the laser designator to a satellite and out of the theater, one reduces the risk to soldiers and eliminates the risk to the weapon platform from a laser-guided weapon released at long ranges. This could enhance the effectiveness of cruise missiles. The number of misses by cruise missiles during the

Persian Gulf War against Iraqi air defense sites could have been reduced if space-based lasers had provided aim points, and coalition forces might have had greater success against the mobile targets that often evaded destruction.

Laser technology is relatively mature, so there are no fundamental impediments to the development of SB-LTDs. The primary challenge is that many satellites would be required to sustain adequate coverage during military operations, which would make this system expensive.

Space-Based Battlefield Illumination
Projecting a laser beam over a large area on the earth's surface would help low-light imaging systems to find targets.[18] The United States has fielded laser illuminators that use semiconductor laser arrays to aid night vision devices. A space-based battlefield illuminator would generate beams from satellites in low-earth orbit and direct them to the target. This technology would allow military forces to acquire targets with low-light imaging systems, insert and remove special operations teams under low light conditions, and increase the security of high-value facilities at night. Because the beam is eye-safe, the illuminator could be used for psychological operations in which U.S. observers search covertly for enemy units.

Battlefield technology requires both lasers that generate enough power to illuminate targets for imaging systems and spacecraft that can produce enough power to compensate for the inherent inefficiency of lasers. This system also requires a highly precise satellite pointing system if the laser is to illuminate the right spot on the ground, which might be as small as 300 feet (100 m) in diameter. Although several satellites would create a significant capability for limited military operations, dozens of satellites would be required to illuminate numerous high-value targets during a large military operation.

One technology now used by U.S. military forces is active illumination for low-light imaging systems. Examples include starlight scopes and night-vision devices (NVDs) that amplify visible and near-infrared light to create images bright enough to be seen or detect the heat emitted by objects. Reconnaissance satellites and other systems also use sensitive sensors to gather the target's reflected and emitted light to create images.

An orbiting laser beam could flood the battlefield at wavelengths that can be detected by the sensor. The ability to point accurately at the desired spot on the earth a laser that is sufficiently powerful to illuminate the ground is essential to the success of this concept. The pointing requirements for this concept are much less demanding than for a laser weapon because the intent is to spread the light over a larger area. The most significant technical challenge is to develop a constellation of satellites with sufficiently powerful, space-qualified lasers that can provide suitable coverage. Although this system would be expensive, the command and control system would be less complex because the illuminator is equivalent to a laser spotlight, which eliminates the need for highly precise pointing.

Space-Based Laser Target Designators
Laser target designation creates highly accurate weapons that home in on the laser light scattered from targets to guide the electro-optical (EO) sensor in munitions. A space-based laser designator must acquire the desired target, place the laser beam on the target at the right time, and steer the laser-guided bomb to the target by providing aim points for guiding laser-guided weapons, gravity bombs, or missiles. The U.S. military demonstrated how effective these weapons could be during the Vietnam and Persian Gulf conflicts.[19] With the shift to precision targeting, U.S. military forces are developing surveillance systems that can locate and identify targets, use enhanced munitions systems to deliver lethal forces against targets, assess the damage, and evaluate whether the strike was effective and whether to attack again.[20] Precision guided munitions supplemented by space-based laser designation are capable of transforming military operations. If targets are attacked with weapons released at greater distances, the overall risk to U.S. forces is reduced. For example, technology can permit U.S. military forces to attack the kinds of mobile targets that worried defense planners during the Persian Gulf War.

One advantage of increasing the standoff range of laser-guided weapons is to reduce the risk to human operators during the terminal phase of delivering weapons. When troops on the ground designate a target with a laser, they are at risk because they must be relatively close to the target and cannot leave the area until the target has been destroyed.

Remote Sensing with Lasers
The idea behind space-based remote sensing with lasers is the ability to obtain actively information about terrestrial locations. This technological trend has significant military implications. With active remote sensing, lasers gather information by projecting a laser beam and gathering the weakly back-scattered, or reflected, light to measure the target's properties. One approach, termed *differential absorption,* focuses two laser beams of different wavelengths to detect differences in the absorption of the beams. In principle, these laser systems can detect a wide variety of chemical compounds, including chemical weapons and pollution, in the air. Not only has this technology been successfully demonstrated in space, the technological trend of using space-based lasers for remote sensing promises to have significant benefits for military operations.[21]

Battle Damage Assessment

Lasers can be used to probe the atmosphere after an attack to measure efflu-ents—chemical agents, propellants, and other militarily relevant compounds—from the target.[22] In principle, lasers could detect biological agents if the sen-sor on a satellite in low-earth orbit was directly overhead just after the attack. The ability to determine whether chemical or biological agents were released after an attack against a bunker, for example, has enormous military and politi-cal implications. The same applies to assessing whether enemy capabilities sur-vived the attack and whether military forces need to attack again.

Space-based BDA requires relatively powerful lasers that could be tuned over a spectrum of wavelengths to stimulate a response from the materials of inter-est. The concept also requires a large optical receiver with highly sensitive de-tectors because the light scattered back to the laser is very weak.[23] The beam must be steered rapidly to scan large regions as the satellite moves overhead. Although many satellites would be needed to cover numerous targets during an extended military operation, even a limited capability would be militarily sig-nificant when weighed against the risks of U.S. military forces being exposed to chemical or biological agents. Although clouds and haze reduce the effec-tiveness of BDA, remote sensing with lasers has significant potential for military operations.

Environmental Sensing

A space-based laser can measure the physical properties of a region of space, land, or the oceans. This is a variant of measurement and signature intelligence (MASINT). For example, the relative smoothness of a surface, which affects the reflected laser beam, could help to identify a target.[24] By scanning the beam over a land area, one can estimate the moisture content of the soil and thereby warn ground forces about the presence of soft soil before they are moved into the area.[25] In this case, lasers and highly responsive detectors are required. For some applications, changes in the reflected light can identify man-made objects from the natural background.

Weather Monitoring

Lasers can be used for remote measurement of meteorological conditions, in-cluding wind speed, cloud density, the height of cloud tops, water vapor con-tent, temperature, and pressure.[26] Short laser pulses would permit measuring the height of cloud tops from which one could infer the intensity of potential storms. Using a space-based weather monitoring system to compute wind speeds over targets would increase the accuracy of unguided bombs, enhance airborne in-fantry operations, and help aircraft land on rough airfields. With developments in wind sensing and ground-based laser radar, several satellites would create a significant military capability. The National Aeronautics and Space Administration (NASA) is also interested in this application given the value of more precise weather forecasting for civilian purposes.

Space Debris Cataloging

The growing number of defunct satellites, spacecraft fragments, and spent rocket boosters in space is an increasingly significant problem. It is estimated that there are 300,000 pieces of debris, principally in low-earth orbit.[27] Even small pieces of debris striking an orbiting system could cause catastrophic damage. The U.S. Air Force catalogues space objects with the Space Surveillance Network (SSN), but this ground-based radar and optical system cannot measure objects that are less than 4 inches (10 cm) in size.

Space-based laser surveillance systems could improve current capabilities to locate, track, and identify space debris. For example, a laser could obtain an optical reflection from the debris and a second pulsed laser would measure the position and velocity of the debris. Because the orbiting laser could be close to the space debris, smaller pieces should be detectable. More detailed knowledge of the debris field could reduce the risk to spacecraft and help to select orbits for new satellites that minimize the probability of collisions. It is not necessary to field a large number of these space-based laser surveillance systems because the debris is not moving and adequate time is available for multiple searches. Thus, the hazard is great and the technology is attainable.

High-energy pulsed lasers can be used to remove orbital debris by projecting a laser beam from a space-based platform to vaporize the surface of the debris. By repeatedly hitting the debris, sufficient energy could be transferred to create thrust and cause the debris to de-orbit and burn up in the atmosphere. Obviously, a great deal of care must be taken to ensure that the thrust slows down the debris, and that debris in lower orbits does not collide with other satellites. A space-based system might offer distinct advantages over ground-based systems. A low-power laser could detect and identify debris, and a high-energy laser could be used to remove the debris. Because we currently do not have a method for clearing space debris, a space-based laser is an option at a time of growing emphasis on the use of space for commercial purposes.

Missile Warning and Attack Assessment

The location of theater ballistic missiles could be identified at launch and their trajectory and impact point estimated by using a space-based laser radar. This technology could possibly recognize transporter erector launchers (TELS) before the missile is launched and then employ a space-based laser designator to guide munitions to the target. This technology could improve the ability to detect missiles and to destroy those targets before the missiles are launched, to detect and to track missiles after they are launched, and to detect and to destroy warheads after their release from the missile. Because laser radar systems have been developed that can act over hundreds of kilometers, it is reasonable to extend these systems to somewhat greater ranges for tracking missiles.

Laser Communications and Data Relay

The use of lasers to transmit information is well developed, for example, in commercial fiber-optic communication networks that handle a tremendous volume of telecommunications. This technology could provide communications links between satellites or between earth stations and satellites in areas in which other communication networks are impractical.[28] For example, the McDonnell-Douglas Corporation developed the technology for providing space-to-space laser links for the Defense Support Program of early-warning satellites for communicating with submerged submarines.[29] This system could be used to communicate with unmanned aerial vehicles or command and control aircraft. For example, the E-3A airborne warning and control system (AWACS) aircraft can track hundreds of enemy aircraft at distances of hundreds of miles.

The Department of Defense's Ballistic Missile Defense Organization (BMDO), which is responsible for developing missile defense technologies, is exploring space-based laser communications. The ability to relay massive amounts of information is critical in modern military operations. The greatest challenges for space-to-space links are acquiring the target, pointing the laser at the target, and tracking the target, whereas the problem for earth-to-space links is that clouds, haze, and other atmospheric effects weaken the laser beam. Using beacons on the receivers would help the transmitters to lock onto the target, and adding ground stations increases the chances that one will be in the clear.

Laser Weapons

This section focuses on various ways in which lasers can be used for military targeting purposes, notably space-based weapons, missile defense, and space- and ground-based antisatellite weapons, and for antiaircraft defense.

Space-Based Counterforce Weapon

The use of space-based lasers to attack military targets—notably military satellites, nuclear warhead reentry vehicles (RV), missiles in the boost phase, high-flying military aircraft, and antisatellite kinetic energy missiles—has been extensively discussed for decades within the defense establishment. The ability to destroy targets at great distances with energy moving at the speed of light has such revolutionary implications for warfare that the U.S. defense establishment has invested billions of dollars in research over recent decades. Even a small number of laser weapons in space would create a significant capability for destroying ballistic missiles that are launched against the United States or against its forces in a regional conflict.

High-energy lasers, which represent an obvious way to destroy missiles, typically seek to destroy the target with thermal effects. The hydrogen fluoride laser, the most mature candidate, would use large-diameter, lightweight mirrors to focus the laser beam onto the target. The ability to acquire targets in near–real-time, perhaps by linking a space-based laser with early warning satellites, is essential because the time between the launch of a ballistic missile and the end of its powered flight (boost phase) is as little as sixty seconds. This laser weapon must be controlled by an automated system that can engage multiple targets by rapidly shifting the beam from one target to another.

A space-based laser weapon involves significant engineering challenges. It would be quite expensive and also vulnerable to attacks by antisatellite weapons, including the co-orbital interceptor developed by the Soviets during the late 1970s. Thus, a space-based weapon requires a system that uses kinetic or directed-energy weapons to defend itself against antisatellite weapons. This technology can be built, but it would involve extraordinary engineering challenges.

Space-Based Ballistic Missile Defense
As articulated by President Ronald Reagan in a speech on March 23, 1983, the goal of the United States was to build a defensive shield with space-based lasers against ballistic missiles. If the laser beam can be focused at an incoming missile's booster, the heat of the laser will weaken the missile skin until internal pressures in the booster's fuel or oxidizer tanks rupture the booster. Because it is difficult to destroy reentry vehicles that are covered with materials protecting against the heat of reentry, the best solution is to destroy the missile in the boost phase. Destroying the booster, which is the most vulnerable component of the missile, might have the collateral benefit of causing nuclear warheads and other debris to land on the territory of the state that launched the missile. This action would also destroy the missile before it could deploy countermeasures to confuse or overwhelm the defenses. Although this technology is promising, it poses serious technical challenges, including the need for an autonomous system that detects the launch, acquires and tracks the target, points the laser at the target, engages the target with the laser until it is destroyed, and shifts rapidly to the next target.

Ground-Based Laser Antisatellite Weapon

Bouncing a laser beam from relay mirrors in orbit requires less power than ballistic missile defense because satellites are relatively vulnerable. To be effective, a ground-based laser should be located at sites that have exceptionally clear weather most of the year. This weapon uses a high-power laser, large telescopes, atmospheric compensation techniques, high-accuracy pointing and tracking systems, and imaging systems to evaluate whether the target was destroyed. Because the laser does not have to be compact and it can use the local electrical grid for power, ground-based laser technology is more developed than its space-based counterpart. The orbiting relay mirrors would be complicated to build and deploy, but they are within existing optical and computer capabilities. These technologies are sufficiently mature for the purposes of developing a limited capability against satellites that are not protected against an attack.

Space-Based Antisatellite Weapon

An alternative is to use space-based lasers for an antisatellite weapon that is in orbit. The relative softness of most satellites, the lack of atmospheric effects, and the shorter range from the weapon to the satellite reduce the power requirements for antisatellite missions below those for missile defense. The problem is that developing a high-power, lightweight, and reliable laser device that can be fired many thousands of times is technologically demanding. An electrically powered laser would be preferable to a chemical laser, which has a limited number of shots before it must be refueled. Placing this, or any, weapon in orbit would create political difficulties because it violates the consensus that states should not place either offensive or defensive weapons in space.

Antiaircraft Weapon

It is possible to use a space-based hydrogen fluoride laser for attacking aircraft that operate above 30,000 feet (10 km). This high-power laser could use a laser beam whose wavelength is stopped by the atmosphere at this altitude, which eliminates the risk of unintentionally illuminating people or targets on the ground.[30] Enemy aircraft could be tracked by infrared or radar sensors, and have their locations relayed to the weapon. With sufficiently large optics, the beam could be focused on a spot that is small enough to damage or destroy aircraft. In general, this system would need far less power than a weapon that destroys missiles because an aircraft's slower speed permits the laser to remain on the target for a longer time. The ability to attack aircraft in regions where the United States could not deploy antiaircraft weapons and to do so without putting friendly forces at risk would represent a significant military advance.

Conclusion

As a result of decades of technological innovation, lasers are revolutionizing how the United States might conduct military operations during the twenty-first century. High-energy lasers can cause substantial damage to a wide range of militarily significant targets, as demonstrated when the predecessor to the airborne laser shot down air-to-air missiles in tests. In the late 1990s, the United States used the mid-infrared advanced chemical laser (MIRACL) to destroy a pressurized booster tank and to blind a U.S. satellite in orbit as part of ongoing research efforts. Laser technology is significant because it can deliver energy over enormous distances for destructive as well as nondestructive purposes, such as imaging, sensing, and communication. It is clear that this technology could have revolutionary effects on military operations.

Laser weapons, however, are not necessarily the most efficient way to destroy military targets. Attempts by the United States to destroy reentry vehicles illustrate the difficulties of efficiently producing laser energy and placing enough laser energy on a target to destroy it. Laser energy also creates opportunities for adversaries to develop countermeasures that can degrade the ability of lasers to destroy targets, classic examples of which are thicker missile skins and spinning missiles to dissipate laser energy.

Whereas continuous lasers must dwell on a target for enough time to damage the target with thermal effects, pulsed lasers also have their weaknesses. To damage a target by blowing off part of the surface of the target, pulsed lasers create a plasma formed by the interaction of the laser and the material of the target that absorbs so much laser energy that it weakens the ability of the laser to damage the target. Although these challenges are well known within the laser weapon community and have spurred numerous innovative solutions, it is essential for the American public to understand that the use of lasers for military purposes is complex and challenging.

Perhaps the most promising laser applications for the military are communications and data relay, space-based target designation, laser remote sensing for battle damage assessment, battlefield illumination, weather monitoring and environmental sensing, and ground-based and space-based antisatellite weapons. There is no doubt that lasers are increasing awareness of, and control over, events on the battlefield, and they are likely to revolutionize warfare.

Notes

1. Jeff Hecht, *Laser Guidebook,* 2d ed. (New York: McGraw-Hill, 1992).
2. Examples of tunable lasers include the titanium sapphire (Ti:S) laser, the chromium:LiSAF laser and the chromium:LiCAF laser.

3. "American National Standard for Safe Use of Lasers," American National Standards Institute (ANSI), Z136.1-1993 (Orlando, Fla.: Laser Institute of America, 1993), 3. A pulsed laser is characterized by the pulse duration, which is measured in seconds. If the laser is repetitively pulsed, the pulse repetition frequency (prf), measured in Hertz, is the inverse of the period from the beginning of one pulse to the beginning of the next pulse. The duty cycle of the laser is the product of the pulse duration and the prf and gives a measure of the percentage of time that a laser is emitting. A duty cycle of 50 percent means that the laser is emitting energy half of the time.

4. U.S. Air Force [hereafter USAF] Scientific Advisory Board, *New World Vistas: Air and Space Power for the 21st Century, Directed Energy Volume* (Washington, D.C.: USAF Scientific Advisory Board, 1996), viii.

5. Ibid. The flexibility of a variable output power is also discussed in the Air Force 2025 study, as cited in John A. Tirpak, "Air Force 2025," *Air Force Magazine* (December 1995), 24.

6. USAF Scientific Advisory Board, *New World Vistas, Directed Energy Volume,* viii.

7. For reference, every compact disk player contains three diode lasers; this fact demonstrates its reliability and affordability.

8. "Pentagon's Mark Sees Pilotless Future," *Defense Week* (May 30, 2000), 6.

9. Hecht, *Laser Guidebook,* 190.

10. Lt. Col. Marc Hallada, Chief, Laser Devices Division, Phillips Laboratory, Kirtland Air Force Base, N.Mex., interview by author, Feb. 19, 1997.

11. The author spent more than three years in leading the Air Force's laser biophysics research program and holds the highest level of U.S. Navy certification in laser safety. The comments in this section are based on this experience.

12. "Air Force Awards Attack Laser Contract," Air Force News Service Release (Nov. 13, 1996.

13. *Air War—Vietnam* (New York: Arno Press, 1978), 79–83.

14. Michael J. Muolo, *Space Handbook,* Air University Report AU-18 (Montgomery, Ala.: Air University Press, 1993), 2:4–5.

15. Kenneth A. Myers and Job G. Tockston, "Real Tenets of Military Space Doctrine," *Airpower Journal* (winter 1988), 59.

16. Although there is some matter even in deep space, the absorption and scattering of the electromagnetic radiation depends on the wavelength. Astronomical spectroscopy of gaseous nebula depends on these effects.

17. Ray Nelson, "Reinventing the Telescope," *Popular Science* (January 1995), 57.

18. R. Benedict, *Laser Mission Study,* AF Phillips Laboratory Technical Report, PL-TR-93-1044, July 1994, 47. See also USAF Scientific Advisory Board, *New World Vistas, Directed Energy Volume,* x.

19. *Air War—Vietnam,* 85.

20. Joint Chiefs of Staff, *Joint Vision 2010,* 1996, 21, available at http://www.dtic-mil/jv2020.

21. David Winker, "LIDAR in Space: The View From Afar," *Photonics Spectra* (June

1995) 102–3. NASA orbited the Laser In-Space Technology Experiment LITE) on Space Shuttle Mission STS-64 to test this concept. See also Carlo Kopp, "Air Warfare Applications of Laser Remote Sensing," Royal Australian Air Force Air Power Studies Centre, No. 33, June 1995.

22. Benedict, *Laser Mission Study*, 47. See also USAF Scientific Advisory Board, *New World Vistas, Space Technology Volume*, 9; USAF Scientific Advisory Board, *New World Vistas, Sensors Volume*, x, 30, 33, 36, 87–89.

23. USAF Scientific Advisory Board, *New World Vistas, Space Technology Volume*, 48.

24. USAF Scientific Advisory Board, *New World Vistas, Sensors Volume*, 88–89.

25. Benedict, *Laser Mission Study*, 53.

26. Ibid., 90. See also USAF Scientific Advisory Board, *New World Vistas, Sensors Volume*, 88; USAF Scientific Advisory Board, *New World Vistas, Space Technology Volume*, 48; Norman P. Barnes, "Lidar Systems Shed Light on Environmental Studies," *Laser Focus World* (April 1995), 87–94.

27. USAF Scientific Advisory Board, *New World Vistas, Directed Energy Volume*, 20.

28. Regis J. Bates, *Wireless Networked Communications* (New York: McGraw-Hill), chap. 3.

29. "Laser, Systems," McDonnell-Douglas Corporation, technical brochure, 1992, 9, 11.

30. USAF Scientific Advisory Board, *New World Vistas, Directed Energy Volume*, 23, 57. If the wavelength is not strongly absorbed, however, one conceivably could attack soft targets on the surface.

2.   Lasers and Missile Defense

William H. Possel

By 2010–2015, the United States could face several states, such as Iran, Iraq, and North Korea, that possess ballistic missiles and nuclear, chemical, and biological weapons capable of killing hundreds of thousands or millions of Americans. Because the United States cannot currently protect itself against missile attack, the growing consensus in Washington is that some form of national missile defense is necessary. Within less than a decade, the United States could be using high-energy laser weapons to defend itself and its allies from missile attacks. During the Cold War, missile defense was viewed as technologically and economically impractical because the Soviet Union had thousands of nuclear weapons. Since the 1980s, however, the Department of Defense has invested billions of dollars in laser technologies designed to destroy a smaller missile attack. As a result of dramatic technological advances, there are now several options for missile defense in the medium term, including spaced-based lasers (SBLS), ground-based lasers (GBLS) with relay mirrors in space, and SBLS with orbiting relay mirrors. This chapter examines the technological risks and economic costs of developing and deploying lasers for missile defense.

Introduction

The laser is the most important optical invention of the latter half of the twentieth century. Since its invention in the early 1960s, the laser has proved to be an extremely versatile and useful device for the scientific, commercial, and military communities. As noted in Chapter 1, the laser redefined the idea of precise military attacks during the Persian Gulf War, and continues to do so as many states develop laser technologies for military purposes.[1]

Since the early 1990s, lasers have produced sufficient energy to be seriously considered, even by the most ardent skeptics, as potential weapons for destroying ballistic missiles.[2] The U.S. defense establishment, notably the Air Force, is developing the airborne laser (ABL) aircraft for the purpose of destroying theater ballistic missiles while they are still over enemy territory, but this is only the first step toward laser defenses (Figure 2.1).[3] The emerging consensus in the defense establishment is that lasers could provide a valuable weapon for defending the United States, while the Congress debates how to reconcile building missile defenses with the Antiballistic Missile (ABM) Treaty.[4] At the same time, the United States has urged Russia to modify the treaty to permit limited defenses.

One technologically feasible and cost-effective approach to missile defense is to deploy lasers in space. An equally tenable option is to use ground-based lasers with a large constellation of relay mirrors to direct the laser beams at incoming missiles. A third option is to combine space-based lasers and optical relay mirrors in order to reduce the overall cost of missile defense. The problem for the defense establishment is that these competing approaches raise a number of significant questions. Are laser platforms that orbit the earth the most technologically realistic and cost-effective means for destroying ballistic missiles? Or, is it more efficient to use orbiting mirrors that relay the laser beam from the ground to the missile? What is the most technologically effective way to defend against ballistic missiles?[5]

While the United States struggles with the best strategy for using high-energy lasers to defend against ballistic missiles, a reasonable estimate can be made that laser missile defenses could cost more than $100 billion during the next several decades. The realization that rogue states armed with ballistic missiles could strike American cities with nuclear weapons or other weapons of mass destruction is moving the United States toward missile defense. By the year 2007, the United States will deploy the ABL that could use a laser to destroy ballistic missiles. As early as 2020, the United States might deploy an SBL weapon system that could destroy ballistic missiles thousands of kilometers away. Another option is to use SBLs in conjunction with orbiting mirrors, which would make missile defenses more effective and less costly.

To offer a better understanding of the most effective, technologically achievable, and affordable high-energy laser weapon system, this chapter discusses technological maturity and cost, reviews the proliferation of ballistic missiles and their vulnerability to laser energy, considers the power and number of laser weapons that are needed, and discusses the critical technologies.

Ballistic Missile Proliferation and Vulnerabilities

During the 1980s, a number of laser weapon studies focused on defending the United States against an attack by the Soviet Union with the use of hundreds

Figure 2.1. The airborne laser (ABL) is a 747 aircraft equipped with a high-energy laser beam for destroying theater ballistic missiles. (Courtesy U.S. Air Force)

of ballistic missiles and thousands of nuclear warheads. The Soviet Union's collapse, however, has prompted defense planners to consider the use of laser weapons to defend the United States and its allies against a smaller number of ballistic missiles.[6]

Missile Proliferation

One conclusion from the Persian Gulf War was that ballistic missiles represent a threat to the United States and its allies. Even though Iraqi short-range missiles were inaccurate and armed only with conventional high-explosive warheads, this technology significantly affected the political and military conduct of the war.[7] Iraq's use of missiles against Saudi Arabia and Israel demonstrated that less powerful states, such as Iraq, were not unwilling to use ballistic missiles against the United States and its allies. During the early twenty-first century, several states could possess ballistic missiles capable of attacking the United States with nuclear, chemical, and biological warheads.[8] Many states are now developing ballistic missiles or importing the technology from such major states as Russia and China that have already developed advanced missile technology.

Because Iraqi ballistic missiles had a decisive political effect on coalition forces during the Gulf War, ballistic missiles might be the preferred weapon when states become involved in a military struggle with the United States. Although these missiles are inaccurate and militarily ineffective, they allow rogue states to intimidate their neighbors at considerably less cost than a buildup of conventional armies.[9] Further, these missiles could become more accurate as advanced states continue to export critical technologies.

The advantages of missiles are that they hit their targets within minutes of launch; they are relatively inexpensive; and, until the Persian Gulf War, they did not encounter active defenses.[10] The consensus is that approximately thirty-six countries possess ballistic missiles and fourteen nations have the technological and industrial infrastructure that is necessary for building them.[11] These missiles range from large ICBMs to small Scud missiles that are dispersed throughout the world. To cite an advanced example, India has developed a space-launch vehicle that could be modified for use as a ballistic missile. Many governments among the major states might help developing states with their ballistic missile programs in order to generate hard currency.[12]

The more immediate problem is the proliferation of short-range ballistic missiles (SRBMs) and intermediate-range ballistic missiles (IRBMs). For example, North Korea's Scud missile can reach cities in South Korea and Japan, and its Taep'o-dong II missile, with a range of 4,500–6,000 miles (7,500–10,000 km), could reach Alaska, Hawaii, or the western United States.[13] To complicate matters, India, Pakistan, and several Middle Eastern countries refused to sign the Nuclear Nonproliferation Treaty (NPT) and are presumed to be importing nuclear technology. Although China adheres to the NPT, it has refused to adhere to the export policies of the Nuclear Suppliers Group, and it is known to sell nuclear energy and research-related equipment to countries that have active programs for developing nuclear weapons.[14]

Missile Vulnerabilities to Lasers

High-energy laser weapons provide a promising technology for defeating ballistic missiles, especially smaller ballistic missiles whose lighter-weight materials and thinner outer skins are more vulnerable to laser weapons.[15] With its tremendous speed, lack of recoil, and extremely long range, the laser beam is the ideal instrument for destroying ballistic missiles, especially during the boost phase when destroying the missile might keep nuclear, biological, or chemical warheads on enemy territory.

An important factor in designing a cost-effective laser weapon is the amount of laser energy that is required to destroy a missile. In practical terms, this translates into holding the laser beam on the missile until there is sufficient energy to heat, melt, or vaporize the missile skin to the point of structural failure. The laser's effectiveness is a function of the power, pulse duration, and wavelength of the beam, as well as air pressure, missile material, missile velocity, and thickness of missile skin.[16] An alternative approach is to direct the beam at the material surrounding the missile's fuel tank until the fuel detonates or to heat the missile skin until the enormous internal forces in the fuel tank rupture the missile skin. Another alternative approach is to target the electronic circuits that are used for guidance control, which are easy to destroy but difficult to target with precision or confidence.[17] The energy required to rupture a missile's skin depends on the type and thickness of the material. The objective is to focus the laser on the target until the skin material absorbs so much radiation that the missile's fuel tank ruptures.[18]

Space-Based Laser

The idea of using SBL weapons for missile defense and offensive and defensive satellite operations originated in the 1970s.[19] The unique characteristic of the space-based laser is its ability to cover large theaters of operations. By placing the SBL in geosynchronous orbit, it could cover about half of the earth's surface, whereas deploying lasers in low-earth orbit increases the number of weapons required for global coverage (Figure 2.2).

The original purpose of the SBL was to destroy Soviet intercontinental ballistic missiles (ICBMs) in their boost phase before each missile released its nuclear warheads. The early SBL concepts were built on the assumption that the Soviet Union would attack with two thousand ICBMs launched simultaneously. To counter this many missiles, the technologists designed a laser system, which would require a 30-megawatt laser and a mirror 33 feet (10 m) in diameter, that could destroy forty missiles per second.[20] With the end of the Cold War, however, American defense planners shifted to using space-based lasers to defend against short-range missiles that are launched from anywhere in the world.[21]

One design concept is to deploy twenty laser platforms at an orbit of 800 miles (1,300 km). Each space-based laser would be designed to destroy a missile in two to five seconds, to retarget another missile in one-half second, and to have the ability to destroy missiles within 2,000 miles (3,200 km) of the laser. After twelve laser platforms are initially deployed, the constellation could be expanded to twenty satellites to protect the United States against a missile attack.[22]

Each space-based laser platform would consist of a laser device; an optics

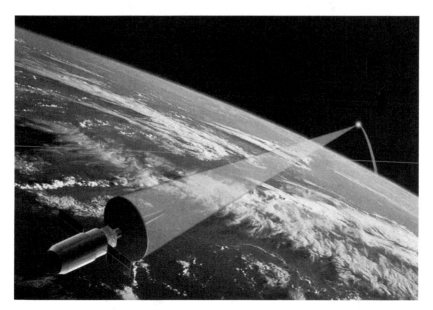

Figure 2.2. The space-based laser (SBL) is a constellation of satellites equipped with a high-energy laser for destroying ballistic missiles launched from anywhere on earth. (Courtesy U.S. Air Force)

and beam control system; an acquisition, tracking, pointing, and fire-control system; and associated space systems. One concept is a laser device with a hydrogen fluoride laser that operates at a wavelength of 2.7 μ and produces about 8 megawatts of power.[23] The primary mirror, with a diameter of 25 feet (8 m), would utilize superreflective coatings to operate without active cooling despite the tremendous heat that is generated by the laser.[24] The purpose of the fire control system is to maintain the beam on the target and reduce the jitter (or vibration) of the high-energy laser produced by the laser's mechanical pumps. The associated space systems provide the necessary electrical power, command and control, laser reactants, and onboard data processing. Each space-based laser is estimated to weigh 77,000 pounds (35,000 kg), which is more than three times the weight of the Hubble space telescope.[25] Before its fuel is depleted, this chemically fueled laser is capable of firing an estimated seventy-five shots against missiles, or an estimated total firing time of two hundred seconds. After the fuel is consumed, the laser must be refueled in space or replaced.[26]

   This approach, however, raises questions about the launch vehicle that is used to place the laser platforms in orbit. The next generation launch booster, which is the follow-on to the Titan IV, could place 48,000 pounds (22,000 kg) into low-earth orbit.[27] With the current dimensions of the laser platform, two rockets will be required to launch each laser platform into space for assembly. The United States has not assembled such a complex system in space, however, and it is unlikely to develop a new launch vehicle specifically for deploying the space-based laser.[28]

Because the United States has never before integrated all of these technologies into a space platform, the Pentagon's Ballistic Missile Defense Organization proposed building the SBL readiness demonstrator, which was a half-scale version of the laser platform. Designed to reduce the risks associated with fielding such a complex entity by integrating the various subsystems into a space-qualified package, it consisted of a high-energy hydrogen fluoride laser that operates at one-third the power of the full-scale SBL.[29] The general consensus in the technological community is that this weapon can be built because many programs have demonstrated that the basic engineering obstacles can be overcome. When ready for launch, the laser demonstrator would have weighed an estimated 36,000 pounds (16,600 kg) and would have been launched on the Titan IV booster or the new rocket for putting payloads into orbit known as the evolved expendable launch vehicle (EELV). Once in orbit, large target balloons would have been used to test the accuracy of the laser tracking and pointing subsystem and rockets launched as test vehicles.[30]

The U.S. Air Force and the Ballistic Missile Defense Organization, recognizing the budget limitations and technological challenges of the readiness demonstrator, are now designing a smaller, more realistic experiment to demonstrate the technological feasibility of destroying ballistic missiles. Known as the Integrated Flight Experiment, this $3 billion program will consist of a megawatt-class laser and large optics that can be launched on the new EELV in 2012.[31]

An operational SBL would be immensely expensive. Early cost analyses conducted by government agencies and defense contractors predict that a twenty-platform space-based laser would cost between $17 billion and $29 billion.[32] These cost estimates, however, are unrealistically low. Based on previous U.S. experience, military satellites, on average cost between $50,000 and $150,000 per kilogram. The SBL constellation is estimated to weigh 1,500,000 pounds (700,000 kg), which is 77,000 pounds (35,000 kg) per platform. Using the historical average cost of $100,000 per kilogram for the development of a space system, the SBL is likely to cost $70 billion, and, with launch costs added, the program could total about $81 billion.[33]

Ground-Based Laser

The second technological option for destroying ballistic missiles is to use large mirrors in space to relay a GBL beam to the missile (Figure 2.3). The GBL con-

Figure 2.3. The ground-based laser (GBL) is a high-energy laser for destroying ballistic missiles from the ground. Typically, it would be deployed with a constellation of relay mirror satellites to direct the laser beams at the missiles. (Courtesy U.S. Air Force)

sists of high-energy lasers at ground stations located throughout the country. Although the concept for SBLs emerged during the 1980s, it received less attention than the SBL concept because of numerous technological difficulties.[34] The GBL's advantage, however, is that keeping the laser on the ground eliminates the need for launching weapons into space and refueling laser chemicals in space. Also, when problems develop, equipment on the ground is radically more accessible than satellites in orbit.

Because poor weather, including clouds, wind, and pollution, distort laser beams, GBLs must be located in regions that have good weather throughout the year. One study determined that, to achieve 99.5 percent availability regardless of weather conditions, the GBL requires five sites, which typically are located in the southwestern quadrant of the United States, notably California, Arizona, and New Mexico.[35]

Each ground system includes a high-energy laser, a beam director, adaptive optics, acquisition and tracking systems, and related support systems. The chemical oxygen iodine laser (COIL) is the preferred laser because the shorter wavelength of the laser minimizes the effects of atmospheric distortion. The GBL requires substantially greater energy than the SBL, however, because atmospheric effects, thermal blooming, and the longer ranges that the beam must travel all reduce its power.

The GBL has a beam director that uses a primary mirror to control the beam and a deformable mirror to compensate for atmospheric distortion.[36] Termed an *adaptive optics system,* such as that used at the Starfire Optical Range in Albuquerque, New Mexico, it determines how the atmosphere would distort the laser, then uses a deformable mirror to "straighten" the laser as it passes through the atmosphere.[37] From the beam director, the laser beam is transmitted through the atmosphere to a constellation of relay mirrors in space that reflect the laser energy to the target. Their altitude is critical because positioning the relay mirrors in a high orbit reduces not only the number of mirrors required to "cover the world" but also the overall complexity of the laser system. Four relay mirrors in geosynchronous orbit would cover the entire planet and always leave one mirror in a position that is sufficiently close to the lasers to minimize atmospheric effects.[38] The higher the orbit, however, the larger the relay mirrors must be to "catch" the laser beam. Because the relay mirrors must receive the incoming laser beam from the GBL and then focus the beam on the target, they also could be in low-earth orbit and use a correspondingly smaller relay mirror. With the relay mirrors in low-earth orbit, however, controlling the system would be more complex because the number of mirrors would increase to provide global coverage and the laser would be relayed by several mirrors before it engaged missiles.

One of the more intriguing concepts for the relay mirror is be a bifocal mirror, which consists of two connected telescopes that transfer the beam from the receiving telescope to the transmitting telescope. The first telescope, the incoming receiver, is pointed directly at the relay mirror so that the laser beam is received directly into the primary mirror. The beam is then transferred to the second telescope, which focuses the beam on the target.[39] For a GBL to have the same capability of the space-based laser, it would require at least twenty relay mirrors.[40] It is estimated that the relay mirror spacecraft will weigh 75,000 pounds (34,000 kg), and the relay mirror satellites will weigh a total of 18,000 pounds (8,500 kg).[41]

The GBL and space mirrors must overcome significant obstacles that do not affect the SBL. For instance, the greater distance between the lasers and the targets dramatically increases the power required for the laser. Further, atmospheric losses will increase the power requirement for the laser and the demands on the adaptive optics that control the quality of the laser beam. The large space mirrors, which must be built to extremely high-quality optical standards, must be capable of high-accuracy pointing and very low jitter (vibration).[42]

The principal technological challenges for the GBL system are the optical systems and generating a laser beam with sufficient power. The National Aeronautics and Space Administration (NASA) has an aggressive program to accelerate mirror technology, but the current generation of relay mirror concept still weighs far more than the capacity of existing launch vehicles, particularly if these mirrors are placed in a high orbit.[43] Further, the power needed for each GBL to destroy missiles is twenty-five times greater than the power that has been demonstrated to date. For these reasons, the GBL is less technologically feasible and mature than the SBL.[44]

The ability to place relay mirrors, each with a diameter of 66 feet (20 m), in geosynchronous orbit with existing launch vehicles requires technological breakthroughs. The consensus in the aerospace community is that for the GBL to be a viable alternative to the SBL, its cost must be the same or less than that of the SBL. Estimating the cost of a ground-based laser involves several factors. The constellation of space mirrors, estimated to weigh 670,000 pounds (306,000 kg), includes four relay mirror platforms that weigh 85,000 pounds (34,000 kg) each and twenty bifocal mirror platforms that weigh 18,000 pounds (8,500 kg) each. The overall development cost is estimated to be $30.6 billion, with the space segment costing $40 billion when launch expenses are included.[45]

When one includes the estimated cost of each ground laser site of $4.13 billion, or about $20.6 billion for five sites, the cost of an entire GBL system, including its space and ground segments, is about $61 billion.[46]

High-energy lasers were built for experimental rather than military purposes, so there are inherent risks in estimating the cost of a laser on the basis of an experimental system. An alternative to estimating the cost of developing a GBL is to compare the cost of developing a GBL antisatellite system.[47] If the laser's power requirement for missile defense is extrapolated, each ground site would cost $26 billion, with five sites costing $130 billion. When launch costs are included, the total system would cost about $170 billion.[48]

In view of the technological challenges associated with the generation of sufficient laser power, the construction and placement of very large mirrors into high orbit, and launch vehicle limitations, the GBL is a less attractive option for missile defense.

Spaced-Based Lasers with Mirrors

Although a GBL involves significant technological challenges, the use of relay mirrors has important implications for missile defense. One option is to use SBLS with large orbiting mirrors in order to reduce the number, weight, and cost of missile defense and to create a more effective system. The use of SBLS with mirrors in space would combine the strengths of both approaches into an effective and technologically achievable system that costs significantly less.[49]

Because a significant source of the SBL's overall cost is the laser platform, reducing the number of platforms cuts the overall cost. If the relay mirrors are positioned between the laser platforms so that the laser fires directly at the missile or relays the laser beam with the mirror, the SBL requires fewer laser platforms because the mirrors provide the global coverage. This was first considered during the 1980s in a study that compared SBLS with a mix of SBL platforms and orbiting mirrors. It concluded that the SBL with orbiting mirrors would lower the overall weight of the payloads that must be placed in orbit, place less stringent constraints on laser beam control, and reduce the vulnerability of the system.[50] The advantage is that, instead of using twenty high-cost laser platforms for missile defense, the same capability can be achieved with ten platforms and ten orbiting mirrors. This constellation would weigh approximately 40 percent less than that of the SBL, which decreases the size of the SBL and frees the United States from developing a new launch vehicle for placing these systems into orbit. The fundamental benefit of adding space-based mirrors to the SBL is to reduce the weight of the laser platforms and to maintain the SBL's ability to destroy missiles.[51]

The Department of Defense estimates that a space-based laser constellation with twenty platforms would cost between $17 billion and $29 billion, but a more realistic analysis suggests that the cost is about $80 billion. An SBL with mirrors would cost about $50 billion because the overall weight is less and involves fewer large lasers. This is about 40 percent less than the cost of the SBL concept and 70 percent less than the $170 billion cost of the GBL. Although these estimates illustrate the magnitude of building these systems rather than providing absolute measures of cost, the SBL with mirrors would cost less than the SBL without mirrors and radically less than a GBL.

Conclusion

For missile defense, the GBL is an attractive but less mature and more expensive option than the SBL. The decision to combine SBLS with orbiting mirrors would result in reducing the overall weight and cost of missile defenses. This has important implications given that the United States is unlikely to spend significantly more money on national missile defense. This logic might be called into question, however, if a state, such as Iran, Iraq, or North Korea, threatens U.S. cities with nuclear weapons. The fundamental conclusion is that high-energy lasers could provide a critical technology for defending the nation against the threat of intimidation or attack by ballistic missiles.

Notes

1. Michael J. Muolo, *Space Handbook,* Air University Report AU-18 (Maxwell Air Force Base, Ala.: Air University Press, 1993), 2:229; Vincent T. Kiernan, "The Laser-Weapon Race Is On," *Laser Focus World,* December 1996.
2. William J. Broad, "From Fantasy to Fact: Space-Based Laser Nearly Ready to Fly," *The New York Times,* Dec. 6, 1994.
3. Suzann Chapman, "The Airborne Laser," *Air Force Magazine,* January 1996, 54–55. See also Kenneth A. Barker, "Airborne and Spaceborne Lasers: Assessing the Compatibility of Technological and Operational Strategies," occasional paper, Center for Strategy and Technology, Air War College, Maxwell Air Force Base, Ala., 1999, and "Airborne Laser," available at http://www.airborne laser.com.
4. Vincent T. Kiernan, "What Is the Future of Space-Based Laser Weapons?" *Laser Focus World,* June 1997, 75.
5. Several studies have recommended space-based high-energy laser programs. See USAF Scientific Advisory Board, *New World Vistas: Air and Space Power for the 21st Century, Summary Volume* (Washington, D.C.: Department of the Air Force, 1996), 46–48; USAF Scientific Advisory Board, *New World Vistas: Air and Space Power for the 21st Century, Space Technology Volume* (Washington, D.C.: Department of the Air Force, 1996), xi–xii, 61–62; USAF Scientific Advisory Board, *New World Vistas: Air and Space Power for the 21st Century, Directed Energy Volume* (Washington, D.C.: Department of the Air Force, 1996), 22–26; *Spacecast 2020,* "Force Application" (Maxwell Air Force Base, Ala.: Air University Press, 1994), O-18; Jamie G. Varni, Gregory M. Powers, Dan S. Crawford et al., "Space Operations: Through the Looking Glass (Global Area Strike System)," in *2025 Study* (Maxwell Air Force Base, Ala.: Air University Press, 1996).
6. USAF Scientific Advisory Board, *New World Vistas, Directed Energy Volume,* 22.
7. Leonard Spector, "Proliferation in the Third World," in *Security Strategy and Missile Defense,* ed. Robert L. Pfaltzgraff Jr. (Hollis, N.H.: Puritan Press, 1995), 13.
8. "Ballistic Missiles within Easy Reach for Many Nations," *The Washington Post,* Sept. 23, 1997. According to the testimony of Dr. George Keyworthy, President Reagan's science advisor, before the Senate Governmental Affairs Subcommittee on Proliferation, "Today, opportunities for developing countries to acquire long-range ballistic missiles are at an all-time high."
9. Missile technology is a profitable export item for several nations. A number of countries export complete systems, technologies, and developmental expertise to generate income from foreign sales. China, North Korea, and several industrial-

ized states in Europe are supplying ballistic missiles and missile-related technologies, which further increases the number of nations with ballistic missile capability. See William Van Cleave, "The Role of Active Defense," in *Security
Strategy and Missile Defense,* ed. Robert L. Pfaltzgraff Jr. (Hollis, N.H.: Puritan
Press, 1995), 101. Further, Iran acquired submarine-launched cruise missiles when
it purchased Kilo class submarines from Russia. To date, United Nations' efforts to
curtail the sale of missile technology through the Missile Technology Control
Regime (MTCR) have not succeeded. See also Spector, "Proliferation in Third
World," 16–17.

10. Spector, "Proliferation in Third World," 13.
11. "The Threat is Real and Growing," Centre for Defence and International Security
    Studies, Oct. 25, 1997, available at http://www.cdiss.org:80/hometemp.htm.
12. Steven Erlanger, "U.S. Telling Russia to Bar Aide to Iran by Arms Experts," *The
    New York Times,* Aug. 22, 1997, A1; "Russia-Israel Strain over Iran Missile Aid,"
    The New York Times, Aug. 25, 1997, A3.
13. "National Briefings: North Korea," Centre for Defence and International Security
    Studies, October 28, 1997, available at http://www.cdiss.org/nkorea_b.htm. See
    also Van Cleave, "Role of Active Defense," 101.
14. "Threat Is Real and Growing."
15. Geoffrey E. Forden, "The Airborne Laser," *IEEE Spectrum,* September 1997,
    40–42.
16. Bengt Anderberg and Myron Wolbarsht, *Laser Weapons: The Dawn of a New
    Military Age* (New York: Plenum Press, 1992), 114.
17. Kosta Tsipis, "Laser Weapons," *Scientific American,* December 1981, 55; Geof-
    frey E. Forden, "The Airborne Laser," *IEEE Spectrum,* September 1997, 46.
18. Muolo, *Space Handbook,* 286-87. See also USAF Scientific Advisory Board, *New
    World Vistas, Directed Energy Volume,* 24, and Forden, "Airborne Laser," 47.
19. This is a conservative estimate because laser weapons must produce even greater
    amounts of energy given the losses to atmospheric absorption, thermal blooming,
    laser beam jitter, and pointing errors. As shown in the following table, several
    factors determine the exact amount of energy that must be absorbed by the missile
    to cause structural failure. If one calculates that the missile skin has 90 percent re-
    flectivity (meaning that only 10 percent of the laser energy on target is absorbed),
    the laser fluence on the missile would need to be ten times greater.

Estimated Missile Vulnerabilities

Name/Country of Missile	Range (km)	Missile Burn Time (sec)	Material	Material Thickness (mm)
Scud B (Russia)	300	75	Steel	1
Al-Husayn (Iraq)	650	90	Steel	1
No Dong-1 (North Korea)	1,000	70	Steel	3
SS-18	10,000	324	Aluminum	2

Source: Geoffrey E. Forden, "The Airborne Laser," *IEEE Spectrum,* September 1997, 47.

19. Originally, the Alpha laser, LODE optics, and Talon Gold ATP/FC were technology development programs for an antisatellite SBL concept. The author was assigned to the Space Laser Program Office, Los Angeles Air Force Base, Calif., from 1981 to 1983.

20. N. Bloembergen, C. K. Patel, P. Avizonis et al., "Science and Technology of Directed Energy Weapons," *Reviews of Modern Physics* 59, pt. II, July 1987, 55.

21. USAF Scientific Advisory Board, *New World Vistas, Directed Energy Volume*, 22.

22. Schafer Corporation, "Space-Based Laser: Pioneering Tomorrow's Defense," CD-ROM, 1997.

23. USAF Scientific Advisory Board, *New World Vistas, Directed Energy Volume*, 24.

24. Ibid.

25. Schafer Corporation, "Space-Based Laser."

26. USAF Scientific Advisory Board, *New World Vistas, Directed Energy Volume*, 23.

27. See "Evolved Expendable Launch Vehicle," Nov. 8, 1997, available at http://www.laafb.af.mil/SMC/MV/eelvhome.htm.

28. USAF Scientific Advisory Board, *New World Vistas, Space Applications Volume*, 88–89.

29. Schafer Corporation, "Space-Based Laser.

30. Ibid.

31. Bryan Bender, "USA Takes Small Steps Towards Space Weapon," *Joint Defence Weekly,* Mar. 22, 2000, 10. See also "Spaced Based Laser," available at www.sbl.losangeles.af.mil.

32. Marc Hallada, Ph.D., and Dustin Johnston, Ph.D., Schafer Corporation, Albuquerque, N.Mex., interviews by author, Nov. 1, 1997.

33. For these and all subsequent calculations in this chapter, the following methodology was used to calculate the cost estimate for the SBL architecture. This is a simplified version of a more detailed calculation that was conducted by the author in the original study. For a complete description of the methodology and assumptions, see William H. Possel, "Lasers and Missile Defense: New Concepts for Space-Based and Ground-Based Laser Weapons," occasional paper, Center for Strategy and Technology, Air War College, Maxwell Air Force Base, Ala., 1998, available at http://www.au.af.mil/au/awc/awcgate/cst.

1. SBL development cost = SBL total weight × cost per kilogram
    = 700,000 kg × $100,000/kg
    = $70.0 × 10^9

2. Added cost for level of technological readiness = development cost × 10%
    = ($7.0 × 10. 10) × 0.10
    = $7.0 × 10^9

3. Launch cost = SBL total weight × cost per kilogram to orbit
    = 700,000 kg × $5,650/kg
    = $3.955 × 10^9

4. Total cost = development cost + added cost for technological readiness + launch cost

$$= (\$70.0 \times 10^9) + (\$7.0 \times 10^9) + (\$3.955 \times 10^9)$$
$$= \$80.955 \times 10^9 \text{ or about } \$81 \text{ billion}$$

34. Numerous architectural studies for a ground-based laser system exist; for a general discussion of the physics of the system, see Bloembergen, Patel, Avizonis et al.,"Science and Technology."

35. R. D. Stark, *RF—Laser Comparison and Considerations,* Aerospace Corporation Report ATR-94 (6486)-8 (El Segundo, Calif.: Aerospace Corporation, July 1993), 52–53. See also Peter B. Ulrich and R. James Morgan, *SDIO Ground-based Laser Support—Laser and Power Technology,* vol. VIB, *Special Tasks in Ground-Based Laser Beam Control,* DNA-R-90-103-V6B (Alexandria, Va.: Defense Nuclear Agency, 1991), B-45.

36. Deformable mirrors use microactuators to change its mirror shape in order to cancel the effects of the distorting effects of the atmosphere on light, as seen by the twinkling of stars. If one can accurately measure the distortion of light as it passes through the earth's atmosphere, then light being transmitted through the atmosphere can be predistorted. And, if the effects of atmospheric distortion on light can be cancelled, these canceling effects of atmospheric distortion have significant implications for astronomy and directed energy.

37. V. Krabbendam and T. Sebring, *Ground-Based Laser System Optical Component Producibility Study—Executive Summary,* RADC-TR-90-355 (Griffiss Air Force Base, N.Y.: Rome Air Development Center, 1990), 3.

38. Relay mirror systems are useful for other missions, including remote sensing, target designation, global wind measurements, and active imaging.

39. Phillips Laboratory personnel, Kirtland Air Force Base, N.Mex., interview by author, Oct. 31, 1997.

40. This estimate is based on a 2,000-km altitude and a 4,000-km range from the relay mirror to the target. Department of Physics, U.S. Air Force Academy, personnel, interview by author, Nov. 26, 1997.

41. The mirror weight estimates for deployable mirrors varies greatly. One estimate provided by Phillips Laboratory, Kirtland Air Force Base, N.Mex., is that the mirror weight scales with $D^{1.3}$, where D is the mirror diameter, whereas another estimate is that the mirror weight scales with $D^{2.3}$ to $D^{2.7}$. To be conservative, this chapter uses $D^{2.7}$ as the scale factor and includes the mirror supporting mass as well as the mirror. It also added 4,400 pounds (2,000 kg) for the spacecraft. The bifocal included another 20 percent to account for the transfer optics. The following calculation uses the weight of 5,900 pounds (2,700 kg) for the next-generation space telescope (NGST), which replaces the Hubble space telescope:

For Relay Mirror at Geosynchronous Orbit:
(Mass of mirror/2,700 kg) = (20 m/8 m)$^{2.7}$;
Mass of mirror = 32,000 kg
+ 2,000 kg (for spacecraft)
= 34,000 kg

For Relay Mirror at Low-Earth Orbit:

(Mass of mirror/2700 kg) = $(8 \text{ m}/8 \text{ m})^{2.7}$;

Mass of mirror = 2,700 kg

$2,700 \times 2 = 5,400$ kg (for two mirrors with bifocal design)

$+ 20\%$ of 5,400 (for transfer optics)

$+ 2,000$ kg (for spacecraft)

$= 8,500$ kg

42. Ulrich and Morgan, "SDIO Ground-Based Laser Support," C-105. See also "Science and Technology of Directed Energy Weapons," 8.

43. See H. S. Stockman, ed., "The Next Generation Space Telescope—Visiting a Time When Galaxies Were Young," June 1997, available at http://oposite.stsci.edu/ngst/initial-study/.

44. This assessment would be closer to the SBL architecture if the development programs involving extremely large deployable optics come to fruition. If such large mirrors could be deployed in space from existing launch vehicles, the rating for this concept would likely improve.

45. The following methodology was used to calculate the cost estimate for the on-orbit segment of the GBL architecture. This is a simplified version of a more detailed calculation that was conducted by the author in the original study.

1. GBL on-orbit development cost = GBL on-orbit weight × cost per kilogram

$= 306,000$ kg $\times \$100,000$/kg

$= \$30.6 \times 10^9$

2. Added cost for level of technological readiness = development cost × 25%

$= (\$30.6 \times 100) \times 0.25$

$= \$7.65 \times 10^9$

3. Launch cost = GBL on-orbit weight × cost per kilogram to orbit

$= 306,000$ kg $\times \$5,650$/kg

$= \$1.729 \times 10^9$

4. Total on-orbit cost = development cost + added cost for technological readiness + launch cost

$= (\$30.6 \times 10^9) + (\$7.65 \times 10^9) + (\$1.729 \times 10^9)$

$= \$39.979 \times 10^9$ or about $40 billion

46. The following methodology was used to calculate the cost estimate for the total cost of the GBL architecture using the "ABL" model. This is a simplified version of a more detailed calculation that was conducted by the author in the original study.

1. GBL ground segment cost/site = GBL power (in watts) × cost/watt

$= 25 \times 106$ W $\times \$165$/watt

$= \$4.125 \times 10^9$

2. Cost for five sites = Cost/site × number of sites

$= (\$4.125 \times 10^9) \times 5$

$= \$20.625 \times 10^9$

      3. Total cost = on-orbit segment cost + ground segment cost
$$= (\$39.979 \times 10^9) + (\$20.625 \times 10^9)$$
$$= \$60.631 \times 10^9 \text{ or about } \$61 \text{ billion}$$

47. Phillips Laboratory personnel, Kirtland Air Force Base, N.Mex., interview by author, Dec. 1, 1997. The estimate was based on a GBL antisatellite (ASAT) system with a brightness of 1.0×10^{18} watts per steradian. The total cost was $1.3 billion over seven years. This extrapolation, which is based on a worst-case analysis, assumes a brightness factor approximately twenty times greater and therefore a cost estimate that is twenty times higher.

48. The following methodology was used to calculate the cost estimate for the total cost of GBL architecture using the antisatellite (ASAT) model. This is a simplified version of a more detailed calculation that was conducted by the author in the original study.

      1. GBL cost/site = GBL brightness (in watts/steradian) × ASAT cost/watt/steradian
$$= 20 \times 10^{18} \text{ W/steradian} \times (\$1.3 \times 10^9/1 \times 10^{18} \text{ W/steradian})$$
$$= \$26.0 \times 10^9$$
      2. Cost for five sites × Cost/site × number of sites
$$= (\$26.0 \times 10^9) \times 5$$
$$= \$130.0 \times 10^9$$
      3. Total cost = on-orbit segment cost + ground segment cost
$$= (\$39.979 \times 10^9) + (\$130.0 \times 10^9)$$
$$= \$169.979 \times 10^9 \text{ or about } \$170 \text{ billion}$$

49. Lawrence Sher and Stephan McNamara, "Relay Mirrors for Space Based Lasers," Research Report, *Laser Digest*, AFWL-TR-88-68, vol. VI, Air Force Weapons Laboratory, Kirtland Air Force Base, N.Mex., May 1989.

50. Ibid. For a more detailed analysis of the physics, see Lawrence Sher, "Optical Concepts for Space Relay Mirrors," Research Report, *Laser Digest*, AFWL-TR-88-68, vol. II, Air Force Weapons Laboratory, Kirtland Air Force Base, N.Mex.: Air Force Weapons Laboratory, May 1989.

51. The following methodology was used to calculate the cost estimate for the SBL platforms with orbiting mirrors architecture. This is a simplified version of a more detailed calculation that was conducted by the author in the original study.

      1. SBL + development cost = SBL + total weight × cost per kilogram
$$= 435,000 \text{ kg} \times \$100,000 \text{ kg}$$
$$= \$43.5 \times 10^9$$
      2. Added cost for level of technological readiness = development cost × 10%
$$= \$43.5 \times 10^9 \times 0.10$$
$$= \$4.35 \times 10^9$$
      3. Launch cost = SBL + total weight × cost per kilogram to orbit
$$= 435,000 \text{ kg} \times \$5,650/\text{kg}$$
$$= \$2,458 \times 10^9$$

4. Total cost = development cost + added cost for technological readiness + launch cost

$$= (\$43.5 \times 10^9) + (4.35 \times 10^9) + (\$2.458 \times 10^9)$$

$$= \$50.308 \times 10^9 \text{ or about } \$50 \text{ billion}$$

3. Airborne and Space-Based Lasers

Kenneth W. Barker

The United States has spent hundreds of millions of dollars for the development of two laser systems for missile defense—the airborne laser (ABL) and the space-based laser (SBL). A strong argument could be made that developing the ABL first will technologically benefit the SBL and that these two weapon systems operating jointly would provide more effective defenses. This chapter examines both technological and operational compatibilities as they relate to developing and operating airborne and space-based lasers, as well as the strengths, weaknesses, and synergies of the ABL and the SBL for ballistic missile defense. In view of the extraordinary investments in lasers for missile defense, the chapter offers the interested public an understanding of how these directed-energy technologies could influence U.S. national security in the medium term.

Introduction

The United States is developing both the airborne laser and the space-based laser for the purpose of defending the country against ballistic missiles. The plan for the ABL program is to deliver seven laser weapon systems, and the current SBL program can deliver one orbiting laser lethality demonstrator, previously known as the Space-Based Laser Readiness Demonstrator but recently retitled the Integrated Flight Experiment (IFX). These two options for missile defense raise a fundamental question about whether the ABL is the technological precursor to the development of the SBL. The relationship between the two systems is termed *technological compatibility*. A second question, which refers to *op-*

erational compatibility, is whether the ABL and the SBL could operate jointly to defend against a missile attack. These questions have profound implications when the United States is investing significant resources in missile defenses.

Essentially, the ABL and SBL have the same primary mission of using high-energy lasers to destroy ballistic missiles during their boost phase. The ABL's primary mission is theater ballistic missile defense, whereas the SBL advertises the two primary missions of ballistic missile defense and counterspace operations. Ballistic missile defense includes both national and theater missile defense. The SBL's national missile defense (NMD) mission involves intercepting strategic missiles in their boost phase when the engines are being fired. Counterspace missions involve assuring access to space, guaranteeing freedom of operations within the space medium, protecting space assets from attack, and denying an adversary's use of space. Examples of counterspace missions are those that deny, disrupt, degrade, or destroy systems in earth orbit, which are classic antisatellite (ASAT) missions. These missions are belligerent by nature, however, and undermine the notion that space is a sanctuary for peaceful purposes; for now, they are politically untenable. Therefore, the ABL and SBL programs are currently moving forward with the same primary mission of theater missile defense. The leadership of the ABL program is planning to intercept a missile by the year 2002 and to start deploying seven ABL aircraft as early as the year 2005. Although the SBL is in an earlier stage of development, with launch dates for a demonstration vehicle that are planned for the year 2012, the plan is to develop a system to demonstrate that laser energy can be used to destroy missiles while not violating the Antiballistic Missile (ABM) Treaty, which prohibits the United States and Russia from developing systems to destroy ballistic missiles.[1]

Considerable debate exists within the technological, policymaking, and operational communities about the value of simultaneously developing the ABL and SBL. The supporters of simultaneous development argue that this approach makes perfect sense because the ABL, as a technological and operational precursor to the SBL, can reduce the overall risk of the SBL program. A related argument is that the ABL can demonstrate the feasibility of destroying ballistic missiles in the atmosphere before the technological and military communities attempt to do the same in space. The competing argument, however, is that because the ABL and the SBL have similar missions, the United States cannot afford to develop both of these weapon systems. At the same time, because the ABM Treaty prohibits the United States from fielding antiballistic missile systems in space, a related criticism is that the United States should not build ballistic missile defenses if it is prohibited from fielding a working system. Finally, there is the technological criticism that the ABL and SBL are high-risk weapon systems whose success depends on a number of technological breakthroughs that have yet to be achieved.

In view of the ongoing debate, this chapter examines the use of laser weapons during the twenty-first century to destroy ballistic missiles. It examines the ideas of technological and operational compatibility and their implications for understanding how to develop and use the ABL and the SBL for missile defense.

Background

The United States and its coalition partners achieved overwhelming victory during the Persian Gulf War, but they were defenseless against Iraq's short-range theater ballistic missiles. Although militarily insignificant, Iraqi Scud missiles were politically lethal. The United States deployed Patriot missile batteries to defend Israel against Iraqi missiles and, as well, to persuade Tel Aviv to refrain from launching the missiles against Baghdad, which would have fractured the military coalition.[2] The Iraqi missiles also caused some damage, however, and, in one incident, twenty-seven American soldiers were killed when a Scud missile hit a barracks in Dhahran, Saudi Arabia.

After the war, the ABL system program office was organized with the objective of delivering seven laser weapons by the year 2005. The ABL consists of a Boeing 747 aircraft that is modified to house a megawatt-class laser, which will destroy missiles launched within its lethal range. The ABL program is based on nearly three decades of high-energy laser research and development by the Department of Defense (DOD) and the Department of Energy. Two earlier programs, the Airborne Laser Laboratory (ALL) and the Airborne Optical Adjunct (AOA), had demonstrated that lasers can track and destroy missiles. As noted in Chapter 1, the ALL shot down several missiles in 1983.[3] The military understood the value of this capability and outlined the need for the ABL in a number of documents.[4] In June 1997, the Air Force selected Boeing Corporation and Lockheed-Martin Corporation to deliver a demonstrator aircraft in 2002 and seven fully functional weapons as early as 2005.

The SBL has a similar technological legacy. Originally designed to defend against missiles of the former Soviet Union, the SBL involves deployment of a constellation of twenty satellites in an orbit of 800 miles (1,300 km) that can attack missiles in their boost phase. With its megawatt-class laser, the SBL could autonomously destroy ballistic missiles at distances of about 2,500 miles (4,000 km). Importantly, the SBL would provide continuous, complete, and instantaneous coverage of the globe against ballistic missile threats that would significantly improve U.S. military capabilities.

A related advantage of the SBL is that it avoids the problem of intercepting thousands of individual warheads because it seeks to destroy missiles before the warheads are released from the missiles. This laser program originated in the Defense Advanced Research Projects Agency in 1977, and, by 1984, the Strategic Defense Initiative Organization had become the executive agent and management authority for all SBL programs. By the late 1990s, these technologies had shown such increased technological promise that the SBL received significant political support from Congress. In 1998, Congress added $100 million to the SBL budget beyond the figure requested by the DOD.[5]

The Meaning of Technological Compatibility

The term *compatibility* has several meanings for large weapon systems.[6] Compatibility is often used inappropriately, however, as, for example, in describing two systems as compatible in political, budgetary, and organizational terms. The term is vague and in need of further explanation. A statement that two systems are compatible could refer to such factors as operations, interchangeability of spare parts, or common software. Unless defined precisely, compatibility can mean everything and nothing at the same time. In this chapter, technological compatibility is assessed by examining both technical risks and challenges, as well as technological similarities and differences.

Because all new weapon systems entail unique technical risks and challenges, it is essential that those risks and challenges are identified so that the technological community can define the proper experiments and demonstrations to reduce risk. When two weapon systems share common risks and challenges, it might indicate that they use or apply compatible technologies. For example, if two systems must employ autonomous navigation in order to accomplish their mission, then demonstrating the feasibility of autonomous navigation will be a significant challenge in developing both systems. If one program successfully demonstrates the feasibility of autonomous navigation, the other program might accept this demonstration as a legitimate way to reduce risk and to demonstrate that the concept is technically valid. If two weapons have no common technical risks and challenges, the technologies in each system might be incompatible. To rephrase, the existence of common technical risks and challenges provides evidence that there is some degree of underlying technological compatibility. Similarities and differences among technologies also point to technological compatibility and can include degrees of form, fit, and function that render pieces of or knowledge about one component or system useful in the design or manufacture of another system. For example, a pop-up toaster and a toaster oven share significant technological similarities and therefore can be considered technologically compatible.[7]

Because systems that share the same mission do not necessarily consist of compatible technologies, a more precise way to discuss technological compatibility is to use the terms *traceable, scalable, leverageable,* and *synergy,* or the phrases *risk reduction, proof of principle* or *concept,* and *stepping stone.*

The term *traceable* describes whether one technology is generally relevant to another. For example, software consists of algorithms or lines of computer code that control system-specific functions. Modern high-performance fly-by-wire aircraft are inherently unstable without a stability augmentation system that is part of the aircraft's avionics. The stability augmentation systems in earlier generations of aircraft are probably not traceable to those that are employed on modern aircraft.

The term *scalable* describes how directly physical principles translate from one technology to another. For example, engineers often construct models to demonstrate the efficacy of a design principle. If the model properly reflects the intended principle, the design can be scaled up to the final dimensions. In bridge building, the engineer might want to demonstrate the ability of a new material to handle loads. If the model uses the same material with the same proportional loading, the model is probably scalable to the real bridge. The art and science of scaling depends on knowing the critical physical principles involved and the influence of other factors on those principles, which might be replicated in models or experiments.

The term *leverageable* is best understood in the mechanical sense as the action of a lever. In this case, leverage simply means to get more out than you put in. In this same sense, programs can gain more than is invested if the investments are wisely made. For example, a program can gain valuable technologies or information from other programs by investing in certain aspects of the other program, such as technology demonstrations or risk reduction experiments.

The term *synergism,* which is both an overused and a misused word, is derived from the Greek word *sunergos* for working together. As long as two entities work together, it is commonly said that there is some synergy between the two. The more precise definition, however, is two or more substances, organs, or organisms achieving an effect of which neither is individually capable and then producing fundamentally different effects. For example, precision bombs increase the ability to destroy targets beyond that achieved with unguided bombs, and stealth aircraft are nearly invisible to radar. The combination of precision bombs with stealth aircraft is synergistic because it produces an effect that neither technology can achieve by itself.

When used synonymously, the terms *proof of principle* and *proof of concept* generally apply to experiments or demonstrations of technologies is a necessary precursor to a future technological development. The Manhattan Project represents a proof of concept for atomic bombs. Never before had the concept of an atomic chain reaction been demonstrated and controlled as an explosion prior to the July 1945 detonation, but it proved that the concept was valid. Another example is the first V-2 launch in October 1942, which proved the concept of ballistic missiles and ushered in the age of intercontinental ballistic missiles.

The phrase *stepping stone* communicates a necessary or beneficial sequence of events. For example, the airplane was a necessary stepping stone to the spaceship regardless of the fact that both systems have few key technologies in common. Psychologically, however, humans probably needed to see themselves safely off the ground in the air before they could grasp the thought of traveling in space. As another example, propeller-driven aircraft were necessary technological stepping stones to jet aircraft because the higher speeds achieved by propeller aircraft drove the development of the designs and manufacturing techniques in airframes that were necessary to support the higher speeds of jet flight.

Technological Compatibility between Airborne Laser and Spaced-Based Laser Weapon Systems

For an understanding of whether the technologies in the ABL and SBL are compatible, this section offers a discussion of the technologies involved in each weapon system.

Technical Risks and Challenges

Both the ABL and SBL programs have identified unique technical risks and challenges that must be overcome in order for the weapon systems to become viable. In part, what makes these risks and challenges unique to each program is their operating environment—the ABL operates in the atmosphere, and the SBL operates in space. In both cases, the environment influences the required technology.

Airborne Laser

The areas of greatest technological risk for the ABL are integrating and testing the system on aircraft; actively tracking theater ballistic missiles, conducting atmospheric compensation of the high-energy laser beam, managing the transition of track from missile plume to missile hardbody (hardbody handover), and developing a "flight-weight," high-energy laser. In relation to these risks, the ABL program office identified the major technical challenges, which are to characterize upper atmospheric turbulence, including meteorological effects; demonstrate active tracking through turbulence; identify weight-reducing laser technology improvements; verify modes for damaging targets; and define the software codes that are used for design analysis and for performance prediction.

Space-Based Laser

The greatest technological risks for the SBL program are development of the spacelift necessary to boost 80,000 pounds (36,000 kg) to a 780-mile (1,300-km) orbit; development of a deployable large primary mirror; development of a space-qualified, megawatt-class laser; integration of the SBL technologies on a spacecraft; and an energy-efficient an energy-efficient way to destroy ballistic missiles. The major technical challenges in the SBL program are to develop a space-qualified laser of shorter wavelength than the SBL's current baseline laser; to demonstrate a lethal laser from space; to develop a heavy-lift booster; and to develop a test and evaluation facility capable of precision alignment of deployable optics and performing a complete test of the integrated system, including the high-energy laser, transfer optics, isolation systems, and beam expander.

Assessment of Compatibility

With the exception of unique aspects of platform integration, the two programs do not share technical risks and major technical challenges. Although this is not conclusive evidence that the two programs are incompatible, it indicates that the ABL and the SBL are deeply entrenched in their own unique technologies that are not common or compatible.

Some technical risks and challenges are common to both the ABL and the SBL but are not identified. One case, for example, is hardbody handover and active track. The fact that the ABL has undergone more mature systems engineering than the SBL might account for some disparity, and it is true that hardbody handover and active track have been recognized for years by both ABL and SBL communities as major concerns for both programs. The failure of SBL developers to identify hardbody handover and active track as risks is more likely due to the fact that other risks in the programs were determined to have higher priority at the time.

The most telling evidence, however, is revealed in the documented assessment of pertinent risk reduction programs for each system. Both the "Airborne Laser Cost Analysis Requirements Document" and the "SBL Technical Requirements Document" discuss in detail the relevant technology programs that are the basis for the overall confidence in the state-of-the-art technologies in these systems. For the individuals who authored the documents, these technology programs are the true risk-reduction and proof-of-concept programs necessary for these weapon systems. From these programs, traceable and scalable technologies have been derived. ABL and SBL developers used their individual technology development programs in ways that were beneficial to them rather than to the other program. Throughout the years, both ABL and SBL program leaders invested in technology development programs. Primarily military or national laboratories and their respective contractor bases have performed these programs, which reduced the risk for both the ABL and the SBL. Prominent examples include the high-altitude balloon experiment (HABE) integrated acquisition, tracking, pointing, and fire control (ATP/FC) architecture and experiments that are relevant to both the ABL and the SBL. Another example is the adaptive optics work, especially the algorithm developed at the Starfire Optical Range at the Phillips Laboratory, which is applicable to both systems. For a variety of reasons—program ownership; mutually exclusive funding sources; and pride in the ability to know, program, and direct one's own technology development requirements—neither ABL nor SBL developers have been eager to acknowledge the mutual benefit provided by some of these technology programs.

Similarities and Differences in Technologies

Both the ABL and the SBL systems can be divided into similar technological subsystems: laser device, beam director, beam control, acquisition, tracking, pointing, fire control, and battle management. The following section addresses compatibility in these areas.

Laser Device

The laser device generates the high-energy laser used to destroy ballistic missiles in flight. The ABL laser device uses a multimegawatt chemical oxygen iodine laser (COIL), whereas the SBL weapon system has a multimegawatt hydrogen fluoride laser.[8] These technologies might sound similar, but the differences are so fundamental that the ABL laser device is not traceable, scalable, or leveragable to the SBL laser device in any meaningful sense. For example, the ABL laser uses different fuels, as well as different injection, cooling, and pressure recovery processes, than those used in the hydrogen fluoride laser in the SBL. The technological, engineering, and integration requirements are so significantly different that developing the ABL laser does not constitute a credible risk reduction or proof of concept for the SBL. Consequently, the ABL laser device is not a stepping stone toward the development of the laser device in the SBL. Although the DOD chose the same defense contractor, TRW, to develop both the ABL and the SBL laser devices, the synergy from sharing ideas, progress, and facilities for the technical teams does not produce technological compatibility.

Beam Director

The beam director functions is the principal optical transmitter and receiver that collects incoming optical signatures and transfers them to the optical beam train and sensors for fire control and beam control. The ABL beam director is a nose-mounted, turret-housed, gimbaled telescope with a primary mirror that is 5 feet (1.5 m) in diameter. The ABL beam director also collects passive and active target signatures for tracking, collects returns for atmospheric compensation, and processes other signatures and images for determining whether the missile is destroyed. By contrast, the SBL beam director, which is located in the forward part of the satellite, will house a much larger, 26–40-foot (8–12-m) primary mirror. The SBL beam director also collects return target signatures and images for tracking, surveillance, and imaging. The SBL's adaptive optics subsystem, with its deformable mirror, also corrects the laser before it enters the beam expander.

Because the operational conditions, range to missiles, and wavelength of the lasers in the ABL and SBL are so different, the beam directors employ fundamentally different technologies. Although the ABL beam director is small enough to fit in the nose of an aircraft, the SBL beam director is five to ten times larger. This technological difference is important because optical manufacturers can fabricate 1.5-m mirrors but not the larger 8-m mirrors. Although this technology is somewhat traceable, it does not scale easily and therefore is not compatible. The fact that plans call for the SBL to use a higher-wavelength high-energy laser (HEL) than the ABL simplifies the task of grinding the SBL's primary mirror surface. Achieving the kinds of specifications required for laser applications on large optics (26–40-foot [8–12-m] diameter), however, poses serious fabrication challenges, including the effects of gravity on the mirror and on grinding tools.

Beam Control

The purpose of beam control is to correct and stabilize the high-energy laser disturbances that distort the beam before it leaves the beam director. Although the ABL and SBL perform the beam control in generally the same fashion by using some similar technologies, the higher-risk technologies tend to be unique to each program. The similar technologies are so similar they are highly traceable and leverageable between programs.

Some technologies, however, are so dissimilar that they share little or no commonality between weapon systems. To cite a technical example, the SBL uses multi-input/multi-output active structural control technology on its truss assembly. The ABL does not use counterpart technologies. The SBL also incorporates holographic gratings on its primary mirror for outgoing wavefront sensing, whereas the ABL incorporates a more complex five-beam track illuminator/two-beam beacon illuminator return path wavefront sensing technology. In these cases, the technologies are so different that they are not traceable, scalable, or leverageable between programs. Neither program reduces the risk for the other, and no synergy exists between the two.

The common technologies between the ABL and the SBL are those with low risk. On the other hand, the higher-risk technologies tend to be those unique to each system. Although there is some compatibility among certain beam control technologies, it primarily involves those with lower risks. Consequently, little real benefit is derived from leveraging between the programs, and little synergy can be expected. The overall degree of compatibility between ABL and SBL beam control technologies is low.

Fire Control System

The purpose of the acquisition, tracking, pointing and fire control system is to acquire and track targets, select points to aim the weapon, point the weapon at targets, control the laser device and beam control system, and assess whether the missile has been destroyed. In the ABL, these optical functions are accomplished through the main aperture. A related idea is "hardbody handover," which refers to switching from passively tracking the missile's plume to actively tracking the missile body. Passive track is performed by using reflected photons from the target that is illuminated only by the sun or other natural phenomena. Active track is performed using reflected photons generated by an illuminating system, such as a laser. This begins when the fire control computer estimates the position of the missile body with respect to the plume by using the laser range finder and imagery from the missile plume. The tracking illuminator lasers then flood the missile's nose to create a spot that acts like a beacon for the active fine tracker. To destroy the missile, the laser beam must focus and dwell on the most vulnerable part of the missile, for example, the pressurized fuel tank in liquid fuel missiles. The final task is to assess whether the target has been destroyed. After the laser is placed on the target, sensors look for indications that the missile has been destroyed, including sudden changes in the missile's velocity and acceleration, sudden changes in the hot spot created by the high-energy laser beam, and human confirmation that the target is disintegrating.

The biggest difference between ABL and SBL fire control technologies is the number of apertures. The ABL uses a single main aperture to gather incoming target signatures and acts as the outgoing beam director for four different lasers: the ranging laser, the track illuminator laser, the beacon illuminator laser, and the high-energy laser (HEL). The SBL, by contrast, uses four separate apertures to accomplish essentially the same tasks. In effect, the ABL trades increased complexity in some optical elements for the simplicity of fewer apertures. Although both systems could use shared or separate aperture architectures, the fact that ABL and SBL have different architectures limits their technological compatibility.

Most of the ABL and SBL fire control technologies are compatible. For example, ABL and SBL coarse track sensors "see" essentially the same bright missile plume. The specific sensor technologies are traceable, but the fact that they are based on different materials severely limits their leveragability. The ABL and SBL fire control rules are quite similar, however, which creates some leverage that reduces overall risk and increases their synergy, but only if there is significant technological and operational coordination between the two programs. For now, the overall degree of compatibility is medium to low.

Battle Management

The concept of battle management includes the overall command, control, communications, and coordination of the weapon system during all phases of operation. The unique operational environments and requirements for autonomy drive choices of the battle management architectures and technologies for the ABL and the SBL. Whereas the ABL will be operated in a fashion similar to other high-value aircraft in the theater, the SBL will be operated much like other communications and intelligence, surveillance, and reconnaissance (ISR) satellites. The SBL, however, will have a more intense system for command and control in view of the fact that it is designed to operate as the first weapon in space.

For this reason, most of the technologies that support battle management for the ABL and the SBL are fundamentally incompatible. For example, ABL communications and intelligence technologies employ frequencies and bandwidths that are typical for air-ground operations while SBL technologies require frequencies, bandwidths, and error rates that are more appropriate for autonomous operations in space. To enable satellite-to-satellite connectivity, the SBL uses laser communications, whereas the ABL does not.

There is, however, some use of similar or compatible technologies. For example, both the ABL and the SBL use similar computer algorithms to identify targets, coordinate the employment of multiple ABLs or SBLs in a military operation, and assess the likelihood of a ballistic missile kill. Although the ABL design currently does not incorporate algorithms to help discern different types of ballistic missiles, the ability to identify friend or foe (IFF) is common to both the ABL and the SBL.

Commonality also exists at the highest levels in the decision algorithms that are embedded in the battle management software. These algorithms employ criteria for making decisions, including handing over targets from surveillance to acquisition; cycling through various modes of laser and beam control operation; assessing the probability of a missile kill; managing overall command, control, and intelligence flow; and resolving anomalies, among others. On the whole, however, the overall compatibility between ABL and SBL battle management technologies is low.

Operational Strategies

The phrase *operational compatibility* refers to weapon systems that can efficiently and effectively work together in combat and whose overall military effectiveness increases when they are used together. Operational synergy exists when a different and better effect is achieved with both systems, when the systems do not conflict with one another, and when employing both systems does not degrade the effectiveness of one system. In the case of using lasers for missile defense, operational strategy involves the functions of deployment, employment, engagement, sustainment, and self-protection, as well as the command and control necessary for integrating lasers into the overall military operation.

Operating the ABL or the SBL on an independent basis would represent a unique challenge for military commanders. With only seconds available for destroying missiles, humans would be required to make extremely fast decisions in highly complex conditions. For missile defenses to be effective, military commanders must integrate the ABL and the SBL into a single missile defense system. Such integration can succeed only if these weapons have compatible operational strategies.

To complicate matters, these lasers have similar primary as well as secondary missions. Secondary missions are referred to as *adjunct missions* in the ABL program and *ancillary missions* in the SBL program. Both the ABL and the SBL share the same primary mission, which is to destroy ballistic missiles in their boost phase. The ABL will focus on theater missile defense, while the SBL will focus on missile defense and counterspace operations on a global scale. Counterspace operations include ensuring access to space, guaranteeing freedom of operations within the space medium, protecting space assets from attack, and denying the use of space to adversaries.

The ABL can also perform the secondary missions of defending against cruise missiles, protecting high-value airborne assets, suppressing enemy air defenses, and conducting surveillance. The secondary missions for the SBL include ground surveillance and reconnaissance, tactical designation, hyperspectral imagery (i.e., identifying targets by using different wavelengths of light), wind sensing, tracking and identifying objects in space, and attacking ground targets with great precision. Although the SBL is designed to perform more secondary missions, there is no fundamental technological limitation on the ability of the SBL and ABL to perform the same missions. A critical point is that the ABL and the SBL can both conduct theater ballistic missile defense, which strengthens the reasons for designing compatible operational strategies. If the SBL focuses on national missile defense and antisatellite operations, however, its operational compatibility with the ABL in terms of intercepting missiles in the theater might be compromised.

Command and Control

The function of command and control, which involves the authority to deploy, employ, engage, and sustain each system in theater and the means to execute that authority, has significant implications for the operational compatibility of the ABL and the SBL. Using the ABL or the SBL against theater ballistic missiles involves a complex command and control process that combines automated and human decision making, precise rules of engagement, and a sophisticated communications network.

Fundamentally, the ABL is designed for theater missile defense and, as such, will operate like the Airborne Warning and Control System (AWACS) and the Joint Surveillance and Target Attack Reconnaissance System (JSTARS) aircraft. This means that the ABL would be physically located in a theater under the control of the theater commander. By contrast, the SBL provides a global capability with limited availability to theater commanders. Tactical control includes controlling the asset during combat operations, but it does not include controlling the asset outside the theater or for any purposes other than direct theater support. The SBL would not be assigned to theater commanders because, according to U.S. law, the U.S. Commander in Chief, Space Command (USCINCSPACE), controls the space forces that support the regional commanders in chief.[9] Although the SBL will be a "national asset," struggles over its use are inevitable as military commanders attempt to integrate it with the ABL in order to achieve a unified system for missile defense.

The ABL and the SBL have sophisticated battle management systems for coordinating automated and positive human control, but the current lack of integration between these systems reflects the human tendency within the programs to focus on the unique operational requirements of each type of laser system. For example, the SBL has a more highly centralized command and control system than the ABL because the authority to release the SBL is likely to reside with the national command authorities, which often means the President. The SBL will be controlled by a highly centralized space-based communications network because any significant degradation in the ability to communicate with the SBL would catastrophically reduce its military effectiveness. Although the ABL is fundamentally reliant on space-based communications, their loss would degrade the ABL's command and control system but not prevent its use.

Deployment and Employment

The term *deployment* refers to moving the weapon into a position so that it is ready for combat operations. Because the ABL would be based in the United States, military planners would assume that it will take about twenty-four hours to move each aircraft to the theater in a fully combat-ready state. Once the full constellation of satellites is in orbit, however, the SBL will be constantly deployed over all potential battlefields.

The term *employment* relates to positioning a weapon system within striking range of potential targets. For the ABL, employment means positioning the aircraft near the forward line of friendly forces, which also happens to be within striking range of enemy air defenses. As with other military systems, military commanders must strike a balance between having the ABL close enough to potential targets to be effective in combat while remaining far enough away to survive enemy attempts to shoot it down.

The current plan for employing the ABL is to use two combat air patrols (CAPs) of fighter aircraft to protect each ABL. Movement of the CAPs within the theater will be based on the threat from enemy aircraft and whether or not the United States has achieved air superiority, among other considerations. Other ABL aircraft that are kept on alert will be capable of rapidly replacing or supporting ABLs that are on combat patrol. Further, the theater commander can employ more than two ABLs independently in order to increase the coverage against theater missiles, to conserve the laser fuel in individual aircraft, and to increase the U.S. military capability against multiple missile launches. While on patrol, each ABL must continuously assess local atmospheric conditions and calibrate the laser.

The employment strategy for the SBL is vastly simplified because it can cover any theater within the limits imposed by its orbit and the lethal range of the laser, regardless of the number or geographic distribution of missiles in the theater. Although a complete SBL constellation will provide nearly global coverage for all theaters of operations, the overall capability of the SBL to provide a sustained response to missile launches is limited. The reasons are that additional satellites cannot be easily or quickly added to the constellation and there are current limitations on refueling SBL satellites.

Engagement

Engagement is the process of detecting, acquiring, tracking, and destroying ballistic missiles. Generally, the ABL and SBL use competing approaches in engaging missiles. The ABL uses infrared detection sensors to observe a missile exhaust plume, generate the target's inertial coordinates for the battle management system, and provide data on the target's location. These coordinates would provide warning to other defense systems, including the Patriot surface-to-air missile and the Theater High-Altitude Area Defense, if the missile is not destroyed. Once the missile is tracked with visible light, the system would determine the exact location on the missile body where the high-energy laser should be pointed.

For the SBL, however, there are two notable differences in the engagement process. First, whereas the ABL can autonomously detects missiles, the SBL relies on information from a number of intelligence, surveillance, and reconnaissance systems. Second, whereas the ABL aircraft remain relatively stationary in the theater, each SBL satellite would provide coverage over the theater for approximately 19 to 20 minutes during each 112-minute orbit at an altitude of 800 miles (1,300 km). To illustrate how dependent the SBL constellation is on its communications and surveillance systems, it is inevitable that an SBL satellite will be tracking a missile launch just before the SBL satellite loses the ability to cover the theater and therefore will pass this information to the next SBL satellite that is entering the same theater. At the same time, the SBL does not perform atmospheric compensation because the laser rarely, if ever, passes through any significant portion of the atmosphere.

Sustainment

The ABL and the SBL must be sustained, which includes refueling the aircraft and laser, rotating crews, and maintaining the aircraft and laser systems. Some sustainment, for example, refueling the laser, is necessary if the weapon was recently fired against missiles, but, in other cases, sustainment is independent of whether the laser was fired, as would be the case with crew rotations. The fundamental difference is that people sustain the ABL aircraft in the theater, whereas the SBL will be designed so that it requires limited sustainment in orbit.

Both the ABL aircraft and the SBL satellites will need to be refueled and the crew members rotated. Although the ABL aircraft can be refueled in the air, the need to rotate aircrews limits the "on-station" time for each ABL aircraft to less than twenty-four hours. Also, to refuel the laser, the aircraft must return to base. By contrast, the SBL has no onboard crew members, but ground station crew members must be rotated in a manner that does not interfere with the SBL's operations. Currently, there are no simple methods for refueling either the SBL laser or the satellite "consumables," which include, among other items, attitude control thrusters, spent batteries, and cryogenics for cooled sensors. Although it is conceivable that manned or unmanned spacecraft could be used to refuel the SBL, that technology does not yet exist. The ABL is designed to be less autonomous than the SBL, but that autonomy is expensive, which means that the ABL will require more frequent maintenance and involve more complex sustainment operations than the SBL.

Self-Protection

Because the ABL and the SBL are designed to operate in hostile environments, these weapons must include self-protection measures. The ABL must survive attacks by hostile aircraft and surface-to-air missiles. The SBL will be at risk from antisatellite or directed-energy attacks, as well as from attempts to interfere with its command and control system. As long as threats to space-based systems are less well developed than threats to airborne assets, the ABL's task of self-protection will be more demanding. This temporary advantage will fade as more states gain the ability to attack satellites, which explains why ABL and SBL program teams are investigating how to use their high-energy lasers for self-defense.

Conclusion

A fundamental conclusion is that the level of technological compatibility between the ABL and the SBL is generally low, but the operational strategies for the two weapons can be compatible. The implications are that the ABL is not a technological stepping stone to the SBL because the degree of technological compatibility between these programs is quite limited. The technological compatibility, to the extent that it exists, involves fairly well developed technologies. Because the development of ABL technologies does not help the SBL program in a technological sense, the term *stepping stone* has more political than technological value within the defense establishment.

There are areas in which greater interaction between the programs would increase their overall compatibility and hence would increase the ability of military commanders to develop an optimal strategy for developing high-energy lasers for destroying ballistic missiles. Greater interaction between the ABL and SBL programs would minimize the degree of risk associated with these programs and therefore would reduce the enemy's ability to exploit their weaknesses.

The weaknesses of the ABL and the SBL suggest that these weapons should not be operated independently of each other. There is merit in combining these laser systems into an integrated weapon because it would allow military commanders to use the strengths of one system to compensate for the other's weaknesses. As the DOD works to integrate these high-energy laser weapons into a unified operational and battle management system, the objective is to combine the capabilities of the ABL and the SBL into a comprehensive system for defending the United States against missile attacks during the twenty-first century.

Notes

1. Boeing Corporation, *Airborne Laser (ABL) System Cost Analysis Requirements Description,* unclassified version 2.1 (Boeing), Aug. 19, 1996, 8; Air Force Space Command, *Concept of Operations for the Space-Based Laser (SBL) System,* draft

document, Dec. 15, 1997. For a more detailed elaboration of the analysis in this chapter, see Kenneth W. Barker, "Airborne and Space-Based Lasers: An Analysis of Technological and Operational Compatibility," Occasional Paper No. 9, Center for Strategy and Technology, Maxwell Air Force Base, Ala., June 1999.

2. See Theodore A. Postol, "Lessons of the Gulf War Experience with Patriot," *International Security* (winter 1991/92), 191–202, for the argument that Patriot surface-to-air missiles did not successfully defend against Scud attacks. Although Patriot interceptor missiles intercepted some Iraqi Scud missiles, there are questions as to whether missile fragments that rained down on U.S. and Allied troops caused damage equal to what a missile would cause.

3. "Pentagon's Mark Sees Pilotless Future," *Defense Week* (May 30, 2000), 6.

4. See, for instance, "Theater Missile Defense Joint Mission Need Statement," November 1991; "Air Force TMD [Theater Missile Defense] Mission Need Statement," October 1991; and "Air Force TMD Concept of Operations," February 1993. See also U.S. Air Force Scientific Advisory Board, *New World Vistas, Air and Space Power for the 21st Century, Directed Energy Volume* (Washington D.C.: Department of the Air Force, 1996), 2.

5. The budget includes funds for the Alpha laser, Large Advanced Mirror Program, Large Optics Demonstration Experiment, Zenith Star, and several acquisition, tracking, pointing, and fire control experiments, including StarLab and the high-altitude balloon experiment. It is also noteworthy that the Airborne Laser Laboratory played a prominent role in the development of the SBL.

6. When used properly, the term *compatibility* means the ability to live or perform in harmonious, agreeable, or friendly association with another or others, as well as the capability of orderly, efficient integration and operation with other elements in a system.

7. A pop-up toaster and a toaster oven both use similar heating elements with similar temperature control electronics. Only the overall size and orientation differ, which is necessary to support the different size and orientation of their unique subjects (slices of bread versus frozen dinners). Interestingly, a toaster oven can perform the same mission as the pop-up toaster for a slice of bread, albeit less efficiently.

8. Because the SBL program is currently using hydrogen fluoride technology in its Integrated Flight Experiment design, hydrogen fluoride technology is used as a point of reference for this discussion of the SBL.

9. According to Title 10, U.S. Code, Section 164, "As a result, USCINCSPACE will likely retain combatant command of the SBL system at all times and may delegate operational control to the Commander Air Forces in Space." See Air Force Space Command, *Draft Concept of Operations for Space-Based Laser System,*14.

4. Directed-Energy and Fleet Defense

William J. McCarthy

Recent advances in directed-energy technologies could alter naval operations during the twenty-first century. This chapter examines the benefits of developing high-energy laser and high-power microwave weapons for maritime operations and naval warfare in the medium to long term. It discusses how an integrated system of microwave devices, high-energy lasers, and surface-to-air missiles for naval operations could provide an important capability for the United States. A number of states are developing weapons, including cruise missiles, that could threaten naval forces operating close to shore (termed the *littoral*). For operational and technological reasons, there will be opportunities to deploy these directed-energy technologies on *Nimitz*-class nuclear-powered aircraft carriers. This chapter evaluates how these technologies could be used in naval operations; whether they might lead to a fundamental shift in the composition of carrier battle groups, as well as naval operations; and whether sea-based directed-energy weapons might alter naval power during the twenty-first century.

Introduction

The use of directed-energy weapons during the twenty-first century could change naval tactics as fundamentally as the transition from sail to steam. As a result of recent advances in directed-energy technologies, it is technically feasible to adapt high-energy laser and high-power microwave weapons for the defense of naval forces. This chapter examines an integrated system of microwave devices, high-energy lasers, and surface-to-air missiles for antiship cruise missile defense, tactical air defense, and fast patrol boat defense.

In view of the proliferation of sophisticated weapons and increasing demands on its ever smaller navy, the United States must reassess its current approach to naval operations. There has been sufficient progress in directed-energy technologies to develop sea-based weapons systems for deployment on a *Nimitz*-class aircraft carrier during the early decades of this century. This development could provoke a fundamental shift in carrier battle group operations from a massed, attrition-oriented defense to a more dynamic, dispersed offense.

Although much has been written about technological innovation and information warfare, less thought has been devoted to the technologies that permit warfare at the speed of light.[1] In the future, naval forces could be threatened by low observable or hypersonic cruise missiles, tactical ballistic missiles with maneuverable reentry vehicles, space-based surveillance systems, fast missile patrol boats, advanced submarines, weapons of mass destruction, and airborne or space-based lasers, as well as explosively driven directed-energy weapons.

Over the last forty years, the United States defense establishment has developed directed-energy technology, and, although the ability to use directed-energy systems to destroy airborne targets was demonstrated more than twenty years ago, the national security community continues to debate their value. Born under the shadow of the "missile gap," directed-energy weapons and lasers in particular were viewed as alternatives to reduce the nation's vulnerability. Iraq's use of ballistic missiles also sparked a resurgence in directed-energy research. The U.S. Air Force study of air and space warfare during the twenty-first century devoted an entire volume to directed energy.[2] The 1997 study, *Technology for the United States Navy and Marine Corps, 2000–2035,* conducted by the National Research Council, however, was not optimistic about using directed energy for defensive systems.[3]

This chapter examines "fleet defense," the use of directed-energy systems for defending naval fleets. It focuses on the first two decades of the twenty-first century, which correspond to the multibillion dollar refuelings of the *Nimitz*-class aircraft carriers USS *John C. Stennis* and USS *Harry S Truman*.[4] The introduction of directed-energy technologies into naval forces is likely to begin with aircraft carriers, whose overhaul represents a unique opportunity in the fifty-year service life of an aircraft carrier. The challenge facing the Navy today is similar to the predicament during the 1950s when submarine-launched cruise missiles were first seen as feasible.[5] Naval strategists already have begun to consider how the capabilities, limitations, and military utility of directed-energy weapons might influence national security. This chapter examines their implications for U.S. naval power.

U.S. Navy Strategic Concepts

The Navy's strategy, as outlined in *Forward . . . from the Sea,* defines five fundamental roles that support the U.S. national security strategy as power projection, sea control, strategic deterrence, strategic sealift, and forward naval presence.[6] Some roles, such as sea control, strategic sealift, and forward naval presence, would be familiar to the classic naval thinkers Alfred Thayer Mahan and Sir Julian Corbett, but strategic deterrence and power projection are products of the twentieth century. The Department of Defense's *Joint Vision 2010* describes the challenge of deterring or prevailing in conflicts that occur when defense budgets are limited and advanced technologies are proliferating. *Forward . . . from the Sea* (1992), which was the U.S. Navy's first effort to articulate a post–Cold War strategy, began the shift from sea control and strategic deterrence to influencing events along the littoral.

Absent a peer competitor and with declining numbers of forces overseas, the United States has renewed its emphasis on expeditionary warfare.[7] Naval expeditionary operations, which are currently built around the structure of a carrier battle group (CVBG) and an associated amphibious ready group (ARG), involve the use of expeditionary forces for peacetime as well as wartime operations. This capability rests on power projection, and, aside from a retaliatory nuclear strike launched from the ballistic missile submarine force, the ultimate projection of naval power and influence is exercised with the insertion of Marine Expeditionary Forces (MEFs).

Projecting combat forces ashore is one of the most challenging tasks faced by naval forces because, as they approach the adversary's coast, the defenders can use less expensive weapons to repel the attackers. Such weapons include mines, small patrol craft, coastal submarines, land-based aviation, and shore-based missiles. The ability of naval forces to remain a significant distance offshore increases their freedom of movement and complicates the enemy's calculations. Once troops are placed ashore, however, naval forces are tied to that area, which increases their vulnerability.

Weapons and technologies largely define the strategy that a navy can undertake, and today the U.S. Navy is in the midst of significant change. For example, guided missile destroyers are highly capable escorts, even in smaller numbers, and can provide area air defense or theater missile defense. This type of deployment, however, can reduce the number of ships available to serve as escorts for high-value ships, such as aircraft carriers, amphibious units, and merchant vessels.

Emerging Maritime Threats

With the rapid advances in computers, less technologically sophisticated states might gain significant military capabilities. Rather than challenging the U.S. Navy directly with expensive, advanced ships and aircraft, the prudent response is to seek advantages with chemical weapons, missiles, and other emerging technologies. Numerous, relatively inexpensive systems that could threaten U.S. naval forces will be available during the twenty-first century.

Cruise Missiles

Despite the proliferation of mines, torpedoes, and ballistic missiles, cruise missiles are the greatest area of concern for naval forces. A number of states are known to be producers and exporters of cruise missiles — Argentina, Brazil, China, France, Germany, India, Iran, Iraq, Israel, Italy, Japan, North Korea, Norway, Russia, South Africa, Sweden, Taiwan, United Kingdom, and the United States. Indonesia, Singapore, and Ukraine also have the aerospace industrial capacity to produce cruise missiles. Approximately seventy to seventy-five countries possess cruise missiles, and nineteen of them produce their own missiles or manufacture cruise missiles under license agreements.[8] Further, both purchasers and producers have demonstrated that they can reverse engineer designs from existing missiles. As examples, China has successfully produced and exported the C-801 and C-802 antiship cruise missiles that were developed from the Exocet missile. The Indian Koral program is allegedly developing an indigenous version of the former Soviet SS-N-22 Sunburn supersonic, antiship cruise missile.

Although India and China now dominate the supersonic antiship cruise missile market, the proliferation of cruise missile technology is not limited to the major powers. The Taiwanese Hsiung Feng II was reverse engineered from the Harpoon, and Iran and Iraq have both developed longer-range variants of the Chinese HY-2 Silkworm (originally developed from the Soviet SS-N-2 STYX). States that can produce jet aircraft generally can produce cruise missiles, and many of them have an interest in doing so.[9]

The two major trends in cruise missile development have been increased speed and reduced radar signature, which is termed *stealth*. The Italian TESEO-3 subsonic missile reduces its radar signature by shaping and coating the missile in ways that make it extremely difficult to detect. Although early cruise missiles, such as the Tomahawk and the Kingfish, used long-range turbofan engines or high-speed rocket motors, respectively, new generations of ramjet engines, such as the French ASMP and ASURA, are capable of speeds in excess of Mach 2. These technologies are creating highly sophisticated and quite affordable missiles.[10]

Remarkably flexible in application, cruise missiles have been adapted from antiship to land-attack missions and from ship-launched to air-launched operations with little difficulty. Although only three nations (France, Russia, and the United States) have developed cruise missiles that can deliver nuclear weapons, cruise missiles could also dispense chemical and biological warfare agents.[11] Public reports indicate that China, Iran, and Syria are developing this capability.[12]

Closely related to the proliferation of cruise missiles is the development of remotely piloted vehicles (RPVs). The Indian Lakshya, the Iranian Baz, and the Israeli Delilah are examples of "harassment drones" that can deliver ordnance. Remotely piloted vehicles can locate and target naval forces operating in the littoral and disperse chemical or biological weapons.[13] States could use cruise missiles to challenge a major naval power for local control of the sea because these weapons offer an economical means for conducting sophisticated attacks with a reasonable probability of inflicting damage.

Theater Ballistic Missiles

The proliferation of theater ballistic missiles has generated considerable public attention since Iraq fired Scud B missiles during the Gulf War, but these weapons are less significant than the threat of cruise missiles. Although about forty nations have fielded or produced ballistic missiles and eleven of these nations can produce nuclear, chemical, or biological weapons, still greater technological challenges must be overcome in order to equip ballistic missiles with chemical or biological warheads.[14]

It is difficult for Scud missiles, which have an accuracy of about 1 km, to damage a ship at sea with a conventional warhead. In certain naval operations, such as traditional amphibious landings, however, a group of ships would be vulnerable to ballistic missiles armed with weapons of mass destruction. The trend in ballistic missiles is to use improved midcourse guidance systems, such as the Global Positioning System, and more accurate algorithms for calculating reentry ballistics. Replacing unitary warheads with submunitions is another low-cost option for improving lethality. Theater ballistic missiles might have a limited maritime role, but they can exert significant political influence, as seen with China's use of missile tests in June 1996 to intimidate Taiwan.[15]

Nuclear, Chemical, and Biological Weapons

Weapons of mass destruction pose a significant concern for naval forces, in part because the risk of collateral damage is so low in the middle of the ocean that it removes one obstacle to their use. These weapons are so potentially dangerous that defensive measures must be taken. Chemical weapons could significantly hamper naval operations even if an attack does not produce significant casualties.

The Soviet Union's chemical arsenal is estimated to have exceeded 50,000 tons of agents, ranging from phosgene, which was used during World War I, to sophisticated nerve agents, including sarin and soman. Equally important, as the vast majority of Soviet weapon systems were designed to be used with conventional or chemical warheads, much of the military hardware in the Third World is readily adaptable to chemical weapons. Reportedly, Chile, Egypt, Iran, Iraq, Israel, Libya, North Korea, and Syria have developed chemical weapons, and Pakistan is reported to have a significant chemical weapons program. Other nations or nonstate actors could hire former weapons technologists or purchase the precursor chemicals on the open market.[16]

Mines and Torpedoes

Following cruise missiles, mines and torpedoes pose the greatest threat to naval expeditionary forces. During the late 1990s, the U.S. Office of Naval Intelligence estimated that more than 150 types of naval mines are in service by at least fifty nations. They range from the simple World War I–vintage contact mines that proved effective in the Arabian Gulf to highly sophisticated propelled warhead mines, which can defend an area up to $\frac{1}{2}$ square mile. Mines remain primarily a threat in shallow waters (less than 200 fathoms), and therefore could pose an obstacle to amphibious warfare.[17]

For an opponent seeking to challenge the United States, torpedoes, like mines, are relatively inexpensive weapons that can destroy high-value targets. As sophisticated torpedoes continue to proliferate, France, Germany, Italy, and Russia actively export wake-homing torpedoes. Germany has offered kits for retrofitting previous models that were sold with Type 209 diesel-electric submarines, which are formidable weapons in littoral areas because they are so quiet. Nevertheless, the popularity of the submarine as the weapon of choice among Third World states might be waning as their military planners learn that it is difficult to maintain these complex systems.[18]

Low-Observable Ships and Aircraft

Surface combatants could employ "stealth" technology in the twenty-first century. In addition to the United States, Sweden, Spain, Israel, Canada, Great Britain, Russia, France, and Saudi Arabia are developing or fielding low-observable ships. Computer-aided design makes this technology accessible to virtually any shipbuilder, and radar absorption materials are now commercially available. Although this technology does not create invisible ships, increasing the difficulties of locating and targeting these ships effectively enhances the effect of decoys or other countermeasures. True stealth aircraft could remain beyond the financial reach of most nations, but applying the basic principles of radar signature management to future tactical aircraft and cruise missiles could complicate the ability to detect and track enemy aircraft, particularly in littoral areas.

Information Warfare

The information explosion is profoundly altering the conduct of war. Satellite imagery and communications, long the province of the major powers, are increasingly available in the world marketplace.[19] Commercial systems now routinely provide encryption and resolution capabilities that until a few years ago were confined to the purely military domain. For maritime commanders, the growth of communication systems offers an unparalleled degree of connectivity between military units, but this development could spur the emergence of new weapons that are designed to destroy high-technology communication, sensor, and computer systems.

The development of radio frequency (RF) weapons has profound consequences for U.S. information systems that could be subject to attack. For example, warships bristling with communication and sensor antennae are prime targets for an attack with RF weapons. These weapons might give an enemy an inexpensive and highly effective system for suppressing U.S. defenses, and they could render the victim virtually defenseless against an attack with conventional guns, bombs, or missiles.[20]

The other important directed-energy weapon is the laser. Since the Vietnam War, lasers have been used extensively in weapon guidance. During the late 1990s, a number of states, including France, Britain, Russia, Germany, and Israel, were using lasers as weapons. The Royal Navy might have fielded a shipboard system as early as the Falklands War.[21] China is the current market leader in antipersonnel and antisensor laser weapons.[22] The U.S. Office of Naval Intelligence predicts the development of high-energy lasers that can damage electro-optical sensors at long ranges during the next fifteen years, and China might have already developed a limited antisatellite laser capability.[23] Because many states are investing in directed-energy research programs, the United States is committing more resources to studies of how these sophisticated, yet low-cost, weapons could be used to gain local control of the sea.[24] The objective for weaker states is not to defeat a major naval power in a battle, but to make the cost of its own defeat prohibitive.

Current State of Directed-Energy Technology

For generations, people have been fascinated with directed-energy weapons. An even earlier legend has Hippocrates defending Syracuse by using Archimedes's idea of reflecting sunlight to destroy the Roman fleet. Historians and scientists have traced the fascination to science fiction writers, such as Jules Verne and H. G. Wells. İn 1938, Generals H. H. ("Hap") Arnold and Ira Eaker of the U.S. Army Air Force wrote that defense against aerial attack would be practically impossible until science developed new inventions such as "an electric ray which has been given credit for being able to stop gasoline engines by putting out of commission their electrical system."[25] Less than ten years later, U.S. Navy scientists proposed using directed energy in the form of radio waves to defeat atomic weapons before they could reach their targets.[26]

Since the 1960s, the senior officials and technologists at the Department of Defense (DOD) had hoped that laser technology would provide a means for countering the seemingly unstoppable threat posed by intercontinental ballistic missiles (ICBMs). The Defense Advanced Research Projects Agency became an early sponsor of the proposal to build a laser.[27] In 1958, the DOD inaugurated a research and development program, known as Project Defender, to search for viable antiballistic missile technologies. Under the charter of Project Defender, the Office of Naval Research managed Project Seaside, a study of whether a ruby laser could be used as an antiballistic missile system. In 1962, the Air Force, given its expertise in nuclear warheads, considered how much energy would be necessary for a laser to destroy an ICBM.[28]

Laser Technology

Laser technology has matured rapidly over the last thirty-five years, as demonstrated by the widespread use of compact, inexpensive, low-power lasers. Although not as rapidly as some proponents had hoped, significant progress in military applications for lasers has also occurred.

Regardless of application, lasers are generally categorized by the substance being lazed (gas, liquid, or solid) and the method of stimulation or "pumping" (pulse discharge, electricity, or chemical reaction) used. The product is a beam of coherent light at a given wavelength. The third component of most laser systems is the resonant optical cavity, which increases the energy in the beam and extracts that energy. In its simplest form, a resonator can be a pair of optical mirrors, of which one is only partially reflective. As the beam traverses back and forth through the lazed media, the photons in the beam stimulate further emissions.[29] Fundamentally, lasers have important military applications because of the beam's unique characteristics. Unlike ordinary incandescent lights that scatter energy in a random fashion, laser beams can be highly collimated. Consequently, the energy deposited on an area of 1 cm^2 by a 100-watt laser might be 1 billion times greater than the energy deposited by a 100-watt incandescent lamp.[30]

In addition to size, weight, volume, power, and cooling requirements for airborne and space-based lasers, atmospheric effects pose the greatest challenge for terrestrial and sea-based lasers. In addition to the effects of atmospheric turbulence, discussed in Chapters 1–3, on airborne, space-based, and ground-based lasers, the effects of absorption, scattering, and thermal blooming also must be considered.

Absorption

The use of lasers for terrestrial and maritime applications is significantly influenced by absorption and refraction because only photons at specific wavelengths are absorbed. Laser energy is diffused by water vapor, carbon dioxide, clouds, and fog, which are found in the lower portion of the atmosphere, termed the *troposphere*. This region extends to an altitude of 11 km, or approximately 36,000 feet.

Scattering

In addition to absorption by individual water molecules, water vapor also causes light to scatter. For example, carbon dioxide typically shows a seasonal variation, with maximum levels in early spring and minimum levels in late summer and fall. For this discussion, atmospheric particles can be divided into two groups, aerosols and hydrometers. For aerosols, which have an average radius of less than 1 micron, scattering is significantly greater than the molecular scattering described above. The "clear blue sky" one observes overhead is due to molecular Rayleigh scattering, whereas the whitish gray haze observed at the horizon is due to aerosol effects as well as smoke, dust, or clouds. There is an overlap of effects when clouds, fog, or smog form a portion of the haze.[31] On the other hand, hydrometers, or water bearing particles, are substantially larger than 1 micron and, given their larger size, are removed by fallout or washout. For these reasons, it is difficult to predict how a laser device will perform on any given day.

Thermal Blooming

As a high-energy laser beam travels through the air, small amounts of energy are transferred to the molecules along its path. As the heated air expands, it effectively creates a lens that distorts the laser beam and produces a spreading effect, termed *thermal blooming*. Blooming is only a minor annoyance for low-power laser applications, such as illuminating a target for a guided weapon, but it severely limits the efficiency of high-power lasers. Although wind and beam motion are significant factors, thermal blooming poses the greatest single challenge for laser applications in the atmosphere.

Radio Frequency Weapon Technologies

The second major category of directed-energy weapons are RF devices that operate in the communications, navigation, and radar frequency bands from approximately 100 MHz to 10 GHz. RF devices are typically categorized as high-power microwave (HPM) or ultra-wideband (UWB) systems. Technically, high-power microwave devices typically operate at frequencies of 1–10 GHz, with large pulse widths (on the order of 1 microsecond) and relatively narrow bandwidths (nominally 1 percent of the frequency, which equates to approximately 10 MHz at the lower end and as much as 100 MHz at the upper end). UWB systems are characterized by narrow pulse widths of less than 100 nanoseconds and bandwidths that can exceed 50 percent of the center frequency. Typical wideband devices have bandwidths that range from 200 MHz to 3 GHz.

Origins

Originating in the radio and radar devices developed during the first half of the twentieth century, microwave devices predate the development of lasers. By World War II, microwave technology had proved its value for communications and sensors. By the 1960s, new solid state transmitters and electronically scanned phased arrays began to replace simple mechanically scanned antennas in many applications.

During the Cold War, the technological community also examined the electromagnetic pulse (EMP) that is associated with nuclear detonations. Scientists learned that EMP probably caused the malfunctions of electronic equipment that occurred during atmospheric nuclear testing. One publicized example was the large-scale failure of streetlights on the island of Oahu, which was caused by a high-altitude detonation 500 miles (800 km) away at Johnston Island, and it provided the impetus for exploring the value of EMP as a weapon during the Cold War. A simultaneous failure of thirty series of connected loops of streetlights occurred on the island of Oahu. Although the effects were little more than an annoyance, this event warned the U.S. military that electromagnetic pulse could have widespread secondary effects. During the Cold War, the Soviet Union had an extensive research program in high-power RF technologies. Soviet work included the successful development of the magnetically insulated linear oscillator (MILO), a device invented in the United States but later abandoned during the 1980s. The Soviets also exploited the work of physicist Andrei Sakharov on the magneto-cumulative generator (MCG) for the development of an explosively driven power supply. Since 1991, Russia and other newly independent states reported the use of MCGs to drive UWB and HPM sources, lasers, and rail guns.[32]

Characteristics

High-power RF systems, which are distinct from traditional electronic warfare systems, overwhelm the target with RF energy and make it susceptible to disruption or destruction. The effects of HPM devices can be categorized as follows: *upset,* a temporary alteration of the electrical state of one or more components, which precludes normal operation until the radiation is terminated; *lock-up,* a temporary alteration, as above, except that an electrical reset is necessary to restore normal operation after the radiation is terminated; *latch-up,* an extreme form of lockup that can result in circuit destruction; *damage,* electrical destruction by a mechanism that causes junctions to burn out. Because certain forms involve charge buildups that decay over time, permanent damage or electrical burnout can be used to distinguish them from less permanent effects.[33] Rather than directly attacking the target system, as do electronic warfare systems, high-power RF techniques exploit electrical pathways to vital subsystems. In general, one of two pathways can be employed to reach a susceptible subsystem. The first path is the so-called *front-door* that directs energy at the antenna. If microwave energy operates in a frequency that falls within the design of the system, the target is particularly vulnerable because its receiver is designed to detect and process relatively weak returning signals—not the high-power energy from a microwave weapon. Although narrowband HPM systems can be particularly effective with front-door techniques, success depends on understanding the characteristics of the target.

The second path is the so-called *back-door* coupling, which refers to radiation that follows any path through the system other than the antenna. Cracks or gaps in an airframe, exposed wires, or any other conductive material can provide a path for energy to reach key electronic components. Although back-door paths require higher energy levels if they are to inflict damage, it is much more difficult for weapons designers to eliminate this path.

Power Systems

There are proposals for RF devices that convert the chemical energy of an explosive reaction into magnetic energy, which is first converted into electrical energy and finally into microwave energy. Although this is an inherently inefficient process, chemical explosives provide a readily available energy source. Because the projected yields of these proposed devices are relatively small, the weapon, to be effective, would have to detonate relatively close to the target, within approximately $\frac{1}{2}$ mile (1 km) or less, to exploit the inherent lack of shielding in most sensor and weapon systems today.

An alternative approach is to develop electrically driven devices that eliminate two of the energy conversion steps and provide a multishot capability. The losses associated with the conversion of chemical energy into an explosion and the conversion of the magnetic energy into electrical energy could be avoided. Explosive reactions represent an inefficient means of transferring energy. Early limitations on power supply and energy storage system have been overcome by technological progress. Russia has developed a system for a ground-penetrating geological sensor that could be used to construct a briefcase-size, adjustable jammer.[34] These pulsed power systems require further development, however, before they can provide weapons with a multishot capability.

Microwave Sources

A number of HPM narrowband sources have been developed over the years. In addition to the magnetically insulated linear oscillator, a number of other technologies are possible.[35] Current technology has produced a 25-gigawatt UWB source, a 100-gigawatt UWB device. Freed from the need to be precisely tuned at a particular frequency, UWB devices use a limited antenna design and switch frequencies quickly. Progress during the last ten years has been so significant that high-power RF weapons could be produced within the next two decades.[36]

Comparison of Radio Frequency Weapon and High-Energy Laser Technologies

When integrated into other weapons, RF weapons and high-energy lasers have complementary capabilities. Whereas lasers are precise weapons that require complex pointing and tracking systems, RF weapons provide the wide-area coverage that reduces the need to track the target. Narrow laser beams can deliver greater energy to point targets over long distances but are severely degraded by weather and atmospheric conditions. By contrast, RF weapons are limited to substantially shorter ranges and are only modestly affected by weather and atmosphere.

As a result of technological advances, laser and RF weapon technologies are on the verge of allowing significantly new military capabilities. Although the volume, weight, power, and cooling requirements of these technologies might limit their airborne and space-based applications for the foreseeable future, there is guarded optimism in the U.S. defense establishment about using laser and RF weapons in aircraft within the next two decades.[37]

Currently, the military utility of these directed-energy technologies is constrained. For lasers, the principal limitations are atmospheric effects, mechanical scanning, and the maximum deliverable power. The effects of absorption and scattering also could preclude lasers from becoming true all-weather weapons in the near term.[38] Thermal blooming is a significant challenge because it offsets many of the advances in power generation. Beyond a certain point, simply adding more power is not the answer. As the National Research Council suggested, the ability to deliver laser power is unlikely to keep pace with the efforts to harden targets, such as missiles. Lasers may be more successful in engaging missiles, however, when the energy is directed at control surfaces and fuselages.[39]

A U.S. Air Force study, known as "Directed-Energy Applications for Tactical Airborne Combat," concludes that microwave devices have significant potential for use in munitions, large and small aircraft self-defense, and unmanned combat air vehicles (UCAV) that suppress enemy air defenses.[40] But RF weapons face numerous limitations, the most notable of which is that increasing the power causes air breakdown. Further, the effective range of RF systems is limited because even focused beams spread dramatically as the range to the target increases.[41]

Although narrowband HPM systems have better operational characteristics and fewer problems with fratricide than wideband systems, narrowband systems have a problem in that their effective use requires prior knowledge about the threat and can be defeated by hardening. UWB microwave systems, however, offer broad coverage even when there is little or no knowledge about the enemy's system. Because less energy is transmitted at a given frequency, current UWB systems have significantly shorter effective ranges than narrowband systems.[42]

Implications for Fleet Defense

Directed-energy systems can contribute to fleet defense by neutralizing or blinding antiship cruise missiles, patrol boats, sensors, and other antisurveillance systems.

Antiship Missile Defense

Advanced antiship cruise missiles pose the most significant threat to naval forces within the foreseeable future. Directed-energy systems provide primary and secondary mechanisms for engaging and destroying cruise missiles. The primary mechanisms disrupt or disable the missile by using electromagnetic effects produced by a UWB microwave system or destroy a missile with a surface-to-air missile. Although direct destruction with a high-energy laser is a secondary mechanism, it might be the first system used in tactical situations. The problem, however, is that atmospheric conditions (e.g., humidity and precipitation) can limit the use of lasers.

A UWB microwave system can temporarily disturb or permanently destroy electronic systems.[43] As their speed increases and altitude decreases, missiles are more susceptible to minor perturbations in the guidance and control system. Sea-skimming missiles require extremely fast control systems to avoid flying into the water, even in relatively benign weather. A Mach 3 missile (3,000 feet [900 m] per second), flying 30 feet (9 m) above the sea, travels approximately 150 feet (45 m) during a 50-millisecond attack with a microwave weapon. Even a minor disturbance of the missile's radar altimeter or guidance software could be sufficient to create a "hard kill" if the missile hits the surface of the sea. If sufficient energy can be deposited to induce latch-up or burnout, the probability of kill increases. The advantage to UWB sources is that they eliminate the need for specific knowledge about the enemy missile, thus it is not necessary to target specific mechanisms in the missile. The wider frequency coverage of the UWB device increases the chance that it will disrupt or damage the missile.

The alternative is to use a high-energy laser system to detect, track, and engage the sensor that guides the incoming missile. For missiles approaching head-on, it may be difficult to obtain a structural or payload kill. Although the radar dome (radome) can be susceptible to damage, the placement of the guidance and control systems within the missile body might preclude a direct kill.[44] The alternative is to use a high-energy laser to detect, track, and attack the sensor that guides the incoming missile. Once the sensor system has been damaged or destroyed, the missile is more vulnerable to both microwave disruption and direct attack. Typically, cruise missiles are programmed to fly to the last known target location if sensor data are lost. Elimination of the missile's ability to maneuver dramatically increases the probability that a conventional surface-to-air missile, such as the RIM-116A, can destroy the missile. Alternatively, if an incoming missile is deprived of updates from its sensor because the missile is momentarily disrupted by microwave energy, it might not be able to reacquire the target.

Crossing targets, which are targets that approach a unit's defensive perimeter, generally pose the greatest difficulties for conventional air defense missile systems, but they are also vulnerable to destruction with lasers. A number of programs have demonstrated that terrestrial and airborne laser systems can successfully engage missile targets.[45] Although such targets were traditionally engaged by area defense systems, the trend toward increasingly sophisticated antiship missiles means that point-defense missile systems can confront maneuvering missiles. The attacker must maneuver to defeat point-defense missile systems or proceed directly at the target to minimize the ability of the laser to engage it. The latter action maximizes the chances of successfully engaging a surface-to-air missile.

The increased speed and reduced signatures of antiship missiles makes defense against them more difficult. A Mach 4 missile skimming the waves at 10 feet (3 m) can be engaged for approximately twenty seconds after it is detected at the radar horizon, which leaves very little time to destroy the missile. The defender is at a disadvantage because the intercepting missile must accelerate from zero to Mach 3 or more in a matter of seconds. Even if the defending missile is fired at the exact moment when the attacking missile crosses the radar horizon, the maximum intercept point is approximately 7 nautical miles (11 km) away from the defended ship. It takes time to train and elevate the launcher for each engagement and to initiate the ignition sequence for each missile, which leaves little time for the defending missile to reach the attacker. When antiship missiles are fired in quick succession, the defender's reaction time is so highly compressed that it is difficult to defend against a "stream raid" even when naval vessels use autonomous weapons, such as the RIM-116A.

The ability to counter this cycle with conventional missile developments could fail because the same technologies that improve the speed, agility, and response time of the defender's missiles also improve the attacker's missiles. Directed-energy systems shift the advantage to the defender because they cut the time required to hit the approaching missile. During the two to five seconds required to deposit laser energy, a missile moving at Mach 4 travels about 3.5 nautical miles (5.6 km). With a sufficiently powerful laser, the missile could be destroyed 16–18 nautical miles (25–29 km) from the defending platform, which is more than twice the best distance attained with conventional systems.[46]

Although air breakdown limits UWB microwave systems to shorter ranges than laser systems, microwave systems still enjoy a significant speed advantage over conventional missiles. The time that is necessary to disrupt the missile's guidance system is 600 milliseconds or less. Unfortunately, reducing the time of flight for directed-energy does not eliminate the time that it takes directed-energy systems to detect, acquire, and identify a target. Depending on the surveillance system, the defender could lose 3–4 miles (5–6 km) before it has the first opportunity to detect the target. The SPS-48E is a three-dimensional air surveillance radar used as the primary sensor for an aircraft carrier's suite of combat systems. Current plans call for integrating the SPS-48E with other elements of the ship's antiship missile defense systems into a networked Ship's Self-Defense System (SSDS). The limiting factor for data updates remains the mechanical rotation of the electronically scanned array. Although plans call for passive sensors to provide 360-degree coverage, electronic surveillance systems depend on the opponent to radiate, and electro-optical sensors that are sensitive to environmental factors.[47] This time delay is critical when defending against cruise missiles with dramatically reduced radar signatures. Although laser trackers and other electro-optical devices marginally improve the acquisition and tracking times, both are affected by weather conditions. Most important, directed-energy weapons increase the time available to the defender for defending against a missile attack.

Antiaircraft Defenses

When cruise missiles approach a ship, there is little doubt about hostile intent, but aircraft present a different problem. During flight operations, aircraft carriers must distinguish between hostile and friendly aircraft. Because directed-energy weapons drastically reduce the time required for defense, the defender has more time to identify aircraft, which reduces the probability that friendly aircraft are inadvertently destroyed. The preferred means of engaging enemy aircraft is to use aircraft that can confirm the target's identity visually or by using other sensors at greater ranges. Such methods are more effective than any ship-based sensor.

Tactical aircraft and missiles can be destroyed, but there are several important differences in their vulnerabilities. For example, destroying the radar dome (radome) might not affect a tactical aircraft's survivability or diminish the effectiveness of antiship missiles, equipped with active seekers, that are launched from the aircraft. The aircraft's control surfaces, fuel tanks, and weapons stores, however, offer numerous aim points, even when the aircraft approaches the ship head-on. Under the right conditions, the laser can precisely track the target and use its short flight time to minimize the risk to friendly aircraft. With lasers, missiles can be engaged at longer ranges, which allows the defender to fire fewer conventional weapons and, in turn, reduces the rate at which the ship's magazine is depleted.

Microwave weapons are the least desirable option for antiaircraft defense. It is unlikely that UWB microwave systems deployed on ships would have lethal effects for two reasons: first, an aircraft that fires a short-range tactical missile or lofts a laser-guided bomb would remain outside the microwave's range, and, second, manned aircraft have far more robust and redundant control systems than unmanned missiles. To affect an aircraft equipped with a digital flight control system successfully, a microwave weapon would have to disrupt simultaneously two or more independent flight control computers.

The ability to disrupt and degrade aircraft sensors and computers could make a successful attack on an aircraft carrier even more difficult. Because the guidance sensors, termed *seekers,* on munitions are vulnerable to disruption, most air-launched missiles must pass an internal self-test before accepting the "launch enable" signal in order to avoid the inadvertent destruction of the aircraft. One advantage of microwave weapons is that the missile guidance and control circuitry can be disrupted, which could prevent the release of the weapon. With the exception of forward-firing rockets and "dumb bombs," all weapons are vulnerable to these microwave effects during the last part of flight. Further, microwave systems could defend against unguided ballistic weapons, such as bombs and rockets, by damaging the fuse or by causing premature detonation of the warhead.

Directed-energy weapons would enhance U.S. defensive capabilities against the "low, slow flyers," which include light civil aircraft, ultralights, and helicopters that operate at relatively low speeds (less than 300 knots [500 km] per hour), have low infrared signatures, and produce few distinctive electronic emissions. Military helicopters pose a slightly different problem. Generally turbine powered, these helicopters can present a significant infrared source if infrared countermeasures (IRCMS) are not employed. They also tend to produce a broad spectrum of Doppler returns as the result of radar reflections from the blades. Nevertheless, their relatively low speeds, combined with the absence of a strong Doppler return, make them a challenging target for conventional defense systems. Under the right weather conditions, the laser is the weapon of choice. For example, an integrated laser tracker, such as the Sea Lite Beam Director, provides an image of the target at long range. In theory, light aircraft and helicopters exploit their small size to identify an aircraft carrier before they can be positively identified. The laser director-tracker shifts the advantage back to the surface ship, since targets that are identified as hostile can be destroyed before they get close enough to friendly units to attack them.

If the target's identity cannot be determined or if the rules of engagement prohibit its destruction at long range, a UWB microwave system might be more successful in engaging the target. The propulsion systems of these aircraft are particularly vulnerable to disruption, which means that a UWB microwave weapon could be used against aircraft engaged in kamikaze attacks by causing premature detonation of the munition.

Military helicopters represent a different problem. Although lightly armed reconnaissance helicopters can be attacked in the same manner as other low, slow flyers, those carrying antiship cruise missiles pose a threat similar to that of tactical aircraft. It is fortunate that, when configured with missiles, helicopters have quite limited tactical ranges. Shore-based helicopters cannot reach aircraft carriers operating more than 100–150 nautical miles (160–240 km) off the coast, but they are still a significant threat. For a helicopter to employ its weapons at the optimum range, it must identify the target vessel by some means. Unless it relies on third parties to target the ship, the helicopter must enter the ship's "surveillance volume," which gives the defender an opportunity to destroy the helicopter. Under the right weather conditions, lasers are an optimum weapon for identifying and engaging helicopters.

Anti–Surface Ship Options

Aircraft carriers must be able to defend themselves against hostile surface ships. Although the primary means of destroying enemy combatants is with antiship missiles and other guided munitions launched from carrier-based aircraft, high-value naval vessels must be able to defend themselves with means other than their own aircraft. For example, the Seasparrow missile has a limited antiship capability. The *Saratoga* (CV 60) accidentally fired a salvo of two Seasparrow missiles at the Turkish destroyer, *Mauvenet,* on Oct. 1, 1992. One of the two missiles, with a nominal 80-pound (38-kg) warhead, struck the ship. The *Mauvenet* was not sunk, but the bridge was destroyed, and the captain and four crew members were killed. This damage equated a "mission kill."[48] The potential effectiveness of the RIM-116A missile against surface vessels is unknown, but its relatively small warhead (25 lb. [11 kg]) might limit its effectiveness.[49] Because directed-energy systems are unlikely to engage surface combatants directly, nonlethal measures can neutralize surface vessels.

Nonlethal Capabilities

Directed-energy weapons can quickly and effectively disrupt the sensors of a surface combatant, which makes them useful against high-speed patrol boats or surface-effect craft that can outmaneuver conventional gun systems.[50] With directed-energy systems, the defender has more control over lethal effects than with conventional weapons. This is particularly important in the territorial waters and harbors of nations where it would be difficult to use conventional weapons. Lasers and microwaves minimize the risk of collateral damage or the ability of the enemy to trace the energy to the ship that fired the weapon.

Anti–Fast Patrol Boat Operations

Although destroying radomes, antennas, and waveguides with microwaves could disrupt enemy radars, electro-optical sensors are even more vulnerable to lasers. Directed-energy weapons can provide the same level of protection as jamming but do not expose the defender to attack with an antiradiation missile. A laser weapon is less vulnerable to detection than a laser illuminator, and, depending upon the laser and the techniques used, the opponent might be unaware that the sensor has failed.[51] Given the lethal ranges of fast patrol boats, microwave systems are useful for disrupting sensitive electronic surveillance and communications systems.

Counterterrorist Operations
By contrast, small craft, such as boghammers or zodiacs, that harass or attack aircraft carriers can be neutralized by directed-energy devices that use antipersonnel or antiequipment effects. These nonlethal options are important when naval forces are operating in areas where conventional weapons cannot be used. For example, microwaves can neutralize the electrical systems of the attacker's boats without creating an international incident because the potential aggressor could not produce tangible evidence that defensive measures were taken. In 1990 the U.K. Ministry of Defense acknowledged that it had developed and fielded a laser dazzle system, manufactured by Irwin Desman Ltd., for use by the Royal Navy's *Broadsword*-class frigates and Type 42 destroyers. Although, reportedly, the system was deployed to the Arabian Gulf for anti–small boat defense, industry sources believe that it is capable of deterring a kamikaze style air attack. Reportedly, it uses a low-power blue laser that does not cause permanent eye injuries. At a nominal range of 1.7 miles (2.75 km), a UWB microwave system would be more effective and preclude concerns about violating Protocol IV to the United Nations Conventions on Prohibitions on Conventional Weapons.[52]

Submarine Defense
A laser director-tracker could detect and destroy submarine periscope sensors. In addition to complicating an immediate attack, it would warn the submarine that it had been detected and identified. As with other antisubmarine weapons, it is essential to ensure that friendly submarines are not mistakenly attacked. Unfortunately, the delay that results from human operation of the weapon might allow all but the least competent submariners to escape destruction. The danger of fratricide in counterperiscope operations probably would require a human to control the laser weapon and make the decision as to when to engage the laser. Because competent submariners leave their periscopes exposed for only seconds, it is unlikely that there would be sufficient time for an operator to identify and engage a periscope target.

Countersurveillance
Using directed-energy weapons against aircraft and surface vessels, particularly when long-range surveillance systems are neutralized, would create a new alternative for dealing with hostile reconnaissance systems. For example, a maritime patrol aircraft that provides targeting information to coastal antiship missile batteries could have its electro-optical sensors destroyed and its radar and communications systems disrupted. Similar techniques could be used to discourage surface vessels from functioning as intelligence collectors. Such ac-

tions against legitimate intelligence collection platforms would have to be consistent with international protocols that permit the observation and collection of missile launch telemetry data. It is conceivable that a ship-based laser system could disable surveillance systems in space.

Directed-Energy Options

Directed-energy systems require large apertures to focus the transmitted energy and power distribution systems that generate megawatts of power. These constraints limit the types of platforms that can economically carry them. Despite the historical emphasis on using directed energy for ballistic missile defenses, this technology could simplify the ability to defend a ship. *Nimitz*-class nuclear-powered aircraft carriers (CVNs), which have a projected service life exceeding fifty years, are scheduled for midlife refueling and major overhaul at twenty-three to twenty-five years. With their dual nuclear power plants, these ships initially could be used to deploy directed-energy systems for tactical defense.

As currently configured, *Nimitz*-class CVNs use Seasparrow surface-to-air missiles and the close-in weapon system (CIWS) Gatling gun for self-defense.[53] Although both the CIWS and the Seasparrow systems have been upgraded since the 1970s, their effectiveness against new threats is in doubt.[54] Replacing these systems with a new generation of self-defense technologies could make the carrier more survivable in the face of more serious threats. The present plan is to replace the CIWS with the RIM-116A rolling airframe missile system and to replace the North Atlantic Treaty Organization (NATO) Seasparrow system with the evolved Seasparrow.

There are four ways to use directed-energy systems for aircraft carrier self-defense. The first option is to replace the conventional gun and missile systems with UWB microwave systems. Given the significant progress in high-power microwave technology, these systems provide the best all-weather option; however, it poses two problems: first, atmospheric breakdown limits the effective range of microwaves, and, second, it is imprudent to depend on one technology for a critical defensive system.

The second option is to replace existing systems with high-energy lasers, in particular, the deuterium fluoride laser technology that has demonstrated its capability against various tactical targets. The principal disadvantages of the high-energy laser are its susceptibility to weather and its limited capability against targets approaching the ship head-on. To be effective in maritime operations, defensive systems must function regardless of the ship's orientation, and relying on a high-energy laser could leave the ship defenseless during severe weather.

The third option is to replace existing systems with a suite of UWB microwave systems and high-energy lasers. The laser's long-range capabilities would complement the microwave's short-range, all-weather capabilities, and both systems can fire as long as the ship has electrical power (a bottomless magazine), which eliminates the need to reload in combat.

The fourth option, which is similar to the third, combines high-energy laser and UWB microwave systems with conventional surface-to-air missiles into a self-defense system that can operate under most military and weather conditions. The rolling airframe missile system is a proven technology that minimizes the overall risks associated with incorporating new weapon systems into naval forces. This option includes two laser tracker director systems, four UWB microwave arrays, and three rolling airframe missile (RIM-116A) launcher systems. With removal of the three Seasparrow magazine launcher assemblies, six associated radar directors, and four CIWS mounts on an aircraft carrier, the weight, space, and power budgets allocated to the existing defensive systems are sufficient to accommodate these directed-energy systems.[55]

The rolling airframe missile will replace the current CIWS and Seasparrow systems.[56] Three rolling airframe missile magazine launchers could replace the three Seasparrow magazine launchers and nearly triple the number of missiles available.[57] Already fielded on large amphibious assault ships, the rolling airframe missile complements directed-energy systems under development with a capability that has been tested in worldwide naval operations. It also benefits from operating in conjunction with a high-energy laser. Two laser tracker-directors could replace a pair of Seasparrow directors.[58] Locating the laser tracker-directors on the aircraft carrier's island maximizes the height of the laser, reduces atmospheric effects from moisture, and minimizes exposure to heavy sea spray.

The CIWS mounts would be replaced with electronically steered arrays for the UWB microwave systems. Installed immediately below the flight deck, the arrays would be approximately the same height above the sea surface as the radar arrays and would be physically isolated from other communication and sensor systems. Although an electronically scanned array is the preferred choice for minimizing response time and reducing mechanical complexity, the current CIWS sites provide satisfactory fields of view for mechanically steered antennas, if necessary.

The propulsion plant on a *Nimitz*-class aircraft consists of two nuclear reactors, but a single reactor can provide steam for the aircraft catapult launching systems as well as routine propulsion. Because two nuclear reactors provide enough power for a directed-energy system, aircraft carrier power plants probably would not require any major redesigns. In view of its size and power generating capacity, the nuclear-powered aircraft carrier is the ideal warship for the experimental use of directed-energy technologies. The U.S. Navy should examine whether the capabilities of directed-energy weapons provide more effective defenses against advanced cruise missiles and evaluate the synergy between high-energy lasers and rolling airframe missiles against sophisticated, high-energy missiles.

These defensive technologies would provide 360-degree coverage and improve the carrier's ability to defend itself against a saturation attack from multiple directions. The overlapping fields of fire and rapid reengagement times eliminate vulnerability where the coverage of defensive systems overlaps, whereas the bottomless magazines of laser and microwave systems would make stream raids by aircraft or missiles of dubious value.[59] Rolling airframe missile launchers need less frequent reloading, which reduces the carrier's vulnerability to mass raids, principally because laser systems can provide long-range defense while the missile launcher is reloaded.[60]

When weather conditions permit, the carrier's optical sensors in high-energy lasers could visually identify aircraft or surface vessels. Directed-energy systems offer numerous nonlethal options, including the ability to blind the sensors on surveillance aircraft and employ antipersonnel effects against speedboats. Thus, the combination of high-energy lasers, radio frequency weapons, and conventional surface-to-air-missiles could increase the aircraft carrier's defensive ability during the twenty-first century.

New Concepts for Employing Naval Forces

World War II and the Soviet blue water fleet during the Cold War influenced U.S. Navy operational concepts. An important naval lesson of the Pacific campaign in World War II was the need for defensive firepower, which led to massing carrier battle groups into the multicarrier battle forces that remain the centerpiece of Navy operations more than fifty years later.[61]

During the post–WW II years, the U.S. Navy and its NATO allies refined the concept of defense in depth to meet the ever-growing challenge from the Soviet fleet. Rings of fighter aircraft, *Aegis*-class cruisers and destroyers, and Seasparrow and Mark-15 CIWS point defense systems were used to defend aircraft carriers. When confronted with raids from Badger and Backfire aircraft; long-range antiship missiles, such as the SS-N-12 and the SS-N-19; and submarines, U.S. military planners assumed that a number of defending aircraft and escort ships would be lost.

The risk in this century is that smaller states could deny control of the seas to the powerful navies, whether at critical choke points or in waters adjacent to their coasts. Unwilling or incapable of investing in forces that can command the sea, these states could use sophisticated, inexpensive weapons to threaten the expensive, multipurpose forces of the major powers. The assumption that naval operations against smaller states are likely to be insignificant could represent a tragic miscalculation.

As the naval strategist Sir Julian Corbett observed almost one hundred years ago, the preferred strategy for weaker opponents is to ensure that powerful adversaries do not have opportunities to engage in decisive battles. Enemy patrol boats hiding in fjords or caves might represent a "fleet in being" that would make it difficult for the adversary to engage in a successful operation. Powerful navies might never have an opportunity to annihilate an enemy's forces in a single crushing blow.[62] For example, four corvettes, each firing four supersonic antiship cruise missiles, could wreak havoc on a carrier battle force. If only one missile hit its target, the prospect of heavy damage to a major combatant ship might dissuade the United States or its allies from taking further action.[63]

The solution for the United States and its allies is to use advanced technologies for developing new fleet tactics against lesser naval opponents.[64] If the U.S. Navy retains the ability to deal with powerful states, it also will develop new approaches for defeating unconventional opponents. The Navy is developing a new doctrine and new equipment to meet the challenges faced by classic amphibious operations,[65] whereas the U.S. Marine Corps is committed to "ship to objective maneuver" and "over the horizon assault."[66] In the future, amphibious forces might not be constrained to a small set of beaches that are suitable for conventional landing craft. For supporting naval forces, the ability to remain at a significant distance offshore increases the freedom of movement, introduces uncertainty in the enemy's targeting, and provides opportunities for deception.[67] Because of these possibilities, the Navy is studying the shift from classic battle group tactics to new ways of conducting carrier operations.

A traditional carrier task force operating in a defensive screen presents a discernible pattern for an adversary that has spaced-based sensors, radar, acoustics, and electronic surveillance. The detection of a single battle group unit helps to orient the enemy's search, and the detection of additional units informs the adversary of their location. The carrier's defender becomes an opportune target whose proximity hampers its ability to engage targets without the risks of damaging friendly vessels, termed *fratricide*.[68] Although escort vessels have been previously considered expendable in the defense of capital ships, defense planners are reconsidering the merit of this approach in cases that do not involve vital U.S. interests.

One answer could involve a dispersed force that combines the carrier's inherent mobility with a robust self-defense capability. Freed from supporting amphibious operations within sight of land, the carrier could exploit its inherent speed, flexibility, and self-sufficiency. Rather than a classic battle group, the future naval task force might be a carrier and a nuclear-powered submarine operating in tandem and employing their mutual strengths of speed and reduced logistical needs to dominate air, surface, and subsurface operations. Once freed from its slower moving escorts that require frequent refuelings, the carrier could sustain cruising speeds of 20–25 knots (32–40 km) per hour on an indefinite basis. Capable of sprinting at higher dash speeds, the carrier can complicate the plans of those who seek to target it. Even when operating at ranges of 100–150 nautical miles (160–240 km) from an enemy's coast, the carrier's operating area could be greater than 10,000 square miles (16,000 km^2). Ambiguity reduces the carrier's vulnerability to attack from both cruise missiles and theater ballistic missiles, and dispersion minimizes the risk that more than one ship would be exposed to chemical or biological attack.

By exploiting the inherent flexibility and mobility of naval forces, adversaries might be compelled to fight on U.S. terms. Any time that an opponent is forced to fight farther out to sea, the advantage shifts to the United States and its allies. The greater the distance from the enemy's coast, the more time it takes for the U.S. Navy to react. Only the major naval powers have vessels with the ability to operate at maximum speeds for extended periods and replenish them without returning to port. The coastal patrol craft of many navies are constrained by their fuel capacity, which is inadequate for combat patrols more than 100 nautical miles (160 km) from a friendly port. Extended distances from land minimize the threats from land-based missiles and helicopters, as well as the threat posed by tactical aviation. Another advantage of a dispersed force is that hostile surveillance units, when confronted with a single contact rather than a formation, must spend time confirming the unit's identity, which effectively gives U.S. forces more time to identify and destroy the attacker.

Sea-based aircraft are the most effective means for destroying hostile patrol craft and tactical aircraft, and, when the use of fixed-aircraft or rotary wing aircraft is not possible, directed-energy weapons enhance the carrier's survivability. The advanced optical sensors for high-energy lasers could assist in positive identification of ships and aircraft at greater ranges, which further helps the defender.

As the U.S. Navy becomes smaller, the capabilities of individual units must increase. For example, during the Cold War, the cruiser provided terminal air defense for the carrier, but, during the first decade of the twenty-first century, *Aegis*-class guided missile cruisers might operate as a launch platform for Tomahawk cruise missiles, provide air defense for an amphibious force, and defend against ballistic missiles.[69] It is highly unlikely that stationing guided missile cruisers 5000–10,000 yards (5,500–11,000 m) from the carrier is the best way to perform these missions. Using sophisticated surface combatants to form a defensive ring of steel around carriers reduces their flexibility and combat capabilities.

Although individual missions might be accomplished within hundreds or thousands of square miles, there is a relatively narrow area within which many missions can be simultaneously conducted. By identifying the missions assigned to a carrier battle group, enemy forces could define the fleet's probable location and target it. On the other hand, dispersion increases the value of deception, which might involve decoys that lead enemy aircraft to an *Aegis*-class cruiser or a full-fledged amphibious feint.[70] Technology can make older tactics more effective. For example, using multispectral passive sensors, block 1 rolling airframe missiles with dual passive seekers, and high-energy lasers with a low probability of intercept would allow the carrier to conduct flight operations without electronic emissions and to avoid choosing between covert operations and robust defenses. The minimum weather condition needed for visual flight operations is likely to be sufficient for the employment of the HEL and its sensors.

The ability of U.S. naval forces to provide the logistics necessary for tactical flexibility contributes to the success of the United States as the preeminent naval power; however, as logistics become more complex, naval forces are more vulnerable. By their nature, replenishment operations establish patterns that adversaries can discern. One reason that the U.S. Navy built nuclear-powered carrier task forces was to create self-contained, agile combat forces that could seize the initiative in combat. The introduction of defensive systems with virtually unlimited magazines is a major step toward that objective.

With directed-energy weapons, carrier battle forces would enjoy the defensive advantages of dispersion and the ability to concentrate offensive naval striking power.[71] The combination of fixed-wing aircraft, helicopters, and unmanned air vehicles in a dispersed force that can strike from multiple axes without an apparent pattern could keep adversaries off balance. With the use of carriers, the ability of combat aircraft to appear simultaneously over many targets puts pressure on the adversary and gives the Navy an unmatched ability to win.[72]

Anticipation of Countermeasures

It is inevitable that every new weapon will be met with countermeasures. The same is true for directed-energy weapons. For example, hardening can reduce the vulnerability of conventional weapons to the effects of microwave devices, but the trend in modern microprocessor electronics is to build the most economical and efficient devices, which are also the most vulnerable.[73] Similarly, antilaser measures, including the use of ablative coatings on missiles, increase the weight and hence drag of the missiles, whereas reflective surfaces tend to increase the electro-optical signature and thereby increase the ability to detect missiles. Also, detection systems for warning aircraft that they are being illuminated with a laser are available, but it is difficult to detect narrowly focused laser beams at short ranges.

The use of directed-energy weapons might give the advantage to the forces that initiate the attack. The large apertures, which give lasers high power and directional control, are highly vulnerable to attack and might compel the belligerent forces to fire first in order to blind the opponent.[74] The less sophisticated opponent might use the electromagnetic pulse from a nuclear weapon to blind directed-energy systems, which increases the risks of nuclear war. The more effective strategy would be to use explosively driven radio frequency munitions to blind the sensors for high-energy laser and microwave systems, but the relatively short ranges of UWB sources suggest that a delivery system must be used. The use of tactical aircraft, unmanned air vehicles, or missiles to deliver this weapon would be vulnerable to attack by the very systems that they are intended to destroy. Finally, other states might perfect weapons that are ideally suited for disrupting and destroying the information systems upon which modern naval forces depend. This implies that information warfare could increase the vulnerability to directed-energy weapons.[75]

Potential Antisatellite Applications

The use of directed-energy weapons by naval forces raises the possibility of antisatellite operations. Although there are significant technical differences between antisatellite and anticruise missile systems, a dual-use system is feasible.[76] It was the potential role of the U.S. mid-infrared advanced chemical laser (MIRACL) as an antisatellite weapon that led the Senate to block any further testing that could be construed as an antisatellite capability.[77]

Although the ability to blind space-based sensors could have great tactical value, it is inevitable that a sea-based antisatellite system would worry many states. The ability to neutralize enemy or third-party space-based sensors would enhance the survivability of naval forces; protect theater missile defense units; and force the opponent to rely on ships, aircraft, and unmanned air vehicles that are vulnerable to conventional defenses. Another possibility is that integrating sea-based lasers with space-based mirrors would create the ability to defend against space-based weapons from any location on the high seas. Sea-based lasers would represent a strategic capability, which could raise concerns that adversaries might field space-based laser systems to attack U.S. military sensors and communications systems. Other states might have fielded laser antisatellite weapons. For example, the U.S. Department of Defense's 1998 Annual Report to Congress declared that the People's Republic of China "may possess the capability to damage, under specific conditions, optical sensors on satellites that are very vulnerable to lasers."[78] Because the physics favor ground or sea-based systems with large apertures and virtually unlimited power sources, lasers on ships would create a highly capable and mobile antisatellite capability.

Conclusion

As the United States embraces a military strategy that depends on expeditionary warfare as a principal component of its military capabilities, directed-energy weapons could have profound implications for naval warfare. The danger is that the ability to project naval power might be increasingly difficult as potential adversaries gain access to sophisticated, low-cost weapons. In the face of overwhelming U.S. naval superiority, adversaries that do not want to risk defeat by directly challenging the Navy may turn to technologies that make it prohibitively expensive to control the sea. Given the development of advanced cruise missiles, the U.S. Navy is developing new defensive systems and approaches to battle group operations. Directed-energy weapons offer a powerful instrument as the result of significant progress in both high-energy lasers and UBW microwave systems, which the United States could deploy within a decade or so. One opportunity could occur when the *Nimitz*–class nuclear powered aircraft carriers, *John C. Stennis* and *Harry S Truman,* upgrade their defensive suites during the refuelings scheduled for the second decade of this century.

With directed-energy weapons, the United States could break the vicious technological race caused by ever faster and more capable missiles. Once freed from a defensive screen of ships, nuclear-powered carriers could operate in tandem with nuclear-powered submarines to exploit their inherent speed and self-sufficiency while preventing adversaries from gaining opportunities for successful attacks against U.S. military forces. Once the carrier battle group is dispersed, each ship could choose the optimum location for launching cruise missiles, defending against theater missiles, protecting commerce, or conducting maritime interdiction. With directed-energy systems, the United States could strengthen its ability to provide the naval presence and military power on which it has depended for centuries.

Notes

1. For a discussion of contemporary views on the implications of the information-dominated environment, see Joseph S. Nye and William A. Owens, "America's Information Edge," *Foreign Affairs* 75 (March/April 1996), 2:20–36; Department

of the Air Force, *Cornerstones of Information Warfare,* 1997, May 9, 1999, http://www.af.mil/lib/corner.html.

2. U.S. Air Force [hereafter USAF] Scientific Advisory Board, *New World Vistas: Air and Space Power for the 21st Century, Directed Energy Volume* (Washington, D.C.: USAF Scientific Advisory Board, 1996).

3. Naval Studies Board, National Research Council, *Technology for the United States Navy and Marine Corps, 2000–2035—Becoming a 21st Century Force* (Washington, D.C.: National Academy Press, 1997), 183–87.

4. U.S. General Accounting Office, *Navy's Aircraft Carrier Program: Investment Strategy Options,* GAO/NSIAD-95-17, Aug. 27, 1998, http://www.fas.org/man/gao/ gao9517.htm.

5. The absence of an effective targeting scheme for employing them resulted in a thirty-year delay in fielding the submarine-launched cruise missile, according to Wayne P. Hughes Jr., *Fleet Tactics: Theory and Practice* (Annapolis, Md.: Naval Institute Press, 1986), 205. See Elting E. Morison, *Admiral Sims and the Modern American Navy* (Boston: Houghton Mifflin, 1942), 106–47. As noted by modern strategists, the Navy was indeed fortunate that the development of large-caliber guns was not delayed until Adm. William S. Sims developed an effective fire control system.

6. Department of the Navy, *Forward . . . from the Sea,* March 1997; http://www.chinfo.navy.mil/palib/policy/fromsea/ffseanoc.html, July 10, 1998.

7. Department of Defense, *DoD Dictionary,* Joint Publication 1-02, December 1997, 172.

8. See Centre for Defence and International Security Studies, "Cruise Missile Capabilities and Suppliers," Oct. 8, 1998, http:/www.cdiss.org/tabanaly.htm.

9. Ibid.

10. Department of the Navy, *Challenges to Naval Expeditionary Warfare* (Washington, D.C.: Office of Naval Intelligence, March 1997), 12–13.

11. "Missile Capabilities by Country," Centre for Defence and International Security Studies, Oct. 8, 1998, http:/www.cdiss.org/table1.htm.

12. "Cruise Missiles and WMD," Centre for Defence and International Security Studies, Oct. 8, 1998, http:/www.cdiss.org/cbwcm.htm.

13. "Selected RPV Capabilities," Centre for Defence and International Security Studies, Oct. 8, 1998, http:/www.cdiss.org/tablef.htm.

14. "Ballistic Missiles and WMD [Weapons of Mass Destruction]," Centre for Defence and International Security Studies, Oct. 8, 1998, http:/www.cdiss.org/cbwbm1.htm.

15. "Challenges to Expeditionary Naval Warfare," 16–17.

16. "Ballistic Missiles and WMD," and "The Devil's Brews: an Introduction," Centre for Defence and International Security Studies, Oct. 8, 1998, http:/www.cdiss.org/cbwintro.htm.

17. Sir Peter de la Billiere, *Storm Command—A Personal Account of the Gulf War* (London: HarperCollins Publishers, 1992), 148.

18. "Challenges to Expeditionary Naval Warfare," 8–11. Effective submarine employment requires a cadre of skilled technicians and tacticians, all of whom must maintain a high level of proficiency. Although the submarine threat to the United States might increase because these nations are willing to commit fiscal and personnel resources, the case might be that the submarines are expensive showpieces with little combat capability.

19. J. Todd Black, "Commercial Satellites—Future Threats or Allies?" *Naval War College Review* (winter 1999), 99–114.

20. Carlo Kopp, "The E-Bomb—A Weapon of Electrical Mass Destruction," *Infowar.com and Interpact, Inc.* (Oct. 9, 1998), http://www.infowar.com/mil_c4i/mil_c4i8.html-ssi.

21. Bill Hillaby, "Directed-Energy Weapons Development and Potential," *National Network News* (July 1997); http://www.sfu.ca/~dann/nn4-3_12.htm, Aug. 12, 1998.

22. In 1995, North China Industries Corporation offered for sale the ZM-87 antipersonnel weapon, which is capable of causing flash blindness at ranges up to 6 miles (10 km) and permanent blindness at ranges of 1–2 miles (2–3 km). See "Challenges to Expeditionary Naval Warfare," 15.

23. Ibid.; "China May Seek Satellite Laser, Pentagon Warns," *Los Angeles Times,* Nov. 28, 1998, 1.

24. Ji Shifan, *Development of Tactical Air Defense Laser Weapons at Home and Abroad: An Outline,* trans. Leo Kanner Associates (Wright-Patterson Air Force Base, Ohio: National Air Intelligence Center, 1996), 10–15.

25. H. H. Arnold and Ira C. Eaker, *This Flying Game* (New York: Funk & Wagnalls, 1938), 130, 135–39.

26. *The New York Times,* Oct.12, 1945, 1; Bernard Brodie, "The Atomic Bomb and American Security," Yale Institute for International Studies, New Haven, Conn., Memorandum No. 18, Nov. 1, 1945, 6.

27. Jeff Hecht, *Laser Guidebook* (New York: McGraw-Hill, 1992), 16.

28. Robert W. Duffner, *Airborne Laser: Bullets of Light* (New York: Plenum Press, 1997), 1–15.

29. Bengt Anderberg and Myron L. Wolbarsht, *Laser Weapons: The Dawn of a New Military Age* (New York: Plenum Press, 1992), 11–42.

30. Richard Saunders et al., *Lasers Operation, Equipment, Application, and Design* (New York: McGraw-Hill, 1980), 10. For reference, the lower limit on the divergence (or spreading) of a laser beam is a function of its wavelength and the size of the aperture. And divergence can be reduced by either using shorter wavelengths (higher frequencies) or increasing the size of the aperture. Lasers whose divergence is reduced to the theoretical minimum are categorized as diffraction limited.

31. See Joseph S. Accetta and David L. Schumaker, *The Infrared and Electro-Optical Systems Handbook,* vol. 2, *Atmospheric Propagation of Radiation* (Ann Arbor, Mich.: Environmental Research Institute of Michigan, 1993), 3–64, 11–12, 100–12.

32. See S. Glasstone and P. J. Dolan, *The Effects of Nuclear Weapons* (Washington, D.C.: U.S. Government Printing Office, 1977), 514–29; see statement of Ira W. Merritt, Chief, Concepts Identification and Applications Analysis Division, U.S. Army Space and Missile Defense Command, in "Proliferation and Significance of Radio Frequency Weapons Technology," testimony before the Joint Economic Committee, U.S. Congress, Feb. 25, 1998, 1–2; http://www.fas.org/irp/congress/1998_hr/s980225m.htm, Aug. 27, 1998. Further, concern in the West solidified in 1994 when Gen. Vladimir Loborev, director of Moscow's Central Institute of Physics and Technology, distributed a paper by physicist A. B. Prishchepenko that described how an explosively driven RF weapon could be employed.

33. See David M. Sowders, Patrick Vail, Kerry Sandstrom et al., "High Power Microwave (HPM) and Ultrawideband (UWB): A Primer on High Power RF," PL-TR-95-1111, Special Report, Phillips Laboratory, Kirtland Air Force Base, N.Mex., March 1996, 81–84.

34. Merritt, "Proliferation and Significance," 4–6. For questions about the reproducibility of some of the Russian claims, see L. L. Altgilbers, I. Merritt, M. Brown et al., "OCONUS Radio Frequency Munitions Test Report," ATD-98-001, Dec. 4, 1997, available at www.house.gov/jec/hearings/espionage/schultz.htm. It is evident from other systems that have been exported to the West that Russian and other former Soviet republic (FSU) laboratories continue to make major strides in this area.

35. They include the relativistic magnetron, an outgrowth of radar development; the large-orbit gyrotron, a form of electron cyclotron maser; the relativistic klystron, which traces its origins to radar and weapons development; and the vircator, a relatively new and elegant design, that is commonly used in single pulse applications.

36. U.S. Air Force [hereafter USAF] Scientific Advisory Board, *New World Vistas: Directed Energy Volume* (Washington, D.C.: USAF Scientific Advisory Board), 1996), 58–60. For an alternative view, see the U.S. Army forecast of *Electronic Warfare/Directed-Energy Weapons,* http://mrmc-www.army.mil/mrmclibrary/astmp/original/original/c4/P4K.htm. The Army projection is that high average power traveling wave tubes and advanced RF weapons could be available by the year 2003. And by the year 2012, advanced conventional source systems and alternate source weapon systems are likely to be available. In addition to developing devices that minimize atmospheric breakdown, other critical technologies include reliable, compact, pulsed-power systems, higher-power microwave sources, solid state switching devices, impulse radiating antennas, and planar arrays with electronic steering for HPM and UWB systems.

37. Naval Studies Board, *Technology,* 184–87, 195–203; USAF Scientific Advisory Board, *New World Vistas, Directed Energy Volume,* 27–29, 35–35.

38. Naval Studies Board, *Technology,* 202–03.

39. Ibid., 184–85.

40. Gen. Ronald Fogelman, USAF (Ret.), "Directed-Energy—Applications in Tacti-

cal Airborne Combat, Phase One Results," address to Directed-Energy Symposium, Kirtland Air Force Base, N.Mex., Nov. 5, 1998.

41. Even a signal originating from a highly directional antenna spreads as the square of the distance.

42. Patrick Vail, Air Force Research Laboratory, Phillips Research Site, interview by author, Nov. 6, 1998.

43. A broader discussion is available in Sowders, Vail, Sandstrom et al., "High Power Microwave and Ultrawideband."

44. RF transmitting materials, such as epoxy/fiberglass, ceramic, and fiberized ceramics, generally serve as good thermal insulators. Similarly, the material used for infrared seeker windows, such as gallium arsenide, quartz, diamonds, fiberized composites, is generally also thermally resistant. The destruction of the radome would likely dissipate much of the energy. See Joung R. Cook, "U.S. Navy HEL Weapons Fundamental Issues," address to the First Directed Energy Symposium, Kirtland Air Force Base, N.Mex., Nov. 6, 1998, slide 11.

45. The MIRACL has successfully engaged five BQM-34 subsonic drones, as well as a supersonic Vandal missile target. The Airborne Laser Laboratory enjoyed similar success against drones and AIM-9 missiles. More recently, the U.S.–Israeli Nautilus Program successfully used the MIRACL to destroy a short-range rocket in flight. Although that rocket's flight parameters were substantially different from those encountered with cruise missiles, the test demonstrated the destructive power of lasers. See "Mid-Infrared Advanced Chemical Laser," *FAS* [Federation of American Scientists] *Space Policy Project* (Mar. 21, 1998), on line (Aug. 27, 1998) at http://www.fas.org/spp/military/ program/asat/miracl.htm. See also "Nautilus—Lasers Are Lethal," U.S. Army Space and Missile Defense Command (October 1997), available at http://www.smdc.army. mil/naut.html; and "Tactical High Energy Laser (THEL) 21st Century Air Defense," U.S. Army Space and Missile Defense Command (Oct. 31, 1998), available at http:// www.smdc.army.mil/THEL.HTML.

46. The assumption is that the laser system employs a phased array of laser diodes that must be trained or elevated prior to engagement. In fact, tests with the Sea Lite Beam Director demonstrated that, although it is capable of rapid engagements, there is a finite amount of time needed to shift from one target to the next. See USAF Scientific Advisory Board, *New World Vistas, Directed Energy Volume*, 67.

47. See Martin Streetly, ed., *Jane's Radar and Electronic Warfare Systems 1997–1998* (London: Jane's Information Group, Ltd., 1998), 170–71.

48. See "The Navy's Year in Review," U.S. Naval Institute *Proceedings* 119, no. 5 (1993), 125.

49. "Facts and Figures," *Sea Power* 41, no. 1 (1998), 198.

50. CVNs typically employ a mix of 50-caliber machine guns and M-60s to deliver harassing fire. Even the 25-mm chain gun, employed on other vessels, such as fast combat support ships, has a limited range and effectiveness.

51. Without careful metallurgical inspection, it might not be possible for an opponent to determine the reason for the hole in the waveguide. The potential subtleties of such an attack mechanism increase the difficulties of incorporating it into the rules of engagement. Nor is it obvious whether this is more or less escalatory than active jamming.

52. A. P. O'Leary, ed. *Jane's Electro-optic Systems 1997–1998* (London: Jane's Information Group, Ltd., 1998), 11, 31–33.

53. *Nimitz*-class aircraft carriers have undergone steady combat system upgrades throughout their service lives. Current plans call for the incorporation of the advanced combat direction system block 1, the advanced integrated electronic warfare system, the cooperative engagement capability, and the Mark 1 ship's self-defense system. See Department of the Navy, *Vision, Presence, Power—A Program Guide to the U.S. Navy 1998 Edition* (Washington, D.C.: U.S. Government Printing Office, 1998), 59, 70–90.

54. Dennis J. Carroll, "Missile Systems and Naval Operations 2010 and Beyond," *Global Defence Review,* November 24, 1998, http://www.global-defence.com.

55. The Mark 15 Phalanx CWIS rolling airframe missile nominally weighs 13,600 pounds (6,200 kg) for the topside weapon assembly with an additional 725 pounds (300 kg) of equipment below the deck. This is equal to the weight and volume estimates for the Naval Research Laboratory's design for a 100 kW–class shipboard laser. See "Facts and Figures," *Sea Power* 41, no. 1 (1998), 198.

56. *Nimitz,* the first aircraft carrier programmed to receive the rolling airframe missile system, is scheduled to be upgraded during its current refueling overhaul. Currently, there are two variants of the RIM-116A, the block 0, which relies on passive RF for both midcourse guidance and passive infrared for terminal homing, and the new block 1, which incorporates an infrared image-scanning seeker that permits autonomous infrared tracking of a nonemitting target. See "Raytheon Awarded $28 Million for Rolling Airframe Missile Work," Raytheon press releases, June 23, 1998, and Dec. 11, 1998, http://www.seiscor/com/pres/1998/jun/ramcon.html.

57. Each NATO Seasparrow missile system (NSSMS) launcher assembly has a magazine of eight missiles. With three NSSMS launchers, the CVN can carry up to twenty-four missiles; reloading the NSSMS launcher takes about one hour. Designed to replace both the NSSMS and CIWS, the rolling airframe missile (RAM) has a twenty-one–missile magazine launcher. Three RAM systems would provide an additional thirty-nine missiles above the twenty-four currently available in the three NSSMS magazine launchers. See Richard Sharpe, ed., *Jane's Fighting Ships 1997–1998* (London: Jane's Information Group, Ltd., 1998), 802.

58. The configuration described is essentially the same as that employed by the Sea Lite beam director during successful engagements.

59. The Royal Navy's experience in the Falklands conflict illustrates that the actual expenditures of weapons far exceeded the models used for an analytical calculation of what would be necessary to neutralize the threat. As the British White

Paper on the Falklands emphasizes, the "rates of usage, particularly of ammunition, missiles and anti-submarine weapons were higher than anticipated." See *The Falklands Campaign: The Lessons* (London: Her Majesty's Stationery Office, December 1982), 25. Anthony H. Cordesman and Abraham R. Wagner, *The Lessons of Modern War*, vol. 3, *The Afghan and Falklands Conflict* (Boulder, Colo.: Westview Press, 1990), 330, 366, quote the White Paper and go on to generalize the same conclusion for all conflicts discussed in the series (1973 Arab-Israeli War, Iran-Iraq War, Falklands and Afghan conflicts), with the exception of the mujahadeen who never had sufficient resources.

60. Although there probably would be more missiles to reload during any given evolution, the smaller size (9.2 feet [3 m] versus 12 feet [3.6 m]) and the lighter weight (approximately one third the weight of the RIM-7) should simplify the loading process. See "Facts and Figures," 196, 198. Any steps that reduce the requirements for handling conventional weapons dramatically simplify defensive measures when chemical or biological weapons are used. The reloading of mechanical gun systems (i.e., Mark 15 CIWS) is particularly challenging for personnel who are attired in full chemical protective gear.

61. Hughes, *Fleet Tactics,* 109.

62. The traditional view of naval strategist Alfred Thayer Mahan was to mass the fleet in order to confront and destroy the opposing force and establish command of the sea. Mahan held this conviction so deeply that he saw no reason to divide the fleet. The depth of his conviction is reflected in his statement that, if the Naval War College "had produced no other result than the profound realization by naval officers of the folly of dividing the battle-fleet, in peace or in war, it would by that alone have justified its existence and paid its expenses." See Alfred Thayer Mahan, *Naval Strategy: Compared and Contrasted with the Principles and Practice of Military Operations on Land* (Westport, Conn.: Greenwood Press, 1975), 6. Corbett took the more contemporary view that, by denying definitive combat, an opponent could continue to contest control of the seas in those areas where he might obtain a local superiority of forces. Corbett suggested that the contest for command of the sea might remain in dispute throughout a conflict; see Spenser Wilkinson, "Strategy in the Navy," *Morning Post* (London*)*, Aug. 3, 1909; reprint on line, Nov. 24, 1998, at http:www.mnsinc.com/cbassfrd/cwzhome/histart/wilk1.html.

63. Hughes, *Fleet Tactics,* 30, quotes T. J. McKearney, "The Solomons Naval Campaign: A Paradigm for Surface Warships in Maritime Strategy," master's thesis, U.S. Naval Postgraduate School, Monterey, Calif., 1985, in which McKearney computes that the overall probability of a torpedo hit by Japanese forces during the Solomon's campaign was 0.06, whereas, in occasional battles, such as Tassafaronga, it reached 0.20. In McKearney's example, an attacker firing 16 SS-N-22 missiles would accomplish his mission if he could match the Japanese Navy's 0.06 success rate.

64. The term *fleet tactics,* as taken from Hughes's classic work, *Fleet Tactics,* is de-

fined as dealing "with operations involving coordination between multiple ships and aircraft." Hughes describes fleet tactics as the analog of *grand tactics* or *operational art,* as the latter terms are used in land combat.

65. During the Persian Gulf War, the threat of amphibious operations was used as a diversion; however, the mine problem highlighted the need for alternatives with greater flexibility and less predictability. See de la Billiere, *Storm Command,*148.

66. See Headquarters, U.S. Marine Corps, *Concepts and Issues '98—Building a Corps for the 21st Century* (Washington, D.C., 1998), 21–23.

67. The practical implications of operational maneuver from the sea are well-articulated in Mark W. Beddoes, USN, "Logistical Implications of Operational Maneuver from the Sea," *Naval War College Review* (autumn 1997); on line, Nov. 19, 1998, at http://www.nwc.navy.mil/press/Review/1997/autumn/art3-a97.htm.

68. The Royal Navy encountered this problem during the Falklands conflict when two Exocet missiles, fired at HMS *Ambuscade,* were successfully deflected. After passing through a chaff cloud, they acquired and struck the *Atlantic Conveyor.* See Sandy Woodward and Patrick Robinson, *One Hundred Days* (London: HarperCollins, 1992), 295.

69. For an elaboration of this discussion see Charles C. Swicker, "Ballistic Missile Defense from the Sea—The Commander's Perspective," *Naval War College Review* (spring 1997), on line, Nov. 19, 1998, at http://www.nwc.navy.mil/press/Review/1997/spring/art1sp97.htm.

70. Geoffrey Till, "Corbett and the 1990's," in James Goldrick and John B. Hattendorf, ed., *Mahan Is Not Enough—The Proceedings of a Conference on the Works of Sir Julian Corbett and Admiral Sir Herbert Richmond,* (Newport, R.I.: Naval War College Press, 1993), 224, reminds readers of Sir Julian Corbett's words, "This power of disturbing the enemy with feints is of course inherent in the peculiar attributes of combined operations. . . . In minesweeping vessels, for instance, there is a new instrument . . . capable of creating a very strong impression at a small cost to the fleet. Should a flotilla of such craft appear at any practicable part of a threatened coast and make a show of clearing it, it will almost be a moral impossibility to ignore the demonstration." See also J. S. Corbett, *Some Principles of Maritime Strategy,* ed. E. J. Grove (London: Brassey's, 1988), 303.

71. Although Naval aviators have long aspired to achieve this goal, the limitations of both offensive and defensive systems previously made it impractical. Hughes, *Fleet Tactics,* 104–5, summarizes the issues that confronted Nimitz during World War II and that led to the adoption of the massed defense.

72. John R. Boyd, "Patterns of Conflict," unpublished briefing, December 1986, 174.

73. Weapons designers seek to minimize heat dissipation requirements and power demands by operating at lower voltages, which reduces the amount of energy that is available to damage or disrupt the device. The one positive development is the trend toward more fault-tolerant architectures that incorporate automatic "soft resets" when disrupted.

74. Sowders et al., "High Power Microwave and Ultrawideband," 19–20.

75. Merritt, "Proliferation and Significance."

76. Sowders et al., "High Power Microwave and Ultrawideband," 30.

77. Senator Tom Harkin (D-Iowa), who has led the fight against the MIRACL testing in Congress, calls it "both unnecessary and provocative." *Inside the Army,* Nov. 30, 1998, 13–17, quotes him as saying: "The Congress, the White House and the Pentagon have to have a serious discussion of our nation's anti-satellite weapons plans before we go down the road of testing these weapons . . . although the Pentagon is spinning the tests as a way to measure U.S. satellite vulnerability, most arms control analysts would describe the test as a major step in developing an ASAT [antisatellite] weapon. These are the same types of tests that I and others in Congress objected to years ago." These remarks were quoted in *AFSPC Legislative Liaison,* Dec. 10, 1998. As they indicate, major unresolved issues regarding the development of antisatellite weapons continue to exist.

78. *Los Angeles Times,* Nov. 28, 1998, 1.

5. High-Power Microwaves and Modern Warfare

Eileen M. Walling

This chapter discusses how high-power microwave weapons could become a decisive directed energy weapon during the twenty-first century. The intriguing aspect of microwave technologies is their ability to have decisive military effects without necessarily creating physical destruction. Microwave weapons destroy the electronic equipment that exists in every modern weapon system and that is exceptionally vulnerable to high-power microwave weapons. The U.S. military is investing considerable resources in microwave weapons in the belief that this technology could disrupt or destroy military and commercial electronics and have revolutionary effects on military operations in the medium to long term. The Air Force leads this development, but microwave technology could have critical implications for all of the military services. This chapter examines the nature of high-power microwave weapons, how they might be used by military forces, the problems posed by integrating this technology into military operations, and its implications for war in the future.

Introduction

The military has exploited the electromagnetic frequency spectrum since the invention of wireless communications during the late 1800s and even more so since the discovery of radar during the 1930s. Although these technologies quickly evolved into military applications, the microwave portion of the directed-energy spectrum historically received significantly less attention and support than did the work in radar or lasers. With technological developments, however, high-power microwave (HPM) technology is becoming a fundamental part of U.S. defense capabilities.

In recent years, the modern battlefield has been filled with targets that are extremely vulnerable to high-power microwaves. Except for the rifle, gun, knife, and grenade, virtually all military equipment contains electronics. During the Persian Gulf War, squads or platoons of soldiers used radios and with Global Positioning System (GPS) receivers to provide communication and information. In recent years, military research laboratories have demonstrated that HPM technologies can produce significant effects, ranging from upsetting to destroying military and commercial electronics. Although much of this research has been conducted by the U.S. Air Force for the Air Combat Command and the U.S. Strategic Command, the development of microwave weapons could have significant consequences for all of the military services.

A number of HPM technologies are sufficiently mature to make the transition from development to active weapons in the U.S. military. This chapter reviews how HPM weapons can be used in military operations, examines how microwave technology can be integrated into weapons, and evaluates the challenges of integrating this new technology into the arsenal. An important conclusion is that high-power microwave weapons could revolutionize the conduct of military operations in the future.

Microwave Developments

Since the early 1980s, the U.S. military has funded scientific and technological programs to explore whether radio frequency and HPM technologies could be developed into directed-energy weapons.[1] Commonly grouped under the umbrella of HPM technologies, they operate in the low megahertz (millions of cycles per second) to the high gigahertz (billions of cycles per second) frequencies (1×10^6 hertz to 1×10^{11} hertz) part of the electromagnetic frequency spectrum. Invisible to the human eye, these frequencies range from wavelengths of 0.1 centimeter (gigahertz frequencies) to 3 meters (megahertz frequencies).

The military's interest in HPM technology is an outgrowth of previous military and civilian research and studies in the field of radar technology that began during the 1930s and continues today. This work also emerged from the U.S. nuclear program with the discovery of electromagnetic pulse (EMP) during the 1950s. Although typically equated with nuclear detonations, EMP is also produced by nonnuclear sources. An example is the static and distorted radio signals that occur when a car is driven beneath high-voltage power. Although, in this case, EMP only disrupts the signals and does no harm to the radio, it can have such serious and catastrophic effects on electronics equipment that the Department of Defense hardens and shields many of its weapons systems and subsystems against the effects of EMP.

Since the mid-1980s, research has expanded into the higher frequencies of the HPM frequency spectrum.[2] Depending on the power, frequency, and distance to the target, microwave weapons can deny the use of electrical equipment, as well as disrupt, damage, or destroy equipment. This is known in military parlance as D4 for "deny, disrupt, damage, and destroy." Because microwave weapon systems can defend themselves, they are D5 weapons, with "defend" added to their capabilities. The implication is that microwave weapons would be the first to defend against enemy attack and simultaneously produce offensive effects on enemy systems. It is commonly assumed that microwave weapons systems are similar to electronic warfare systems. Although both systems use the frequency spectrum against enemy electronics, microwave weapons differ from electronic warfare systems on several counts. Electronic warfare systems are limited to jamming, and they affect enemy systems only when the electronic warfare system is operating. When an electronic warfare system is turned off, the enemy capability returns to normal operation. Electronic warfare also requires prior knowledge of the enemy system because the jamming function works only at the enemy system's frequency or modulation. The enemy system also has to be operating for electronic warfare systems to be effective in jamming it, and there are numerous ways to counter the effects of electronic warfare signals. For reference, *bandwidth* is defined as the range of frequencies within which a system receives, transmits, or operates. For example, a radio that operates between 10 MHz and 50 MHz has a bandwidth of 40 MHz, whereas a radio that operates between 75 MHz and 100 MHz has a smaller bandwidth of 25 MHz. Electronic warfare systems are designed to attack specific frequencies, but they cannot attack all frequencies. A system that operates over a large-frequency bandwidth is less vulnerable to an electronic warfare attack because the attack is limited to a few frequencies. Ultimately, microwave weapons overwhelm the ability of a target to reject, disperse, or withstand energy, which has significant and often lethal effects on electronic systems.[3]

There are four differences between microwave weapons and electronic warfare, which seeks to jam or interfere with electronic systems. First, microwave weapons do not rely on exact knowledge of the enemy system. Second, they can have persistent and lasting effects on enemy targets by damaging and destroying electronic circuits, components, and subsystems. Third, microwave weapons affect enemy systems even when those systems have been turned off. Fourth, the only way to counter the effects of microwave weapons is to harden the entire system, not just individual components or circuits.

Current State of Technology

The high-power microwave program at the U.S. Air Force Research Laboratory investigates the effects of microwave and radio frequency emissions on electronics and develops technologies for integrating directed energy into weapons. As a result of significant advances in antennas, pulsed power technologies, and microwave sources on the offensive, defensive, and protective capabilities of microwaves, the United States has gained a deeper understanding of how susceptible and vulnerable weapon systems are to HPMs. This technological understanding forms the basis for shielding and hardening efforts to protect current and future weapons systems from microwave weapons that are developed by other states. It also helps to protect weapon systems from "friendly" microwave system emissions that can inadvertently damage or destroy U.S. weapons.

High-Power Microwave Terminology and Characteristics

Several distinctive characteristics of HPMs influence how they can be utilized in weapon systems. Although microwave weapons are not widely understood in the U.S. defense establishment, they could potentially create a dramatically new class of weapons whose distinctive characteristics would redefine military operations of the twenty-first century.

Critical to understanding microwaves is learning about their entry points into electronic systems. Entry points are the numerous pathways through which microwave emissions can penetrate these systems. When microwave emissions travel through the antenna, dome, or other sensor openings, the pathway is known as the "front door." When microwave emissions travel through cracks, seams, trailing wires, metal conduits, or seals, however, the pathway is known as the "back door."[4]

Because microwave emissions affect electronic targets from the inside, they do not physically destroy the target, but they can destroy or disrupt individual components, including integrated circuits, circuit cards, and relay switches. In addition, the effects caused by microwaves can be gradually increased, depending on the amount of energy that the target absorbs. Scaling, or changing, the effects is known in the microwave technical community as "dial-a-hurt."

The underlying phenomenon is that the integrated circuits, microelectronics, and components found in modern electronic systems are extremely sensitive to microwave emissions. The effect caused by microwaves can vary from denial, which means to upset or jam the system, to degrade, damage, or destroy the system. Microwave effects on targets vary based on the distance between the microwave weapon and the target, the power generated by the weapon, the emission characteristics (notably frequency, burst rate, and pulse duration) of the microwave, and the target's vulnerability.

In the language of military operations, to *deny* means to eliminate the enemy's ability to operate without physically harming the system.[5] For example, microwave weapons could cause malfunctions in relay and processing circuits within the enemy target, analogous to the static and distortion that high-voltage power lines have on a car radio, but which have no lasting damage on the radio after the car leaves the area. Thus, deny does not cause permanent effects because the affected systems are easily restored to their previous condition.

The meaning of *degrade* is to remove the enemy's ability to operate while inflicting minimal injury on electronic systems.[6] Examples of this capability include signal overrides and power cycling (turning power on and off at irregular intervals) that cause systems to lock up. These effects are not permanent because the target system returns to normal operation within a specified time, depending on the weapon. In most cases, the target system must be shut off and restarted, but, in some instances, the system might require minor repairs before it can operate normally again.

The principle behind the use of microwaves to *damage* systems is to inflict moderate injury on enemy communications facilities and weapons systems in order to incapacitate them.[7] Examples include damaging individual components, circuit cards, or motherboards in desktop computers. Although the effects might be temporary, this attack could have permanent effects, depending on the severity of the attack and the ability of the enemy to diagnose, replace, or repair the affected systems.

Finally, to *destroy* refers to the use of microwaves to cause catastrophic and permanent damage to enemy functions and systems.[8] In this case, the enemy might have to replace entire systems and facilities before it could return to normal operations.

Because electronic systems can be affected by microwave weapons, military organizations actively train technicians and electrical engineers who can diagnose and repair the components or circuits that are damaged or destroyed. It can take weeks of detective work, including sophisticated "autopsies" of the damaged or destroyed items, however, before repairs can be made. Although, in theory, once the cause has been diagnosed and determined, the damaged system can be repaired or replaced if there are adequate parts, the reality is more complex. Because microwaves can enter a weapon system through many entry points, numerous circuits and components are likely to be damaged.[9] The technician's job is complicated by the fact that, even after the system is evaluated and repaired, it might not regain its full capabilities. Then, the entire system must be reexamined. Damage caused by microwaves is often difficult to diagnose.

A further problem is that microwave weapons do not discriminate between friendly electronics and enemy electronics. The terms *susceptibility* and *vulnerability* are sometimes used interchangeably. Susceptibility means that a system can be affected by a specific frequency or set of frequencies, whereas vulnerability means that the system can be exploited by those frequencies. A system might be susceptible to microwave radiation but not be vulnerable, especially if it has been hardened. To protect its forces from enemy microwave emissions, U.S. military systems must be hardened against microwave frequencies. Although the United States leads in the development of microwave weapons and the threat from enemy microwave weapons is small, the more immediate problem is the potential for fratricide or suicide caused by its own microwave weapons. Countermeasures and hardening techniques are being developed to protect U.S. forces and systems, but relatively few of these techniques have been incorporated into current or planned U.S. or allied weapon systems.

A microwave weapon is an area weapon whose footprint is determined by the frequency, range to the target, and antenna field of view that is measured from several to tens of degrees. The fact that microwave weapons cannot be aimed precisely means that pointing and tracking these weapons is far less demanding than comparable laser weapons or conventional "smart" munitions. The footprint of a microwave weapon can be a two-dimensional area for targets on the ground or a three-dimensional volume for targets in the air or in space. By implication, microwave weapons can simultaneously attack multiple targets. For example, the primary target might be an enemy communications van, but an enemy surface-to-air missile that happened to be within the weapon's footprint also would be affected. Moreover, microwave weapons can be designed to fit into most weapon systems, including the wing or fuselage of an aircraft.

As with lasers, high-power microwave emissions travel at the speed of light, but, unlike lasers, microwave frequencies are insensitive to weather and thus can penetrate clouds, water vapor, rain, and dust. Microwave weapons can be used in all weather conditions. This has profound advantages for military operations where relatively few weapons in military arsenals can function regardless of the weather.

Microwave emissions, traveling at the speed of light, are 40,000 times faster than a ballistic missile.[10] With current technology, microwave weapons could have a range of tens of kilometers, and, as the technology develops, they could operate over even greater ranges. Another benefit of microwave weapons is that they can emit energy as long as there is sufficient power. The implication is that most microwave weapons would not be single-use systems that emit expendable bombs and bullets. Microwave weapons can be built to fit the nature of the target and the desired effects and thus would be well suited to covert military operations. Conceivably, handheld microwave weapons that weigh less than 10 pounds (4.5 kg) could be developed, and man-portable microwave weapons could weigh tens of pounds. Although it is possible to build vehicular or pod-mounted devices that weigh hundreds of pounds, as well as airborne systems that weigh thousands of pounds, the broader point is that microwave weapons have great operational flexibility.[11]

To operate, microwave weapons draw their power from electrical energy that is stored in batteries or that can be drawn from an internal power source, such as an aircraft engine. Most microwave weapons can fire multiple bursts of microwave power over a long period of time. When one considers that microwave weapons do not consume expendable fuel or ammunition in the traditional sense, the logistical support for these weapons is significantly less than conventional weapons.[12] In those cases where the microwave weapons are single-shot devices powered by an explosively generated electrical pulse, the logistical support for these microwave weapons systems would be equal to conventional munitions.

Finally, microwave weapons are distinguished by their ability to minimize collateral damage. In recent conflicts, U.S. civilian and military leaders emphasized the importance of minimizing collateral damage. With the exception of explosively driven microwave weapons, these weapons affect only electronics and do not cause physical or structural damage to facilities. Although any vulnerable electronics system within the weapon's footprint could be harmed by microwave emissions, the same is not true for physical facilities and structures. By far, the most important reason that microwaves minimize collateral damage is that these emissions do not harm people or structures.[13] To reduce the effects on noncombatant systems in an area, such as medical systems within a hospital zone, microwave weapons can be programmed to cease or reduce their emissions over that area.

High-Power Microwave Technology Development
Major technical activities central to the development of microwave weapon systems include choosing the microwave source and antenna, testing the effects and lethality of microwaves, hardening U.S. systems, and developing applications for microwave weapons.

Microwave Sources and Antennas
In recent years, the technological community has made great progress in developing HPM sources that operate at different frequencies and antennae that transmit at higher power levels. The technological community has developed innovative ways to reduce the size, weight, and volume of microwave sources

and antennae and has simultaneously increased their power. For example, one microwave source produces 1 gigawatt of power in a few nanoseconds and weighs less than 45 pounds (20 kg), and another microwave source radiates 20 gigawatts of power and weighs 400 pounds (180 kg). In comparison, the Hoover Dam generates 2 gigawatts each day.[14] As a result, these technological developments are transforming microwave devices into practical weapons.

Because microwaves do not discriminate and therefore attack all unshielded electronics, the U.S. military must assess the vulnerability of all weapon systems, both its own and foreign, to microwave effects and take steps to protect or "harden" its systems against microwaves. These tests are usually performed at low-power levels in order to prevent damage to expensive and, often, unique systems. Some weapons, including the F-16 aircraft and the low-altitude navigation and targeting infrared for night (LANTIRN) pod, have been modified to withstand microwaves.[15] With a significant testing program, the military can understand the lethal frequencies and power levels that deny, disrupt, damage, or destroy foreign systems. This program also gives the technological community opportunities for improving microwave weapons and countermeasures.

Microwave Weapons Applications
The technological community has devised military uses for microwave weapons that satisfy the requirements of the military commands, particularly in the areas of information warfare (IW), suppression of enemy air defenses, and aircraft self-protection.[16] In 1997, the Department of Defense approved the first Advanced Concept Technology Demonstration for an HPM device, and various military commands are evaluating the military value of microwave weapons.

Types of High-Power Microwave Weapons

An enduring objective for the Department of Defense is to develop and field weapons that permit the U.S. military to defend its national security interests and prevail when it is necessary to use force. The U.S. Air Force Research Laboratory's Directed Energy Directorate at Kirtland Air Force Base in Albuquerque, New Mexico, has programs to evaluate the ability of directed-energy technologies to satisfy the military's needs.[17] In 1998, the Air Force Research Laboratory commissioned a study to identify promising applications for using directed-energy weapons on airborne platforms. The purpose of the "Directed Energy Applications for Tactical Airborne Combat" study was to outline how to translate directed-energy technologies into weapons. Somewhat surprisingly, microwave weapons, rather than lasers, constituted the most promising applications for precision-guided munitions, self-protection for large and small aircraft, and unmanned combat air vehicles.[18] The fifth application is advanced sensors, which use laser technologies for numerous applications, including confirmation of the effects of military attacks, air-to-ground combat identification, detection of chemical and biological weapons, and above-ground target identification. The term *war effects confirmation* is the new phrase for battle damage assessment.

Precison-Guided Munitions

The lethality of conventional precision-guided munitions is limited by the blast and fragmentation footprint (or area). For example, a 2,000-pound (900-kg) precision munition has a blast and fragmentation radius of about 115 feet (35 m) and a footprint of approximately 13,000 square feet (4,000 m^2). In the comparison of a conventional precision-guided munition and a precision-guided microwave device, the blast and fragmentation areas are similar. The lethal radius and the footprint of the microwave weapon, however, are hundreds of times larger because the primary reason for generating energy is to power the microwave device rather than to generate blast effects. A 2,000-pound (900-kg) microwave munition would have a minimum radius of approximately 650 feet (200 m), which produces a lethal area of about 400,000 square feet (126,000 m^2). Further, targets that are not vulnerable to blast and fragmentation would be exposed to microwave energy.[19]

A significant opportunity for the use of microwave munitions is against the hardened targets that can be extremely difficult to damage or kill with conventional munitions. For example, during the Gulf War, the U.S. Air Force developed the GBU-28, which is a 5,000-pound (2,200-kg) guided bomb for destroying hardened Iraqi targets.[20] Even highly accurate munitions, however, cannot guarantee that the target will be killed because impact errors of even several feet can leave it intact. Finally, microwave munitions are not limited to precision-guided weapons but can be incorporated into artillery shells, scatterable mines, and 2,000-pound (900-kg) munitions.

Self-Protection Systems for Large and Small Aircraft

During the last several decades, surface-to-air and air-to-air missiles have become more significant threats to aircraft. Guided by infrared, radio frequency, electro-optical, or laser sensors, the majority of missiles on the global market pose a threat to U.S. military forces, but the United States does not have weapon systems that can actively defeat these missiles.[21] During recent years, rebel forces and terrorists have acquired many shoulder-mounted, man-portable air defense systems, including the Russian SA-8 and the U.S. Stinger missile, which are relatively inexpensive, easy to operate, and extremely lethal. Larger vehicle-mounted missiles, such as the Russian SA-10, are also appearing throughout the world.

Large, relatively slow-moving military aircraft, such as the C-17, the C-130, and the airborne laser (ABL), are not highly maneuverable during takeoff and landing. Although these large aircraft, as well as most smaller fighter aircraft, are equipped with self-protection systems, notably the chaff and/or flares that might defeat the older, less sophisticated missiles, these systems cannot defeat newer missiles. An HPM system, however, could actively engage incoming missiles. When triggered by the aircraft's missile warning sensor, which would provide information on the missile's location and trajectory, a microwave system could flood a region of the sky with microwave energy. If the microwave can induce rapid changes in the missile's trajectory, it could produce catastrophic missile failures, ranging from destruction of the missile body caused by extreme turns, detonation of the warhead fuse, and a force that causes the missile to change direction and eventually run out of fuel.

For these purposes, a microwave weapon offers three significant advantages over other types of weapons. First, it is an "area weapon" that can engage all missiles within the target area. Second, microwave beams can be rapidly retargeted, especially with a phased-array antenna that provides protection in several directions. Third, the microwave weapon can be sized and packaged to protect most aircraft. Microwave systems for large, less maneuverable, and slower aircraft can be mounted internally but still possess sufficient power to engage missiles at longer ranges. Rough calculations suggest that placing a microwave weapon on a large aircraft would not severely reduce its cargo capacity or range.[22] Microwave systems for smaller, faster, more maneuverable aircraft could be mounted in pods; although pods produce drag, the increased protection might outweigh the penalty.

Other U.S. military services can use microwave weapons to protect their systems, including Navy fighters and Army tanks, helicopters, and ground vehicles, from guided missiles. Larger microwave weapons can protect Navy and Coast Guard ships, as well as ground facilities, from surface-to-surface or air-to-surface weapons. For additional information on U.S. Navy applications, see Chapter 4.

Unmanned Combat Air Vehicles

A number of unmanned air vehicles, including Predator, Hunter, Dark Star, and Global Hawk, have reconnaissance and surveillance capabilities. There would be several advantages to adding a microwave weapon system to transform them into combat vehicles.

An unmanned combat air vehicle (UCAV) armed with a microwave weapon could operate as an autonomous vehicle or be linked to a controller on the ground or in an airborne platform. Examples of airborne platforms are the Airborne Warning and Control System (AWACS) and JSTARS aircraft. Although these aircraft can be programmed to fly against fixed targets, a microwave UCAV controlled by a human operator could also search for and attack mobile targets. These weapons could fly deep into hostile territory, especially if designed with low-observable technology; cruise at high altitude; and descend to conduct the attack.

During an attack, the UCAV engines would generate the power for the microwave energy, which means that the vehicle can attack targets as long as it has fuel. The projected maximum capability for a microwave UCAV is approximately 100,000 pulses (or shots) of microwave energy per mission. During a typical engagement, a microwave weapon could fire multiple pulses until the target is destroyed or disabled. Assuming 1,000 pulses per target, a microwave UCAV could attack about one hundred targets during a typical mission, and, during the attacks, the microwave system could simultaneously protect the UCAV from enemy missiles. The High Power Microwave Division at Kirtland Air Force Base, New Mexico, performed the preliminary analysis for a microwave unmanned combat air vehicle in 1998.

Strategic and Operational Capabilities

Microwave weapons offer such significant offensive and defensive capabilities that they might change the conduct of military operations. To clarify this possibility, this discussion focuses on the types of military operations that microwave weapons could perform.

Suppression of Enemy Air Defenses

To gain air superiority and supremacy, U.S. military aircraft must be able to attack targets in the enemy's territory without being destroyed by enemy aircraft or missiles. What is termed *air supremacy* begins with attacks that seek to suppress the enemy's air defense systems, including the tracking and targeting radars, communications, and missile guidance, and to control and intercept the enemy's functions necessary for locating, tracking, targeting, and attacking friendly aircraft.

Another option for destroying an enemy's air defense system is to use a combination of precision-guided and "dumb" conventional munitions. Because the damage radius of a 2,000-pound (900-kg) bomb from explosive and fragmentation effects is about 115 feet (35 m), military systems that are farther away than that distance might suffer only minimal effects. One way for the enemy to increase the chances that an air defense system will survive is to separate physically the individual systems, such that the tracking radar is kept far enough away from the targeting radar and missiles to prevent one bomb from destroying both. This strategy has the practical effect of forcing the attacker to strike the air defense system with several weapons to ensure its destruction. A reasonable estimate, however, is that one microwave weapon on a precision-guided munition, unmanned combat air vehicle, or self-protection pod on fighter aircraft could destroy most, if not all, of an unshielded air defense system.

Microwave precision-guided munitions could be employed in the same way as conventional munitions. Although their blast and fragmentation pattern would be the same as conventional munitions, which would allow each one to operate as a single-shot device, the primary kill mechanism is microwave energy rather than explosive effects. The footprint of microwave munitions is at least one hundred times greater than conventional munitions. The detonation of a microwave weapon could damage or destroy enemy air defense systems located within this area, although blast and fragmentation effects also could physically damage or destroy those targets. In addition, UCAVs armed with microwave weapons could destroy the numerous targets that comprise an air defense network. Operating as a multiple-shot weapon that emits microwave energy for as long as it has sufficient fuel to continue flying, a UCAV armed with a microwave weapon could fly over known mobile air defense sites. If a microwave UCAV could destroy the electronics in the air defense network, it would compromise the performance of the entire air defense system.

Command and Control Warfare or Information Warfare

The objective of command and control, or information warfare, is to limit the enemy's ability to control its military forces. The present approach is to use conventional munitions to attack enemy command and control facilities in order to prevent enemy commanders from maintaining contact with their forces. Because the modern military commander is dependent on radios, telephones, satellite communications, computers, and faxes for communicating with military units, the use of microwave weapons against such systems would present an extremely effective instrument for disrupting enemy command and control systems.

A microwave UCAV could be either preprogrammed or actively controlled to conduct attacks against enemy command and control facilities, as well as against individual units dispersed on the battlefield. A microwave weapon that attacks individual units could sever the communication networks and inhibit enemy forces from effectively coordinating combat operations. Such a microwave UCAV weapon could attack commercial radio and television stations and thereby limit the enemy society's sources of information. Microwave munitions, which rely on explosive mechanisms to produce microwave energy, would damage facilities and produce collateral damage, depending on the distance from the target.

Close Air Support

The objective of close air support is to assist friendly ground forces when they are fighting enemy ground forces by using conventional munitions and large-caliber (20–30-mm) aircraft guns to attack enemy tanks, artillery units, and forces. Microwave weapons could damage or destroy electronic systems, including command and control systems, radio and satellite communications, artillery targeting capability, and guidance and control functions on guided munitions, in the enemy's frontline equipment. The ability to destroy the enemy's command and control and targeting functions would effectively prevent it from using its weapons. The two microwave options for close air support are microwave weapons mounted on UCAVs and aircraft, such as Air Force A-10 aircraft or Army helicopters. It would be a great advantage to have microwave weapons that could blanket enemy forces with energy and weaken their ability to fight in an organized and effective fashion.

Battlefield Air Interdiction

By their nature, microwave weapons could strike supplies, equipment, and troops located behind the enemy's front lines. These weapons could attack and disable enemy airfields by damaging and destroying electronics in airborne aircraft, aircraft on the ground, air traffic control equipment, communications facilities, radars, and ground defense systems. In addition, microwave weapons could attack industrial or manufacturing facilities, as well as supply lines and transportation vehicles, which would interfere with the flow of supplies to enemy forces. Finally, microwave munitions would be highly effective against railroads because the explosive detonation would damage the tracks and trains and the microwave emissions would damage the electronic equipment in locomotive engines.

Space Control

Microwave weapons have significant potential for space control missions. Their principal roles would be to protect satellites from weapons and to attack satellites that provide information to enemy forces. Direct information includes GPS coordinates, reconnaissance/surveillance activities, communications, and weather forecasting. By contrast, indirect information involves radio and television broadcasts, which could provide valuable intelligence information to the enemy. One advantage of microwave weapons is that they do not physically destroy satellites and thereby produce the debris that would harm other satellites. Another advantage is that microwave weapons have an unlimited magazine, whereas lasers often use limited supplies of chemicals that must be replenished to produce the beam. Unlike single-shot explosive or kinetic kill weapons, microwave weapons use electrical energy obtained from the host vehicle's engine, rechargeable batteries, or solar panels.

Conclusion

Although the extent of their potential is still unknown, microwave weapons could have a decisive effect on military capabilities during the twenty-first century. Because microwave technologies are the first directed-energy weapon to be equally adept at both offensive and defensive operations, they could spur the U.S. military to develop a new generation of innovative weapons and doctrines. The military is also taking steps to deal with the emerging vulnerability of its weapons to microwaves by ensuring that they are hardened against microwave emissions.

Notes

1. Prior to 1984, the funding for high-power microwave research was organized into multiple project lines in two program elements, PE 0602601F and PE 0603605F, at the Air Force Weapons Laboratory. In 1985, separate and distinct project funding lines were established for this research in these two program elements. Air Force funding for electromagnetic pulse hardening research was held in two program elements: PE 0604711F and PE 0604747F.
2. This discussion on microwaves excludes specific details on frequencies, power levels, susceptibilities, vulnerabilities, weapon effects, and lethality. More detailed information is available from High Power Microwave Division, Directed Energy Directorate, Air Force Research Laboratory (AFRL/DEH), 3550 Aberdeen Drive, Kirtland Air Force Base, NM 87117.
3. Sowders et al., "High Power Microwave (HPM) and Ultrawideband (UWB)," 7.
4. Ibid., 76–79.
5. Ibid., 81.
6. Ibid.
7. Ibid.
8. Ibid.
9. This general principle is based on analyses and reports, related to damaged circuitry, of senior electrical engineers and technicians at Kirtland Air Force Base, Albuquerque, N.Mex.
10. Jeff Hecht, *Beam Weapons, The Next Arms Race* (New York: Plenum Press, 1984), 266.

11. HPM Overview Briefing," High Power Microwave Division, Directed Energy Directorate, U.S. Air Force Research Laboratory, Kirtland Air Force Base, N.Mex., February 1998.

12. Given a preliminary cost analysis, an unmanned combat air vehicle would require approximately 70 percent fewer logistics personnel and support than conventional weapons. This analysis was performed by the High Power Microwave Division, Kirtland Air Force Base, N.Mex., 1998.

13. Biological and biomedical research in the electromagnetic spectrum is performed by researchers, scientists, and medical personnel for the U.S. Air Force Research Laboratory. This research is conducted by the Human Effectiveness Directorate, Brooks Air Force Base, Texas.

14. HPM Source Technology Review and Assessment, High Power Microwave Division Overview Briefing, n.d. See also "Hoover Dam—How It All Works," Jan. 4, 1999, http://www.hooverdam.com/workings/main.htm.

15. William Baker, "Air Force High-Power Microwave Technology Program," *JTCG/AS Aircraft Survivability* (Kirtland Air Force Base, N.Mex.: High Power Microwave Division, Directed Energy Directorate, 1998), 9.

16. These programs are managed within the High Power Microwave Division, Directed Energy Directorate, Air Force Research Laboratory, Kirtland Air Force Base, N.Mex.

17. Barry Hogge, Chief Scientist, Directed Energy Directorate, Air Force Research Laboratory "Assessment of the Aerospace Expeditionary Forces Studies Recommendations," briefing, Kirtland Air Force Base, N.Mex., May 1, 1998.

18. Office of Public Affairs, Directed Energy Directorate, Air Force Research Laboratory, "Directed Energy Study Kicks Off," Release No. 93-32, June 26, 1998, http://www.fas.org/spp/ starwars/program/news93/93-32.html.

19. The blast and fragmentation radius of a 2,000-pound (900-kg) microwave bomb is slightly less than that of a conventional 2,000-pound bomb.

20. During Operation Desert Storm, the author served as a member of the Air Force's Rapid Response Team at the Pentagon and was directly involved in the evaluation and selection of the GBU-28.

21. The Air Force is actively pursuing a technology program to develop a laser-based weapon system, known as the infrared countermeasure (IRCM) program. This technology, however, is being designed to defeat only the existing inventory of infrared-guided missiles. Given the technical challenges and limitations of this laser program, it is unclear whether this IRCM system can defeat advanced infrared missiles or other types of guided missiles.

22. Cargo aircraft reach their volume limitations long before their weight limitations. Rough calculations suggest that the weight penalty imposed by a microwave system would represent a reduction of less than 100 nautical flight miles (160 km).

PART TWO
Military Targeting and Its Effects

6.   Cruise Missiles and War

David J. Nicholls

Cruise missiles are emerging as a critical weapon technology at the beginning of the twenty-first century. Several decades of technological progress have transformed cruise missiles into highly effective weapons that could become more cost-effective and militarily effective than manned aircraft and ballistic missiles. It is no accident that, when the United States conducted air campaigns against Iraq in 1991 and Serbia in 1999, the strikes began with cruise missiles. This chapter discusses how the proliferation of cruise missile technologies in the 1990s has transformed the cruise missile into a significant weapon that poses a threat to the United States and other states. Because the U.S. military recognizes that it is vulnerable to cruise missile attacks, which are extremely difficult to detect and shoot down, this chapter discusses how cruise missiles could alter the use of force in the short to medium term.

Introduction

The concept of the cruise missile predates the outbreak of hostilities in World War I and has inspired a number of devoted advocates ever since then. As early as 1915, the *New York Tribune* referred to the progenitor of the cruise missile as "a device . . . likely to revolutionize modern warfare."[1] Later, U.S. Army Gen. William "Billy" Mitchell described the cruise missile as "a weapon of tremendous value and terrific force to airpower," and proposed that it be used in his famous bombing tests against battleships to prove the effectiveness of attacks from aircraft.[2]

Only recently, however, have cruise missiles begun to live up to the expectations that emerged during the first half of the twentieth century. Since a number of their fundamental shortcomings have been resolved by technological developments, cruise missiles have begun to emerge as modern weapons that could give states an unprecedented ability to destroy important targets in military campaigns. For example, in the spring of 1999, the North Atlantic Treaty Organization (NATO) air campaign against Kosovo began with cruise missile strikes against communication facilities and air defense sites.[3]

Advances in guidance and control technologies have dramatically improved the lethality, reliability, and accuracy of cruise missiles. New propulsion technologies, for instance, now permit cruise missiles to operate at significant ranges, and stealth technology increases their survivability. States will learn how to exploit the inherent advantages of cruise missiles because they are relatively inexpensive, uninhabited, and hence expendable. With the end of the Cold War, there is a potential for technologically advanced states to sell their cruise missiles and technologies.

The allure of cruise missiles has been strengthened by the effectiveness of U.S. strikes against Iraq, Sudan, Afghanistan, and Yugoslavia. As the United States demonstrated that cruise missiles are militarily useful weapons, other states might be persuaded that cruise missiles could be militarily advantageous for them. This could strengthen the global demand for these weapons. For numerous reasons, cruise missiles could be an important part of the military arsenals of developed and developing nations.

This chapter explores how technological developments have remedied the historical shortcomings of cruise missiles and produced weapons with significant military capabilities. As cruise missiles become more cost-effective weapons for developing states than manned aircraft and ballistic missiles, the widespread proliferation of these systems and technologies could transform cruise missiles into decisive weapons for conflicts during the twenty-first century.[4]

A related issue is whether the United States could defend itself against a cruise missile attack. The Department of Defense continues to study national cruise missile defense, which reflects growing concerns that the United States and its military forces are increasingly vulnerable to cruise missiles.[5] It is unlikely that defenses could entirely defeat a significant cruise missile attack, given how difficult it is to detect and engage cruise missiles. When one considers that adversaries could develop significant numbers of cruise missiles, they will be drawn to attack U.S. supply lines and logistics centers. The United States, in turn, must reduce its vulnerability to cruise missiles.

Improving Cruise Missile Technologies

The principal value of airpower is the ability to destroy targets that are well behind the enemy's front lines. This idea of "deep attack" is important because aircraft or missiles can destroy the power grids, command and control facilities, social and economic infrastructure, and logistics systems that constitute the foundation of modern societies. With its technological superiority, the United States has preserved its monopoly in deep attack and denied this capability to its adversaries. This is one reason for its unprecedented military superiority at the start of the twenty-first century.

Almost since the origins of powered flight, cruise missiles have competed with manned aircraft for deep-strike attacks. Until recently, the military potential of cruise missiles has been limited by low reliability, poor accuracy, vulnerability to intelligence deception, inability to adjust to changing battlefield conditions, limited range, predictable and hence vulnerable flight paths, and vulnerable launch platforms. As the result of several decades of significant technological advances, however, cruise missiles have been transformed into reliable weapons with militarily significant ranges, extraordinary accuracy, and a significant degree of survivability against sophisticated defenses. Not surprisingly, cruise missiles are now a fundamental part of the U.S. arsenal for conducting deep attacks against military and economic targets. This transformation is based on technological developments in range, survivability, and precision.

Increased Range

The range of a cruise missile fundamentally defines the depth of attack and the number of targets that it can attack. A long-range effect is to prevent the enemy from establishing sanctuaries within which its military forces are safe from attack. For example, during the 1991 Persian Gulf War, the range of Iraq's Scud missiles forced the United States and its coalition partners to station high-value systems, including the Airborne Warning and Control System (AWACS) and JSTARS, in Yemen to keep those critical weapon systems beyond the range of Scud missiles.

An important focus of technological innovation has been to improve the range of cruise missiles. The range of a cruise missile is a function of the efficiency of its propulsion system and the drag of the vehicle itself. Further, the increased range of cruise missiles allows these weapons to maneuver around threats, which, in turn, increases their survivability. In order to increase the propulsion efficiency of cruise missiles, the United States developed small and highly efficient turbojet engines during the early 1960s. In recent years, these engine technologies have spread to many states through a number of routes. For example, the United States sold the Harpoon missile to twenty-three countries, many of which have the technological and industrial ability to reverse engineer those engine technologies. China, France, India, and Russia also have developed similar technologies.[6] In effect, states have invested in technologies that increase the range of cruise missiles, and this technology continues to diffuse to other states.

Survivability

Because a cruise missile does not possess defensive capabilities that would permit it to withstand an attack, its survivability after launch depends on minimizing the time between the moment it is detected by enemy air defense systems and its arrival at the target. This time span depends on the speed of the cruise missile and the distance at which it is detected, therefore, one way to increase the survivability of the cruise missile is to significantly increase its speed. Although significant improvements in speed are unlikely for now, an important exception is Russia's Alfa cruise missile, which flies faster than Mach 4 or four times the speed of sound (i.e., it travels 4,000 feet [200 m] per second).

Another approach to increasing the survivability of cruise missiles is to develop technologies that reduce their detectability. The most prominent method is to reduce the radar cross section (RCS) of cruise missiles, which is known as low-observable or "stealth" technology. As with speed, stealth technologies reduce the time between the initial detection of a cruise missile and its arrival at the target. Importantly, stealth technologies reduce the defender's reaction time, which puts the cruise missile closer to the target before it is detected. For example, if an AWACS-type radar could detect a cruise missile with a 75 square-feet (7-m) radar cross section moving at 500 miles (800 km) per hour at a distance of 230 miles (370 km), the defender would have about ten minutes before the cruise missile arrived at the target.[7] If the same radar is used to detect a stealthy cruise missile, however, the cruise missile might be detected less than two minutes before it arrived at the target.

Other technological developments could minimize the time between detecting a cruise missile and its arrival at the target. For example, with terrain maps and radar altimeters, cruise missiles can fly at such low altitudes, often less than 50 feet (16 m), that the chance of detection by radar or other sensors is quite low. The principal reason for this is that ground clutter, which occurs when radar bounces off trees, buildings, and other structures, makes it difficult to detect cruise missiles. Operating at low altitudes also improves a cruise missile's survivability against ground-based defenses because low-flying missiles are easily hidden by terrain. Also, survivability can be increased by using cruise missiles to attack radar sites in order to create holes in the radar coverage or by programming missiles to fly around defensive radars in order to avoid detection altogether.

Another factor that contributes to the increased survivability of cruise missiles is the development of relatively small launch facilities. For example, a significant tactical weakness of the German V-1 missile during the World War II was the need for a fixed ramp that was 180 feet (54 m) long. As a result of technological advances, however, Tomahawk cruise missiles can be launched from tubes on surface ships or submarines that are about the same dimensions as the missile. As shown by the failure of U.S. and coalition forces to locate Iraqi Scud missiles during the Persian Gulf War, it can be extraordinarily difficult to detect cruise missiles.

Precision Targeting

A fundamental feature of cruise missiles is the highly precise guidance system. The power of an explosive decreases as distance from the detonation increases, so the relatively small warhead on a cruise missile must detonate quite close to the target to ensure that it is destroyed. The technological innovation of the late twentieth century that gives cruise missiles phenomenal accuracy is the GPS. With GPS technology, cruise missiles can be guided toward their targets with constant position updates to produce levels of accuracy that often can be measured in feet.

Before the development of GPS, cruise missiles used inertial guidance systems to measure the missile's position in terms of the rate at which it drifted from its initial launch position. If inertial guidance systems are updated periodically with an accurate and independent source of navigation, such as GPS, cruise missiles can achieve extraordinary accuracy. For example, a cruise missile with a high-quality inertial guidance system that has a drift rate of 0.1 degrees per hour would produce a guidance error equal to 580 feet (190 m) over a distance of 250 miles (400 km) at a speed of 500 miles (800 km) per hour. But, if this system receives a GPS update at 50 miles (80 km) from the target, the error could be reduced to 23 feet (7 m).[8]

The accuracy of GPS guidance technologies for cruise missiles can be further improved by differential techniques, which require a reference transmitter whose location is precisely known. This transmitter is located so that it receives the same GPS satellite signals as the missile. By comparing its actual known location to the calculated location based on the GPS satellites, the transmitter can instantaneously calculate the error of the GPS signal and transmit that information to the missile. In tests conducted by the U.S. Air Force with munitions guided by inertial systems and differential GPS, the average miss decreased from 40 feet (12 m) to 16 feet (5 m). Not surprisingly, this technology has attracted the attention of other states, including China.[9]

A further advantage of GPS is the ability to determine the position of targets with great accuracy. One method is to use GPS receivers and laser range finders to determine the precise GPS coordinates of potential targets. Although this technique is limited to nonrelocatable, or fixed targets, most ports, airfields, electrical power units, pre-positioned logistics supplies, transportation nodes, and military bases can be located. This targeting information is available from high-resolution satellite imagery that can be easily obtained from commercial firms.

Precise knowledge about the locations of the target and of the incoming cruise missile is essential if the flight control system is to guide the missile accurately to the target. As technological innovation increases speed and accuracy, the military capabilities of cruise missiles will significantly increase to the point where their lethality will be equal to manned aircraft.

U.S. Experiences with Cruise Missiles

During the Persian Gulf War, the Allied coalition fired 288 Tomahawk cruise missiles with only six launch failures. These figures attest to improvements in reliability as compared with earlier generations of cruise missiles. Tomahawk cruise missiles destroyed 85 percent of their assigned targets.[10] Also, they were the only weapons used to attack Baghdad during daylight, which makes the percentage even more significant given the air defenses that protected the city. Tomahawks were used against a wide variety of targets, including command and control centers, electric power plants, industrial facilities, and Scud missile sites.

Tomahawks did not have a decisive effect on the outcome of the Persian Gulf War or the December 1998 attacks against Iraq, but, as unmanned vehicles, they reduced the risk to U.S. military personnel. This feature made them the weapon of choice in the raids against Sudan and Afghanistan in August 1998, against Iraq in December 1998, and during the Kosovo air campaign in the spring of 1999.

Although the consensus in the defense establishment is that Tomahawk cruise missiles are highly effective weapons, they have four limitations. One, their relatively predictable flight path makes them more vulnerable to defensive weapons. Second, planning military missions for terrain-following guidance systems is time consuming and complicated in terms of intelligence requirements; for example, U.S. targeting groups must request a targeting package from the Defense Mapping Agency to gather mapping data for a cruise missile mission. Third, a Tomahawk cannot be used against hardened targets because the 1,000-pound (450 kg) warhead, the weapon's accuracy, and its kinetic energy (speed) as it hits the target do not produce high probabilities of kill. Fourth, Tomahawk cruise missiles cannot attack moving targets because they are guided to a position rather than to a specific target, nor could they attack relocatable (mobile) targets because these targets could move while the mission is being planned or during missile flight.

Proliferation of Cruise Missiles

Numerous technologies are improving the range, accuracy, and survivability of cruise missiles. To deploy significant numbers of cruise missiles, however, nations must have access to the technologies that make the cruise missile a cost-effective weapon. Cruise missiles can give a state such a significant advantage that the result is a revolutionary improvement in its military capabilities. The availability and cost-effectiveness of cruise missiles have accelerated their proliferation.

Availability

The commercial availability of critical technologies; widespread arms sales; and the indigenous development of guidance, propulsion, and survivability technologies have enhanced the capabilities of cruise missiles. The commercialization of technology has improved electronic and digital components, including the computers in autopilots and the GPS receivers that locate targets and guide missiles to those targets. In addition, the commercialization of computer-aided design technologies, when coupled with computer-assisted, precision-machining capabilities, greatly enhances the ability to manufacture the precise parts necessary for modern cruise missiles. As a result, the number of states that can build cruise missiles has substantially grown. Nineteen countries currently produce cruise missiles, fifty-four countries possess them, and China reportedly could field a stealthy cruise missile.[11]

States that cannot build their own cruise missiles can buy them, principally because the Missile Technology Control Regime (MTCR), a multinational agreement designed to prevent the proliferation of missiles, does not effectively restrain cruise missile technologies. The MTCR focuses on missiles that have strategic uses, so it is concerned primarily with missiles that have ranges in excess of 180 miles (300 km) and 1,100-pound (500-kg) warheads. Suppliers of cruise missiles tailor their missiles to meet these requirements so that they are exempt from the restrictions imposed by the MTCR. In addition, some countries, including China, have not signed the MTCR.[12]

Although many cruise missile components and manufacturing technologies are widely available, the knowledge required to integrate those components into weapon systems remains quite restricted. Despite its advanced capabilities, the United States experienced difficulty in developing advanced missile technologies. For example, the Tri-Service Standoff Attack Missile (TSSAM) was canceled in 1994 because of technical problems and cost.

Another factor that accelerates the rate at which states acquire cruise missiles is the proliferation of antiship missiles, currently operated by seventy countries. Antiship tactical missiles are beyond the focus of the MTCR, but they are so functionally similar to land-attack cruise missiles that they are often converted into land-attack missiles. Tomahawk and Harpoon missiles are prime examples of systems that share both land-attack and antiship functions. In Asia, Taiwan is modifying its Hsiung Feng antiship missile into a cruise missile version that would allow it to strike China's land-based missiles.[13]

Cost-Effectiveness

Cruise missiles are becoming more cost-effective weapons. The unit cost of a U.S. cruise missile has historically exceeded $1 million, but it might decrease in the future. For example, although the Tomahawk cruise missile costs about $1.2 million, the Navy's new tactical Tomahawk is projected to cost one half as much. The Air Force will field the Joint Air To Surface Standoff Missile (JASSM) at a projected cost of $300,000 each, compared with $2.4 million for the functionally similar, but canceled, TSSAM.[14] Russian-made missiles, such as the Alfa, are expected to cost less than $300,000 each.

The fact that a cruise missile is less expensive to purchase than some other weapons might not convince countries to acquire them. The situation could change, however, as cruise missiles become more cost-effective overall when compared with manned aircraft and ballistic missiles. The basic approach to comparing the cost-effectiveness of cruise missiles and aircraft for delivering munitions is to compare the expected rate of attrition. Without attrition, all bombs, even smart bombs dropped from aircraft, would be more cost-effective than cruise missiles because bombs do not require propulsion and guidance systems. The total cost of munitions dropped from aircraft, however, must include the cost of the aircraft that could be shot down while delivering munitions and the costs of operating and maintaining the aircraft. Even if one includes the cost of the cruise missile infrastructure, cruise missiles are likely to be far less expensive overall than manned aircraft for probable aircraft attrition rates against U.S. forces.

A simple way to compare the cost-effectiveness of cruise missiles and munitions delivered by aircraft is to use the following assumptions. First, one can assume that the cost of acquiring an airplane is $30,000,000, which is the rough cost of an F-16 aircraft, and the cost of a cruise missile is $300,000, which is the cost of a JASSM. Second, it is assumed that each airplane carries four munitions per mission (termed a *sortie*), and that each munition costs $20,000, which is the cost of the Joint Direct Attack Munition. Third, based on U.S. experience, it is assumed that the cost of aircraft operations and support is twice the procurement cost and that each aircraft shot down is halfway through its operational life. The final assumption is that cruise missile operations and support are 10 percent of the procurement cost. Using these assumptions, one can calculate the costs of delivering munitions with cruise missiles and with aircraft for different attrition rates. Such calculations show that, even if the aircraft attrition rate is only 5 percent, cruise missiles are more cost-effective than aircraft until the cruise missile attrition rate reaches 80 percent.

For decades, military theorists have argued that the fundamental value of airpower was its ability to destroy a state's key military and economic nodes, to cripple its military forces, and to prevent it from effectively fighting, which was the stated objective of the air campaign in the Persian Gulf War. Although it is unlikely that any nation, within the foreseeable future, would have aircraft capable of achieving air superiority over U.S. military forces or could mount a strategic bombing campaign, cruise missiles are so inexpensive and expendable that even a developing state could conduct a strategic bombing campaign with them. This development would represent a fundamental change in the nature of airpower. Ballistic missiles cost six to seven times more than cruise missiles. Because cruise missiles and most ballistic missiles each deliver just one weapon, cruise missiles must suffer an attrition rate six to seven times higher than ballistic missiles before ballistic missiles are as cost-effective as cruise missiles. For this reason, many states are adding cruise missiles to their arsenals. Although most of them are relatively unsophisticated antiship cruise missiles, the demand for cruise missiles might increase once states realize how effective these weapons were in the U.S. attacks launched against Iraq, Serbia, Sudan, and Afghanistan.[15]

Reasons for Employment of Cruise Missiles

The fundamental value of cruise missiles rests in their ability to overcome defenses. There are several strategies involving cruise missiles that states could use to prevent the United States from achieving its political and military objectives. These strategies could deter the United States from taking action; prevent the United States from deploying forces, which is important in view of the fact that the U.S. geographical position requires it to deploy forces before it can execute a military campaign; attack the political will of the United States and thereby persuade the public that further action will produce levels of casualties that are politically unacceptable; and, finally, inflict a tactical defeat that causes the United States to reassess the costs and benefits of further action.

Deterrence of U.S. Involvement

The first option a state might employ to deter the United States is to use cruise missiles armed with conventional warheads in a regional conflict. The deterrent effect of using conventional cruise missiles would be to delay the deployment of U.S. forces, cause an unacceptable level of casualties, or help the state to achieve a tactical victory. Cruise missiles have significant deterrent value if American policymakers believe that the adversary has a credible capability.

The second, more credible option is to arm cruise missiles with weapons of mass destruction. As relatively slow flying aircraft, cruise missiles are better able to disperse chemical and biological agents over a wider and more controlled area than ballistic missiles. For example, a cruise missile carrying 1,000 pounds (500 kg) of the chemical agent sarin could contaminate about 600,000–990,000 square feet (190,000–320,000 m^2). An even more lethal situation would result from a cruise missile armed with 1,100 pounds (500 kg) of a biological agent, such as anthrax, that could deliver lethal doses over hundreds of square miles.[16] Because of their small size, minimal launch facility requirements, and easily survivable basing schemes, cruise missiles represent a highly credible threat to military forces. U.S. scientists and military personnel have known for decades that cruise missiles armed with weapons of mass destruction represent a highly credible deterrent threat, especially if deployed in a way that would make their destruction difficult. The principal reason for deploying nuclear weapons on submarines was to enhance the survival of nuclear weapons, which rested on concealing the location of the launch sites.

Although cruise missiles are a credible platform for carrying weapons of mass destruction, it is unclear whether other nations would risk using this option against the United States. During the Gulf War, Iraq probably refrained from using weapons of mass destruction against the United States and its allies even though it had the capability to do so, in part because of explicit threats that the United States would retaliate with devastating force.[17] The Iraqi leadership also probably feared that using weapons of mass destruction would provoke the United States to expand its military objectives and demand that Iraq not only withdraw from Kuwait but also agree to an unconditional surrender.

A related factor that affects a cruise missile's survivability is its low cost. With the cost of a cruise missile about 15 percent of a ballistic missile, a state could build so many cruise missiles that an attacker could not destroy enough cruise missiles to prevent at least some from reaching their targets.

Perhaps the most important deterrent effect of cruise missiles armed with weapons of mass destruction is their ability to deter or limit the conflict. For example, a state could threaten to use cruise missiles armed with nuclear warheads against U.S. military forces. This would allow the state to pursue an aggressive path, secure in the knowledge that it can back down before using those weapons rather than face the prospect of total defeat should it use them.[18]

Delay in Deployment

In the event that deterrence fails, a state could use cruise missiles to delay the deployment of U.S. troops, or at the very least, delay a U.S. counteroffensive and thus disrupt U.S. logistics plans.

Cruise missiles can be used to delay the deployment of U.S. military forces by attacking key logistics nodes; these assets are highly vulnerable to attack. In most regions, only a small number of ports or airfields can support large-scale deployments, so destroying or damaging critical nodes could sharply reduce the capacity of these facilities. Moreover, these points of entry often have bottle-necks, such as heavy cranes or docks, that indicate their capacity, and such information is readily available to adversaries. For example, the number and size of the cranes that hoist cargo from ships determine the logistics capacity of a port. Even the roll-on, roll-off ships require a dock and access to the port. Airfield capacity depends on cargo-handling equipment, availability of an air traffic control tower, amount of ramp space, and intact runways. In addition to these targets, cruise missiles could attack equally vulnerable power genera-tion facilities, bridges, marshalling points, and other fixed-logistics infrastruc-ture sites.

An adversary could attack logistics units en route to the region of hostilities. The sites that contain pre-positioned supplies, whose locations are known and easily found, especially with GPS guidance systems, could be attacked by cruise missiles launched from land, ships, or submarines. Using antiship cruise mis-siles, a state could attack supply ships that are en route to the theater or are still in port. The vast majority of American military equipment is transported by ships, most of which are vulnerable because relatively few merchant ships can defend themselves against cruise missiles. The need to use convoys to protect supply ships from cruise missile attacks would delay the arrival of equipment and materiel. It is also possible that a state would attack U.S. logistics units at sea with weapons of mass destruction because collateral casualties in the middle of the ocean, far removed from population centers, would be minimal. Cruise missile attacks would create significant delays if the equipment had to be de-contaminated or if personnel were unsure that decontamination was complete.

The use of cruise missiles to attack supply lines would force the United States to devote a number of significant combat forces and logistics supplies to counter this threat. If supply ships were vulnerable to attack, the United States would require convoys to protect its merchant fleet. Organizing convoys would take additional time, and the process would slow the deployment and create bottle-necks. Moreover, defending against cruise missiles would reduce the airlift and sealift assets that are available for deploying other forces, principally because missile defenses require a significant amount of airlift and sealift. For example, deploying one Patriot battalion of ninety-six missiles requires approximately sixteen C-5 aircraft.[19]

Undermining of Public Support for Military Action

An adversary might use cruise missiles to exploit the American people's aversion to casualties, particularly in situations that do not involve vital U.S. interests. For example, Iraq's strategy in the Persian Gulf War was to force the United States to fight the ground battles that would create more casualties than the American people would accept. Although the strategy failed, Iraqi President Saddam Hussein apparently believed that he could create enough public pressure on the administration of U.S. President George Bush to force Washington to settle on terms advantageous to Iraq.

There is no doubt that cruise missiles, armed with weapons of mass destruction, would create significant casualties and political difficulties, especially if innocent civilians were attacked indiscriminately. Even conventionally armed cruise missiles would create political difficulties. The historical record of U.S. aversion to casualties, however, is not reassuring to adversaries. For example, in the Korean War, 33,651 U.S. soldiers were killed and another 103,284 wounded; in the Vietnam War, 58,161 U.S. soldiers were killed, and 153,303 were wounded. Even with these levels of casualties, particularly during the Vietnam War, only a minority of the American population favored withdrawal; the majority wanted to escalate the war in order to achieve the nation's objectives. During the fall before hostilities erupted in the Persian Gulf, the estimates of casualties were much higher than those actually experienced, but, in a February 1991 poll, 83 percent of Americans approved U.S. intervention. Interestingly, 80 percent of the American people polled believed that "the situation will develop into a bloody ground war with high numbers of casualties on both sides."[20]

One option for an adversary of the United States would be the use of cruise missiles to threaten countries that offer basing rights and port facilities to U.S. forces. Countries that are the least capable of protecting themselves might be bullied into neutrality rather than risk an alliance with the United States. If this strategy were successful, the United States might lose basing rights, overflight authorizations, local supplies, and port facilities that are necessary for sustaining overseas military deployments and combat operations. In this sense, cruise missiles would help a state to achieve its political objective of undermining American public support.

Infliction of Tactical Defeat

Cruise missiles also might be used to inflict a tactical defeat on the United States. Most states possess a relatively small number of cruise missiles, but an attack on critical nodes in the U.S. military would constitute an efficient use of them. Although U.S. military capabilities are robust, several vulnerabilities, including tankers, airborne warning and control aircraft, command and control nodes, and satellite ground stations, could be exploited.

As defense budgets decline and the costs of advanced weapon systems increase, economic forces complicate American military strategy. This could force the United States to purchase fewer high-value combat systems and supporting systems, such as transport air or ships. This would further reduce the number of high-value assets, including tankers, AWACS, command and control nodes, Patriot missile batteries, and satellite ground stations. In addition, if the United States entered a crisis with relatively few assets in theater, it would confront difficult choices about which forces should be deployed first. The danger is that military assets deployed early in the crisis might not include the forces that can defend against cruise missiles and that depend heavily on considerable airlift and sealift assets. It is conceivable that an adversary could achieve tactical victories with cruise missiles by attacking the critical nodes that support military operations.

There is considerable utility to using cruise missiles for attacking the airpower assets that represent the center of gravity for U.S. forces, at least during the early stages of a conflict. To date, the United States has kept its airpower relatively invulnerable to enemy attack, but it is conceivable that the use of cruise missiles to destroy aircraft and supplies on the ground could severely weaken the strength of its airpower.

All military organizations contain critical nodes essential to the conduct of effective military operations that are vulnerable to attack.[21] Although adversaries could attack logistics nodes, command and control centers, personnel, and airfields with cruise missiles, it is difficult to attack aircraft on the ground because their location varies over time. This is fortunate because a successful attack can be extremely effective in a military sense, as demonstrated during the first two days of Operation Barbarossa in 1941, when German forces destroyed 1,489 of 1,811 Soviet aircraft on the ground.[22] Although cruise missiles are more capable against fixed targets because their guidance systems can steer them to fixed points or home them in on targets that are actively emitting, aircraft deployed at bases are not kept in fixed positions, are moved quite frequently, and do not emit sources of radiation that could be tracked by incoming cruise missiles.

As a practical matter, a successful attack against aircraft on the ground would involve significant numbers of cruise missiles. Although cruise missiles can carry clusters of highly effective submunitions, most states do not possess the technical capability for effective dispersion of these weapons. This limitation could be minimized by using biological or chemical agents, as long as the adversary understands their political consequences.

Defense against Cruise Missiles

In light of the vulnerabilities outlined in the previous section, U.S. government and military personnel must understand the nature and problems of defending against cruise missiles. Current U.S. doctrine for dealing with cruise missiles divides its defenses into active defense measures; attack operations; passive defense measures; and command, control, communications, computers, and intelligence (C4I).[23] *Active defense measures* are operations that seek to destroy the cruise missile during its flight. *Attack operations* are those that destroy launch sites, command and control nodes, or missile stocks and the supporting infrastructure. *Passive defense measures* include steps that are taken to reduce the vulnerability of targets and minimize the damage caused by a cruise missile attack. *C4I* refers to the command and control systems that coordinate and integrate defenses.

This language helps to differentiate between tactical defenses and strategic defenses. Active defense operations and attack operations are essentially tactical missions that rely on destroying cruise missiles in tactical engagements. If the United States were able to destroy sufficient numbers of cruise missiles, the adversary could not use those missiles to achieve a strategic effect. By their nature, attack operations depend heavily on technology, notably in the area of sensors, because it is inherently difficult to detect and engage cruise missiles. The objective of passive defenses, by contrast, is to minimize the ability of the adversary to use cruise missiles to achieve strategic effects in war. This section focuses on tactically oriented attack operations and active defense, while the subsequent section examines passive defenses.

Offensive Attack Operations

Offensive attack operations seek to destroy cruise missiles before they are launched, which translates into attacking cruise missiles located deep within the adversary's territory. The objective is to locate and attack successfully cruise missile launch sites, command and control nodes, and missile stocks and infrastructure in enemy territory. Because cruise missiles can be moved to different locations around the countryside, attack operations depend on providing accurate targeting information to military forces as quickly as possible so that the missiles can be attacked before their launchers are moved to other locations.

These operations are extremely challenging, principally because of the countermeasures that are available to the adversary. During World War II, for example, the Allies conducted a massive bombing campaign against the launching sites for V-1 missiles. By the end of the war, they had expended about 98,000 tons of bombs. The Germans, however, had built numerous secret, smaller sites that were difficult to attack, often because these sites were concealed by vegetation and other nonstandard configurations.[24] German deception measures also succeeded because the sites were constructed without French workers, which deprived the Allies of an important source of intelligence about their location. To deceive the Allies further, the Germans repaired some of the larger V-1 launch facilities to create the impression that the bombing campaign was effective and that these sites were still active. Although the Allies were eventually successful in destroying two out of three V-1 sites, these attack operations consumed significant Allied bombing resources for several years.

Attack operations are a highly desirable method for defeating cruise missiles. Although their purpose is clear, it is difficult to conduct these operations. An example was the failure to find and destroy Iraqi Scud missiles during the Persian Gulf War. Because cruise missiles do not require an extensive launch infrastructure, the problems of finding launch sites or storage facilities are complex. Attack operations can succeed if timely and accurate information is available, but adversaries who have competent counterintelligence and deception operations can reduce the effectiveness of such information and operations.

Active Defenses

The aim of active defense is to intercept and destroy incoming cruise missiles targeted against the United States or its overseas military bases through the use of radar, antiaircraft missiles, and guns. As with defenses against aircraft, active defenses against incoming cruise missiles require an extremely capable command and control system. It must be able to detect incoming missiles, select the proper defensive forces, communicate with those forces, and move them to the best location for attacking the cruise missiles. This process starts from the moment that the cruise missile is initially detected to the time that it strikes the target.

The principal decision for the defender involves the allocation of defensive weapons against incoming cruise missiles in order to disable or destroy them before they arrive at the target. Attacks of individual cruise missiles vastly simplify the defender's command and control problem because this avoids prioritization decisions and allows the defender more time from the initial detection of the missile. The optimum strategy for the attacker is to launch multiple cruise missiles, termed *mass attacks,* to saturate the enemy with more missiles than it can handle. This chapter focuses on mass attacks with cruise missiles because they constitute the most dangerous and demanding type of attack for the United States.

Time is the critical constraint because it determines whether the defender could engage the cruise missiles, the number of times that each missile can be attacked, and the time that it takes the defender to assess the nature of the attack and respond accordingly. Further, if the attacking cruise missiles are not destroyed the first time, the defender must decide whether to reengage the attacking cruise missiles and communicate that decision to its forces.

One approach for saturating the defenses is to launch more cruise missiles against the defender than it can manage. Consider, for example, a defensive combat air patrol in which four F-15 aircraft are each armed with eight air-to-air missiles. Against this force of thirty-two missiles, an attack with thirty-three cruise missiles would exceed the ability of that combat air patrol to defend a target. This is true even if one assumes that the F-15s have sufficient time to maneuver as they engage the cruise missiles before they arrive at their targets and that each defending missile disables one cruise missile during each engagement.

A second approach for saturating the defenses is to minimize the time for the defender to engage the cruise missiles. In the case of the four F-15s in the combat air patrol, if this force engages cruise missiles that are flying at 500 miles (800 km) per hour during their last 50 miles (80 km) of flight, the total time available to engage those cruise missiles is about six minutes. If one further assumes that the defender's missiles have a 70 percent probability of kill and that each engagement requires two minutes, eight cruise missiles would saturate the defenses rather than the thirty-two previously calculated. In order to engage all thirty-two cruise missiles, it would be necessary to decrease the engagement time to thirty seconds, increase the number of fighter aircraft to sixteen, or increase the engagement range to 200 miles (320 km).

This logic leads to the conclusion that the defender's effectiveness is determined by the weapon system. To use the current generation of weapon systems to defeat cruise missiles, the defender's choices are to buy more weapons or to increase the total time between the detection and impact of the cruise missiles. Although these alternatives present equally effective ways for minimizing the attacker's ability to saturate the defenses, with early detection, cruise missiles can be engaged and destroyed. This choice would have profound significance if the incoming cruise missiles were armed with nuclear, biological, or chemical weapons. The value of early detection offers insights into why the Department of Defense is improving its early-warning capability against cruise missiles, including links between sensors that create a "system of systems" for characterizing the nature of the attack.

The implication is that the number of cruise missiles that can saturate the defenses is determined by the defender's response time, which would be longer during the early stages of a deployment into a theater of operations. Because theater missile defenses require significant amounts of airlift and sealift, the most effective strategy for the adversary would be to launch a mass cruise missile attack as soon as U.S. forces arrived in the theater. The problems of detecting incoming cruise missiles and saturating the defenses reduce the chances that defenses could intercept all cruise missiles.

Because current defensive weapons have a low probability of destroying cruise missiles, the U.S. Department of Defense is investing in technologies for defending against them.[25] An approach is to use directed-energy weapons for cruise missile defenses, which would essentially reduce the engagement time to zero because the energy travels to the cruise missile almost instantaneously. It takes some time to engage a cruise missile, however, because time is required to aim the beam at the cruise missile and to employ the kill mechanism. The principal disadvantage to directed-energy systems is that they are essentially line-of-sight weapons, which means that the view of an incoming cruise missile is obstructed by the ground, whereas air-based systems could be obstructed by clouds. Nevertheless, the Navy, which has a significant interest in defending against cruise missiles, favors line-of-sight defensive weapons because aircraft might not be in the proper position for engaging the incoming missiles.

These alternatives are influenced by the tactical situation. For example, it is less important to detect conventionally armed cruise missiles early than those carrying nuclear, biological, or chemical warheads. In the latter case, the defender would want to detect the missile as early in its flight as possible to minimize the collateral damage from such weapons. A problem arises, however, in that a defender always has more high-value targets than it can protect with point defenses; point defenses, including the Patriot missile, are not very effective against cruise missiles, so perhaps less than 10 percent of them would be shot down.[26]

Passive Defenses

By contrast, passive defenses seek to reduce the effects of cruise missile attacks.[27] The doctrinal foundation for responding to cruise missiles, as contained in the U.S. Joint Chiefs of Staff's *Joint Publication 3-01.5*,[28] is the ability to be warned about an attack, to reduce the effectiveness of the adversary's targeting, to reduce the vulnerability of U.S. military forces, and to reconstitute U.S. military capabilities.

Fundamentally, the U.S. military doctrine for passive defense does not distinguish between defending against cruise missiles armed with conventional warheads and those armed with weapons of mass destruction. The warhead dramatically alters the number of missiles that the adversary might launch, the size and type of defenses necessary to defeat the attack, and whether the attack might succeed. For example, precision guidance significantly improves the capabilities of conventional cruise missiles because even relatively small warheads are militarily effective if detonated near the target. Passive defenses could be designed to interfere with cruise missiles by using intelligence techniques that deceive adversaries about the locations of key targets through camouflage or that interfere with the GPS signal that guides the missile.

The U.S. military doctrine for passively defending against cruise missiles fails to deal explicitly with the vulnerabilities of the U.S. logistics and supply system. Its logistics system is inherently vulnerable because U.S. military forces must be transported across the oceans to the crisis, whereas the adversary would have its forces in the theater. Although dispersing forces once they arrive in the theater can help, the larger problem is protecting forces while they are in transit to the theater. Cruise missiles with GPS guidance are well suited to attacking port facilities, which are fixed, known targets. Because the logistics system depends on the use of ships, the problem is complicated by the fact that most cruise missiles are designed as antiship missiles.

The doctrine for passive defenses does an adequate job of dealing with the nation's aversion to casualties, achieving tactical victories, and deterring the United States. With respect to casualties, the object of passive defenses is to disperse U.S. forces in order to minimize the number of lucrative targets, to train civilian authorities to deal with missile attacks, and to defend against weapons of mass destruction. If the adversary's strategy is to defeat the United States tactically, it might be useful for the adversary to attack in ways that enhance its combat capabilities, such as destroying air bases. Passive defenses include other techniques, however, such as deception and dispersal, that could be effective. If deterrence depends on possessing a credible threat and the will to use it, cruise missiles armed with weapons of mass destruction represent a credible threat, but U.S. doctrine does not address this problem.

It should be understood, however, that *Joint Publication 3-01.5* is the U.S. military doctrine that defines technologies for passive defense against cruise missiles. After all, Great Britain developed its doctrine for air defense during the early 1920s, well before it had developed the technology, notably radar, that allowed the British to make dramatic improvements in their air defenses. Doctrine provides a framework for organizing the methods for using technology to solve the military problems of defending the United States and its military forces against cruise missiles.

Conclusion

The challenge is to understand how technology is transforming cruise missiles into militarily significant weapons. If cruise missiles become more cost-effective than manned aircraft and ballistic missiles and as widely available, they could become essential weapons in twenty-first–century military arsenals. A worrisome conclusion is that states might consider cruise missiles to be weapons of choice as improvements in precision, survivability, and propulsion dramatically improve their tactical capabilities. These tactical capabilities may make it exceedingly difficult to defend against them, especially when the defenses are saturated with mass attacks.

The U.S. Department of Defense, which is investing in cruise missile defenses, is not proceeding on the assumption that defenses could entirely defeat a cruise missile attack in view of the difficulties of detecting and engaging cruise missiles, particularly if tens or hundreds are launched. Because many states could deploy large numbers of cruise missiles, an optimum strategy for an adversary is to use cruise missiles to exploit vulnerabilities. Although numerous countermeasures are available for neutralizing this threat, the supply lines that stretch from the United States to potential theaters of operation are inherently vulnerable. This, unfortunately, is precisely the type of strategic vulnerability that states could exploit with cruise missiles.

Given their ability to deliver ordinance over great distances with a high degree of accuracy and in a cost-effective fashion, cruise missiles could be strategically significant weapons during the twenty-first century. By combining cruise missiles with technologies that enable precise attacks, states could use cruise missiles to prevent the United States from establishing secure sanctuaries for its military forces. For example, bases in another country could be vulnerable to attack. Even including the cost of stealth technology, cruise missiles could be more cost-effective than air power.[29] For minor powers, the most effective use of cruise missiles, particularly if armed with weapons of mass destruction, is to persuade Washington that the risks of military involvement outweigh the gains.

Cruise missiles represent a critical defense technology that other states could use to exploit U.S. vulnerabilities and complicate defense planning. This technological development has the potential to revolutionize the military capabilities of states that seek to counterbalance overwhelming military superiority at the beginning of the twenty-first century.

Notes

1. "Aerial Torpedo Is Guided 100 Miles by Gyroscope," *New York Tribune,* Oct. 21, 1915, 1.

2. W. Mitchell, *Lawrence Sperry and the Aerial Torpedo* (Washington, D.C.: U.S. Air Services Publishing Company, 1926), 1.

3. "NATO Hits Serb Targets," *The Washington Post,* Mar. 25, 1999.

4. See John R. Harvey, "Regional Ballistic Missiles and Advanced Strike Aircraft: Comparing Military Effectiveness," *International Security* (fall 1992), 41–83.

5. Office of the Under Secretary of Defense, memorandum, June 2, 2000.

6. See www.cdiss.org/tabanaly.htm, 2.

7. Irving Lachow, *GPS-Guided Cruise Missiles and Weapons of Mass Destruction* (Santa Monica, Calif.: The RAND Corporation, 1995), 12. From radar physics, there is a fourth-order relation between the size of the RCS and the range at which it can be detected.

8. This analysis is based on the author's calculations.

9. Gregg D. Constabile, *Exploitation of Differential Global Positioning System (DGPS) for Guidance Enhancement (EDGE) Test and Evaluation,* Air Force Development Test Center, Technical Report 95-31, January 1996, 3-2. For references to China, see Liao Chaopei, "Precision Strike Concepts Associated with the Utilization of Relative GPS Technology," *Feihang Daodan (Winged Missiles Journal)* 1 (1996), 55–61.

10. W. Seth Carus, *Cruise Missile Proliferation in the 1990s,* The Washington Papers (Washington, D.C.: Center for Strategic and International Studies, 1982), 1.

11. See http://www.cdiss.org/cmthreat.htm.

12. Although China is not a signatory to the MTCR, it has pledged to adhere to the guidelines established in the MTCR. Nevertheless, there are reports that China has sold missiles or missile technology to Syria, Saudi Arabia, and Pakistan, among others.

13. Carus, *Cruise Missile Proliferation,*15. For references to Taiwan, see "Taiwan Puts $600m into Missile Programmes," *Jane's Defence Weekly,* Mar. 10, 1999, 4.

14. These cost figures are based on the author's experience as a missile analyst in the Directorate for Program Analysis and Evaluation within the Office of the Secretary of Defense in the Pentagon.

15. See www.cdiss.org/tabanaly.htm, 1.

16. Lachow, *GPS-Guided Cruise Missiles,* 18–20.

17. See Janice Gross Stein, "Deterrence and Compellence in the Gulf, 1990–91: A Failed or Impossible Task," *International Security* (fall 1992), 147–79.

18. See Henry A. Kissinger, *Nuclear Weapons and Foreign Policy* (New York: Harper and Row, 1957), 201, for the comment: "A power possessing thermonuclear weapons is not likely to accept conditional surrender without employing them. . . . It is the task of our diplomacy to make it clear that we do not aim for unconditional surrender." Several thousand years earlier, the Chinese strategist Sun Tzu said: "To a surrounded enemy you must leave a way of escape. Show him that

there is a road to safety and so create in his mind that there is an alternative to death. . . . Do not press an enemy at bay. Wild beasts while at bay, fight desperately. How much more this is true of men." See Sun Tzu, *The Art of War,* ed. Samuel B. Griffin (Oxford University Press, 1963), 109.

19. Air Mobility Command Studies and Analysis Division personnel, Scott Air Force Base, interviews by author, February 1999.

20. Eric Victor Larson, *Ends and Means in Democratic Conversation—Understanding the Role of Casualties in Support for U.S. Military Operations* (Santa Monica, Calif.: The RAND Corporation, 1994), 1–2, 24.

21. See J. A. Warden, *The Air Campaign: Planning for Combat* (Washington D.C.: Brassey's, 1989), 35, for the argument: "The layman tends to associate air superiority with destruction of enemy aircraft . . . it is not the only approach. A potentially vulnerable sequence of events (the aircraft chain) must take place before an aircraft fires a missile or drops a bomb . . . it is possible to eliminate an air force by successful attacks at any point in this chain."

22. Richard Muller, *The German Air War in Russia* (Baltimore, Md.: Nautical and Aviation Publishing Company, 1993), 44.

23. *Doctrine for Joint Theater Missile Defense, Joint Publication 3-01.5,* Feb, 22, 1996.

24. F. W. Heilenday, *V-1 Cruise Missile Attacks against England: Lessons Learned and Lingering Myths from World War II* (Santa Monica, Calif.: The RAND Corporation, 1995), 5.

25. S. B. Frosch, *A Critical Analysis of Ground-Based Air Defense during Joint Expeditionary Operations* (Leavenworth, Kans.: U.S. Army Command and General Staff College, 1997), 82.

26. Ibid.

27. It is difficult to define precisely what is meant by the strategic effects that could be achieved with cruise missiles. One example is the U.S. experience during the Persian Gulf War, in which 8,000 tons (7.3 kg) of precision-guided munitions were dropped for the explicit purpose of producing strategic paralysis in Iraq. See Buster C. Glosson, "Impact of Precision Weapons on Air Combat Operations," *Airpower Journal* (summer, 1993), 5. If one assumes that conventional cruise missiles have 1,000-pound (450-kg) warheads, an equivalent attack would involve 16,000 cruise missiles, which exceeds by an order of magnitude the cruise missile production capacities of most nations. A preliminary analysis suggests that precision guided munitions are about thirty times more effective than imprecise munitions. This estimate of the number of cruise missiles required for strategic attacks is low, however, for three reasons. First, U.S. and coalition delivery platforms used during the Persian Gulf War suffered no significant attrition. The only real source of attrition would be that inflicted by the defenses, and, historically, the only relevant data relate to the British experience of shooting down 50 percent of the V-1s launched against them. If this is a realistic attrition rate, then the number of cruise missiles necessary for strategic attacks would double to

32,000. Second, the low estimate relates to the increased effectiveness of munitions used during that war, notably the ability of the United States to choose tailor-made munitions for specific functions (weapons designed for soft, dispersed targets versus weapons designed for hard targets). Other states might not have the same options. Third, this approach assumes that a nation expends its cruise missiles without keeping any in reserve, which is highly unlikely. A broad conclusion is that adversaries could not use cruise missiles to conduct strategic level attacks against the United States without dramatic increases in production. Thus, the better strategy for adversaries is to focus their strategic attacks on potential U.S. military vulnerabilities, rather than seek to generate strategic paralysis, such as the U.S. air campaign against Iraq in 1991. The more practical conclusion is that an adversary would seek to exploit an asymmetric vulnerability in the United States rather than try to conduct strategic attacks.

28. *Doctrine for Joint Theater Missile Defense.*

29. See George Donohue, *The Role of the B-2 in the New U.S. Defense Strategy* (Santa Monica, Calif.: The RAND Corporation, 1991), for the observation: "Stealth technologies would only marginally improve the B-2's ability to penetrate Soviet air defenses, and would certainly not justify the system's tremendous cost. More importantly, even if stealth technologies guaranteed that every B-2 would penetrate, it would still be a less cost-effective weapon than . . . the cruise missile."

7. Nonlethal Technologies and Military Strategy

Joseph W. Siniscalchi

Historically, military organizations have made their weapons more lethal in order to strengthen their military and political power. Mounting political pressure to limit war casualties, however, suggests that making weapons more lethal is not necessarily the most rational and effective strategy. The development of nonlethal weapons that began in the 1990s could provide a more decisive means for dealing with military challenges in the medium term, especially the peacekeeping and peace enforcement operations that are becoming more prominent. This chapter examines nonlethal weapons, the military options created by these weapons, and whether this technology might represent a significant development in how states use military force.

Introduction

Despite the military success of U.S. forces during the Persian Gulf War, military operations in Somalia, Bosnia, Rwanda, Haiti, and Kosovo suggest that the United States needs to develop the appropriate political will and military tools for future conflicts. Perhaps among the nonlethal technologies that the U.S. military is now developing will be an important instrument for coercing or deterring adversaries while keeping casualties and destruction to much lower levels than is the case in present war-fighting concepts.

Nonlethal weapons represent a shift from the increasingly lethal evolution of military arms. Not surprisingly, the defense establishment has been slow to accept these technologies despite support from Congress and the academic community.[1] Although the debate has focused on the military and moral advantages of nonlethal weapons, interest within the defense establishment peaked when the military services struggled to forge effective employment doctrine and tactics for the peacekeeping and humanitarian operations in Bosnia and Somalia. As a result of these experiences, the Department of Defense (DOD) consolidated procurement priorities and employment policies for nonlethal technologies in peacekeeping and humanitarian operations.[2] A review of proposed nonlethal funding indicates that more than 70 percent of projected research and procurement funds are dedicated to these efforts.[3]

Although the use of nonlethal technologies for tactical applications is maturing, the development of protocols for their use in broader military applications is still in a formative stage. A fundamental issue is whether nonlethal technologies will provide a compelling advantage and result in a radically new type of war that justifies their expansion. This chapter examines the implications of nonlethal technologies for the military and whether these technologies could result in decisive tools for use during the twenty-first century.

Definition of Nonlethal Technologies

Nonlethal technologies cover a broad range of capabilities, including biological and chemical weapons, information warfare, crowd-control measures, and the latest in exotic weapons. This section reviews the promise of nonlethal technologies and assesses their strategic value.

Serious interest in *nonlethality* as a technology and as a distinct class of weapons is fairly recent. A 1970 study, "Nonlethal and Nondestructive Combat in Cities Overseas," is a seminal assessment of potential applications for nonlethal technologies in operations in urban areas and serves as the intellectual template for current research and development efforts.[4] Many of today's nonlethal technologies emerged from these concepts at the end of the Cold War. To strengthen their relevance, the national laboratories turned from nuclear warfare technology to less conventional research areas, of which the subject of nonlethal weapons is one example. Because nonlethal weapons are a product of *technology-push*, in which technology creates new military options, this technology has lacked the traditional base of well-defined military requirements and doctrine.[5]

The original phrase *nonlethal* caused confusion concerning the realistic capabilities and intent of these weapons. The vision of future wars being transformed into short "bloodless conflicts" drew a cautionary reaction from the defense community.[6] As a result, the debate did not rest on realistic expectations about how these technologies could be employed.

The DOD defines nonlethal weapons as those that are explicitly designed and primarily employed to incapacitate personnel or materiel while minimizing fatalities, permanent injury to personnel, and undesired damage to property.[7] Unlike conventional lethal weapons that destroy their targets principally through blast, penetration, and fragmentation, nonlethal weapons employ means other than gross physical destruction to prevent the target from functioning. Nonlethal weapons are intended to have one or both of the following characteristics: first, they have relatively reversible effects on personnel or materiel; second, they affect objects differently than destructive weapons within the area of their influence. Three important points are implicit in this definition.

The first point is nonlethal intent. Nonlethal weapons, when properly employed, should significantly reduce lethal effects, but there is no guarantee that fatalities or permanent injuries will be eliminated.[8] Although even the most benign weapon technologies can create lethal effects under some conditions, the intent separates nonlethal weapons from conventional munitions. The second point is that nonlethal weapon employment is not limited to less intense conflicts, notably peacekeeping, peace enforcement, and humanitarian missions. Rather, their employment can be applied across the range of military operations to enhance the effectiveness and efficiency of military operations.[9] The recent DOD study, "Policy for Nonlethal Weapons," leaves the door open to apply these weapons in numerous military contingencies, even though the rationale for expanding their use might not be well developed. The third point is that information warfare generally is excluded from the definition of nonlethal technologies. Information warfare, however, is a form of nonlethal warfare when it indirectly seeks to deny or disrupt war without actually destroying personnel or materiel. Its means of application is distinctly different from other forms of nonlethal weapons and, therefore, should be addressed separately.

Given that conventional munitions have evolved over centuries, nonlethal technologies are in their infancy, which explains why their advancement is still largely unfocused. Recent DOD policy corrects this deficiency by establishing specific responsibilities for the development and employment of nonlethal weapons. The Commandant of the Marine Corps is identified as the DOD executive agent for nonlethal technologies, and oversight for the development and employment of nonlethal weapons is assigned to the Assistant Secretary of Defense for Special Operations and Low-Intensity Conflict.[10] This initiative helps to focus future policies for developing the employing these weapons.

To establish a common point of reference for understanding nonlethal weapons, it is relevant to examine current research activities in nonlethal technologies and the limits of their use. Nonlethal weapons can be classified by either function or technology, but the most effective approach is to categorize nonlethal weapons in terms of *antipersonnel* and *antimateriel* effects. These are not absolute categories because some technologies can be used for both purposes.

Antipersonnel Technologies

The purpose of antipersonnel technologies is to target people with nondestructive means, which includes paralyzing or disabling effects that are generally temporary in nature or reversible with minimum lasting effects.

Chemical Agents

Nonlethal chemicals generally include agents that induce sleep or produce irritation, such as calmative agents, neural inhibitors, irritants, and odor-producing chemicals. Chemical agents are not new. They have been used by military forces during combat in more lethal forms and by law enforcement agencies to disrupt riots and to control crowds. As a result, considerable experience exists in employing chemical munitions and taking protective measures against them. Many types of chemical agents, such as pepper spray, are used for crowd and riot control.

The quick-acting effects of these chemicals can be used to disrupt military operations or to achieve a military advantage. They can be specifically utilized to disable individuals, large groups of people, or troop assemblies and to attack precision targets, such as ventilation intakes in leadership bunkers. Military employment of chemical agents, however, is limited by four factors. First, protective equipment is readily available, and tactics for dealing with these agents are routinely practiced by most modern military units. Second, their effective radius can be limited by weather conditions, including precipitation and winds. Third, the unpredictable reaction of some individuals to the agents, even at low dosages, could unexpectedly produce more lethality than is desired. Fourth, various international conventions limit the offensive use of chemical and biological agents, which raises questions concerning the legality or morality of these agents. Thus, although chemical agents can be useful for crowd or riot control, their effectiveness in other military operations depends on the vulnerabilities of the target and the restrictions of legal agreements.[11]

Optical Weapons

Low-energy lasers, such as night vision devices, target acquisition devices, or range-finding equipment, can disrupt human vision or optical sensors and, temporarily or permanently, damage the optic nerves in humans to the extent of causing blindness. The magnitude of the effect depends on the laser's power, the range to the target, and whether the target is moving. Not surprisingly, it is difficult to target a moving object for a sufficient amount of time to achieve the desired effect. A similar capability is created by isotonic radiators or optical bombs, which produce an extremely intense flash with an explosive burst. This flash can radiate a burst of energy equivalent in intensity to a laser and produce effects similar to those of low-energy lasers, including disorientation and temporary or permanent optic nerve damage to humans and damage to optical sensors.

This capability can achieve a temporary military advantage within the limited range of the weapon, which is small enough to be mounted on aircraft or carried by an individual. The proliferation of advanced optical sensors in precision weapons creates vulnerabilities that can be exploded by optical weapons. A laser could "sweep" an area to damage the optical sensors in precision weapons; although destroying the optical sensors rarely disables the weapons, their effectiveness could be reduced. The U.S. Army investigated the employment of lasers to blind optical sensors used for targeting or acquisition. One of these systems was deployed during the Persian Gulf War, but it was not used because American soldiers had not received sufficient training. In addition, illumination lasers on individual weapons were deployed to Somalia during peacekeeping operations, but their use was limited.[12] The use of lasers to disorient combatants could prove effective, but it has generated significant opposition because of concerns about the humanity of using weapons that can indiscriminately blind both combatants and noncombatants.

Acoustics

There has been considerable interest in acoustical weapons, which generate low-frequency sounds (below 50 Hz) that can disorient or cause nausea in personnel. The distress is reported to be temporary and stops when the acoustic source is stopped. At high-power settings, these weapons can have an antimateriel capability if "tuned" to the appropriate frequencies. Acoustic weapons, however, have two important limitations. First, this technology requires large amplifiers and large-volume speakers (or a phased array of speakers), which limit the mobility of the weapon. Second, range of the weapons is limited because acoustic energy dissipates quickly, which makes it difficult to deliver acoustic effects at an extended range. The use of these weapons on aircraft will require significant engineering advances.

Acoustic "bullets," high-powered, low-frequency blasts that generate an impact wave to incapacitate people, are being explored. In general, acoustic technology is immature. Modern capabilities would limit acoustic weapons to close-in engagements, but they might become useful for additional military situations in the future if the technical difficulties can be solved.

Directed-Energy—High-Power Microwave
High-power microwaves are normally considered an antimateriel weapon, but they might have significant antipersonnel capabilities as well. Some directed-energy weapons, such as microwaves, produce a variety of effects on humans, including pain, incapacitation, and disorientation. With current research efforts, as discussed in Chapters 4 and 5, the range and power of a high-power microwave weapon might be useful for keeping enemy forces out of an area or for protecting U.S. military forces.

Restraining Mechanisms
A variety of devices to restrain personnel, including polymer adhesives or "sticky foam," ensnaring nets, and ultra slick liquids that can impede personnel movement, are being developed. Although most of these restraining technologies are being developed for tactical situations, they could have strategic value for disrupting personnel movement or for preventing enemy movements toward an area or facility.

Antimateriel Technologies
The purpose of antimateriel technologies is to disrupt partially or to destroy military equipment, vehicles, facilities, weapons, or supplies. Their advantage is the ability to achieve the desired effects while minimizing the need to use lethal force. These technologies could have significant value in military operations.[13]

Chemical and Biological Agents
Research is under way to create chemical or biological agents that have various antimateriel effects. Supercaustic agents, which can rapidly deteriorate rubber and plastics or spoil petroleum supplies, are claimed to be "millions of times more caustic than hydrofluoric acid" and can be delivered as liquids or aerosols. Liquid metal embrittlement agents, normally formulated for specific metals or alloys, alter the molecular structure of metals and make them weak and susceptible to structural failure. Polymer agents (termed *stick-ems*) are extremely strong adhesives that can be applied as liquid or foam to prevent the movement of equipment and personnel. Alternatively, superlubricants (termed *slick-ems*) now being developed have an antitraction capability of disrupting the movement of vehicles. Combustion-inhibiting substances could shut down the engines in ground and small maritime vehicles. Many of these types of agents have proved effective in laboratories but have not been fully tested in the range of weather conditions that exist in combat.

Antimateriel chemical agents can be used to disrupt enemy supply lines by attacking critical transportation nodes, denying the use of critical supplies and equipment, or disabling the infrastructure. These capabilities offer significant options to a military commander, but they suffer several limitations. For instance, the effective reaction time and difficulties in delivering these agents in a precise fashion limits their use. The application of such agents over a broad area might require such significant amounts as to complicate effective targeting. As a result, antimateriel chemical agents might be best employed against smaller choke points, such as airfield taxiways, critical intersections, and inclines on railroads. Because, in most cases, the effects last until the substances are removed or countered, they might be best employed in tactical situations where small delays in the ability to maneuver or deliver supplies can be critical.

For some proposed weapons, it is difficult to discriminate between the effects of lethal munitions and nonlethal substances, such as metal embrittlement or supercaustic agents. The destruction of a bridge by nonlethal chemicals or by kinetic munitions achieves the same results. Hence, the advantages of nonlethal technologies must be weighed against the commander's confidence that the weapon will achieve the desired effect.

Electromagnetic Pulse and High-Power Microwave Weapons
Electromagnetic pulse (EMP) and HPM weapons offer significant capability against modern electronic equipment, which is vulnerable to power surges, as described in Chapters 4 and 5. These weapons generate very short, intense energy pulses that produce transient electrical surges capable of destroying semiconductors. Conventional EMP and HMP weapons can disable practically all modern electronic device within their effective ranges that are not shielded. The effectiveness of an EMP device is determined by the power that is generated and by the characteristics of the pulse.

Microwaves are highly effective against electronic equipment, and it is more difficult to harden potential targets against them. Current research efforts focus on converting the energy from explosive munitions into an EMP, which can produce significant levels of highly focused electromagnetic energy. Future technological advances could provide the compactness needed for a bomb or missile warhead. Currently, the effective radius of the weapon is not as great as nuclear EMP effects, but the effective radius could be hundreds of meters or more. Because these devices can disable a large variety of military or infrastructure equipment over a broad area, they would be useful for dispersed targets. Determining the appropriate level of energy, however, is difficult and requires detailed knowledge of the target. The obvious countermeasure is to shield or harden electronic equipment, but, at present, only critical military equipment is hardened, which significantly increases its weight and expense. Because many commercial and military systems could be susceptible to this type of attack, EMP and HPM weapons are emerging as leading contenders among nonlethal technologies.[14]

Characteristics of Nonlethal Weapons

Nonlethal technologies could strengthen military capabilities, but whether they will represent a revolutionary development depends on their characteristics. The extent that nonlethal weapons will evolve as credible weapons will depend on how technological developments are focused on these unique characteristics.

Precision Effects

There is no clear line between precision lethal and nonlethal capabilities, principally because nonlethal weapons are part of a continuum to increase the effectiveness of the attack while limiting lethal and collateral destruction. Although precision-guided lethal weapons control the extent of destruction by using highly accurate delivery, nonlethal weapons directly control the weapon's destructive effects. The implication is that conventional munitions destroy everything within their effective radius, whereas nonlethal weapons precisely attack specific components of the enemy's infrastructure or military force. Nonlethal weapons are more precise because they increase the radius of effects and focus the attack, both of which are important in areas where the risk of lethal effects or collateral damage rules out the use of conventional weapons.

Radius of Effects

Nonlethal weapons differ from precision munitions because their radius of effects can be considerably greater. Chemical, acoustic, or directed-energy weapons can have an effective range that is measured in the hundreds of meters. If one minimizes the lethal effects, the effective radius of future weapons could be expanded to cover large geographic areas and perhaps even entire countries. By filling a niche that precision weapons cannot fill, nonlethal weapons permit the destruction of dispersed equipment in a large area or facility or the disabling of infrastructure targets, such as manufacturing facilities, where it is difficult to identify the critical nodes or to target them. The ability to attack diverse targets might require nonlethal weapons in which the radius of effects is controlled. The ability to match the weapon radius to the desired target allows greater discrimination and more precise effects and thereby allows the military commander to match the weapon precisely to the objective.

Repeatable Effects

Nonlethal weapons must produce reliable and repeatable effects, and political authorities and military commanders must be confident that the weapons will achieve the desired nonlethal effects. If they are not confident that they will perform as desired, military commanders might be reluctant to risk lives and equipment by using nonlethal weapons. Further, subsequent military actions could depend on the effectiveness of a nonlethal attack. Confidence in the ability of the weapon to deliver the intended effects is imperative if these weapons are to enable new military strategies. Many of their capabilities, however, depend on a singular mechanism to produce the effect, which makes the development of countermeasures easier. As examples, antimateriel chemical agents depend on a single effect that can be eliminated with the use of the proper chemical antidote, EMP weapons can be nullified by the use of hardened electronic equipment, and antitraction agents can be countered by applying sand to add traction. For nonlethal weapons to become viable options that commanders freely choose, national leaders and military commanders must be confident that the technology will have the same effects each time that it is used in combat.

Selectivity of Effects
Nonlethal intent is the aspect of these weapons that permits political and military authorities to pursue strategies that would be impractical with conventional munitions. This feature of nonlethal weapons has many advantages, including greater flexibility to attack politically sensitive and broad-area targets without risking extensive collateral damage. Another aspect is the desire for reversible materiel damage when the United States and international agencies attempt a rapid reconstruction of an economic infrastructure. In general, this technology provides a partial answer to the moral imperative that military forces should minimize combat casualties.

Weaponized Capability
In the future, nonlethal weapons must be capable of delivery on cruise missiles or unmanned aerial vehicles (UAVs) because this type of delivery would reduce the risk to friendly forces and equipment and increase the ability to strike strategic targets. These considerations are critical if nonlethal weapons are to have strategic effects in military operations.

Utility of Nonlethal Technologies
The U.S. military is embracing nonlethal technologies for dealing with modern foreign policy problems. Nonlethal technologies, however, are not a panacea because several contentious issues complicate whether these technologies can meet the promises made by their advocates.

Unrealistic Expectations

Because many nonlethal technologies remain in research and development, no objective data are available for evaluating their effectiveness. Lack of combat testing, exercises, and military experience with nonlethal weapons rightly leaves the military services unconvinced of their merits. In principle, nonlethal employment is compelling because the ability to use technology to defeat an enemy without casualties appeals to American political sensibilities. This vision is inspiring, but, unfortunately, it is unrealistic. Although thoughts of "bloodless battlefields" have been abandoned, the capabilities posed by nonlethal weapons could foster two dangerous and misleading misconceptions about war.[15]

The first caution stems from interpreting nonlethal characteristics too literally. Nonlethal weapons consist of a large array of technologies with varied characteristics and effects. The application of these weapons, which are intended to minimize materiel and personnel damage, could kill both combatants and innocent civilians. An antipersonnel attack with a chemical or directed-energy weapon could be fatal to individuals with low tolerance for particular weapons effects. Another example is an antimateriel attack on an electrical grid that could prove fatal to civilians who require life-sustaining electrical equipment. Further, the incomplete testing of nonlethal technologies leaves doubt about the significance of the long-term effects on humans and on the environment. The political and moral advantages of nonlethality are of little value if nonlethal weapons pose significant, if unintended, health or environmental risks. Military commanders must consider the target and the weapon as they evaluate the balance between the desired effects and unintended consequences of using nonlethal weapons.

The second caution refers to the premature perception that nonlethal technologies offer a revolution in warfare. Scenarios are being hypothesized where the application of a nonlethal strategy during the Persian Gulf war would have subdued the enemy without a shot being fired.[16] This perception can lead to the misapplication of nonlethal force, unrealistic expectations, and disappointing results. Separating the promise from reality is critical for both military and political authorities if they are to avoid the failures that lead the military to reject nonlethal technologies.

Legal and Ethical Implications

The employment of nonlethal technologies has legal implications that can affect their development and limit their use. Historically, any new class of weapons provokes legal debates, and nonlethal weapons are no exception. The debate focuses on the just war doctrine and compliance with biological and chemical weapons conventions.

The just war doctrine (*jus ad bellum* and *jus ad bello*) attempts to limit or restrain the ways in which states utilize military force by requiring them to refrain from using unnecessary force and conducting hostilities with regard to proportionality.[17] *Jus ad bellum* governs when a state may resort to war and establishes specific ethical criteria. *Jus ad bello* establishes the conduct of war and sets limitations to military force once conflict is justified. The key tests to determine compliance are using military necessity to guide targeting while minimizing human suffering and ensuring that the level of damage is consistent or proportional with military significance.[18] A general interpretation is that nonlethal weapons, because their objective is to "humanize" military conflict, are consistent with the goals of the just war doctrine. Problems can occur, however, because of the relatively indiscriminate nature of some nonlethal technologies. The greater number of noncombatants that can be affected by a nonlethal weapon increases the risks of unintended consequences. These effects must be minimized in order to maintain the moral "high ground" when employing nonlethal weapons. Antipersonnel nonlethal weapons, such as chemical and biological technologies, generate the most dissension because of historic opposition to such weapons.

Ensuring compliance with international treaties and conventions further complicates the debate. Several nations and organizations oppose the use of antipersonnel lasers (blinding) and are initiating efforts to prohibit their use. This problem was highlighted during debates of the Certain Conventional Weapons Convention (CCWC) of 1982 (properly, the Convention of Prohibitions or Restrictions on the Use of CCWs Which May Be Deemed to Be Excessively Injurious or Have Indiscriminate Effects) ratified by the United States in March 1995. The United States maintains that employing nonlethal blinding lasers is consistent with the laws of armed conflict, but, under pressure from international agencies, the Clinton administration adopted a ban on "laser weapons specifically designed, as their sole combat function or as one of their combat functions, to cause permanent blindness to unenhanced vision."[19] Other nonlethal technologies, such as directed-energy weapons and acoustic devices, are subject to international legal review and debate.

Of greater significance is compliance with the chemical and biological weapons conventions. The future employment of several nonlethal weapons must be carefully weighed in the context of these agreements. The 1972 Biological Weapons Convention, signed by the United States on April 10, 1972, and ratified in 1975, prohibits the development and use of certain biological agents. Specifically, the convention prohibits the development or production of biological agents of "types and quantities that have no justification for prophylactic, protective, or other peaceful purposes."[20] Current U.S. policy strictly interprets this convention by prohibiting the use of any substance that causes the deterioration of food, water, equipment, or supplies. Further, the Chemical Weapons Convention, signed by the United States on 13 January 1993, and ratified in 1995, prohibits the use of chemical weapons as a method of warfare. The prohibition restricts the use of chemicals that affect "life processes" but, interestingly, does not restrict these same chemical agents in peacekeeping or humanitarian operations. Chemical agents that are used for antimateriel purposes are not addressed in this agreement and are considered legal. Ultimately, existing international conventions and U.S. policy prohibit chemical agents for antipersonnel purposes.

Because significant issues relate to compliance with international conventions, the United States must carefully consider whether modifying or denouncing existing agreements to accommodate nonlethal technologies might raise questions about the proliferation of lethal biological and chemical weapons. A chemical agent used by one nation to limit the human cost of warfare could be used by another state for mass destruction. The challenge is to strike a balance between prohibiting weapons of mass destruction and developing nonlethal technologies that minimize human casualties. Paradoxically, only a few nonlethal technologies are free from legal restraints. Antipersonnel uses of chemical weapons and low-power lasers are already restricted, and other antipersonnel nonlethal technologies face critical review. As noted by an independent task force study on nonlethal weapons, "It would, of course, be a tragic irony if nations used lethal means against noncombatants because nonlethal means were banned by international convention."[21]

Proliferation Risks

Adopting nonlethal technologies could promote the spread of nonlethal weapons to states and terrorist organizations. As future generations of weapons are fielded, the existing generation of nonlethal capabilities might spread throughout the world and eventually be targeted against the United States. When that occurs, it might be difficult to implement nonproliferation measures. The real danger is that reliance on advanced technology and sophisticated electronics makes the United States more vulnerable to a nonlethal attack. For example, an EMP attack against critical computers or the contamination of petroleum reserves by biological or chemical agents would pose a significant threat. Protective measures must be developed with the same urgency as with the nonlethal weapons themselves.

Implications for Adventurism or Deterrence

One risk in using nonlethal technologies is that a state might be persuaded to intervene at an earlier stage in a crisis or to intervene more frequently when its marginal interests are involved because the danger of escalation seems quite low. By virtue of their attractiveness, nonlethal weapons could persuade political authorities to become involved when the response appears to be low risk, which could lead to intervention in inappropriate cases—the stuff of military quagmires.

The availability of effective nonlethal weapons might lead to adventurism, but it is dangerous for a state to defer the development of more effective and humane military capabilities on the grounds that the political authorities might not have the judgment to refrain from using military force. Rather, political authorities must understand the dangers of inappropriate use and indications for nonlethal weapons to be a useful component of military capabilities.[22]

A second risk in using nonlethal technology is that an opposing state or subnational group, which is unable to respond in kind, might respond with lethal force, terrorist attacks, or weapons of mass destruction. If a state loses electrical power, how the loss occurred might not matter as much as the fact that it has no power. Although using nonlethal technologies increases the risks of escalation, it also underscores the need for decision makers to define strategies that permit a lower threshold of conflict without encouraging intervention because the risks appear low. If military force is used only when U.S. interests are threatened, the development of nonlethal weapons might not necessarily lead to adventurism.

Nonlethal weapons could create an effective instrument for coercion if the United States maintains the political will and military capability to apply lethal force when necessary. One study of military coercion concluded that conventional coercion is most effective when the adversary's military forces or war-making capabilities are threatened.[23] Nonlethal means can effectively increase a state's vulnerability to lethal attack if U.S. military forces destroy early warning and communications, disrupt supply lines, or immobilize equipment. Nonlethal means used to increase vulnerabilities of an enemy's military capability, when backed up by a credible lethal threat, can be an effective tool for coercion. Although states commonly assume that their opponents are rational actors, the emergence of intense national and religious passions in many states could produce unexpected reactions to the use of nonlethal weapons. This statement does not mean that Washington should refrain from using nonlethal weapons, but it does sound a cautionary warning.

Operational Considerations

Several considerations can influence the debate about the employment of nonlethal technology. Many of the scenarios used to demonstrate the effectiveness of nonlethal weapons fail to consider countermeasures, but, as the nonlethal arsenal expands, states could acquire effective ways to counter these technologies. Nonlethal weapons might be particularly susceptible to countermeasures because of the nature of the weapons' effects. For now, many of these counter-measures might be technically or financially beyond the reach of many states. For example, hardening existing electronic equipment against EMP could be difficult given the vulnerability of power lines and antennas. Other protective measures, however, such as protective goggles against lasers and protective covers to limit the effectiveness of antitraction substances on runways or bridges, could be relatively low-cost and effective options. The failure to consider the evolution of air defense weapons contributed to excessive aircraft losses during strategic bombing campaigns over Germany in World War II. For similar reasons, failure to consider the development of nonlethal countermeasures might be equally as costly.[24]

Difficulties with assessing the effectiveness of nonlethal attacks complicate the effective use of these weapons. It is difficult to evaluate the damage caused by nonlethal weapons principally because the external indicators of damage are not as obvious as the destruction caused by lethal munitions. Assessing a bridge whose metal has become brittle, the acoustic effects on personnel, or an EMP attack on air defense systems is not as easy as making traditional imagery-based assessments used by the intelligence community. Confidence that an attack was successful might not be confirmed until the enemy uses, or attempts to use, a particular piece of equipment. In the case of air defense or offensive military equipment, it is too late to wait until enemy forces are engaged to confirm their disablement. Thus, nonlethal weapons might be a technically elegant solution to war but might not represent a credible capability until we possess the means to verify a successful attack.

The intelligence system must develop new methods to assess the effects of nonlethal technologies, which could involve new multisensor reconnaissance methods and detailed analyses of their effects.[25] Determining the level of damage, the sequence of subsequent military or political actions, or whether to reattack a target is critical to the success of nonlethal weapons. The fast pace of modern battle demands that the United States operates within an enemy's decision cycle, which will require new technologies and methods. The Persian Gulf War highlighted the problems of assessing bomb damage and fueled a debate on the measures of success. If it is difficult to assess the effectiveness of a 2,000-pound (900-kg) bomb, assessing the effects of nonlethal weapons will be even more challenging.

Nonlethal Missions and Strategies

To date, no serious effort to incorporate nonlethal weapons into U.S. military strategy has occurred.[26] Although there is general acceptance of using nonlethal weapons in peacetime operations, their role has not been widely accepted within the Department of Defense or the foreign policy establishment. This discussion focuses on the role of nonlethal technologies in military operations that extend beyond peace enforcement.

Strategic Implications
Nonlethal technologies might provide effective solutions for dealing with political and military problems during the twenty-first century by offering a credible military option that minimizes risk and maximizes success. In general, nonlethal technologies could fill the gap between political coercion and lethal force.

Emerging Conflicts
Nonlethal weapons will permit a state to demonstrate its political commitment in most military operations without the risk of significant casualties and damage to the enemy. In lesser contingencies, nonlethal technologies could make traditional political and economic strategies more effective, for example, by stopping or inspecting suspect shipping and selectively disrupting transportation. Nonlethal sanctions might achieve more immediate results by selectively focusing on vulnerabilities and varying the effects.[27] In addition, nonlethal technologies might offer the means to intervene with military force when the combatants are in close proximity to civilians. In theory, these effects might compel an adversary to change its behavior to the point where intervention with lethal force is not necessary.

Nonlethal technologies permit the state to intervene at a lower threshold of conflict. The precise effects that are possible with nonlethal weapons, especially if used with cruise missiles or aircraft, might decrease the political and military risks associated with intervention. Whereas military intervention might not resolve the problem, nonlethal technologies could provide the opportunity to deescalate a crisis. Nonlethal intervention preserves political options because it can help to avoid alienating a population against future diplomatic efforts.[28] Most importantly, states no longer have to contend with the paradox of engaging in peacekeeping operations with lethal military tools.

Nonlethal weapons create a lower risk option for intervention because, with their large radius of effects, they can have significant political visibility and impact without the need to use ground troops. States are well aware that the American public's aversion to casualties has important its implications for continued support of a military operation. As many incidents have demonstrated, American forces represent a lucrative target when an adversary seeks to undermine public support. Reducing the number of forces and using less destructive technologies can reduce the overall political and human costs of intervention. The reduced risk of noncombatant casualties is also significant. In 1950, noncombatants accounted for approximately 50 percent of worldwide casualties during war, and, in 1980, the rate was 80 percent.[29] Nonlethal weapons might reduce the motivation for the targeted group or state to escalate the conflict. For example, an EMP attack against the state's communications system, although damaging, might produce a less emotional response than a lethal attack. This technology preserves political conditions that could be conducive to negotiations.

Nonlethal weapons could increase the ability to terminate a conflict because the reversibility of most nonlethal effects limits the extent of damage. If the political objective is stability, nonlethal weapons will help the failed state to restore its economy and political system. As long as military doctrine continues to emphasize that the destruction of national leadership, infrastructure, and economic capabilities is essential to strategic paralysis, the reversible effects of nonlethal weapons will remain important. The ability to rapidly rebuild infrastructure avoids the creation of economically and politically failed states whose legacy is permanent instability.

Major Conflicts
Nonlethal technologies will also provide a significant complement to lethal force during a major conflict, particularly as nonlethal technologies become more effective. Their precise effects are unknown because the technologies are immature, but they could expand as the technologies evolve.

For instance, airpower seeks to attack the fundamental centers of gravity in the state's leadership, infrastructure, and war-making capabilities, as demonstrated by the air campaign during the Persian Gulf War. Nonlethal weapons provide a natural complement to this military strategy. The precise effects and selective nature of engagement can support strategic attacks against vital targets while limiting the level of violence. The larger radius of effects for future weapons can enable devastating, simultaneous effects on a national scale. Although this option has political problems, one ballistic missile armed with EMP munitions could disrupt a nation's vital communications centers. Achieving this effect during the Persian Gulf War often required scores of sorties that were conducted over many days. Nonlethal technologies might allow modest-size forces to apply overwhelming pressure on the state's leadership and war-making capabilities during the initial stages of a campaign.

The ability of nonlethal weapons to delay, disrupt, and disorient enemy forces could make them more vulnerable to lethal attack. The destruction of electronic devices could force the enemy leadership to consider whether to discontinue military action or to suffer the consequences of a lethal attack. For example, a nonlethal attack could disrupt air defenses, degrade sophisticated electronics in fielded military forces and aircraft, and render many vehicles unusable, which would mean that the military forces are vulnerable. A subsequent attack on the disabled forces with conventional munitions could be conducted at the discretion of political authorities and military commanders.

In some cases, nonlethal weapons could be more effective than traditional lethal means. The greater radius of the effects of EMP or HPM offers a significant capability for electronic attack or for suppressing air defense equipment that is more efficient than precision munitions. An EMP or HPM attack on air defense can destroy the radar and support equipment associated with an air defense site. This attack is equivalent to multiple missions with conventional munitions and provides more sustainable results than electronic jamming. Also, nonlethal technologies offer flexible targeting options because reducing the risk of collateral damage allows nonlethal weapons to attack higher-risk targets. Although the location of command and control facilities or infrastructure targets in highly populated areas poses significant targeting problems, nonlethal weapons can provide a better alternative than lethal munitions.

In a strategic sense, nonlethal weapons are more than an adjunct to lethal force. Nonlethal weapons provide the ability to strike early in a conflict, significantly disrupt military actions, and increase the vulnerability of the aggressor's military force. This combination of effects could permit decisive intervention with smaller military forces, thus allowing nonlethal weapons to substitute for large-scale military forces. The future military requirements for intervening in a major conflict might shift from a force that is sized to fight on the scale of a Desert Storm operation to a much smaller force.

Conceivably, nonlethal technologies could allow military forces to reduce the risk of intervention, permit intervention at a lower level of conflict, preserve the political will to intervene, allow more rapid reconstitution of attacked infrastructure, and create greater harmony between political and economic tools. If such hopes prove true, nonlethal technology could weaken the restraints on intervention to the point where intervention is more effective and less risky and costly, both to the intervening forces and to the enemy. Further, nonlethal technologies allow smaller forces to be more decisive. Two caveats about nonlethal technologies, however, are in order. First, nonlethal technologies involve political and military risks that the political authorities must understand. Second, the use of nonlethal technologies is not equally useful in all military contingencies.

Employment of Nonlethal Weapons

The following discussion of nonlethal employment uses the examples of enforcing sanctions and fighting a major conflict to highlight the scenarios in which nonlethal technologies could enhance political options and military effectiveness.

Enforcement of Sanctions

Sanctions are traditionally the first option to coerce or weaken a potential threat when the risk to the state's interests do not justify the use of military force. The goal of international sanctions is to inflict sufficient economic hardship in order to persuade the target state to modify its behavior by prohibiting the flow of goods in or out of a targeted country or of specific goods. Traditionally, economic sanctions have been only marginally effective because of the problems of enforcement and the lack of credible means to escalate the sanctions; however, nonlethal weapons can make sanctions more effective. The precise and nonlethal effects of these weapons complement economic sanctions by providing greater freedom of action to the state using nonlethal weapons, by increasing the immediacy of the effects, and by reducing the risk to civilians and military forces.

Traditional sanctions are often ineffective because it is difficult to enforce compliance across a large geographic area, especially when neutral states choose not to cooperate and resist shipping inspections. The obstacle tends to dilute the effectiveness of sanctions and prolong the commitment that is needed to achieve the intended results. Nonlethal technologies add a new dimension to sanctions by increasing the ability to deny or disrupt the movement of critical goods and technologies to, and within, the targeted nation. The ability to shut down illegal shipping with EMP or HPM weapons gives a new level of effectiveness to the enforcement of sanctions. Further, the ability of nonlethal technologies to disrupt port facilities, equipment, and transportation nodes selectively can restrict shipping at vulnerable choke points, and thereby increase the effectiveness of sanctions.

The ability to adjust the radius of the nonlethal effects to incorporate broader geographic areas or more categories of targets allows the military commander to apply or relax expanded sanctions as part of a graduated response to a crisis. Using nonlethal technologies to strengthen sanctions creates more immediate effects and limits the risk to friendly forces, civilians, and neutral noncombatants. Minimizing permanent collateral damage can help to maintain a favorable political climate and contribute to diplomatic efforts.

The nonlethal disruption of electrical power, communications, or transportation systems in all or part of a nation could create a new category of more decisive and effective sanctions, perhaps in combination with economic sanctions. Preventing the enemy from using its critical infrastructure can have the same effect as military force but achieve the result with greater speed and precision. For example, disrupting television, radio, and commercial communications could isolate a state's leadership or shutting down electrical production could bring an economy to a grinding halt. This category of sanctions increases both the economic cost of noncompliance and the vulnerability of the state's military forces. Also, because such options are more intrusive and offensive in nature than economic sanctions, they could invite retaliation.

The following examples indicate how nonlethal technologies can be employed to enforce sanctions. EMP munitions, delivered by cruise missiles, could disable illegal or suspicious shipping within a designated restricted area, and EMP sea mines could be used in the restricted area to deter maritime traffic, as well as disable the electronic ignition of transportation vehicles at port facilities. In addition, transportation nodes can be disrupted with antitraction materials or superadhesives applied to selected roadways and rail routes. If the sanctions are not heeded, their radius could be expanded. Thus, the ability to deny electrical power, disrupt transportation, or disable communications in the targeted nation could signal that sanctions are not easily circumvented.

Major Theater Wars
Nonlethal weapons are well suited to blunt an imminent military invasion because they can attack the enemy's leadership, military forces, and infrastructure and thereby increase their vulnerability to lethal attack. One option is to rely on EMP or HPM munitions to disable the enemy's communications, logistics, and transportation infrastructure. Antimateriel chemical agents could disrupt transportation long enough to delay the movement of essential military equipment and forces.

Disabling air defense sites significantly increases the vulnerability of the enemy's military forces to a lethal attack. Further, the use of EMP or HPM weapons against invading forces could disable the sophisticated military electronics upon which military forces depend. The overall effect is to paralyze temporarily the political leadership and military forces, persuade the enemy to stop military operations, and increase its vulnerability to a follow-on military counterattack. Many of these objectives can be accomplished with nonlethal, standoff weapons that reduce the risks of intervention and provide a climate for diplomatic efforts.

The threat of posed weapons of mass destruction is so significant that the ability to neutralize related production or storage facilities remains the critical military objective. Interestingly, nonlethal technologies might provide a means for destroying these weapons without the risk of contamination that results from lethal attack. For example, EMP or HPM technologies could destroy the navigation, guidance, and detonation circuits in nuclear, biological, or chemical weapons or their delivery systems and hence neutralize these weapons. Various nonlethal technologies could be employed to deny access to storage facilities, antimateriel chemical agents could disrupt vehicle access to the facility, and polymer foams could contain the weapons in storage facilities. The ability to deny access to these weapons might be sufficient to deter their use.

Nonlethal technologies, in conjunction with lethal force, can be employed in four ways during a major conflict. First, a nonlethal strategic attack can disrupt the enemy's key leadership, organic essentials, and infrastructure. The attack could be accomplished with air-delivered EMP and conductive particle munitions to shut down the electric power grids that support military facilities and logistics, or EMP munitions could target commercial communications (radio and television) and military command and control to degrade the state's ability to control the population and military forces. Second, EMP could disable electronic equipment on aircraft, neutralize computer systems, and disable other sophisticated electronic equipment and vehicles. Third, to neutralize weapons of mass destruction, unmanned air vehicles could deliver HPM weapons against assembly and storage areas in order to destroy the guidance, navigation, detonation, and delivery systems of nuclear, biological, or chemical warheads. To deny access to weapons of mass destruction (WMD) storage areas, unmanned aerial vehicles could deliver polymer foam agents that render the facility temporarily inaccessible. Fourth, nonlethal technologies could be used with lethal munitions to disable key air defense sites. EMP munitions could disable radar, fire control, and associated electronic systems that are concentrated in urban areas. The effective radius of EMP weapons can be adjusted to match the target requirements and to minimize collateral effects.

These technological and operational developments point to the emergence of a doctrine for employing nonlethal technologies that, if properly employed, can provide considerable flexibility and credibility. To be effective, however, nonlethal weapons must be consistent with the nation's political, economic, and military strategies, as well as the vulnerabilities of the intended target. Political and military authorities are likely to demand a doctrine that balances the strengths and weaknesses of nonlethal weapons with the necessity to break down institutional military barriers against the use of nontraditional types of military force. A doctrine for the U.S. military that is integrated into the existing continuum of military capabilities could be based on three principles.

First, nonlethal weapons are inherently precise, selective, and versatile. By using them as flexible instruments of military power, states can control military effects and minimize violence. The implication is that nonlethal weapons provide a range of options between diplomacy and lethal force, which can allow political and military authorities considerable flexibility. The use of nonlethal force can strengthen sanctions and protect diplomatic efforts.

Second, the availability of nonlethal options permits a state to intervene earlier in a crisis, which could reduce the overall costs of intervention and the risk of escalation. To the extent that nonlethal options permit preemptive intervention, their use reduces the risk of escalation and lethal destruction. At the same time, nonlethal weapons can be highly effective in war, particularly when they are combined with lethal weapons for a military operation. Nonlethal weapons should be used, however, when they can provide the equivalence of a lethal force or even more effective capability. The implication is that nonlethal weapons are part of a synergistic strategy that, to be effective, must be closely coordinated and executed in conjunction with political and economic policies. The intent is to produce an instrument by which the state can achieve its goals without the risks inherent in traditional military actions.

Third, nonlethal technologies are not usable in all contingencies and are not a universal replacement for lethal force. Military commanders whose forces are at risk must retain the means and authority to respond with lethal force to ensure that nonlethal capabilities do not put U.S. resources and lives at risk. To be used properly, nonlethal technologies must be employed in concert with the enemy's vulnerabilities, the state's political objectives, the dangers of unintended consequences, and compliance with international conventions. Any one of these factors can render nonlethal technologies ineffective. Together, these principles provide a foundation on which to develop a doctrine for employing nonlethal technology.

Conclusion

Efforts to defeat an enemy without using lethal force are as ancient as warfare itself. With the development of nonlethal technologies, perhaps "victory without battle" no longer will be confined to political and economic tools. In principle, nonlethal technologies could give the United States a decisive tool for diplomacy and war that, if properly employed, could invigorate diplomatic actions, enhance the flexibility of military commanders, and give policymakers new strategic options. At the same time, nonlethal technology might strengthen U.S. military capabilities if it increases the vulnerability of enemy military forces and permits the U.S. military to prevail with smaller forces.

The degree to which nonlethal weapons influence strategy depends on the nature and pace of technological innovation. With the exception of tactical applications, nonlethal weapons have not evolved into an effective instrument of military power, and, until these technologies are developed into weapons, the military will not be able to gain confidence in them. Nevertheless, nonlethal technologies are promising because they are consistent with the American desire to use military force as precisely and selectively as possible. With nonlethal weapons, military commanders could affect enemy military systems and thereby focus their attacks on the enemy's strategic vulnerabilities.

A strategy that relies on nonlethal weapons would require technological innovation in weapons as well new ways of determining which centers of gravity are vulnerable to nonlethal technologies. This technology could result in new demands on intelligence collection and assessment processes, as well as closer integration among the state's political, military, and economic strategies. If nonlethal technologies are consistent with the political will of the state, they could change the nature of war during the twenty-first century.

Notes

1. Greg Lynch, "The Role of Nonlethal Weapons in Special Wars," master's thesis, Navy Postgraduate School, Defense Technical Information Center, Fort Belvoir, Va., ADA 297651, 1995, 19–23; Charles Swett, "Strategic Assessment: Nonlethal Weapons" (Office of the Assistant Secretary of Defense for Special Operations and Low-Intensity Conflict, staff paper, November 1993), 1–3.

2. Charles Swett, Office of the Assistant Secretary of Defense for Special Operations and Low-Intensity Conflict, interview by author, Dec. 12, 1996; Department of Defense, "Policy for Nonlethal Weapons," Department of Defense Directive, July 9, 1996, 1–4.

3. Commandant of the Marine Corps (Executive Agent), Nonlethal Weapons FY 98–03 Augmentation Program Objective Memorandum, Oct. 3, 1996.

4. Joseph Coates, "Nonlethal and Nondestructive Combat in Cities Overseas," Study Paper for Institute for Defense Analysis, Science and Technology Division, May 1970; also see Lynch, "Role of Nonlethal Weapons," 19.

5. Swett, "Strategic Assessment," 4–6; John Barry, Michael Everett, and Col. Allen Peck, "Nonlethal Military Means: New Leverage for a New Era," National Security Program Policy Analysis Paper 94–01, John F. Kennedy School of Government, Harvard University, 1994, 9.

6. Alvin Toffler and Heidi Toffler, *War and Anti-War* (Boston: Little, Brown, 1993), 128.

7. Department of Defense, "Policy for Nonlethal Weapons," 1–2.

8. Ibid., 2.

9. Ibid.

10. Ibid., 3.

11. For general information on antipersonnel capabilities, see Steve Aftergood, "The Soft Kill Fallacy," *Bulletin of Atomic Scientists,* September–October 1994, 43–45; John Collins, *Report to Congress: Nonlethal Weapons and Operations: Potential Applications and Practical Limitations* (Washington D.C., Congressional Research Service), 1–2; Paul Evancoe, "Nonlethal Technologies Enhance Warriors

Punch," *National Defense* (December 1993), 27–28; Dennis Evans and William Howard, "Nonlethal Arms," Secretary of the Army Staff Study, February 1993; Timothy Hannigan, Lori Raff; and Rod Paschall, "Mission Applications of Nonlethal Weapons," JAYCOR Technical Study for Office of the Assistant Secretary of Defense for Special Operations and Low Intensity Conflict, August 1996, Appendix C; Jonathan Klaaren and Ronald Mitchell, "Nonlethal Technology and Airpower: A Winning Combination for Strategic Paralysis," *Airpower Journal* 9 (1995), 42–51; Barbara Starr, "Pentagon Maps Nonlethal Options," *International Defense Review* 7 (1994), 33–39; Stephen Pope, "Nonlethality and Peace Operations" (master's thesis, U.S. Army Command and General Staff College, 1995), 54 59; Greg Schneider, "Nonlethal Weapons: Considerations for Decision-Makers" (unpublished National Defense Fellow research paper, Program in Arms Control, Disarmament, and International Security, University of Illinois, June 1996).

12. Neil Munro, "Peacekeeping Requires Special Tools," *Defense News,* Apr. 4, 1994, 14; Schneider, "Nonlethal Weapons," 23.

13. For general information on antimateriel capabilities, see Aftergood, "Soft Kill Fallacy," 43–45; Collins, *Report to Congress,* 1–2; Evancoe, "Nonlethal Technologies, 27–28; Evans and Howard, "Nonlethal Arms"; Hannigan, Raff; and Paschall, "Mission Applications," Appendix C; Klaaren and Mitchell, "Nonlethal Technology and Airpower," 42–51; Starr, "Pentagon Maps Nonlethal Options," 33–39; Stephen Pope, "Nonlethality and Peace Operations," 54-59; Schneider, "Nonlethal Weapons, 23.

14. For an excellent account of EMP and HPM capabilities, see Carlo Kopp, "A Doctrine for the Use of Electromagnetic Pulse Bombs," Royal Australian Air Force staff paper, July 1993, 1–14; Winn Schwartau, *Information Warfare: Chaos on the Electronic Superhighway* (New York: Thunder Mouth Press, 1994), 269–96.

15. Lexi Alexander and Julia Klare, "Nonlethal Weapons: New Tools for Peace," *Issues in Science and Technology* (winter 1995–1996), 67–74; "Non-Lethal Technologies: Military Options and Implications," report of an independent task force, sponsored by the Council on Foreign Relations, 1995.

16. Barry, Everett, and Peck, "Nonlethal Military Means." 13.

17. See Michael Walzer, *Just and Unjust War* (New York: Basic Books, 1977).

18. Miguel Walsh, "New Technology, War, and International Law," Office of the Secretary of Defense, Policy and Planning staff study, 1993; Joseph Cook, David Fiely, Maura McGowan, et al., "Nonlethal Weapons: Technologies, Legalities, and Potential Policies," *Airpower Journal* 9 (1995), 79–81; Hannigan, Raff, and Paschall, "Mission Applications," 13–18.

19. Schneider, "Nonlethal Weapons."

20. Hannigan, Raff, and Paschall, "Mission Applications," 15.

21. "Non-Lethal Technologies."

22. Roger Hunter, "Disabling Systems and the Air Force," *Airpower Journal* 7 (1994), 43–47; "Non-Lethal Technologies."

23. Robert Pape, *Bombing to Win* (Ithaca, N.Y.: Cornell University Press, 1996), 314–30.

24. Alexander and Klare, "Nonlethal Weapons," 72; "Non-Lethal Technologies," 9.
25. Edward O'Connell and John Dillaplain, "Nonlethal Concepts: Implications for Air Force Intelligence," *Airpower Journal* 8 (1994), 26–33.
26. "Non-Lethal Technologies," 3.
27. John B. Alexander, "Non Lethal Weapons and the Future of War," Los Alamos staff paper for Harvard-MIT Seminar on the Future of War, Mar. 9, 1995, 5.
28. Barry, Everett, and Peck, "Nonlethal Military Means," 9.
29. Hannigan, Raff, and Paschall, "Mission Applications," 13–18.

8.   Space Operations Vehicles
Commercial and Military Applications
John E. Ward Jr.

After several decades of launching vehicles into space, the United States is on the threshold of developing a new generation of reusable space launch vehicles that can be used for commercial and military purposes during the medium to long term. Despite the presence of the military in space, space vehicles in the future should not be designed for solely military purposes. Reusable launch vehicles can be used in many ways, including reconnaissance and targeting, but the fundamental reason for developing reusable space vehicles is to put satellites into orbit as inexpensively as possible. Because efficiency is not the primary consideration when the U.S. military places satellites into orbit, the development of reliable and inexpensive spacelift is likely to shift to commercial firms. This chapter discusses the development of reusable launch vehicles, their potential military and commercial applications, and their influence on the use of space.

Introduction

The conventional wisdom is that using space for commercial and military purposes is likely to influence the political, military, and economic interests of the United States. At present, the DOD exploits space by launching and operating sophisticated satellites that provide intelligence, surveillance and reconnaissance, communications, navigation, early-warning, and weather monitoring services. Commercial firms are also heavily involved in space, principally in the area of communications satellites.

The economic impact of space is significant. More than $500 billion in both public and private funds was invested in space between 1998 and 2000.[1] Constituting a global enterprise in developing, manufacturing, and operating space systems, more than 1,100 commercial companies in fifty-three countries engage in space activities. The U.S. government and U.S. commercial firms are annually investing about $100 billion in space, and their investment is increasing. At least 500 U.S. companies are directly involved with space activity, with their revenues totaling about $122 billion in 2000. Twenty-seven American states are seeking to become involved in space activity, such as developing licensed commercial spaceports.[2]

Despite these economic benefits, the high cost of getting into space is a fundamental impediment to using space. On the governmental side, the U.S. Air Force's Evolved Expendable Launch Vehicle Program seeks to reduce the costs of spacelift by 25–50 percent, but cost reductions on the order of ten to one hundred times the current costs are needed to make the use of space economically viable.[3]

The idea of sturdy and lightweight reusable launch vehicles (RLVs) has emerged as an important option for reducing launch costs, providing routine access to space, and dramatically expanding the ability to operate in space. Reusability is an attractive feature because it reduces the cost of placing objects in orbit. The traditional way to increase the amount of payload that can be put into orbit is to discard unneeded weight. For example, after the two solid fuel rocket motors are jettisoned from the space shuttle, they are recovered, refurbished, and reused. After the space shuttle lifts the bulk of the international space station into orbit, it will be replaced with a vehicle that performs resupply missions; however, this is an expensive form of reusability.[4]

Although the space shuttle is effective, it is highly inefficient. It is the most expensive and technically complex project in the history of space exploration, principally because military requirements were incorporated into its design at the urging of the Air Force.[5] The Air Force viewed the space shuttle as a replacement for expendable boosters, but the program expanded into a multipurpose vehicle for manned spaceflight, surveillance, and reconnaissance.[6] Today, the space shuttle is the only reusable launch vehicle in operation.

The DOD is interested in RLVs for reconnaissance, servicing satellites, military strikes, global transport, space control, and spacelift missions.[7] RLVs can carry at least 20,000 pounds (9,000 kg) into low-earth orbit, return to earth for servicing, and return to space within days. Although there have been numerous proposals for RLVs, including single-stage to orbit, two-stage to orbit, and transatmospheric vehicles, the fundamental objective is to gain routine access to space in a less costly fashion. A reasonable estimate is that the United States could produce an RLV within the first decade of the twenty-first century.

Although the use of RLVs in a manner similar to using aircraft is logical in a technological sense, it would be unwise to design these vehicles for solely military applications because the fundamental objective is to reduce the cost of access to space. The first-generation RLV should emphasize cost-effectiveness rather than military performance. Despite the numerous national security benefits associated with RLVs, they are more cost-effective in the long term for the United States if civil or commercial firms dominate their development.

The first generation of RLVs refers to concepts that are likely to result in production vehicles, whereas later generations of vehicles could exhibit higher performance (e.g., altitude and payload), more durable airframes, more durable propulsion, and generally faster turnaround times between missions. For example, a first-generation vehicle might have a flight propulsion system that lasts for twenty-five flights, whereas a second-generation vehicle might push that to fifty flights, and a third-generation vehicle might have a five-hundred–flight propulsion system.

Demand for Access to Space

The key to exploiting space is to have satellites in orbit. During the early days of the space program, the government was the only customer, but commercial satellite users soon entered the market. By 1996, there were more commercial launches than military launches from the United States, and, because 75 percent of all satellites worldwide are commercial, the commercial sector dominates the space industry.[8] In 2001, about 600 active satellites are in orbit, 134 of which were launched in 1998.[9] It is estimated that, by the year 2007, about 1,700 commercial communication satellites will have been launched, but Western military satellites will number only 129. An estimated 2,700 satellites will have been launched by 2017.[10]

Today, the United States places satellites into orbit primarily with unmanned, one-time use, expendable boosters that are derived from intercontinental ballistic missiles developed during the 1950s and 1960s. This approach has been very profitable for firms providing launch services. An estimated 1,700 expendable launch vehicles, worth about $110 billion, will be produced during the first two decades of the twenty-first century to meet the growing demand for launch services.[11] The company that develops the first practical RLV could dominate the global market for spacelift, but it will succeed only if it can develop a space launch capability that is routine, reliable, flexible, and affordable.

There are many potential uses for commercial RLVs, including satellite servicing, manufacturing, space tourism, and transporting cargo or personnel through space. For example, the commercial market might support a high-speed, point-to-point parcel delivery service with delivery prices up to $500 per pound.[12] RLVs could generate ten times more revenue than cargo aircraft and do so at only twice the cost. The idea of the RLV, however, is not new. The United States has conducted numerous technology programs to explore the options for building RLVs, including the DynaSoar (X-20) in the late 1950s, the space shuttle in the early 1970s, the National Aerospace Plane (X-30) in the 1980s, and the Delta Clipper Experimental Advanced (DC-XA) program in the 1990s.[13] Not surprisingly, both private firms and governments are investing in RLVs.[14]

Review of Reusable Launch Vehicle Programs

The U.S. Air Force has invested in RLVs for decades. It spent approximately $115 million on RLV studies between 1992 and 1997, and the National Aeronautics and Space Administration (NASA) invested more than $1 billion in RLVs during this same period.[15] The investment in 1998 was $86 million, with an additional $29 million for technology development. Most of these funds were spent on programs that evolved from the Delta Clipper Experimental program, which is still in various stages of development.

Delta Clipper Experimental

The DC-X (Figure 8.1) began as a private initiative funded by the Strategic Defense Initiative Organization and managed by the U.S. Air Force Phillips Laboratory at Kirtland Air Force Base in Albuquerque, New Mexico.[16] The McDonnell-Douglas Corporation built the DC-X in the early 1990s as a model for single-stage to orbit vehicles. The eight DC-X test flights, which occurred from August 1993 to July 1995, lasted from 59 to 136 seconds and reached an altitude of 8,200 feet (2,500 m). The DC-X demonstrated that it is possible to develop vehicles for relatively low-cost operations and showed how to integrate critical subsystems for RLVs with suborbital or orbital operations.[17]

Delta Clipper Experimental Advanced

The DC-XA was the DC-X modified for NASA and DOD under the RLV program. The first flight of the DC-XA occurred in May 1996, lasted 62 seconds, and reached an altitude of 800 feet (250 m); the third flight lasted 142 seconds and reached an altitude of 10,300 feet (3,100 m). The DC-XA successfully completed three test flights before human error on the fourth flight resulted in damage so severe that it has not flown since July 1996.[18] Its most significant contribution was to demonstrate that technologies permitting quick turnaround operations are feasible.

Figure 8.1. The Delta Clipper Experimental (DC-X) is an unmanned rocket that will use a single-stage engine for carrying payloads into orbit. (Courtesy National Aeronautics and Space Administration)

NASA X-33

The X-33, which is the NASA–Lockheed-Martin program (Figure 8.2) for demonstrating "aircraftlike" performance, uses a longer, shallower reentry profile than the space shuttle to reduce reentry heating. The X-33 will be unmanned,

Figure 8.2. The X-33 is an unmanned and reusable launch vehicle for carrying payloads into orbit. It will take off vertically and land like an airplane. (Courtesy U.S. Air Force)

take off vertically, and land like an airplane. NASA plans the first test flight in late 2001, which is designed to reach an altitude of 60 miles (37 km) and speed of Mach 15.[19] The program seeks to produce a cost-effective rocket system that will replace the space shuttle and reduce costs from approximately $10,000 to $1,000 per pound of payload that is put into low-earth orbit.[20]

NASA X-34

The X-34 is a NASA program conducted with the Orbital Sciences Corporation for the purposes of designing, developing, and testing key RLV technologies. The X-34 will use a single-engine rocket in an airplanelike vehicle, and serve as the link between the DC-XA and X-33 programs.[21] Plans call for the Orbital Sciences Corporation to build the vehicle and the government to provide the engine. The principal objectives of the program are to conduct twenty-five test flights within one year, engage in autonomous flight operations, use composites, and produce low cost avionics.[22]

U.S. Air Force Space Operations Vehicle

Known as a military space plane, the space operations vehicle (SOV) is an Air Force concept that is similar to the X-33. Based in the United States, it will exhibit aircraftlike operations; launch directly into low-earth orbit; and perform a wide variety of manned or unmanned reconnaissance, global strike, satellite service, space control, and spacelift missions. The SOV payload could include a number of space maneuver vehicles (see next section) and orbital transfer vehicles designed to transfer payloads to higher orbits.[23]

U.S. Air Force Space Maneuver Vehicle

Envisioned as a reusable orbital vehicle that deploys from an expendable launch vehicle, the space maneuver vehicle (SMV), performs missions while in orbit, returns to earth for refurbishment, and prepares for the next mission. The SMV involves a reusable upper stage for on-orbit maneuvering and functions as a space-based platform that can carry and deploy various payloads. After its return to earth, the SMV can be loaded with different payloads and launched again. The Air Force is currently testing a 90 percent scale version of an SMV atmospheric vehicle built by Boeing and designated the X-40A. The full-scale version should be capable of carrying 1,200 pounds (550 kg) of payload after it is deployed from an SOV.[24]

Commercial Reusable Launch Vehicle Programs

In addition to U.S. government partnerships with private industry, commercial contractors are developing their own versions of RLVs in order to reduce their cost of access to space. The Kistler Corporation plans to use the K-1 RLV to capture a substantial share of the market for low-cost launches of small communication satellites. The firm estimates that it will cost $17 million per launch, in comparison with $55 million for the U.S. government's Delta II booster.[25] Kistler signed a contract with Space Systems/Loral to launch ten Globalstar satellites.[26]

Kelly Space and Technology has an agreement with the Motorola Corporation to launch ten replacement satellites for the Iridium constellation of mobile satellites for global communications at a reported price of $89 million.[27] Kelly's vehicle, the Eclipse Astroliner, is designed to carry small to medium payloads into low polar or equatorial orbits.

Another promising commercial program is the Pioneer Corporation's Pathfinder, which will utilize aerial refueling of conventional jet engines. At

25,000 feet (7,500 m), the Pathfinder will meet with a tanker to load 130,000 pounds (6,000 kg) of liquid oxygen for the single RD-120 rocket engine that propels the Pathfinder to a suborbital trajectory of 80 miles (128 km), where the payload is released. After the payload is placed in orbit, the Pathfinder will land with conventional jet engines.[28]

The Rotary Corporation's Roton vehicle launches vertically like a conventional rocket but deploys rotors after reentry to land vertically like an autorotating helicopter. With a 7,000-pound (3,100-kg) payload, the Roton would meet the demand for launching low-earth orbit communication satellites. Launch costs for the first operations are estimated to be about $7 million per launch.[29]

VentureStar, Lockheed Martin's full-scale version of the NASA X-33, targets the traditional spacelift mission with a cost of $1,000–$2,000 per pound of payload, seven-day turnaround, and extremely high reliability.[30]

Foreign firms are also developing RLVs. For example, the European Space Agency, with Great Britain in the lead, initiated the Skylon program during the 1980s to investigate cheap and easy access to space without the traditional infrastructure. The program centered on a 270-foot (87-m) space plane that was capable of carrying 20,000 pounds (9,000 kg) into low-earth orbit.[31] Other European states also have an interest in RLVs.

Recent research by the European Space Agency includes the Ascender project. A suborbital airplane suitable for carrying passengers, the Ascender takes off from an ordinary airfield with the use of a turbofan engine that, at 26,000 feet (105,000 m), starts a rocket engine. The airplane climbs vertically at a speed of Mach 2.8 to reach a maximum altitude of more than 325,000 feet (105,000 m). The Ascender RLV will carry two crew and two passengers. A follow-on plan is to develop a space plane, known as the Spacecab, that can put small satellites into orbit. It is designed to be one hundred times less expensive than the space shuttle. An even larger vehicle, called the Spacebus, is designed to carry fifty people to and from orbit or to fly passengers from Europe to Australia in seventy-five minutes.[32]

The Japanese government has actively pursued research and development for an unmanned, winged space vehicle, known as HOPE-X (Figure 8.3). This technology, which will be launched from a Japanese H-IIA rocket, was scheduled to make its first flight in 2000, but it has been delayed. The Japanese have conducted several technology demonstration flights and experiments in support of HOPE-X. Although the purpose of HOPE-X is unclear, the vehicle demonstrates Japan's active involvement in RLV research and development.

Commercial firms are interested in RLV technology as well. The Lawrence Livermore National Laboratory proposed the HyperSoar, an aircraftlike vehicle that serves as the first stage of a two-stage launch system. It will achieve alti-

Figure 8.3. The H-2 Orbiting Plane Experimental (HOPE-X) is a reusable space shuttle being built by Japan's National Space Development Agency. (Courtesy National Space Development Agency of Japan)

tudes of 115,000–200,000 feet (37,000–64,000 m) at speeds of Mach 10–12 and use the upper stage to place satellites into orbit.[33]

Military Uses for Reusable Launch Vehicles

Because space plays a critical role in U.S. national security, the United States is investing in programs that seek to reduce the cost of spacelift. The Air Force vision for RLVs rests on SOVs and SMVs, which could be the first U.S. space superiority weapons.[34] The military's appraisal of the utility of RLVs, as outlined by the Air Force Space Command, describes how the SOV should be deployed, employed, and operated. The Air Force Space Command's argument is that RLVs should support, rather than replace, the roles performed by conventional air-breathing aircraft, including air superiority, strategic bombing, mobility, and close air support.

Reconnaissance

The aim of using reconnaissance and surveillance satellites is to cover military theaters of operations, but satellites are limited by the time delay between requesting and receiving data. RLVs with reconnaissance payloads could supplement systems because they can respond rapidly and maneuver in orbit.[35] Using RLVs for reconnaissance, however, could change how the United States organizes its intelligence community and disseminates reconnaissance information, as well as how long it takes to get information to the right organizations. A system in which RLVs collect high-quality reconnaissance data and deliver them directly to the consumer would be radically different from the existing intelligence system that tightly controls access to satellite imagery.

The principal advantage to using RLVs for reconnaissance is the ability to provide intelligence information quickly to military forces. The use of RLVs to deploy reconnaissance sensors would improve the ability to collect images of targets and revisit them regularly, but it would increase the complexity of who owns, operates, tasks, and decides to launch RLVs. The problem with RLV reconnaissance is that regional military commanders, known as commanders in chief (CINCS), prefer intelligence systems that are under their exclusive control.

Numerous alternatives to RLVs can provide critical intelligence information to military forces. An important example is commercial sources. With the proliferation of imagery systems by numerous commercial companies and nations, the United States is exploiting commercial products. For example, the Air Force spends $10 million per year on commercial satellite imagery to plan military operations and to meet imagery requirements when the competition for scarce satellites causes gaps in coverage. The Air Force predicts that the next generation of U.S. and foreign commercial satellites will provide military capabilities that are comparable to government sources.[36]

The comparisons between RLVs that deliver reconnaissance satellites and existing satellites raise questions about the advantages of RLVs. For example, satellites deployed by RLVs will provide limited access to targets because they operate in low-earth orbit. Although the deployment of additional satellites increases the coverage and revisit rates of satellites, each new satellite complicates command and control arrangements. Because the ideal spacing of sensors requires a substantial degree of separation between individual sensors, the United States would have to launch many RLVs to place sensors into the proper orbits or rely on highly maneuverable upper stages for deploying sensors from one RLV. There are military benefits from using RLVs for reconnaissance, but they are not significant reasons for developing the vehicles.

Global Strike

Global strike is the application of military power directly against enemy military forces or institutions. The role of RLVs in global strike is to deliver precision-guided weapons to enemy targets. This tactic would allow military forces to respond globally on a rapid basis, conduct highly precise targeting, and reduce the need for forward deployment of U.S. units. With this capability, the United States could reduce the number of personnel at risk, respond to crises anywhere, operate from bases in the United States, and eliminate the need to obtain permission from states to fly over their sovereign territory. For example, the common aero vehicle, a maneuvering reentry vehicle, is carried by the SOV and dispenses weapons in the atmosphere with accuracy approaching 10 feet (3m). Although this RLV would operate much like an aircraft that launches precision-guided munitions, the technological challenge is to design RLVs that provide a cost-effective alternative to aircraft.[37]

The range of RLVs is important if they are to be capable of striking targets anywhere in the world. Their response times might be similar to those of cruise missiles, however, because air-launched cruise missiles, which have a range of 1,500-plus miles (2,400 km), and Tomahawk submarine or ship-launched land attack cruise missiles, which have a range of 1,000 miles (1,600 km), travel more slowly than RLVs.[38]

Global strike differs fundamentally from space launch because placing weapons in orbit involves different payloads, propulsion systems, and landing concepts. The military commonly argues that global strike RLVs should be manned to preserve human control over the use of lethal force. Because the placement of weapons in space has significant implications for national security, U.S. policy is that the United States will not be the first nation to put weapons in space.[39] For now, using RLVs to launch weapons from space would radically change how states conduct war.

Global strike RLVs that do not penetrate hostile airspace or confront conventional air defenses could be highly survivable. Because the United States would procure few of these weapons, political and military authorities probably would hold this technology in reserve for critical circumstances. Even if they are reserved for serious contingencies, however, there are limits to how many RLVs it could afford to build.

Arguably, the development of global strike RLVs would strengthen the military's ability to project power globally and might reduce the size of conventional aerospace forces. If RLVs could perform 50 percent of precision strike missions, the United States would need fewer F-16s, F-117s, and F-15Es, but it is unlikely that the military would eliminate fighter squadrons or aircraft carriers to fund the development and operation of global strike RLVs.

It is estimated that manufacturing costs would be $750 million to $1 billion for each global strike RLV. The costs of ground facilities, training, operations and maintenance, and ordnance costs would equal that of the B-2 bomber program.[40] A global strike RLV has enormous military potential but would be so expensive that building large numbers of them is not economically feasible. Although global strike is not sufficiently compelling to fund a major new program, it will be a better option for second- or third-generation RLVs.

Satellite Servicing

RLVs could be used for refueling, upgrading, repositioning, or recovering satellites. Orbiting and rendezvousing with spacecraft without human intervention, however, requires a level of technological sophistication that the United States has yet to demonstrate. Although the servicing of satellites has broad appeal, given NASA's success with the Hubble space telescope, the orbits that RLVs could reach do not contain DOD satellites and will not do so for the foreseeable future.[41]

Nevertheless, on-orbit satellite servicing is worthwhile if the United States deploys space-based lasers or kinetic energy weapons for missile defense. In either case, satellite servicing might become necessary for replenishing fuel and weapons. Before the military pursues this mission, however, it must have evidence that defense contractors could not perform this mission. Servicing space-based weapons is analogous to servicing military aircraft, which is often performed by private firms. In any event, until the military designs and deploys satellites in the low-earth orbits that RLVs can reach, satellite servicing has little military value.

The alternative to satellite servicing is disposable satellites. Although the United States has designed spacecraft, with limited lifetimes, that are not intended for retrieval and refurbishment, there is a shift toward less expensive, disposable satellites. If it disposes of satellites, rather than refurbish them, the United States must maintain an inventory of inexpensive satellites that are ready for launch. Although satellite servicing might be relevant for later generations of RLVs, it does not provide a compelling reason for developing military RLVs.

Global Transport

RLVs could be used for rapidly transporting troops or materiel around the globe. The primary constraint, however, is cost. If it costs $1,000 for an RLV to put 1 pound (0.45 kg) of payload into orbit, this is radically more expensive than using conventional airlift. For example, the cost of shipping cargo on a C-17 aircraft flight from Charleston, South Carolina, to Ramstein Air Base, Germany, is $0.88 per pound of cargo for a ten-hour flight.[42] RLVs could deliver high-priority cargo more quickly, but the cost would be about one thousand times more than the cost on a conventional airlift. Although there are cases when eight hours might make a critical difference in military operations, this is not a compelling reason for building RLVs. As with aircraft, RLVs that are optimized for delivering cargo will be different from those that conduct global strike and different still from those that are optimized for placing satellites in orbit. Shipping cargo via RLVs would require fleets of specialized RLVs, and economic constraints on defense spending would appear to make this scenario unlikely.

The bases for global transport must be able to handle RLV operations. Unless the United States uses existing airfields and supplies, it would have to invest in new facilities. Although development of global transport RLVs is logical, their vastly greater costs do not justify reducing cargo delivery times by eight hours. Nor are later generations of RLVs likely to be viable candidates for global transport.

Space Control

The objective of space control is to disrupt hostile space systems temporarily while protecting military and commercial space systems. By using this tactic, termed *defensive counterspace operations*, RLVs could prevent the adversary from using space and protect U.S. satellites, communication links, and ground stations from attack. The concept of space control has two elements, negation and protection. Protection of space-based assets does not mean that satellites must be "escorted" around their orbits, or that the United States must ensure that no commercial losses occur. Protection might be as simple as putting the weight of the U.S. military behind the promise that any attack on a U.S. satellite would be considered an attack on U.S. sovereign property and dealt with harshly.[43]

The Air Force Space Command has argued that RLVs will provide "the means by which USCINCSPACE [U.S. Commander in Chief, Space] can maintain freedom of space for friendly forces."[44] Nevertheless, the role of RLVs in space control is unclear. In principle, RLVs could launch sensors and decoys for protecting friendly forces; degrading or disabling hostile space systems by nonlethal means, including jamming; identifying objects; determining if U.S. systems had been attacked; and assessing damage. Although these are viable concepts, the fact remains that space control could essentially weaponize space and raises concerns about an international incident or an arms race.[45] Space control might become necessary if a satellite were intentionally destroyed and other satellites harmed by the debris, but this contingency alone is a not a compelling rationale for building RLVs. Whether or not using RLVs for space control is escalatory, other states could believe that the United States has acquired potentially destabilizing capabilities.

The ability to control space is essential in war. For example, the United States could place sensors on satellites to provide unambiguous information about military events. It also could attack ground stations or control nodes, jam or disrupt communication links, and achieve space control through diplomacy.[46] Although the best approach might be to use RLVs for placing sensors and emitters into orbit, space control is not a compelling reason for pursuing RLV technology.

Spacelift

The purpose of spacelift is to place materiel into space as inexpensively and rapidly as possible. RLVs could be used to replenish satellites and to increase the number of satellites in orbit during a crisis.[47] Four problems with these missions, however, could arise. First, rapidly reconstituting (or replenishing) satellites requires a large inventory of satellites, but, with the exception of the GPS of navigation satellites, the United States cannot afford to maintain large satellite inventories.

Second, the military does not maintain large inventories of weapon systems. For example, when the U.S. military exhausted its supply of conventional air-launched cruise missiles during the Kosovo conflict, it had to build more missiles and convert nuclear air-launched cruise missiles.

Third, scenarios in which the United States would lose the ability to use space (i.e., nuclear detonations in space or antisatellite weapons) would also prevent other states from using space. Even if the United States could launch additional satellites, it might be beneficial to delay launches given the effects of radiation or debris. Without an overwhelming reason for placing large numbers of new satellites into orbit, there is no compelling reason for military spacelift RLVs.

Fourth, the development of RLVs for military spacelift is not likely to lower the costs of spacelift for the DOD because RLV research and development expenditures, which would be substantial, are unlikely to be as cost-effective as the continuing use of existing expendable launch vehicles. In any event, the current generation of expendable launch systems is sufficient to meet the needs of the military.[48]

Commercial Uses for Reusable Launch Vehicles

Beyond deploying satellites into orbit, there are other commercial uses for RLVs, which include satellite servicing, rapid delivery of cargo, global travel, and, possibly, space tourism. For example, it is estimated that the international space station will require substantial logistical support, perhaps a mission every two weeks that carries about 50,000 pounds (22,700 kg). Studies of the market for the rapid delivery of cargo suggest that there might be a commercial market for delivering cargo at $500 per pound.[49] An even more radical idea is that some private ventures might offer space tourism flights with ticket prices starting at about $40,000, whereas other studies indicate that, with estimated ticket prices at $17,000, demand could exceed 900,000 passengers annually. Although commercial passenger service with a one-hour flight from New York to London might be interesting, commercial spacelift remains the most important application for RLVs.[50]

Spacelift
In principle, commercial spacelift would provide routine, reliable, cost-effective, and user-friendly access to space at much less than current costs. The challenge is to develop commercial RLVs that are reliable and cost-effective. One alternative to developing RLVs for commercial spacelift is to develop expendable vehicles or to use surplus military systems, of which the Minuteman and Peacekeeper missiles are interesting examples. Despite the hopes that commercial RLVs could provide satellite servicing, parcel and cargo delivery, global travel, and space tourism, these possibilities are more relevant for future generations of RLVs.[51]

Space Tourism
Although a commercial market for touring space might exist, an initial step is to develop technology that is reliable, affordable, and safe. Some market surveys have estimated that space tourism might be viable if people could travel into space for less than $20,000 per round trip.[52] Launch failures might be tolerable if aborted takeoffs were followed by safe landings and if missile reliability were equal to commercial airliners. Such reliability, however, far exceeds the reliability of the current generation of expendable launch vehicles. For space tourism to succeed, a reusable system whose efficiency is two hundred times greater than that of the space shuttle would be necessary.

Conclusion
Despite technological advances that permit the development of cost-effective RLVs for military and commercial purposes, there are currently no compelling reasons for developing them. Because the United States needs a more cost-effective form of spacelift, however, the military could help commercial firms develop these vehicles and use them to meet the needs of the Department of Defense. If RLVs are cost-effective, the emphasis could shift to reliability, rather than to strict military requirements. After the military developed the first generation of commercial vehicles, it would have the experience to develop later generations for military missions. The military should not own and operate militarily unique RLVs, however, because commercial vehicles could satisfy most military requirements. Commercial firms could place payloads into orbit for the military, while economic forces shape the design, development, manufacture,

and operation of RLVs, which would allow the military to adapt commercial RLVs for military missions.

The fundamental reason for the United States to develop these vehicles is to reduce the cost of access to space. By harnessing technological progress in the commercial world, the military could acquire cost-effective reusable launch vehicles that revolutionize how military and commercial organizations use space during the twenty-first century.

Notes

1. Director of Plans, "Future Strategic Environment," in "U.S. Space Command Long Range Plan," Peterson Air Force Base, Colo., March 1998, 3.
2. The White House, *A National Security Strategy for a New Century* (Washington, D.C.: Government Printing Office, 1999), 25. See also Andrew J. Butrica, "Commercial Spaceports: Hitching Your Wagon to a VentureStar," *Space Times* (October 1998), 6–7.
3. John A. Tirpak, "The Flight to Orbit," *Air Force Magazine* (November 1988), 41. See also John J. Egan, "Perspective on Space Commerce—Is It Real?" *Space Energy and Transportation* 2, no. 1 (1977), 12–19.
4. John R. London III, *LEO on the Cheap: Methods for Achieving Drastic Reductions in Space Launch Costs,* Research Report No. AU-ARI-93-8 (Maxwell Air Force Base, Ala.: Air University Press, 1994), 98.
5. Ibid., 175; Roger D. Launius, "Toward an Understanding of the Space Shuttle: A Historiographical Essay," in *Air Power History* (Lexington, VA: Air Force Historical Foundation, 1992), 8.
6. David N. Spires, *Beyond Horizons: A Half Century of Air Force Space Leadership* (Peterson Air Force Base, Colo.: Air Force Space Command, 1997), 181–82.
7. The global transport mission was originally of high interest to the military for moving equipment and Special Operations Forces. First drafts of the "Space Operations Vehicle Concepts of Operation" (SOV CONOPS) contained this mission as a priority, but the final Phase I SOV CONOPS no longer actively pursues this mission. See Headquarters, Air Force Space Command, Directorate of Operations, Nuclear Operations and Future Concepts Branch [hereafter HQ AFSPC/DOMN], "Concepts of Operations for the Phase I Space Operations Vehicle System," Air Force Space Command, Peterson Air Force Base, Colo., 1998, 5–6.
8. Director of Plans, "Future Strategic Environment," 3, in which a former commander in chief of the U.S. Space Command (SPACECOM) acknowledged, "The shift will continue from the military to the commercial sector as the dominant receiver and provider of space services."
9. In 1998, seventy-three space launches worldwide (thirty-six from the United States) attempted to place 149 satellites in orbit, to resupply the Mir space station,

or to begin construction of the International Space Station. Of the seventy-three launches, which carried 15 satellites, four launches failed to achieve orbit. The 149 satellites that were launched included 115 commercial satellites, 17 civil satellites, and 17 military satellites. See http://www.flatoday.com/space/next/ 98log.htm, Dec. 28, 1998.

10. This forecast does not include scientific, technology development, or remote sensing spacecraft and excludes classified programs. See Terri Lehto, "Space Systems Analysis 3—Commercial Communication Satellites 1998–2017," in *DMS Market Intelligence Reports* (Alexandria Va.: Janes Information Group, 1998), 23, 28; "Space Systems Analysis 4—Western Military Satellites—1998–2007," Janes Information Group, July 1998, 13. The projection of 2,700 satellites is not equal to 2,700 launches because individual rockets can launch multiple satellites. This forecast also excludes "eastern military satellites" and western classified satellites for which there are no reliable estimates. See Terri Lehto, "Space Systems Analysis 2—The World Market for Expendable Launch Vehicles—1998–2017," in *DMS Market Intelligence Reports*, 4.

11. This estimate includes twenty-eight distinct types from at least nine countries. The U.S. share of this launch market is estimated at 48 percent. See Lehto, "Space Systems Analysis 2," 2–7.

12. William B. Scott, "McPeak, Hecker Head 'Space-Plane' Project," *Aviation Week & Space Technology,* March 10, 1997, 22–23.

13. David N. Spires, *Beyond Horizons: A Half Century of Air Force Space Leadership* (Peterson Air Force Base, Colo.: Air Force Space Command, 1997), 4.

14. Jay P. Penn and Charles A. Lindley, "RLV Design Optimization for Carrying People to and from Space," *Space & Energy Transportation* 2, no. 3 (1997), 153. This analysis theoretically would yield a profit that is five times greater than current values. See also William B. Scott, "Airbreathing HyperSoar Would 'Bounce' on Upper Atmosphere," *Aviation Week & Space Technology,* Sept. 7, 1998, 126. See also Egan, "Perspective on Space Commerce," 17.

15. See "Military Space plane Briefing," Air Force Research Laboratory, Wright-Patterson Air Force Base, Ohio, February 1998.

16. See http://www.hq.basa.gov/office/pao/History/X-33facts_1.htm.

17. The key areas that were demonstrated and evaluated included flight controls, reaction control systems, vertical takeoff and landing systems, in-flight abort, in-flight vertical rotation maneuver, and auto-land capability. See http:// www.hq.nasa.gov/office/pao/History/X-33/dc-xa.htm, Oct. 8, 1998. The DC-X was 40 feet (13 m) high, 13.5 feet (4 m) across at the base, and conical in shape. When empty, the DC-X weighed 20,000 pounds (roughly 9,100 kg) and could carry 21,600 pounds (9,800 kg) of liquid oxygen and liquid hydrogen. The DC-X was powered by four RL-10A5 rocket engines, each of which generated 13,500 pounds (6,100 kg) of thrust. The primary structural components of the DC-X were aluminum, titanium, and steel. The DC-X used off-the-shelf avionics, including an F-15 navigation system, an F-18 accelerometer and rate gyro pack-

age, and a GPS code receiver. See "DC-X Fact Sheet," Oct. 8, 1998, 2. See also http://www.hq.nasa.gov/office/pao/History/x-33/dcx-facts.htm.

18. "The Delta Clipper Experimental: Flight Testing Archive," Oct. 8, 1998, http://www.hq.nasa.gov /office/pao/History/x-33/dc-xa.htm, 2–3.

19. "Space Plane Grounded," *Technology Review,* July/August, 2000, 28. For flight test plans, see Lehto, "Space Systems Analysis 2," 5; http://www1.msfc.nasa/gov/NEWMSFC/xplanes.html, 1.

20. See "X33, What Is X33?" Oct. 8, 1998, http://stp.msfc.nasa.gov/stpweb/x33/x33about.html.

21. The X-34 vehicle is 58.3 feet long, 27.7 feet wide at the wingtips, and 11.5 feet tall. NASA awarded a contract to Orbital Sciences Corporation for $50 million to build and test-fly the X-34. The government has increased funding for long lead items and has an option to build a second X-34. See Lehto, "Space Systems Analysis 2," 5.

22. National Aeronautics and Space Administration, "X-34 Objectives," Oct. 8, 1998, 1–2. See also http://stp.msfc.nasa.gov/stpweb/x34/x34objectives.html.

23. HQ AFSPC/DOMN, "Concepts of Operations," 5–6.

24. Action officers at Headquarters Air Force Space Command report that the X-40A completed its first drop test in August 1998 and successfully completed an autonomous landing. NASA's Advanced Technology Vehicle program plans a drop from the space shuttle in the near future. See Tirpak, "Flight to Orbit," 43.

25. Headquarters Air Force Space Command, Division of Operations personnel, interviews by author, Feb. 26, 1999.

26. Ray Peterson, "Space Systems Update," in *DMS Market Intelligence Reports* (Alexandria, Va.: Janes Information Group, January 1998), 2.

27. Payment is contingent on successful launches. See http://msia02.msi.se/~lindsey/RLVCoundown.html, Dec. 18, 1998, 2.

28. Scott, "McPeak."

29. Ray Peterson, "Space System Forecast," in *DMS Market Intelligence Reports* (Alexandria, Va.: Janes Information Group, January 1998), 2.

30. Penn and Lindley, "RLV Design Optimization," 154.

31. "Britain's Space Plane," *Futurist* 28, no. 4 (July/August 1994), 6.

32. See http://www.bristolspace planes.com/projects/ascender.html, Nov. 21, 1998, 1–5.

33. Scott, "Airbreathing HyperSoar," 126–30.

34. HQ AFSPC/DOMN outlined ways to use the SOV for counterspace operations; real-time protection of domestic and friendly force on-orbit assets; rapid recoverable intelligence, surveillance and reconnaissance; satellite deployment, redeployment, recovery, upgrade, refueling and repair; space-based deterrence in areas unreachable by land, sea, and air forces; space-based resource integration into the conventional force package; and worldwide weapons delivery within minutes of launch. See HQ AFSPC/DOMN, "Concepts of Operations," v–vi.

35. Time delays are often attributed to physical positioning of reconnaissance assets, the administrative process for requesting support, and the relative priorities assigned to users. See ibid., 7.

36. Headquarters U.S. Air Force, Division of Operations, "Commercial Satellite Imagery Integration Plan," July 15, 1998, 1–5.

37. These key attributes were provided by Headquarters Air Force Space Command, Director of Requirements (Space and Support) [hereafter HQ AFSPC/DRS], e-mail to author, Feb. 5, 1999. The assumption is that any such system would have to pass internal DOD review for affordability before moving from the drawing board to the flight line.

38. See http://www.af.mil/news/factsheets/AGM_86B_C_Missiles.html, Dec. 28, 1998, 3. See also http://www.chinfo.navy.mil/navypalib/factfile missiles/ wep-toma.html, Dec. 28, 1998, 1. This capability could complement the Air Expeditionary Force by enabling rapid strikes in regions without deployed forces.

39. Scott, "Airbreathing HyperSoar," 126–30. Also, HQ AFSPC action officers, interviews by author, Feb. 26, 1999; see also William A. Gaubatz, "Specific Inputs to National Security Space Master Plan, Space Sortie and Military Operational Space," McDonnell-Douglas Corporation, Huntington Beach Calif., June 7, 1996, 10; HQ AFSPC/DOMN, "Concepts of Operations," 7, 25.

40. Jamie G. G. Varni, Gregory M. Powers, Dan S. Crawford et al., "Space Operations: Through the Looking Glass (Global Area Strike System)," in *2025 Study* (Maxwell Air Force Base, Ala: Air University Press, 1996), 227, 233.

41. This statement is based on DOD missions in orbits that are less than 250 miles in altitude and less than 60 degrees in inclination.

42. S. Maeurer, Warner Robins Air Logistics Center, e-mail to author, Nov. 19, 1998, provides the following cost and flight-time data for round-trip highest priority airlift: Dover, Del., to Ramstein Air Base, Germany, C-5, 17 hours at a cost of $240,000, and C-141, 18.5 hours at $100,000. C-17s operate from Charleston, S.C., to Ramstein Air Base, Germany, 20.5 hours' flight time at $150,000. The maximum payload for a C-17 is 170,000 pounds.

43. HQ AFSPC/DOMN, "Concepts of Operations," 9.

44. Quote in ibid., 7.

45. The current U.S. national space policy directs the military to prepare to protect space assets. What the United States views as defensive efforts might be viewed by others as offensive efforts. Although this statement can be true for all weapon systems, there is a difference when dealing with the medium of space. At some point, U.S. allies might view the United States as a potential aggressor that has grown too powerful. U.S. actions pursuing space control must consider unintended consequences, which is difficult to do, given the relative newness of space control.

46. This idea was derived from author's correspondence with HQ AFSPC/DRS, Jan. 3, 1999. Interestingly, the previously mentioned Air Force war games report identified "military space planes" as favored systems, whose primary uses were space launch and global precision strike, rather than space control. See HQ USAF, DCS [Deputy Chief of Staff], Air and Space Operations, Directorate of Command and Control, Strategy, Concepts and Doctrine Division, U.S. Air Force, "Space Doctrine and Strategy Issues," Apr. 9, 1997, 10–11.

47. HQ AFSPC/DOMN, "Concepts of Operations," 10–11. Paul Kennedy, *The Rise and Fall of the Great Powers* (New York: Random House, 1987), 524, makes this very point for all of today's modern weapon systems, including satellites: "It is clear that today's complex weaponry simply cannot be replaced in the short times which were achieved during the Second World War."

48. The DOD does not perform spacelift today, and, with the exception of several Atlas launches during the 1960s, it never has done so. Spacelift operations and maintenance functions are conducted by contractors. Uniformed personnel do not turn wrenches or push buttons; essentially, they are quality assurance evaluators and safety monitors. The primary duties of U.S. Air Force operations crews on launch day are to verify safety procedures and practices and to keep the leadership informed.

49. See http://stp.msfc.nasa/gov/stpweb/x33. See also Scott, "McPeak," 23.

50. Based on early cost goals for the Delta Clipper, the price for a space trip was estimated to be less than the cost of a round-the-world trip on the *Queen Elizabeth II,* or from $40,000 to $140,000. See http://www.hq.nasa.gov/office/pao/History/X-33/dc-xa.htm, Oct. 8, 1998. See also Penn and Lindley, "RLV Design Optimization," 154–56; and Scott, "McPeak," 23.

51. Egan, "Perspective on Space Commerce," 15–16.

52. The figure of $20,000 is in 1997 dollars, and estimates are derived from Penn and Lindley, "RLV Design Optimization," 157–58.

9.   Unmanned Aerial Vehicles

David B. Glade II

With considerable investments in computer and communications technologies, it is possible to develop unmanned aerial vehicles (UAVs) that could conduct certain missions more effectively, less expensively, or at less risk than manned aircraft. Although the U.S. military is developing these technologies, it has not fully explored the possibilities for unmanned aircraft and space vehicles or the interesting questions about the role of humans in war that are raised by these technologies in the short, medium, and long terms. This chapter examines these critical technologies, how such vehicles might be used to employ lethal force in military operations, and the consequences of an era in which military operations could be performed by unmanned vehicles. It also discusses the ultimate prospects of an era in which humans do not pilot future generations of aircraft and space vehicles.

Introduction

As a result of technological progress, military systems, including UAVs, are being built that can conduct military operations with less human intervention. The development of UAVs raises the possibility that states could conduct military air operations more effectively and at less risk than conducting them with aircraft piloted by humans on board.[1] Although the United States has gained experience with UAVs during recent military operations, such as Kosovo in 1999, the American defense establishment has not fully explored how unmanned aircraft technology might influence the nature and conduct of future military operations. The prospect of adding UAVs to the U.S. arsenal raises significant questions about the nature of military operations in the future and how these technologies might influence international security. Taken to the extreme, it also raises significant military and ethical questions.

The principal conclusion of the U.S. Air Force Scientific Advisory Board (SAB), following a 1996 study on the role of UAV technologies in military operations, was that UAVs would enhance the ability to project military power.[2] The Pentagon's Director of Defense Research and Engineering predicted that pilotless aircraft are likely to play a major role in military operations.[3] An equally important conclusion is that these vehicles could perform tasks that pose increasing difficulties for manned aircraft, two of the most important examples being attacks on chemical warfare (CW) or biological warfare (BW) facilities and suppression of enemy air defenses. The SAB study concluded that, because UAVs are more survivable than manned aircraft, this technological development has profound implications for the military forces in the future.

The idea of building unmanned air vehicles is not new. For most of the twentieth century, states investigated the feasibility of building unmanned aerial vehicles and their potential value in military operations. The principal reason for the interest in UAVs was a desire to reduce the risk to humans in combat. A related reason was that freeing aerial machines from the constraints imposed by onboard humans could increase performance of the vehicles. From the beginning of the development of aircraft, hopes have been that UAVs would be less expensive to develop and manufacture than manned aircraft and that they would reduce the demand for the supporting facilities and manpower that modern aircraft require. As a result of technological advances in flight controls, navigation, data and signal processing, sensors, communications links, and integrated avionics, UAVs are now becoming a more practical option.

Another hope of technologists, as yet unfulfilled, is that UAVs will be able to perform the "dull, dirty, and dangerous" military missions.[4] The "dull" missions require aircraft personnel to be on station for hours or days to keep watch on the enemy or to wait for an event or target to appear. The "dirty" missions, including attacks against chemical or biological facilities, and the "dangerous" missions involve attacking targets that are heavily defended by surface-to-air missiles and antiaircraft artillery or directly attacking those missiles and artillery. An unmanned ability to attack fixed and mobile ground targets effectively, and perhaps enemy aircraft, could represent a revolution in military capabilities.

Far more than technological advances are accelerating the development of UAVs. Since the end of the Cold War, the United States has been spending less on defense, and, in the future, it is more likely that it will be involved in peacekeeping and humanitarian operations rather than in major theater wars. In addition, U.S. security depends on rapidly deploying mobile forces rather than relying on large forces that are based overseas. In all of these operations, the political culture emphasizes minimizing casualties, specifically when the nation's vital interests are not at stake. If the United States could employ technology to minimize the exposure of military personnel in the lesser contingencies that dominate American military operations, policymakers could gain more flexible instruments for defending American interests. A primary reason for developing UAVs is the need to destroy what are termed *time critical targets,* especially those armed with weapons of mass destruction.

A number of technological factors suggest that unmanned weapon systems might be important in future military operations. To understand how the technology behind the development of UAVs is changing the nature and conduct of military operations, this chapter examines the role of three categories of air vehicles in military operations: aircraft operated by traditional pilots and onboard crews, vehicles operated remotely by pilots or other operators, and vehicles operated autonomously. After discussing the advantages and disadvantages of these categories of aircraft, this chapter considers some of the implications of using UAVs in military operations.

Definition of Unmanned Aerial Vehicles

The Department of Defense defines *unmanned aerial vehicle* as "a powered, aerial vehicle that does not carry a human operator, uses aerodynamic forces to provide vehicle lift, can fly autonomously or be piloted remotely, can be expendable or recoverable, and can carry a lethal or nonlethal payload."[5] This definition also includes aerodynamic drones and remotely piloted vehicles. Strictly interpreted, it also includes systems typically thought of as weapons, including various types of air-to-air– and air-to-ground–missiles.[6] It excludes ballistic or semiballistic vehicles and artillery. Cruise missiles, which meet this definition, are viewed as nuclear delivery systems in arms control treaties, but this discussion also includes vehicles that behave like cruise missiles. The term *pilot* can refer either to an onboard pilot or to the operator of a remotely piloted vehicle. To differentiate, this chapter refers to an aircraft with an onboard crew as a *manned* vehicle and uses the term *operator* to refer to the crew of a remotely operated vehicle.

Within these terms, UAVs can be remotely piloted or they can operate autonomously, and control that is exercised by a remote pilot can be continuous or episodic. In some cases, autonomous vehicles follow preprogrammed courses and lack the capacity for retargeting, whereas, in other cases, autonomous UAVs follow preprogrammed courses but can be rerouted or retargeted by a remote operator.[7] According to military terminology, vehicles are *reusable*, but weapons are *expendable*. In addition, UAVs typically have shorter life spans than manned aircraft and can suffer attrition in military operations, which means that they would survive for a relatively small number of sorties until failures, accidents, or hostile action destroy them.[8] Ultimately, UAVs are more expendable than manned aircraft. Importantly, modern American society might have great difficulty in accepting the losses encountered by combat aircraft during World War II. For example, 10 percent of the aircraft and six hundred airmen were lost during a single raid over Germany. Relative loss rates for manned aircraft and UAVs should be a factor in evaluating their cost-effectiveness.[9] Thus, it is likely that several types of UAVs, ranging from simple, inexpensive vehicles that last for several missions to complex, expensive UAVs that survive for thousands of missions, will emerge.

Categories of Air Vehicles

The nature of the UAV as a military instrument can be understood by tracing the development of manned and unmanned air vehicles, by assessing the technological state of the art in aircraft and computer technologies, and by considering its use in military operations.

The simplest approach is to divide aircraft into manned and unmanned vehicles and then to subdivide unmanned vehicles into those that are remotely operated and those that are autonomous. This framework rests explicitly on the human role in perceiving and influencing events during the operation of air vehicles. Manned aircraft are dependent on direct human presence for firsthand perception of events and conditions around the vehicles, whereas the use of remotely operated vehicles keeps the human presence at a distance.

A critical factor that distinguishes between aircraft and UAVs is the amount of information available to the human. Although the technological and operational communities have invested considerable resources in using visual and data displays to provide information to the human operator about conditions in and around the remotely operated vehicle, these technologies have been inadequate because the human operator is deprived of significant information about the vehicle's performance, including the field of view, attitude, vibration, and sound. In the case of vehicles that are operated only periodically by a human, such as the *Global Hawk* UAV (Figure 9.1), the operator must make decisions with much less information than an onboard pilot would have about the vehicle. The amount and type of information provided to a remote operator have significant implications for UAVs, principally because such information directly increases combat effectiveness, ability to survive, cost, and complexity of these vehicles.[10]

In autonomous vehicles, the human presence exists at a distance, is confined

Figure 9.1. The Global Hawk is a high-altitude, long-endurance, unmanned aerial re-connaissance system. Providing high-resolution, near–real-time imagery of large geographic areas, it uses synthetic aperture radar and electro-optical and infrared sensors. It can fly 3,000 nautical miles and collect data for twenty-four hours up to altitudes of 65,000 feet. (Courtesy U.S. Air Force)

to receiving little or no information about the vehicle, and does not exercise direct control over the vehicle. By definition, humans lose control of an autonomous vehicle once it is launched, which implies that information about the vehicle's status will be quite limited. Given these limitations, autonomous vehicles are well suited to attacking targets whose location is precisely and accurately known. The value of the autonomous vehicle diminishes, however, when searching for mobile targets, such as Scud missile launchers, and targets, such as command and control centers, whose location might not be precisely known.

Perhaps the best way to differentiate between types of manned and unmanned aerial vehicles is to consider the role of human presence, which can be immediate or distant and can involve large or small amounts of information about the vehicle's operation. The information provided to human operators, however, is not the same for all piloted aircraft. For example, the Russian MiG-23 and U.S. F-15 are both manned fighter aircraft, but the F-15 pilot has greater visual perception outside the aircraft than the MiG-23 pilot because of the F-15's larger and less restrictive canopy. As another example, the F-15 pilot has vastly more tactical information than did the World War II P-51 Mustang pilot, principally because the F-15's radar greatly extends the pilot's ability to perceive objects and events scores of miles away.

In principle, all unmanned vehicles possess some degree of automation. Automated flight control systems in contemporary manned combat aircraft also provide vast amounts of information. Completely autonomous operations must be able to cope with unexpected situations, which was reaffirmed during tests of the *Global Hawk* UAV.[11] Not surprisingly, the price of automation is a significant increase in the cost of engines, hydraulics, electrical, and avionics systems, which makes them more expensive than the less automated counterparts in aircraft controlled by humans.

Categories of Military Operations

The roles of UAVs can vary widely based on the difficulty of the military operations in which they are involved. An example of simpler aerial operations are attacks against exposed, fixed ground targets, whereas more challenging operations involve attacks against concealed targets, mobile ground targets, and other air vehicles. An attack against an exposed, fixed target is the simplest type of operation because it is relatively easy to find a visible target whose location is known with great accuracy. Concealed targets are more difficult to attack because the attacker does not have accurate information about their locations. Mobile targets are the most difficult to attack because of the need to identify and intercept them before they move to another location.

An attack against an air target is more difficult than an attack against a ground target because the air target's mobility makes it more difficult for the attacker to find, identify, and destroy it and because the target itself can maneuver away from the attacker. After an air target has been located, the simplest form of attack is hitting the target before it is aware of the attack. By contrast, an observed attack against a highly maneuverable target flown by an experienced pilot is the most difficult type. For instance, an unobserved attack from behind a large bomber is easier to conduct than an attack against an opposing fighter, whose experienced pilot is aware that an attack is under way and takes active defensive measures. A smart opponent will make targets more difficult to locate by camouflaging and concealing them. In addition, terrain, vegetation, weather, and composition of the targets complicate these operations.

Attacks against enemy targets that are out of contact with friendly forces are simpler than attacks in which enemy targets are relatively near friendly forces. The principal reason for the difficulty of conducting attacks against enemy forces fighting in proximity to friendly forces is the high level of coordination that is necessary if friendly vehicles are to avoid fratricide, or destroying one another. The difficulty of a combat situation increases as the number of enemy threats increases, which has important implications in air-to-air and air-to-ground operations when friendly and enemy forces are interspersed throughout the battle area. The ideal condition for attack is one in which all of the forces in an area belong to the enemy and are readily identifiable. In reality, it is likely that distance, as well as concealment, will make it difficult to identify individual vehicles and aircraft, and often enemy and friendly aircraft will be mixed in the same area. The problem is more complex in operations other than war because military forces, as well as neutral forces and civilians, are scattered throughout the battlespace.

The points discussed above have two important implications for UAVs. First, a human pilot has a vastly greater ability to understand and respond to the conditions around a vehicle during combat than does a human who operates the vehicle from a distance. Second, the number and type of threats; the degree of mobility of targets and threats; and the degree of sorting that is necessary to locate, identify, classify, and separate threats determines whether UAVs can be used in military operations. So far, UAVs have been used in intelligence gathering and surveillance roles, and the military is beginning to explore their use in limited combat roles. This shift could transform the nature of war.

Automation

It is difficult to discuss the success of UAVs without considering advances in automation, which is defined as acting in a manner that is essentially independent of external influence or control. A successful shift in the nature of war might depend on the ability to develop technologies that automate many of the functions performed by humans in military operations. In essence, a vehicle is said to be autonomous when it can conduct operations without human intervention. In the current generation of automated fighters, the U.S. F-117 stealth fighter can complete an entire mission virtually autonomously with the pilot intervening to identify and track the target and to release weapons. Vehicles being conceived by the defense industry include those with varying degrees of human control, in which the remote operator identifies the target and the UAV executes coordinated attacks. Truly autonomous vehicles, such as cruise missiles, do not require any form of human intervention once they are launched.

The military value of UAVs depends partly on automating many of the functions that historically have been performed by humans. Such functions range from guiding a vehicle to delivering ordnance against legitimate military targets.[12] A simple form of automation is represented by the Kettering Bug of World War I, which was guided by a gyroscope and barometer.[13] A more complicated example of an automated aerial vehicle is the modern cruise missile, which is guided by the global positioning system (GPS) or by a terrain map stored in the guidance computer.

A subset of the concept of automation is automated decision making, which uses programmed rules to guide decisions. An example would be a UAV that relies on rule-based artificial intelligence or an expert system to detect, identify, and attack mobile targets. Any form of rule-based decision making, however, is a highly complex problem in war. This complexity is illustrated by the air campaign during the Persian Gulf War, which involved about 2,600 Allied aircraft of at least forty-one types and 950 opposing enemy aircraft of seventeen types, of which at least six types shared common features with Allied aircraft. All of these aircraft could be attacked by various air-to-air weapons—16,000 surface-to-air missiles in ten types and 7,000 antiaircraft guns.[14] For automation to succeed in military operations, a program would need to sort through large numbers of choices and make good decisions about the use of lethal force in a reliable and timely fashion.[15] At the present time, rule-based decision-making technology is not sufficiently reliable to permit autonomous vehicles to make the kinds of wartime decisions in which humans could have high confidence, especially when failure can result in the deaths of hundreds or thousands of innocent civilians.

Given that enemy forces likely will seek to confuse the attacker, these rule-based systems will not be able to compensate for changes on the battlefield. Although automated systems might recognize legitimate targets in complex situations more quickly and effectively than humans, these systems might not be able to distinguish legitimate military targets, which could increase the potential for collateral damage or damage to civilians or protected sites. Thus, automated decision making might not be practical or desirable in some circumstances.

Evaluation of Aerial Vehicles

This chapter, thus far, focuses on understanding the differences among piloted, unmanned, remotely piloted, and autonomous vehicles. This section considers the advantages and disadvantages of these vehicles in the context of the role of air vehicles in military operations.

A few comments about cost comparisons are in order. It is difficult to compare the cost of manned aircraft and unmanned aircraft, partly because of the higher expected attrition of unmanned vehicles versus the longer lifetimes and lower attrition of manned systems. In addition, an unmanned vehicle should cost less than a manned aircraft of comparable capabilities, including the unmanned vehicle's launch and mission control facilities. The manned aircraft likely will be more useful because it is capable of more tasks and has a longer lifetime.

It will not be possible to estimate the overall cost-effectiveness of manned or unmanned systems until the actual life span of a vehicle is determined and its worth measured in a concrete way, such as by counting the number of targets photographed or destroyed. In general, cost-effectiveness comparisons should be treated with caution and examined in detail, and preconceived notions that UAVs will be more cost-effective than their manned counterparts should be avoided.[16]

Characteristics of Piloted Vehicles
Although there are many ways to characterize modern piloted aircraft, speed, range, altitude, and payload are among the most important characteristics when examining the differences between piloted and unpiloted vehicles. Removing the crew from the vehicle gives the designer more flexibility in aerodynamic and structural design, but there are still tradeoffs among the vehicle's required payload, range, speed, maneuverability, and other characteristics. In order to increase its range, for example, the designer might need to reduce its payload. So far UAV designs have been able to exploit niches—extreme endurance, for example—by trading off other design parameters, such as speed or structural strength. Removing the crew also increases the requirements for automation and communication.

The fact that a vehicle is unmanned does not change the required payload, range, or speed, but it removes the requirements for accommodating humans while adding the need for automation. Beyond that, the most fundamental characteristic of piloted vehicles is that they rely on the presence of a human crew to detect and respond to changes in the vehicle's operation and environment. Even though human sensors have their own limitations and shortcomings, it is still true that the current state of nonhuman sensors is not sufficiently developed to replace their human counterparts.

Aircraft have historically relied on pilots because technology has not been able to assess and respond to the operation of the aircraft without the presence of a human. The human can deal with the condition of the aircraft, including unusual vibration, smoke, and odor, that could indicate structural damage or impending engine failure. The value of the human crew is their ability to absorb and analyze larger volumes of more diverse and ambiguous information than can any machine. A related characteristic is that piloted aircraft are designed for longer lifetimes than their unpiloted counterparts, principally because the human crew is intrinsically valuable.

Perhaps the most important military characteristic of piloted aircraft is their ability to deliver weapons against a wide array of targets. Modern tactical aircraft can carry a variety of munitions that can produce wide-area, as well as precise, effects and do so at standoff distances ranging from thousands of feet to thousands of miles. In addition, designers have been able to increase the accuracy of munitions by reducing the size of the warhead, which permits weapons to achieve the same effects while reducing unintended damage. Finally, while conventional aircraft require long runways and large numbers of supporting personnel, facilities, and supplies, the shift toward weapon systems with increasing degrees of automation could reduce the reliance on supporting facilities.

Advantages
The most significant advantage of piloted vehicles is the ability of onboard humans to sense the environment and events within and outside the vehicle, known as *situational awareness,* and to make decisions based on that awareness.[17] A related advantage is that pilots create uncertainty for the enemy because no two pilots react the same in every situation. Each will react differently when identifying threats and targets, making decisions in unfamiliar and ambiguous situations, and functioning in an analytic and creative fashion. Human pilots can adapt readily to new and different circumstances, make decisions on the basis of incomplete or ambiguous information, and deal with unexpected situations, such as damage or malfunction. Automated vehicles cannot possess these human qualities. The human operator can adapt relatively quickly to the unique circumstances of conflict, whereas an automated decision-making system might require extensive planning, reprogramming, debugging, and operational testing in order to adapt to new rules or conditions. Although piloted vehicles use electronic devices, such as radio, radar, radar warning, and electro-optical sensors, to supplement the pilot's senses, the most fundamental characteristic of piloted military vehicles is that the human makes critical decisions about using lethal force and is held accountable.

A related advantage of piloted vehicles is that people can solve problems that machines cannot solve, and, further, that humans can tolerate greater confusion than machines and can make decisions that computer programs cannot. Ultimately, humans must maintain responsibility for supervising war machines.[18]

According to the SAB, the reason for using piloted vehicles is to maintain human control over the critical functions that are executed during combat operations. The SAB argues that human controllers have unique abilities that have not been replicated in machines and that represent a decisive advantage in combat as long as humans can think, synthesize, and comprehend faster than machines.[19] Although unmanned vehicles can conduct military operations with minimal risk to humans, the trade-off is a reduction in the ability of human operators of such vehicles to make timely decisions in military operations. Unless UAVs can gain this ability through advances in sensors, automation, and communication systems, their role in military operations is likely to remain limited. In any case, war machines must remain under timely human control.

Disadvantages

Two principal disadvantages of manned aircraft, compared with unmanned aircraft, are that human physiology limits the performance of aircraft and complexity and weight penalties are associated with systems that support humans—notably the seat, canopy, life support, displays, and other human accommodations. A principal argument for UAVs is that manned vehicles are likely more vulnerable in combat than UAVs designed to accomplish the same mission because the manned vehicle presumably would be larger and hence more susceptible to attack than smaller UAVs. In practice, this idea is difficult to prove because few UAVs are designed for precisely the same mission requirements as manned aircraft and because there are no comparable combat data.

An additional disadvantage is that piloted aircraft are vulnerable to political exploitation. In several cases during the latter part of the twentieth century, the loss of aircraft and crews created political difficulties for the United States. Notable examples were lost aircraft and crews in raids against Libya in 1986 (Operation Eldorado Canyon) and in Bosnia in 1995 and the loss of an F-117 stealth fighter over Serbia in March 1999. A wayward cruise missile that strayed into an unintended country during an August 1998 raid against a terrorist camp in Afghanistan did not create the same level of political difficulties as the loss of aircraft and crews.

Characteristics of Unmanned Vehicles

Unmanned vehicles fall into two groups: remotely operated vehicles in which the human operator is removed from the vehicle, and autonomous vehicles in which the vehicle is removed from human control.[20] This section examines the general characteristics of UAVs, and subsequent discussions focus on the characteristics unique to remotely piloted and autonomous vehicles.

UAVs can be built with endurance and altitude capabilities that enhance their ability to project military power, as demonstrated by the Predator (Figure 9.2) and Global Hawk UAVs, whose endurance is greater than that of typical manned vehicles. Because they are free of constraints from onboard crews, other UAVs

Figure 9.2. The Predator is a medium-altitude unmanned aerial vehicle (UAV) developed for military surveillance in all-weather and day or night conditions. Carrying electro-optical and infrared sensors and synthetic aperture radar (SAR), it can fly for twenty-four hours up to an altitude of 25,000 feet. (Courtesy U.S. Air Force)

can accomplish tasks that are increasingly difficult for manned aircraft, such as attacking chemical and biological warfare facilities and suppressing enemy air defenses. In addition, UAV capabilities are reaching the level of technological maturity where, when coupled with maturing sensor, automation, and weapon technologies, they might be able to inflict devastating damage on many targets.[21]

In historical terms, the development of UAVs has been marked by extending the range or distance between the target and the person who is responsible for using the system. The use of UAVs began with the Kettering Bug (aerial torpedo) during World War I and continued with German guided-weapons experiments, including the V-1 buzz bomb, during World War II. The development of UAVs for photo reconnaissance was spurred in the United States during the early 1960s by the downing of Gary Francis Powers's U-2 aircraft over the Soviet Union in May 1960 and the downing of another U-2 during the 1962 Cuban missile crisis.[22] Subsequently, the United States used UAVs for photographic, communications, and electronics reconnaissance; surveillance; and electronic combat during the Vietnam War. Israel used UAVs for photographic and electronic reconnaissance and as decoys during the 1973 Yom Kippur War and 1982

Lebanon operation.[23] More recently, the U.S. Army, Navy, and Marine Corps used the Pioneer UAV for tactical reconnaissance, surveillance, and target acquisition during the Persian Gulf War.[24]

UAVs can be designed to operate at altitudes exceeding 70,000 feet (22,500 m) and can carry optical sensors and radar.[25] The development of new warhead technologies allows UAVs to deliver compact precision weapons that can inflict significant damage against ground targets. Automatic target identification capabilities are being developed to help remote operators to identify and attack mobile targets. In view of recent successes with the development of automatic target recognition software, an interesting possibility is using UAVs to locate and destroy mobile targets.[26] Still, care must be taken to ensure that the human is given sufficient information to determine that the attack is lawful and that collateral damage will be kept to a minimum.

Advantages

The principal advantage of the UAV is its ability to reduce the risk to humans and thus provide cost-effective military options that can be used when military or political risk prohibits the use of manned systems. Other advantages are the ability to free the aircraft from the human's limited ability to withstand acceleration (g forces) and fatigue and to eliminate the life-sustaining systems that increase the weight, complexity, and cost of piloted aircraft. Once freed from these constraints, UAVs can be more maneuverable, enjoy longer endurance or loiter times, and be less observable than their piloted counterparts. Another important advantage is their ability to fly close to highly defended targets, as well as nuclear, biological, and chemical targets, all of which pose significant risks for onboard crews.

Disadvantages

The primary disadvantages of UAVs are cost, the need for large bandwidth communications and the resulting vulnerability to jamming and exploitation, and low survivability in military operations.[27] Although it is commonly assumed that UAVs are relatively inexpensive in comparison with manned aircraft, the current generation is relatively expensive to develop and build. This cost disadvantage might be overstated if the expected operating costs of the Global Hawk UAV are half the operating costs of U-2 aircraft. For now, the production costs are relatively high because these systems typically involve small production runs and the avionics and weapons are sophisticated and expensive. UAV losses could be prohibitively expensive if large numbers were lost in military operations.

A second disadvantage is the UAV's need for sufficient bandwidth to permit the remote operator to maintain an adequate data link with the vehicle for controlling it and its payload. The need for large bandwidth also increases its vulnerability to jamming and exploitation. Exploitation occurs when an adversary electronically jams data links, disrupts or prevents the flow of information, or uses that information for its own purposes. For example, jamming could prevent the vehicle from receiving reconnaissance images or could send signals to take control of the vehicle.

A third disadvantage is survivability. The UAV lacks situational awareness and is not technologically sophisticated enough to warn the operator (in the case of remotely piloted vehicles) that it is under attack. In addition, it cannot operate in adverse weather, and it has a low level of reliability, which reduces its value for military operations.[28]

Characteristics of Remotely Piloted Vehicles

Remotely piloted vehicles (RPVS), which have remote operators, can be smaller, enjoy greater endurance, and cost less than manned vehicles while maintaining comparable capabilities. An RPV relies on sensors and communication links to inform the operator of the condition of the vehicle. The current approach is to use this type of UAV for intelligence, surveillance, and reconnaissance missions. Some thought has been given to using RPVS in air combat missions to protect other fighter aircraft or high-value assets, such as the U.S. Airborne Warning and Control System (AWACS). Their ability to perform these missions, however, will require vehicles with highly automatic functions, which typically increase development and acquisition costs.

Advantages

The principal advantage of RPVS is their ability to use human reasoning so that the vehicle itself is less complex and less expensive than its autonomous counterpart.[29] RPVS can be smaller and lighter; they can have greater endurance than piloted vehicles; and they can be stealthy, depending on the design of the aircraft and its communication system. Although they enjoy many of the advantages of human decision making, these vehicles are limited by their reliance on sensors and communications links and by time delays that exist when the aircraft and the operator are in different locations.

The roles of the remote operator are similar to the roles of the pilot, which are to make decisions in the presence of incomplete or unambiguous information, deal with unexpected circumstances, and take measures to protect the vehicle. Success, however, requires the operator to have access to timely information about threats to the vehicle, to identify an attack that is contemplated or in progress, and to take measures to protect the vehicle. By contrast, the current generation of UAVs, such as the Predator, however, lack the technological sophistication to perform these measures.

Disadvantages

The principal disadvantage of the RPV is that the operator is fundamentally unaware of the tactical situation around the vehicle, which translates into a greater probability that the mission will fail or that the vehicle will be lost.[30] At present, the RPV is susceptible to the loss of the electronic link with the human operator, which has catastrophic implications for failure of the mission or the loss of the vehicle. Another important disadvantage, often ignored or minimized, is that the distance between the vehicle and the operator causes a time delay that reduces the responsiveness of the RPV during combat.

Characteristics of Autonomous Vehicles

Autonomous vehicles, by definition, perform their functions without a human operator and as a result tend to be smaller and less costly than piloted vehicles. The need for automation means that an autonomous vehicle with any degree of capability will be more complex than remotely piloted vehicles.

Simple autonomous vehicles that lack any ability to adapt to changing conditions can be made smaller than remotely operated vehicles with similar capabilities. Two reasons are the absence of communications systems and the relatively simple guidance systems in these vehicles. Currently fielded autonomous vehicles, such as cruise missiles, are limited to attacking fixed targets that remain in a constant position during the flight of the missile. Their autonomous functions are limited to guiding toward a target selected before launch by human crews. An unresolved question is whether autonomous vehicles with simple guidance systems will be able to adapt to changing conditions in battle or to attack mobile targets, such as missile launchers or mobile surface-to-air missile sites.

Military commanders will want relatively inexpensive vehicles that are equipped with complex sensors that can interact with other weapons and react reliably and correctly to rapidly changing conditions. Any autonomous vehicle that can function in this way will be more complex and costly than its remotely piloted counterpart. At the present time, the United States does not have the technological capability to build autonomous vehicles that can reliably perform relatively complex missions in combat.

Advantages

Autonomous vehicles are useful in military missions that require relatively simple guidance systems. They are primarily expendable systems that normally would be classed as weapons rather than unmanned vehicles. The primary advantage of autonomous vehicles is their relatively small size and expendability. The cost of autonomous vehicles relates directly to their capabilities, and, currently, an autonomous vehicle with a simple guidance system cannot adapt to changing conditions on the battlefield as it flies toward the target. At the present time, the United States does not have the technological capability to build autonomous vehicles that can perform even relatively complex missions.

Autonomous vehicles, as well as remotely piloted vehicles, might be designed for greater endurance than manned aircraft, and they can operate with impunity despite the effects of nuclear, chemical, or biological weapons.[31] Also, they can be designed to operate from short runways and catapults and for use with other launch and recovery methods, and they can be dispersed to a large number of small sites. Finally, autonomous vehicles can be sufficiently small that they are difficult to observe and destroy.

Disadvantages
The primary disadvantage of an autonomous vehicle is that human controllers have little to no information about how the mission is progressing or how the vehicle is performing. Although an autonomous reconnaissance vehicle could be used to provide bomb damage assessment in much the same fashion as electro-optically guided weapons, none has yet been designed or fielded.

Another significant disadvantage of autonomous vehicles is that their systems could be susceptible to ambiguities or simple programming errors that cause them to attack friendly forces or that cause collateral damage in civilian areas or to other unlawful targets. The broader disadvantage with purely autonomous systems is that computers cannot make decisions in complex or ambiguous situations without humans to supervise their behavior.[32] Autonomous vehicles that possess sophisticated artificial intelligence or expert systems would be expensive, complex, and prone to behave in ways that an adversary might be able to recognize and exploit. The time required to plan, design, implement, debug, and test reprogrammed rules could limit their usefulness or render them useless, especially in military operations other than war. In general, these machines cannot adapt to or exploit the factors that are essential to success in combat.

A reasonable assumption is that autonomous vehicles cannot analyze events or display the flexibility or freedom of action that is essential for success in military operations. Autonomous vehicles cannot replicate the human ability to understand the nuances that make the difference between success and failure in war.[33] Such vehicles cannot demonstrate initiative; they must rely on other expert systems or artificial intelligence that, in itself, is a product of lists of explicit rules and contingencies. These systems would lack the human ability to adapt and behave in creative ways, which increases their vulnerability to enemy actions. This limitation derives from the fact that expert systems do not react well to inputs at the edge of their "knowledge." This is termed *brittleness,* which effectively increases the vulnerability of an autonomous vehicle to enemies who can use deception or ambiguity to confuse it.[34] Given the sheer number of objects that highly automated systems could encounter and the number of decisions that must be correctly and rapidly made, it would be relatively easy for an adversary to exploit autonomous vehicles.

Military Roles for Unmanned Aerial Vehicles

Manned aircraft dominated twentieth-century warfare, but technological advances are leading to the development of UAVs that could perform military missions once reserved for piloted aircraft. UAVs can, and probably will, perform a number of roles in future military operations.

Transportation

It is unlikely that passengers will travel via UAVs, at least in the near future. A more realistic possibility is that UAVs could transport cargo, especially in the relatively small quantities that would apply in tactical situations. The current state of technology might be sufficient to create remotely piloted or autonomous helicopters that are capable of delivering supplies and ammunition to troops in the field, as long as these UAVs are guided by specific instructions and restrictions and have trained operators.

Intelligence, Surveillance, and Reconnaissance

UAVs are being used extensively for intelligence, reconnaissance, and surveillance missions, which take advantage of the fact that specially designed UAVs have long loiter times, can be positioned flexibly near potential targets, and are small and relatively difficult to detect. The long endurance of UAVs is particularly important for surveillance missions that could extend over several days. In this role, UAVs relieve manned platforms of the need to maintain the high operational tempo for extended periods, which is becoming the norm in modern military contingencies.

The U.S. military uses a number of UAVs in surveillance missions. The U.S. Air Force is developing the Global Hawk for surveillance missions, and the U.S. Army and Navy have developed the Predator for tactical reconnaissance.[35] The

Congressional Budget Office recommended the purchase of UAVs in order to reduce the Army's purchase of *Comanche* reconnaissance helicopters, which would save several billion dollars.[36] Meanwhile, the military is developing UAVs that can fly autonomously and broadcast real-time information, which the Army will use for reconnaissance, jamming, chemical or biological detection, and the placement of remote sensors on the battlefield.[37]

Attacks on Fixed Targets

UAVs can be used to attack high-value, fixed ground targets in military operations. The U.S. military has developed UAVs that have demonstrated the ability to launch weapons against air defense sites. As early as 1972, a Ryan Lightning Bug drone successfully launched an AGM-65 Maverick electro-optical missile against a radar control van.[38] In addition, UAVs could be used to attack facilities that produce or store weapons of mass destruction, as well as to attack critical fixed and, possibly, moving targets.[39] It is conceivable that UAVs could detect whether states are involved in manufacturing or storing weapons of mass destruction and attack those facilities. The U.S. Air Force's SAB has suggested that, to attack these facilities, the military should develop dual-equipped UAVs with multispectral sensors and weapons. Surveillance UAVs could fly with others that are armed with precision-guided penetrating weapons or weapons designed to prevent the spread of these materials. Once military commanders give the location, type of target, and desired weapons effects to a UAV system, it would determine the proper way to attack the targets with a remote operator or some form of automation.

Attacks on Mobile Targets

Methods for attacking mobile targets have been pursued with increasing urgency since the Persian Gulf War. One concept for attacking mobile targets with UAVs involves using sensors on high-altitude, long-endurance UAVs in conjunction with armed aircraft. The fundamental problem is detecting and identifying targets in modern combat operations. One fundamental reason for developing unmanned vehicles is to locate and destroy what are termed *time-critical targets,* especially if they are armed with weapons of mass destruction. A remotely operated vehicle in this role could loiter for hours or days near a suspected target, identify the target, and destroy it or pass on the information to an armed aircraft. The relatively long endurance of these vehicles, when coupled with helping the human operator detect and identify targets, could make remotely operated UAVs a viable option for this type of mission. For now, the problems of finding and destroying the right targets lessen the value of using armed autonomous UAVs for destroying mobile targets.

Air-to-Air Combat

In the foreseeable future, technology could increase the ability of UAVs to conduct offensive and defensive combat operations against aircraft, cruise missiles, and ballistic missiles. For example, modern air-to-air missiles fit the definition of autonomous vehicles, even if they cannot autonomously detect and identify targets. These vehicles could be equipped with technologies that permit detecting and identifying targets, and their range could be increased. In the longer term, it might be technologically feasible to develop UAVs that can supplement the current generation of combat aircraft with vehicles whose performance and survivability exceed that of piloted vehicles. If equipped with sensors, high-altitude and long-endurance UAVs could detect ballistic and cruise missiles. Although some form of remotely piloted vehicle might be valuable in air combat, it would rely on levels of automation that exceed existing technological capabilities, which raises concerns about using UAVs in this role.

Combat Support Missions

UAVs might be used for electronic support operations that are currently performed by manned aircraft. Such operations could involve using UAVs in conjunction with manned aircraft to target and jam fire-control radars. This category of UAV could function as a decoy that duplicates the radar, infrared, and radio signatures of fighter aircraft to increase the survivability of manned aircraft. Once UAVs detect and identify the location of enemy air defenses and transmit that data to manned attack aircraft, these or other UAVs could deliver weapons to destroy enemy air defenses, as noted in the earlier section, Attacks on Fixed Targets.

Conclusion

Using UAVs in military operations will remain speculative until these technologies demonstrate their operational value and cost effectiveness.[40] Significant problems currently limit the ability to use unmanned vehicles, especially those that rely on advanced automation technologies to identify and select among alternatives in combat. As the SAB concluded, automation is the critical technology that will determine the roles that UAVs can perform effectively in military operations.[41] Simply because cruise missiles use inertial navigation systems, automated terrain-comparison, or GPS technologies does not mean that UAVs will assume a dominant role in military operations.[42] Their development was hampered throughout the twentieth century by the problems of building autonomous machines that can perform human functions. Making correct decisions in combat about the use of lethal force will be the most difficult challenge.

The United States has invested in UAV technology to increase the cost-effectiveness of weapon systems and to reduce the risk to humans in combat. The prudent option, however, is to maintain significant capabilities in manned aircraft until sensors and automation develop to the point where they can perform the functions in war that historically have been controlled by humans.

It is likely that unmanned vehicles will not be able to fulfill all of the missions now performed by manned aircraft.[43] A fundamental technological problem is that UAVs have a limited ability to deal with ambiguity. In major wars and humanitarian operations, military commanders make mistakes in identifying friendly and enemy forces, as well as civilians. For example, the failure to realize that civilians and military force were crossing a bridge in Kosovo at the same time led to an attack by North Atlantic Treaty Organization (NATO) aircraft.[44] To be truly valuable in military operations, UAVs should be able to deal with ambiguity, but this ability exceeds the existing technological capabilities of sensors and computers.

The development of UAVs could lead to the technological obsolescence or extinction of piloted aircraft and the U.S. Air Force. Alternatively, excessive reliance on unmanned machines would weaken the Air Force's ability to deal with opponents, whereas the failure to adapt technologically would herald its demise.[45] Although technology makes the modern battlefield more lethal, technological progress is unlikely to erase the need for placing humans in harm's way. Political and military authorities should cautiously proceed before allowing automated systems to select targets and weapons. One could imagine an armed autonomous vehicle that attacks a school bus filled with children because its technology mistakenly indicated that the bus was a Scud missile launcher. Although a compelling reason for developing UAVs is to save lives in war, the United States has not reached the point when technology permits automated systems to make decisions about the use of lethal military force.

Notes

1. Throughout this work, the terms *unmanned air vehicles, uninhabited air vehicles,* and *unmanned* (or *uninhabited*) *combat air vehicles* are used by the contributors. The terms *unmanned* and *uninhabited* are essentially interchangeable. The term *combat* signifies that the vehicle is designed to employ weapons, although UAVs can have provisions for weapons added after their introduction to service. This usage reflects the fact that this technology exists in several forms, and that it is developing at a rapid pace.

2. U.S. Air Force [hereafter USAF] Scientific Advisory Board, *Report on UAV Technologies and Combat Operations,* vol. 1, *Summary,* SAB-TR-96-01, Washington, D.C., November 1996.

3. "Pentagon's Mark Sees Pilotless Future," *Defense Week,* May 30, 2000.

4. Paul Geier, U.S. Air Force Battlelab, interview by author, Nov. 17, 1998.

5. *Department of Defense Dictionary of Military and Associated Terms* (Washington, D.C.: Department of Defense, Mar. 23, 1994 [as amended through Apr. 15, 1998]), 138, 369, 459.

6. Edward E. Huling III and James D. McCormick, Reconnaissance Systems Program Office, Aeronautical Systems Center, interview by author, Nov. 24, 1998. The definition of aerial vehicles includes the AIM-9 Sidewinder and the AGM-130 electro-optically guided missile. See Susan H. H. Young, "Gallery of USAF Weapons," *Air Force Magazine* 83, no. 5 (May 2000), 155–56.

7. Brian T. Kehl and Michael D. Wilson, "Manned versus Unmanned Reconnaissance Air Vehicles: A Quantitative Comparison of the U-2 and Global Hawk Operating and Support Costs," (master's thesis, Air Force Institute of Technology, 1998).

8. USAF Scientific Advisory Board, *Report on UAV Technology,* 4–6.

9. William Wagner, *Lightning Bugs and Other Reconnaissance Drones* (Fallbrook, Calif.: Aero Publishers, 1982). See also Christopher A. Jones, *Unmanned Aerial Vehicles (UAVs): An Assessment of Historical Operations and Future Possibilities* (Maxwell Air Force Base, Ala: Air Command and Staff College, March 1997), 11.

10. In terms of cost, the least expensive weapon is a dumb bomb, the next more expensive option is an expendable cruise missile or a precision standoff weapon that is delivered from a manned platform, and the most expensive option is a precision weapon that is delivered by a reusable vehicle, either remotely piloted or autonomous.

11. "Global Hawk 2 Flight Sets Stage for Airborne Sensor Tests," *Aviation Week & Space Technology,* Nov. 30, 1998, 32, states, "Operators had one unexpected event. While on approach, the Global Hawk was told by the Edwards [Air Force Base] tower that heavy traffic required it to hold. The aircraft's flight plan was suspended, and the UAV was put into a holding pattern [by the remote operator] at 5,000 ft. until it was permitted to land. It then conducted an autonomous landing."

12. Stan Gibilisco, ed., *The McGraw-Hill Illustrated Encyclopedia of Robotics & Artificial Intelligence* (New York: McGraw-Hill, Inc., 1994), 405–6. For reference, there are at least eight levels of automation: (1) manually operated tools and manipulators, (2) machines that perform a series of tasks in a fixed sequence, (3) programmable manipulators, (4) numerically controlled robots, (5) sensate robots or robots that incorporate any type of sensor, (6) adaptive robots that compensate for changes in their environment, (7) smart robots with artificial intelligence, and (8) smart mechatronic (mechanical-electronic) systems that can control a fleet of robots or robotic devices.

13. Stuart W. Leslie, *Boss Kettering* (New York: Columbia University Press, 1983), 82.

14. James P. Coyne, *Airpower in the Gulf* (Arlington, Va.: Air Force Association, 1992), 19–35. For some sense of the complexities involved, one can consider the

chess-playing computer program Deep Thought, which "evaluated up to 125 million possible alternatives within the span of one move of a chess game, three minutes. The 125 million alternatives were bounded by no more than thirty-two pieces, whose possible moves are specified by well-defined rules belonging unambiguously to only two players, on exactly sixty-four potential spaces in two dimensions, and whose moves occur sequentially. The expert human chess player is said to have an intuitive understanding of the board positions and a compelling sense of the winning move, whereas the program must calculate all possible moves in order to select the winner." The military situation is more challenging by orders of magnitude. See Daniel Crevier, *AI: The Tumultuous History of the Search for Artificial Intelligence* (New York: Basic Books, 1993), 234.

15. Gibilisco, *McGraw-Hill Illustrated Encyclopedia,* 62–63. See Daniel Crevier, *AI: The Tumultuous History of the Search for Artificial Intelligence* (New York: Basic Books, 1993), 234.

16. Kehl and Wilson, "Manned versus Unmanned Reconaissance Air Vehicles," 51, 84, 88, 91.

17. The military concept of the term *situational awareness* relates to what artificial intelligence researchers call the *frame of reference*. See Crevier, *AI: Tumultuous History,*119.

18. Giblisco, *McGraw-Hill Illustrated Encyclopedia,* 62.

19. See USAF Scientific Advisory Board, *Report on UAV Technologies,* 4-3, which notes that, "Humans can *learn* to perform control functions and can thus *adapt* to unexpected inputs and demands. Humans can also *reason* effectively under conditions of uncertainty and perform higher order integration tasks." See also Boyd, "Patterns of Conflict," in which Boyd argues that "to win, we should operate at a faster tempo or rhythm than our adversaries—or, better yet, get inside an adversary's Observation-Orientation-Decision-Action time cycle or loop." See also Giblisco, *McGraw-Hill Illustrated Encyclopedia,* 63, which notes that real-world problems have subtle aspects and subjective variables, such as personality, expression, and other cues "that no electronic brain comes close to understanding."

20. Another possible group might consist of autonomous vehicles that can be retasked or reprogrammed periodically, such as satellites that operate autonomously but whose orbits or payloads can be altered.

21. USAF Scientific Advisory Board, *Report on UAV Technologies,* 2-2.

22. Wagner, *Lightning Bugs,* Foreword; Jones, *Unmanned Aerial Vehicles,*1–3.

23. Dana Longino, *Role of Unmanned Aerial Vehicles in Future Armed Conflict Scenarios* (Maxwell Air Force Base, Ala.: Air University Press, 1994), 6.

24. Jones, *Unmanned Aerial Vehicles,* 5.

25. USAF Scientific Advisory Board, *Report on UAV Technologies,* 4-1, 2.

26. Ibid., 2, 3-2–3-4.

27. Ibid., 9-3.

28. Ibid., 1-1, 4-2.

29. Ibid., 4-3, 7-1, 2.

30. Ibid., 1-1, 9-3.

31. Ibid., 3-2, 4-2.

32. Gibilisco, *McGraw-Hill Illustrated Encyclopedia,* 23, 62–63.

33. Boyd, "Patterns of Conflict," 74–79.

34. Crevier, *Tumultuous History,* 207.

35. Geier, interview.

36. David A. Fulghum, "U.S. Army Debates Tactical UAV Requirements," *Aviation Week & Space Technology,* Nov. 23, 1998, 50.

37. David A. Fulghum, "Miniature Air Vehicles Fly into Army's Future," *Aviation Week & Space Technology,* Nov. 9, 1998, 37.

38. Jones, *Unmanned Aerial Vehicles,* 13.

39. USAF Scientific Advisory Board, *Report on UAV Technologies,* 4-3.

40. Kehl and Wilson, "Manned versus Unmanned Reconnaissance Vehicles," 57–60.

41. USAF Scientific Advisory Board, *Report on UAV Technologies,* 4-3.

42. "Gallery of USAF Weapons," *Air Force Magazine* 81, no. 5 (May 1998), 155.

43. See Kehl and Wilson, "Manned versus Unmanned Reconnaissance Vehicles," 51, 81–88.

44. "Kosovo Air Attack," *ABC News,* June 1, 1999, available at abcnews.com.

45. See Carl H. Builder, *The Masks of War: American Military Styles in Strategy and Analysis* (Baltimore, Md.: Johns Hopkins University Press, 1989); Carl H. Builder, *The Icarus Syndrome: The Role of Air Power Theory in the Evolution and Fate of the U.S. Air Force* (New Brunswick, N.J.: Transaction Publishers, 1994).

PART THREE
Command and Control

10.　　　　　Directing War from Home
Scott M. Britten

Planning and conducting military campaigns are extremely complex tasks. For example, each day during a major war, thousands of aircraft sorties from dozens of bases are organized into a coherent war plan for destroying enemy forces. This chapter discusses how the United States could use modern computer and communications technology to perform many of the tasks required to plan and execute wars from its homeland. Through such operations, termed *reachback operations,* military commanders could use electronically connected, but geographically separated, computers to direct wars from secure locations, such as the middle of the United States, rather than moving troops and weapons overseas where they would be vulnerable to attack. This technological development is significant because states could wage wars from the security of the homeland and reduce the risk to troops and equipment. This chapter discusses how reachback operations might alter how wars are planned and waged during the short term, as well as the long-term implications for national security.

Introduction

During each day of an air campaign, thousands of aircraft sorties from dozens of bases must be coordinated into an organized effort that will have the maximum effect on the enemy. In the past, the nerve center for military planning was located in the theater of operations; thus, it was as close to combat operations as possible. With advances in communications and computer technologies, however, it is possible for military commanders to plan and execute air wars from the security and safety of the United States. This strategy would keep most of the personnel and equipment in a secure location rather than facing the risk of being attacked.

War is an extraordinarily complex human endeavor. As an example, during the 1991 Persian Gulf War air campaign, 2,400 coalition aircraft flew day and night with precise synchronization from more than twenty airfields and six aircraft carriers.[1] In most cases, air campaign planners, while selecting the missions, types of ordnance or cargo, targets, flight paths, and refueling routes required for attacking hundreds of targets each day, minimized the risk to air crews, ground forces, enemy civilians, religious and historically significant buildings, and other proscribed sites.

What tools did the planners have for this daunting task? Despite the presence of more than three thousand computers in the war zone that were linked to computers in the United States, aspects of this process were conducted with paper charts and grease pencils.[2] Retired U.S. Air Force Lt. Gen. Charles A. Horner, Joint Force Air Component Commander (JFACC), formed a planning staff whose nucleus was aptly named the "Black Hole." These experts, as well as the entire JFACC staff, used rudimentary computer tools to organize the air campaign.[3]

During the twenty-first century, modern data processing and communications technologies could transform how air wars are planned and fought far beyond the rudimentary tools used during the Persian Gulf War. Since the late 1980s, the Air Force has developed computer systems, collectively known as the Contingency Theater Automated Planning System (CTAPS), to lessen the war planner's burden. This is the foundation for planning and executing modern air campaigns.

Some inefficiencies encountered by military forces during the Persian Gulf War could be resolved with advanced communication and distributed data processing systems. In practical terms, the complex computational task of planning air campaigns could be performed by geographically separated computers. Firms in the private sector, as well as the Department of Defense (DOD), perform such tasks all the time. In fact, the Air Force's Tactical Air Command headquarters at Langley Air Force Base in Virginia used reachback operations extensively during the Persian Gulf War.[4] Technological innovation now permits most of the individuals and computer systems that organize air campaigns to remain in the United States, while only the commander of air operations and the smaller supporting staff and equipment are at risk in the theater.[5]

This chapter examines how the military could use reachback operations to fight future wars with devastating lethality and efficiency from U.S. bases. It discusses how communications capabilities can make reachback operations possible, examines the implications of reachback operations for planning and executing air wars, and considers specific actions for implementing a reachback system. Although this chapter focuses on air wars, this technology has important implications for how the U.S. military fights all types of wars in the future.

Modern Air Campaigns

The need for flexible planning in war has been evident for millennia, and air campaigns, which are no exception, involve choreographing numerous aircraft to achieve the overall objectives of the military commander, known as the Joint Force Commander (JFC). Since World War II, when air power often failed to mass against enemy forces wherever it was most needed in the theater, centralized control over air operations has been the foundation of U.S. Air Force doctrine.[6] The U.S. Navy learned the need for maritime air and surface force coordination when it developed carrier air doctrine during the 1930s.

Even before the Persian Gulf War, Air Force officials understood that planners needed a new generation of automated tools to make air campaigns more responsive, especially during attacks on moving targets, such as mobile missile launchers. During the late 1980s, the Air Force started the CTAPS program in order to establish a technological basis for planning and executing air campaigns by automating the activities of the joint air tasking cycle.[7] With minor exceptions, these computer programs freely interchange data and products to give any operator access to information about the air campaign.[8] The following discussion, beginning with how air campaigns are currently conducted, provides a foundation for understanding reachback operations.

Joint Air Tasking Cycle

In essence, a modern air campaign dynamically allocates weapons against targets as efficiently and logically as possible. The air campaign is the product of the air tasking order (ATO), which should be completed before the enemy can respond in order to prevent the enemy from controlling the war. The joint ATO is organized into six steps[9]:

1. *Coordination between Joint Force Commander and Component Commanders:* The Joint Force Commander evaluates the most recently completed combat assessment and, with the advice of component commanders for air, land, and maritime forces, issues guidance and objectives for the next targeting cycle. For example, if air superiority has been achieved, the commander might shift the emphasis to attacking other targets.
2. *Target Development:* Once the commander's guidance and objectives are understood, the component commanders nominate the tar-

gets that they cannot attack with their own military assets. These targets are derived from previous target lists, intelligence reports, and electronic warfare systems. Once the commander establishes the priority of the targets to be attacked, the joint integrated prioritized target list (JIPTL) documents the commander's recommendations for detailed planning.

3. *Weaponeering/Allocation:* Targeteers use this approved target list to match the types and numbers of aircraft and weapons that are best suited to attack these targets, aim points for these targets, and other critical mission-planning factors. This master air attack plan (MAAP), which the commander reviews, forms the foundation for the ATO.

4. *Joint Air Tasking Order Development:* The staff in the joint air operations center turn the high-level master air attack plan into the detailed ATO by generating directions so that the assigned forces can plan and execute their missions. Some tasks, such as determining the types and settings of weapon fuses, are normally performed by planning cells in the air wings.[10] When a small number of units are involved, the ATO is a relatively short message to the tasked units, whereas in large operations that require precise coordination among many units, the ATO can be quite lengthy. For example, air tasking orders during Desert Storm were typically six hundred pages long and contained data for 3,000 aircraft sorties.[11] This process also generates special instructions (SPINS) and the airspace control order (ACO) that help air crews to complete their missions without interfering with other military operations.

5. *Force Execution:* This step in the cycle relates to execution of the missions assigned by the atoand includes redirecting previously planned sorties in real time so that forces can react to time-sensitive targets. For example, a case of real-time redirection occurred on the night of January 30, 1991, when, based on a real-time warning from a Joint Surveillance, Targeting, and Reconnaissance System (JSTARS aircraft,[12] more than 140 tactical aircraft sorties were redirected to interdict an Iraqi attack on Khafji, Saudi Arabia. These sorties were devastatingly effective and decisive.[13] Although the ATO cycle is ponderous, it allows the commander to react immediately to take advantage of opportunities as these arise.

6. *Combat Assessment:* Although listed as the final step in the cycle, this step is actually continuous throughout the cycle. The purpose of combat assessment is to determine what happened during military strikes, as well as to evaluate the results of friendly sorties, enemy

actions, and other tactical changes. The foundation for this process is bomb damage assessment, which involves analyzing the results of all military strikes for the duration of the military campaign.

Vulnerabilities of the Contingency Theater Automated Planning System

Despite its obvious technological leap over "paper charts and grease pencils," the CTAPS requires that large amounts of manpower and equipment be deployed in the theater, which make it vulnerable to attack and difficult to deploy and support.[14] Several critical vulnerabilities are associated with the CTAPS.

Survivabililty

When military equipment involves lots of space, a large number of people, or an easily detectable signature, it has a large "footprint." Even in rear areas of the theater, the electronic and physical footprint of the joint air operations center with the CTAPS is vulnerable to air raids, missile attacks, guerrilla actions, or sabotage. Losing highly trained personnel or critical air combat planning capabilities would significantly disrupt the ability to conduct an air campaign.

The loss of the CTAPS during wartime could severely disrupt the coordinated air war until a new Joint Air Operations Center (JAOC) could be constituted. Its loss would restrict the types of sorties that are flown as well as the control that military commanders could exercise. This loss of effectiveness would impede the war and produce more casualties among friendly forces. Any prudent adversary would conclude that it is a critical center of gravity that should be attacked.[15]

Deployability

It is extremely difficult to deploy an air operations center equipped with the CTAPS. A large campaign, such as the Persian Gulf War, would require forty-one C-141 aircraft to deploy the JAOC equipment and three airliners to deploy the nine hundred people who operate the center. Because airlift is always in short supply, transporting a center with its CTAPS is a burden.[16] More important, because it requires such a massive amount of airlift, the U.S. military cannot mobilize beyond a small, quick reaction package for the short term.[17] In a fast-breaking crisis, the air component commander might depend on the CTAPS based on a ship or in the United States. But, as it maintains global commitments with smaller forces, the military must be organized to fight immediately and deploy the air operations center as quickly as possible.[18] The United States has pre-positioned a considerable amount of war materiel overseas, but many sophisticated and expensive systems, such as CTAPS, remain in the United States for both security and training reasons. If there is no operations center with the CTAPS already located in the theater, the military would benefit from having access to systems located in the United States that can immediately operate.

Supportability

A fundamental problem with deployment of an air operation center to the theater is providing facilities and supplies for nine hundred people. The CTAPS was not in use during the Persian Gulf War, but computers, generators, and other sophisticated equipment regularly broke down in the harsh climate which meant that spare parts and replacement equipment had to be moved thousands of miles.[19] Although on-site service in a war zone is practical, flying in replacement parts adds to the airlift burden.

System Deficiencies

The CTAPS has deficiencies that relate to its computer systems. First, these enormous databases contain sensitive data that are crucial to the conduct of modern air warfare. For example, this system includes precise information on the commander's guidance and direction, disposition of friendly and enemy forces, target vulnerabilities, aircraft capabilities, weapons effects, terrain data, political boundaries, surface and foliage composition, current and predicted weather, supply status, combat assessments, and air-to-air refueling orbits, among other information.[20]

Second, Air Force databases might not be compatible with those of the other military services, which can have disastrous effects. For example, during a theater missile defense exercise, the Air Force and Marine Corps used different missile-warning grid coordinate systems, even though the two services coordinated the grids before the exercise. When Air Force units warned Marine units of incoming missile attacks, the Marines were confused until they received the correct grids. Although Air Force and Marine staffs worked closely together before the exercise to avoid this problem, it is an example of the ample opportunities for confusion that can exist even in well-planned military operations.[21]

Third, it might be necessary to station the commander on an aircraft carrier or a command and control ship.[22] The latter has better facilities than an aircraft carrier, but the staff on a command and control ship is limited to about 280 personnel and similar restrictions on the number of computer tools.[23] These limitations will remain unless the United States builds a new class of ships with significantly more room and facilities. Although it was adapted for command and control ships, the commander on a ship is limited to planning and executing about eight hundred sorties per day, or one quarter of the sorties required in a major conflict. Given these problems, reachback systems may provide a more effective and efficient way to plan and execute future air wars.

Conceptual Reachback System

In essence, a reachback operation uses data-linked, but geographically separated, computer systems to plan and execute air campaigns in a manner that is
more survivable, deployable, and supportable fashion than the CTAPS. A reachback system consists of communications equipment, computer hardware, and
software deployed both in the theater and in the garrisoned segment in the
United States. Located at a distance from the immediate dangers of the theater,
the garrisoned segment could be in the continental United States (CONUS) or another secure geographic location. Staffs of both the deployed and the garrisoned
segments are collectively referred to as the JAOC staff because they function as
one team. The combination of the deployed and garrisoned segments constitutes
a reachback system.

To be effective, a reachback system should not reduce the ability to prose-
cute an air campaign and should minimize the vulnerabilities of personnel and
equipment in the theater to attack. To function effectively, a reachback system
must use high-capacity, reliable, secure, and survivable communication links to
form its deployed and garrisoned segments into a "virtual" center. To succeed,
a reachback system must support the commander and staff, but decisions about
the air campaign could be influenced by the location of the commander and the
center staff (including coalition officers) and by the distribution of equipment
between the garrison and the theater. The JAOC is organized into four groups.
The first group, the command section and staff, performs administrative duties.
The second group, combat plans, anticipates the future needs of the theater commander. In addition to supporting the ATO, combat planners also generate se-
quels, or plans for the upcoming phases of the campaign. Based on the most recent combat assessment and the commander's guidance, the combat plans group
develops the master plan and ultimately the ATO. The third group, combat operations, oversees the execution of the air tasking order. The fourth group consists of the liaison officers from land, maritime, space, and special operations
forces, who represent their commanders' interests and keep their commanders
informed about air operations. This organization raises fundamental questions
about where each member of the operations center should be located.

One option is to locate the commander in the United States for three reasons[24]: he would have better access to information, which would improve its effectiveness; forward-deployed headquarters are inherently vulnerable, difficult
to deploy, slow to set up, and are less well connected to communications systems; exposing the commander to enemy action could be an unnecessary risk,
particularly when considering that many air forces under its control might not
be based in the theater. These arguments, however, contain serious flaws in
many operational scenarios.

The alternative is to place the commander in the theater. With advances in communication technologies, more information will be available in the theater, which is where most of the information that he needs to conduct an air campaign is generated. If communications between the theater and the United States were interrupted, it would be better to have the commander in the theater because the data originate in the theater and he could still communicate with air forces in the theater.

There are several overriding advantages to forward-deployed headquarters. Because the United States is likely to fight major regional contingencies as part of multinational coalitions, the deployed headquarters should be located in the same place as the military commanders and staffs of other coalition nations.[25] Personal interactions with commanders in the theater are absolutely necessary if the commander is to perform properly during the war.

A related argument for a forward-deployed commander is that a significant portion of air assets still will be based in or near the theater. Although some aircraft, notably intercontinental bombers, can operate from the United States, such an operation would be cumbersome and would not alter the fact that most air assets would be shifted to the theater. Because most forces will be based in the theater, this is the best location.

In addition to planning and executing air wars, the commander has equally important responsibilities to all of the military personnel in the theater. As the commander, this is the most duty-bound position in a military organization and must stay in touch with the airmen, eat in their mess tents, shake their hands, and thank them for their sacrifices. No video teleconference can ever become a substitute for personal interaction. A commander could be killed while serving in a combat zone, but death is one of the risks of war.

Assuming that the commander is located in the theater, the senior deputies and advisors must be in the theater to help coordinate operations with other command elements and serve as the "brain trust." A majority of the command section and administrative staff, however, can operate in the garrison with a reachback capability. For example, many personnel in the combat plans group could work effectively in the garrison, including most targeteers, weaponeers, and specialists. By contrast, a much larger percentage of the combat operations staff—the personnel who are constantly communicating with flying units, liaison officers, and senior staff—must be deployed. Liaison officers must be located in the theater because, as links between the air operations center and the supported commanders on the ground or at sea, they must interact extensively with the commander and the senior staff in order to maintain close communications with the commanders.

The actual number of personnel who could operate in the garrison depends on the specific configuration of the reachback system, the theater commander's concept of operations, and the decision on how best to support the senior military commander. A reasonable estimate is that about eight hundred of the nine hundred personnel in a typical center could be based in the United States with a reachback system, which is a 90 percent reduction in the number of deployed personnel. While eliminating eight hundred people in the theater's headquarters is trivial in comparison with the tens of thousands of personnel deployed with an Army corps, there are considerable advantages to having these eight hundred people in the United States. For example, if the garrison is in a protected location, not all of the garrison personnel must be military. Although the garrison commander should be a military officer who is an experienced senior JAOC staff member and who has earned the commander's absolute trust, many workstation operators could be civilian employees with extensive military experience.[26]

If the United States fights in coalitions, as it did during the Persian Gulf War, coalition members will rely on U.S. command, control, and intelligence systems.[27] Although some countries, such as France and Australia, are investing in these technologies, coalition air campaigns will need to use U.S. automated capabilities, as seen in Bosnia.[28] Reachback operations do not preclude multinational involvement because the presence of Allied military officers enhances operations at both the deployed and garrisoned segments. To prepare for future contingencies, Allied air force officers should serve on both the theater and garrison JAOC staffs during regular multinational exercises. One challenge is to protect sensitive intelligence information, but these security restrictions will be manageable as the United States develops computer operating systems that permit individuals with lower security clearances to operate workstations containing more classified information. Since the Persian Gulf War, the United States has relaxed restrictions on intelligence information, which will allow Allied officers to become more involved in center activities.

Regardless of location of the reachback system, a 90 percent reduction in personnel would not necessarily reduce the size (or "footprint") of the center by 90 percent. The reason is that not all of the staff uses the same amount of computer hardware and supporting infrastructure. A reasonable estimate is that a reachback system might reduce the equipment in the theater by 50 percent to 70 percent, personnel in the theater by about 90 percent, and the deployed hardware by 50 percent to 70 percent,[29] depending on the contingency.

A related problem is the garrison's location. Although its functionality does not depend on its location because the technology works wherever the garrison is located, the advantages of reachback operations stem from its location. In all probability, one or several garrisons would be located in the United States, but other locations are conceivable and perhaps desirable. For example, a garrison in Japan or Guam could support reachback operations in a Korean theater of operations.[30] If the objective is to support contingencies in various theaters, however, the most cost-effective option is to place the garrison in the United States.

In the long run, a phased approach to locating the garrisons has advantages. During the first phase, one reachback garrison would be established temporarily at a numbered Air Force headquarters. During this phase of initial training and operations, the commander could manage the inevitable problems while gaining confidence in reachback operations. The second phase would establish the garrison at a permanent location. For the third phase, placing a second garrison at a different location, which is linked electronically to the first garrison to ensure its survivability, would give military commanders enough reachback capability to fight wars on two fronts simultaneously.

One factor that influences the location of reachback garrisons is to ensure the physical security of the garrisons. As prime wartime targets, these facilities must be secure against terrorist or guerrilla attacks and conventional cruise missile or ballistic missile attacks. Although nuclear weapons might threaten the garrisons, the detonation of nuclear weapons on American soil would involve catastrophic consequences for the attacker that go far beyond the U.S. military's loss of a garrison. To be survivable, garrisons must be located on military bases in America's heartland that are hardened against attack and possibly located underground. It would be quite difficult for most states to attack these locations successfully with cruise missiles or ballistic missiles.

The notion of dual garrisons is important if one garrison were destroyed or damaged, because the commander could continue to fight the war from the alternate garrison. Although constructing and operating costs for two garrisons are twice those of a single garrison, these costs must be weighed against protecting the ability to conduct effective air campaigns.[33] Because the garrisons would be centers of gravity for U.S. air combat capabilities, their survivability must be certain.

Although a number of locations, including Offutt Air Force Base in Nebraska and Schriever Air Force Base in Colorado, are feasible, one location that would unify opposition among military commanders is the Pentagon (or any location in the Washington, D.C., area). Because the success of reachback operations depends on the ability of the commander to command the garrisoned detachment, garrisons located near Washington would undermine confidence in the commander's authority. Worse, it would increase the ability of high-level military and political authorities to interfere with a war.

Another consideration with reachback operations is the connection between the theater and the garrisons in the United States. To be effective, reachback garrisons must be connected by high-capacity, reliable, secure, and survivable global communications. The necessary communications technologies already exist, such as the Global Broadcast System, which is designed to support combat operations of the early twenty-first century.[34] Depending on the required communications speed, other commercial and military communications systems could handle some of the data. Because of rapid advances in communication technologies, the system chosen to support reachback operations will be based on existing technologies.[35]

U-2 Reachback Example

The U.S. military has some experience with reachback operations. One example is the reachback capability developed during the 1980s for U-2 aircraft. Rather than using this reachback capability for remote data processing, however, the Air Force transmitted data from U-2 aircraft to in-theater ground stations, which allowed U-2s to conduct operations in Europe until the end of the Cold War, during Desert Storm, and in South Korea. Theater commanders believed that a co-located ground station was a viable option because they could use assets in the theater, which was preferable to relying on assets outside the theater that were beyond their control and thus less reliable. When U-2 support for Bosnia was necessary, the last available ground station was located at Beale Air Force Base in California. Because moving the ground station to Europe would have made it unavailable for training and military contingencies, the Air Force established data links between U-2s that were supporting operations in Bosnia and the ground station in California where the data was processed. This arrangement worked well because the European Theater was adequately supported, personnel of the ground station in California could train and simultaneously support worldwide U-2 operations, and transmittal of U-2 results to the Combined Air Operations Center in Italy added only several seconds to data processing.[31] The fact that this U-2 reachback capability was accepted by the military is a positive sign that a reachback system can be developed.

Just as theater commanders were unwilling to relinquish control over U-2 ground stations, senior Air Force officials might be reluctant to endorse reachback operations.[32] But this concern can be resolved by locating reachback garrisons at the home bases of the Air Force and other military units that would be used in air campaigns. In this case, military commanders could more easily oversee training, orchestrate exercises, refine their concepts of operations, and increase their familiarity with reachback operations, even if this leads to some duplication of equipment.

Advantages of Reachback Operations

A reachback system would have three significant advantages, related to survival, deployment, and support, over the current system used by the U.S. military to plan and execute air campaigns.

Survivability

The large physical and electronic signature of a modern air operations center raises significant questions about its survivability. Simply reducing the number of personnel and deployed equipment in the theater could decrease its size and increase its overall security. A second aspect that affects the survivability of U.S. garrisons is that threats in the theater will not interrupt military operations, as did threats of missile attacks by Iraq during the Persian Gulf War. The ability to operate in the face of enemy attacks is a significant advantage in an era when more states could possess ballistic missiles and weapons of mass destruction. Although the U.S. homeland will not be absolutely free from this threat, the existence of two geographically separated and electronically linked garrisons would reduce the risks and increase the effectiveness of air campaigns.

Deployability

Another concern is the ability to deploy forces overseas rapidly and to project military power as the military shifts toward expeditionary forces.[36] If only one hundred of the original nine hundred staff members must deploy, transportation requirements would shrink. The resulting savings in airlift would equal nineteen C-141 sorties, which could be used to ferry other critical supplies.[37] A related factor is the time that it takes a deployed unit to reach its full capability. In addition to reducing the need for aircraft to ferry supplies, reachback systems would permit earlier planning and execution of air campaigns because most of the system and its operators would not have to relocate. For many contingencies, the garrison staff could generate the initial air campaign plans while the deployed segment is traveling to the theater. If it were necessary to start air combat immediately, the commander could organize and direct the air war from the United States, as happened during U.S. military intervention in Haiti in 1994.[38] In these ways a reachback system better fits the demands of an expeditionary military.

Supportability

The two principal aspects of supportability are people and equipment. While supporting eight hundred people in the theater is manageable, the larger challenge is supporting the JAOC equipment. Many geographic regions pose significant challenges to electronic equipment, particularly if the equipment is built to commercial standards rather than more rugged military specifications. Although a reachback system would use the same commercial electronics as CTAPS, it is more supportable because spare parts and maintenance for the garrisoned segment are more available in the United States than overseas.

Drawbacks of Reachback Operations

Although reachback systems using advanced communications and distributed data processing technologies to improve the ability to conduct air operations have some compelling advantages, they might be offset by equally compelling drawbacks related to resistance by senior officers, vulnerability of the operation, operational efficiency, remote leadership, and intelligence produced in the theater.

Reservations of Senior Officers

Because poor decisions in war can have catastrophic consequences, military commanders are trained to be cautious and averse to risk.[39] Thus, it is not surprising that they might question the wisdom of dividing the JAOC's resources by physically separating the two segments of the operation and locating one in the United States. Further, senior officers undoubtedly understand that placing the reachback garrison in the United States would reduce their ability to conduct autonomous operations.

For thousands of years, military commanders have resisted political direction from their capitals. In 168 B.C., Lucius Aemilius Paulus, the consul in charge of the Macedonia campaign, warned the citizens of Rome that: "Generals should receive advice . . . from those who are on the scene of action, who see the terrain, the enemy, the fitness of the occasion, who are sharers in the danger."[40]

Today, military commanders believe that direction from Washington is counterproductive, and, in this respect, the Persian Gulf War was no exception. Following the public relations disaster when hundreds of civilians in the Al Firdos bunker were killed, Gen. Colin Powell's pressure to stop the bombing of Baghdad influenced the conduct of the air campaign and caused resentment within the Air Force.[41]

The concern of military commanders is that they are losing control. The "principle that Washington should . . . leave the details up to the theater commander" is sacrosanct.[42] Admittedly, a reachback system at a garrison increases the risk that policymakers in Washington might give military commanders more help than they need. The U.S. military operates on the principle that experienced military commanders use their initiative to react to unforeseen circumstances and capitalize on fleeting opportunities, which political or military leaders in Washington cannot hope to achieve. For example, the U-2 ground station high-lighted the fact that theater commanders are unwilling to depend on assets that are not within the theater and thus beyond their control. This does not mean that losing control of the reachback garrison is inevitable, especially if the JFACC operates the garrison, but military commanders will be skeptical.

Locating these garrisons far from Washington would lessen the opportunities for political authorities to provide unsolicited direction. Although military commanders might believe that reachback systems encourage unwelcome "help" from Washington, their concerns might disappear after several exercises and a major theater war were conducted without advice from Washington. Even though the prospect of political control influences the argument that reachback garrisons should not be located in or near Washington, a critical operational reason is apparent—Washington's coastal location provides less warning time for a cruise missile or ballistic missile attack than locations in the middle of the country provide.

Communication Vulnerabilities

A prominent reaction among military commanders is that reachback operations can succeed only if there are secure and reliable communications. Reachback operations and all aspects of modern warfare depend on robust, reliable communication systems, but there cannot be absolute guarantees that communications will survive. The reality is that communications systems are plagued with vulnerabilities, including such natural phenomena as sunspots and lightning, as well as enemy actions ranging from selective jamming techniques to the indiscriminate electromagnetic pulse from a nuclear detonation. All of these can disrupt communications links, ground stations, and data being transmitted.

A related concern is the available bandwidth, or the range of frequencies that can be transmitted.[43] Recent technological developments have vastly increased the bandwidth that was available during the Persian Gulf War. Data transmission speeds approaching 23 million bits per second have been available since 1997, and the local area network for the CTAPS transmits data at 10 million bits per second.[44] Although existing communications technologies can handle a reachback system, the tendency is for additional capacity in a communications channel to be used until that channel is saturated.

U.S. communications systems use numerous features to ensure that systems remain connected and reduce vulnerabilities, including distributed and redundant links, jam-resistant frequencies, spread-spectrum signal hiding, automated frequency hopping, error-correcting data encoding, encryption, ground station security, and other techniques.[45] Also, new technologies, such as the Global

Broadcast Service, are likely to ensure robust communications between the United States and the theater. If communications between the garrison and the theater were disrupted, the JAOC must be designed so that its deployed component would have sufficient computational power to plan and execute air campaigns, albeit at reduced capacity. Uninterrupted communications between a garrison and theater cannot be absolutely guaranteed, but safeguards exist for minimizing this vulnerability.

Establishing a reachback system would require additional communications systems that electronically link the garrison and deployed segment, including video teleconferencing to connect the commander with the garrison and to link workstation operators as substitutes for face-to-face interactions. The deployed and garrisoned units would need additional liaison officers to coordinate operations between the two locations, especially in the case of simultaneous contingencies or exercises.[46] It is likely that total manpower would increase by 10 percent to 20 percent, most of which would occur in the garrisoned staff.[47] Although geographic separation of the planning system into two components would increase its opportunities for survival, deployment, and support, the separation would not improve its operation. This loss of efficiency must be acknowledged as a drawback to reachback operations.

Challenges of Remote Leadership for Garrisoned Personnel

The commander would have little face-to-face interaction with the garrison's staff during hostilities because the commander and the airmen in theater would have the greatest need for the commander's presence. In addition, because military personnel generally prefer combat assignments, those who are assigned to a garrison could believe that their positions are less responsible and that their contemporaries in the theater will gain the combat experience that leads to better jobs and promotions. If highly qualified individuals from the fighting commands shun garrison assignments, the morale and performance of the military staff at the garrison could suffer.

To ensure the effectiveness of garrison personnel, senior military officers must be highly attuned to leadership and morale. The air commander and subordinate commanders can minimize these problems by extensive personal contact with the garrisoned detachment during peacetime. During deployment, the commander could use video teleconferencing technology to communicate with the garrison and to provide the personal interaction that is necessary to maintain morale. Historically, personnel in the United States have supported overseas combat operations to the utmost of their abilities, as seen by the assistance provided by the Tactical Air Command at Langley Air Force Base, Virginia, to General Horner during the Persian Gulf War.[48]

It is equally critical for the commander to counter the perception that the garrison is a backwater assignment by assuring the garrison staff that they are critical to any war effort. In addition, the military should see that duty in reachback garrisons counts toward the critical joint tours that enhance its officers' professional capabilities. By emphasizing that the garrison is a key component of U.S. military capabilities, the commander and other senior officers can minimize the morale and performance problems that might result from placing the garrison in the United States.

Lack of Theater-Produced Intelligence

The Persian Gulf War demonstrated that satellites do not produce all of the intelligence information and that critical intelligence often is produced in the theater by numerous sources, including pilot reports, gun camera film, infrared imagery, synthetic aperture radar, and the traditional photography and electronic intercepts from intelligence, surveillance, and reconnaissance platforms. In recent years, the value of human intelligence, including prisoner of war interrogations and reports from agents in the theater, has been as important as technical intelligence systems.[49]

Obviously, the intelligence produced in the theater must be available to the intelligence analysts and those responsible for targeting and assigning weapons in the reachback garrison. Separating the garrison from the theater will complicate the ability to assimilate theater-produced intelligence because the analysts, interrogators, and other intelligence specialists in the theater could not directly discuss this information with their counterparts in the United States. The ability to use theater-produced intelligence can be solved, however, if the theater digitizes data and sends the information to the garrison. Just as the garrison must send data to the theater, the garrison must receive all of the intelligence information produced in the theater. Transmittal of intelligence is especially important in order to lessen the security consequences should the deployed unit be attacked or evacuated. If it were necessary to evacuate the unit in the field, personnel in the deployed segment could erase the electronic data stored in the jaoc with a few emergency software commands and feel secure in the knowledge that the garrison has a complete backup.

Technology also could minimize the problems of physically separating members of the intelligence team. Video teleconferencing could reduce the barriers to interacting with the analysts and specialists in the theater who produce intelligence data. As the day crew in the theater interacts with the night crew in the garrison, productive work can be accomplished with some thoughtful scheduling. But, to be effective, data from the theater must be shipped to the United

States and data from national sources must be shipped to the theater. Neither task is an insurmountable problem in view of the capabilities of modern communications systems.

In summary, many of the difficulties with reachback operations are the product of human, rather than technological, shortcomings. The challenges are not overwhelming, but they must be addressed if the U.S. military is to be successful in implementing a reachback system.

Conclusion

The Persian Gulf War was significant because it demonstrated that technological innovation could change how the U.S. military plans and executes modern air wars. It showed that joint air campaigns are feasible, that airpower provides a powerful tool for decimating an enemy's military capabilities, and that synchronization of massive and prolonged air campaigns cannot be managed with "paper charts and grease pencils." The commanders of future air campaigns are likely to use sophisticated computer tools, advanced communications, and distributed data processing to manage air campaigns. These forms of technological innovation could allow the United States to take the first step toward the ability to fight wars from the relative security of its homeland.

Although there always will be compelling reasons for military commanders and their staffs to deploy to the theater to fight an air war, reachback systems could allow the U.S. military to keep most of its air campaign planning personnel and equipment at home or in protected rear areas. This is particularly important at a time when more states possess the ballistic missiles and cruise missiles that could attack such facilities. The revolution will be complete when the military links equipment and personnel to the theater without sacrificing combat effectiveness. Several disadvantages to reachback operations exist, but none of them reverses the ability of technology to allow military forces to plan many aspects of operations from the relative security of the homeland. Ultimately, reachback operations could alter how the United States and other nations use military force during the twenty-first century.

Notes

1. Williamson Murray, *Air War in the Persian Gulf* (Baltimore, Md.: Nautical & Aviation Publishing Company, 1995), 12, 41.
2. Alan D. Campen, *Information War* (Fairfax, Va.: AFCEA International Press, 1992), 33; David R. Stinson, "Improved Air Campaign Planning through Cyber-

netics and Situation Control," paper presented at Mershon Center Program for International Security and Military Affairs, Ohio State University, May 1995, 7. See also Nick Cook, "USA Plots Mission Support Revolution," *Jane's Defence Weekly* (Nov. 19, 1994), 29.

3. Thomas R. Gorman, Training Program Director, U.S. Air Force Air Ground Operations School, Hurlburt Field, Fla., communication to author, Mar. 5, 1997.

4. Stephen B. Croker, interviews by author, Feb. 20–21, 1997.

5. Carl DeFranco of Rome Laboratory, in conjunction with the Defense Advanced Research Projects Agency, is developing a system that employs a distributed data processing version of CTAPS. This system is called the Distributed Air Operations Center.

6. Stephen J. McNamara, *Air Power's Gordian Knot—Centralized versus Organic Control* (Maxwell Air Force Base, Ala.: Air University Press, 1994), 7–19.

7. Thomas R. Gorman, interview by author, January 1997. The term *tool* refers to a software program and its associated hardware, such as the Sun Microsystems SUN SPARC workstations that CTAPS typically uses. Also, Carl H. Steiling, Theater Battle Management Core Systems Program Manager, communication to author, Feb. 24, 1997.

8. Gorman, communication.

9. *Command and Control for Joint Air Operations, Joint Publication 3-56.1* (Washington, D.C.: Joint Chiefs of Staff, Nov. 15, 1994), IV-6–IV-11.

10. Gorman, communication.

11. U.S. Air Force Air Ground Operations School, *FY97 Multimedia CD-ROM,* December 1996.

12. Charles A. Fowler, "The Standoff Observation of Enemy Ground Forces from Project Peek to Joint STARS: A Prolusion," prepublication draft, n.d., 17.

13. Murray, *Air War in Persian Gulf,* 252–53.

14. Carl DeFranco, Rome Laboratory, Rome, N.Y., interview by author, Oct. 22, 1996. In addition to other shortcomings, CTAPS depends on a lengthy air tasking cycle. The Defense Advanced Research Projects Agency (DARPA) program, "JFACC after Next," is exploring the feasibility of real-time, continuous ATO generation, as well as designing a geographically distributed data processing version of CTAPS. in conjunction with Rome Laboratory, Air Combat Command, and other organizations.

15. U.S. Air Force [hereafter USAF] Scientific Advisory Board, *Vision of Aerospace Command and Control for the 21st Century,* SAB-TR-96-02ES, Nov. 26, 1996, http://web.fie.com/htdoc/fed/afr/sab/any/text/any/sabvis.htm, 5.

16. Thomas A. Keaney and Eliot A. Cohen, *Gulf War Air Power Survey Summary Report* (Washington, D.C.: Government Printing Office, 1993), 4.

17. William Hoge, Director, Shaw Air Force Base, N.C., paper presented at Joint Air Operations Senior Staff Course, Jan. 7–10, 1997.

18. Chairman of the Joint Chiefs of Staff, *National Military Strategy of the United States of America* (Washington, D.C.: Joint Chiefs of Staff, 1995), 7.

19. John A. Leide, U.S. Central Command, briefing to senior officers at Electronic Systems Center, Hanscom Air Force Base, Mass., June 12, 1996.

20. Defense Advanced Research Projects Agency, "JFACC Concept: Jump Start to Future," JFACC after Next Program Review briefing, Aug. 14, 1996, 61.

21. Croker, interviews.

22. *Command and Control for Joint Operations,* 8–9.

23. Donald W. McSwain, Naval Ocean Systems Center, San Diego, Calif., lecture presented at the Joint Air Operations Senior Staff Course, Jan. 7–10, 1997.

24. Jeffrey R. Barnett, *Future War: An Assessment of Aerospace Campaigns in 2010* (Maxwell Air Force Base, Ala.: Air University Press, 1996), 65.

25. Office of the President, The White House, "A National Security Strategy of Engagement and Enlargement (Washington, D.C.: Government Printing Office, 1996), 14.

26. Croker, interviews.

27. Leide, briefing.

28. Charles T. Fox, Air War College, Maxwell Air Force Base, Ala., interview by author, Mar. 14, 1997.

29. More precisely, the reduction is between 47 percent and 73 percent, but this notional division of workstations is not sufficiently accurate to provide estimates to the nearest percentage point. The lower bound was calculated by assuming that eighty workstations are equivalent for additional support equipment in the JAOC, whereas the upper bound was based on the assumption that no additional support equipment would be needed.

30. Steiling, communication.

31. Ronald L. Thompson, Deputy Director, U-2 System Program Office, Robins Air Force Base, Ga., interview by author, Mar. 8, 1997.

32. Carl H. Steiling, communication.

33. Although the software must be developed only once, the cost is influenced by facility construction, equipment procurement, and operations and maintenance. Thus, building and operating two garrisons instead of one would generate little or no cost savings.

34. John S. Fairchild, "A Jointly Focused Vision Charting the Course for the 21st Century Air Force," *Armed Forces Journal International,* Jan. 24, 1997, available at http://www.dtic.mil. See also Thomas S. Moorman Jr., "The Challenge of Space Beyond 2000," remarks to the 75th Royal Australian Air Force Anniversary Airpower Conference, Canberra, Australia, June 14, 1996, available at http://www.dtic.mil.

35. USAF Scientific Advisory Board, *Vision of Aerospace Command,* 5.

36. Ibid., 2.

37. This result is derived from the number of C-141 aircraft sorties that are required to fully deploy CTAPS with its current architecture, which includes 146 workstations in addition to the equivalent of 80 workstations worth of additional remote terminals, radar repeaters, and communications equipment. Based on the assump-

tion that the number of sorties varies approximately with the number of workstations and the amount of support equipment, reducing the number of workstations by 107 would save about 19 C-141 sorties to the theater.

38. Croker, interview.
39. Richard A. Stubbing with Richard A. Mendel, *The Defense Game* (New York: Harper and Row, 1986), 110.
40. Quoted in Alfred C. Schlesinger, trans., *Livy,* vol. 13 (Cambridge, Mass.: Harvard University Press, 1951), 161–63. Following is the entire passage that is instructive of Paulus's point: "In all the clubs and even—God save us!—at dinner tables there are experts who lead armies to Macedonia, who know where camp should be pitched, what places should be held with garrisons, when or by what pass Macedonia should be invaded, where granaries should be set up, by what routes on land or sea provisions should be supplied, when we must join battle with the enemy and when it is better to remain inactive. Not only do they decide what should be done, but when anything is done contrary to their opinion, they accuse the consul as if he were in the dock. Such behavior is a great obstacle to the men in the field. For not everyone is as unwavering and as steadfast of spirit against hostile gossip as was Quintus Fabius, who preferred to have his independence of command lessened by popular folly rather than to neglect the best interests of the state for the sake of acclaim. I am not, fellow citizens, one who believes that no advice may be given to leaders; nay rather I judge him to be not a sage, but haughty, who conducts everything according to his own opinion alone. What therefore is my conclusion? Generals should receive advice, in the first place from the experts who are both specially skilled in military matters and have learned from experience; secondly, from those who are on the scene of action, who see the terrain, the enemy, the fitness of the occasion, who are sharers in the danger, as it were aboard the same vessel. Thus, if there is anyone who is confident that he can advise me as to the best advantage of the state in this campaign which I am about to conduct, let him not refuse his services to the state, but come with me into Macedonia. I will furnish him with his sea-passage, with a horse, a tent, and even travel-funds. If anyone is reluctant to do this and prefers the leisure of the city to the hardships of campaigning, let him not steer the ship from on shore. The city [Rome] itself provides enough subjects for conversation; let him confine his garrulity to these; and let him be aware that I shall be satisfied with the advice originating in camp."
41. Michael R. Gordon and Bernard E. Trainor, *The Generals' War* (Boston: Little, Brown, 1995), 326.
42. Ibid.
43. The larger the bandwidth, the greater the maximum transmission speed that the communication channel can support.
44. Fairchild, "Jointly Focused Vision."
45. Bruce M. DeBlois, School of Advanced Airpower Studies, Maxwell Air Force Base, Ala., communication to author, Feb. 24, 1997.

46. If real-world contingencies automatically take precedence over exercises, there should not be any resource conflicts between contingencies and exercises.

47. Croker, interview. Because these figures are approximate, the staffing estimates of eight hundred personnel in the garrison and one hundred personnel deployed in the theater have not been adjusted to account for inefficiencies in operations. All estimates illustrate the possible staffing levels for a reachback system until more a detailed concept of operations is created.

48. Ibid.

49. Stansfield Turner, *Secrecy and Democracy: The CIA in Transition* (New York: Harper and Row, 1985), 91.

11.   Computers and Controlling War

William B. Mcclure

The U.S. military's investment in information technology could redefine the identity of the fundamental decision makers in the use of military force. The prospect of computers making significant decisions in war represents a radical departure from current command models that mandate that humans must make the life-or-death decisions in war. As military operations put increasing pressure on commanders to operate at a faster pace, the next step could be reliance on computers to make those decisions. This chapter discusses how the U.S. military might seek to use information superiority in the form of a machine commander to make critical decisions in military operations more quickly and efficiently than humans. Such a step would be a logical extension of existing systems, where, for example, Navy-guided missile cruisers rely on computers and radars to decide when to attack approaching cruise missiles or aircraft.

Introduction

The introduction of advanced technologies into the military, known as the "revolution in military affairs," could significantly change how the United States controls its military forces. If military commanders are to operate more efficiently and at a higher operations tempo, they must use modern technologies to allow machines, notably computers, to make significant command decisions in war. This entity might be viewed as a machine commander. Although current U.S. military doctrine is unclear on the acceptability of this entity, developments in information technology are on the threshold of delivering the components for constructing the first-generation machine commander and using it for making complex command and control decisions.

As a result of remarkable technological progress during the twentieth century, the U.S. military is on the threshold of an era in which humans can control time, long recognized as a critical dimension to warfare. Time is formalized in current U.S. military doctrine through its focus on the pace of military operations, which enables military forces to exploit their own capabilities while preventing the enemy from prevailing in war.[1]

The current U.S. joint military doctrine, known as *Joint Vision 2010,* argues that U.S. military forces will win by fighting and moving at a faster pace, termed *operational tempo*. Speed of action complicates enemy efforts to target forces and permits the U.S. military to seize the initiative.[2] A faster tempo in battle puts pressure on the commander's ability to coordinate and synchronize forces as effectively and efficiently as possible.

For military commanders, increased combat tempo increases the complexity of the battlefield. The integration of weapons, soldiers, sensors, and communications systems hold the promise of revolutionary advances in military effectiveness. Meanwhile, expectations that these same technologies will improve combat efficiency will result in fewer combat systems and personnel, thus raising the value of each weapon and individual. Adversaries are expected to challenge U.S. conventional military strength through asymmetric or disproportionately destructive means, such as weapons of mass destruction. Finally, military commanders could be connected in real time with senior political and military leaders, including the national command authorities, the Joint Chiefs of Staff, or the theater commander in chief, which will expose military commanders to micromanagement of military operations. All of this raises problems for modern military commanders who must operate at a rapid tempo to retain the initiative.[3]

One casualty of this technological revolution could be the U.S. military's model for command. Historically, the pace of war allowed the commander, with assistance from the staff, to gather and process the information that is necessary to develop and execute command decisions. Although the speed of mental and organizational activity did not substantially constrain the conduct of war, the speed, range, lethality, and tempo of future combat might significantly shorten the commander's time to make decisions. In essence, the speed of the decision cycle could outpace the ability of the human brain to absorb information and to make decisions.[4]

The amount of information that the human mind can receive, process, remember, and act upon is quite limited.[5] The human brain can scan about seven words per second and process this information at a rate of about one symbol ("bit") every twenty-five milliseconds. Although there are advantages to collecting and organizing a large amount of information, more time is required to process that information. These constraints on the information "bandwidth" of the human mind impose a fundamental limit on a human's ability to guide events in war. Put differently, the tempo of battle could exceed the ability of commanders to make timely decisions in war (also known as "operating inside the commander's observe, orient, decide, act [OODA] cycle").[6]

While the U.S. military doctrine emphasizes access to a great amount of information, the same volume could result in paralyzing information overload. The corollary is that modernizing the command and control infrastructure could threaten the ability of the human commander to make decisions and to conduct military operations in high-tempo wars. For this reason, the U.S. military is looking to take advantage of military and commercial investments in information technology to supplement the overloaded human commander with machine-based decision-making systems. In principle, machines would make and execute some military decisions in ways that were once reserved to humans, thus freeing human commanders to focus on the most critical aspects of war.

The accelerating pace of technological progress in computers and information systems, when combined with the resources being invested, suggests that the time might be approaching when the defense industry could build a *machina sapiens,* or thinking machine, for the military.[7] If the U.S. military leadership is to make prudent decisions about this technological possibility, it is imperative that it consider competing arguments about the proper role of *machina sapiens* in warfare.[8] Under the assumption that it is technologically feasible for the military to build a machine commander, the United States could do so within a decade or two. Although this technology has benefits for military command and control, the broader argument is its larger effect on the U.S. military and society. Following a brief review of the history of the relevant aspects of command and control, this chapter examines a military decision cycle and its relationship to a machine commander. It concludes with thoughts on how political and military authorities could approach the role of a machine commander in war.

Background

As a general principle, military commanders achieve their objectives by exercising command over people and resources. This circular relationship between command and the commander is reflected in Joint Publication 1-02, which states that "[Command is] the authority that a commander in the Armed Forces lawfully exercises over subordinates by virtue of rank or assignment. Command includes the authority and responsibility for effectively using available resources and for planning the employment of organizing, directing, coordinating, and controlling military forces for the accomplishment of assigned missions. It also includes responsibility for health, welfare, morale, and discipline of assigned personnel."[9] The commander's goal and basis for authority rest on unity of effort, which is the foundation for the synchronized, effective, and efficient use of military power. The primary function of the commander is the ability and authority to make and execute decisions in war.

When a commander's span of control is confined to an immediate geographic area, command can be executed by issuing verbal orders directly to soldiers. Known as command by direction, it represents "the commander's dream . . . of direct[ing] dynamically all of the forces all of the time," and centers all responsibility and authority in one individual.[10] Because the commander is located in the same area as the troops and uses the same sensors as these troops, the commander is the focal point for acquiring and fusing information.

As new weapons, communication technologies, and military doctrines increase the geographic span of control, command by direction is increasingly impractical. In response, commanders have introduced command by plan, a form of scripting war based on the assumption that the commander understands the salient features of the battlefield and creates a vision of how events will unfold before the battle begins. Its execution requires strictly disciplined soldiers who adhere to the plan because, even if the fog of war weakens their ability to understand events, they are confident in the commander's abilities. Once the script is written, however, the commander cannot readily adjust it to the changes on the battlefield that result from unforeseen acts of nature or enemy actions.

An integral part of command by plan is the staff, who help the commander to acquire and process information, to develop courses of action, and to communicate the commander's orders to units in the field. Because the commander no longer is the focal point for information, data must be captured and consolidated to help the commander understand how the battle will develop.[11] Through such efforts, the staff seek to assist the commander develop what von Clausewitz referred to as coup d'oeil—the inward eye, "the quick recognition of a truth that the mind would ordinarily miss or would perceive only after long study and reflection."[12] As a result of the growing complexity and speed of events in twentieth-first century warfare, command by direction is increasingly inadequate.

One way to solve the problem of maintaining unity of effort toward the commander's objective, while simultaneously remaining responsive to the uncertainties and rapidly changing face of battle, is termed *command by influence*. Through this approach to command, which is applied through the use of *auftragstaktik* (mission-type orders), combat objectives are defined at the minimal level of detail, and the commander expects lower echelons of command to use their knowledge of immediate battlefield conditions to adapt their operations to meet the commander's intent. This approach found initial notoriety in German military operations during World War I.[13] Command by intent and its implications for decentralized control are useful when resources are abundant, speed is important, and failures of individual units do not threaten the success of the strategy. This is the preferred method of command for modern military leaders, particularly for the U.S. Army and Marine Corps, which depend heavily on the traditional roles and capabilities of the soldier. The introduction of twenty-first century information technologies and the growing dependence of the U.S. military on information, however, will change the philosophy of command.

The end of the Cold War has resulted in public and political pressure on the military to provide for the national defense in a more economical manner.[14] As U.S. military forces shrink in size, it is unlikely that the conditions and resources that favored command by intent will endure. To compensate for its smaller force, the U.S. military expects to retain its combat power by enhancing its awareness of events on the battlefield. Not surprisingly, these developments could increase the commander's reliance on command and control technologies for three reasons. First, the loss of overwhelming advantage in combat forces will limit a commander's ability to exploit opportunities. Second, with less information about enemy actions and intentions, the commander is more vulnerable to catastrophic losses in battle. Finally, fewer forces translate into fewer options for the commander, which increase the chance that the fast pace of battle will strain the commander's ability to make the right decisions.[15]

These pressures on command and control suggest a return to command by direction. Unlike previous applications of this approach to command, the modern commander's span of control will significantly expand, which will creates two fundamental problems for the commander. First, the ability to gain access to so much information could tempt the commander regularly to direct tactical operations, rather than to develop and execute an overall strategy and allow subordinates to make lower-level decisions. Second, the sheer quantity of information and speed with which it is available could exceed the commander's ability to absorb all of the information and act on it. The rule of thumb, that a good commander can make consistently appropriate decisions with 80 percent of the necessary information, might have to be dramatically revised. If these problems inhibit the commander's ability to control the tempo in battle, it is inevitable that the military will turn to technology for assistance.

Technology and Command

Technological innovation, a fundamental force in American society, represents the fulcrum of American economic and military power. One observer described

America's fascination and growing dependence on technology as the "ratchet of progress."[16] This technological dependence applies to all U.S. military services. Technology has been described as the U.S. Air Force's "altar of worship," as evident from the Wright Flyer, SR-71 aircraft, the airborne laser, and F-22 aircraft.[17]

The U.S. Navy's dependence on technology is evident from its nuclear submarines, aircraft carriers, and Aegis guided-missile cruisers. Some of the Navy's most far-reaching doctrinal changes involve movement toward "network centric warfare," which seeks to use information to improve its support of combat operations. By linking sensors and communication systems, the commander will be able to rely on automation to increase the speed of decision making in war.[18] The Army, which is imbued with the culture of the solitary, minimally armed soldier, is using technology to create and field lighter, more lethal "strike forces."[19]

Enabling Technologies

This affinity for technology is leading the military toward technological solutions that could help military commanders to increase their span of command and control without sacrificing the ability to operate at a faster pace. Technological advances in hardware, software, and communication systems could lead to the development of the machine commander. These developments are analogs of the commander's brain, mind, and nervous system.

It is essential to create central processing units that are fast enough to form the basis for the machine commander's brain. Currently, the Department of Energy, through its accelerated strategic computing initiative, is sponsoring the development of supercomputers that have demonstrated the ability to execute several trillions of operations per second (teraflops), which is about 15,000 times faster than state-of-the-art personal computers.[20] It is likely that further developments will produce processors that can store trillions of bytes and execute thousands of teraflops. It is also likely that computer technologies will continue to be miniaturized, thus reducing cost and support requirements.

If the processor is equivalent to the physical brain of the machine commander, its "mind," or the logic on which its decisions are based, is derived from the software that drives it. A variety of activities could provide the basis for this "mind." An important source is combat modeling and simulation. The Department of Defense is developing a number of models to represent land, sea, and air warfare that will help to train military forces, select new weapons, and evaluate military tactics. These models are exercised regularly during service and joint war games and reviews of U.S. military forces, during which military leaders become more familiar with model strengths and weaknesses.

The Department of Defense requires that the models and simulations use a common technical framework that will allow individual modules to be reused in other models.[21] These plug-and-play modules will make it possible to build and update the "mind" of the machine commander to keep pace with how humans understand decision making, technology, and doctrine.

Another potential source for shaping the "mind" of the machine commander is the automated planning tools that are being integrated into military operational units. As described in Chapter 10, the Contingency Theater Automated Planning System (CTAPS) produces the air tasking orders for air campaigns. Its successor, under development by the Defense Advanced Research Projects Agency's (DARPA's) Joint Forces Air Component Command Program, will use computer technologies to help the air component commander plan and operate at a faster pace. With the ability to plan military strikes within minutes of changes in the tactical situation, this technology will inform the commander about how new missions relate to one another, to the overall air campaign, and to the entire theater strategy. The Army demonstrated the value of automated planning aides during operational experiments conducted in 1995.[22]

The final technological component is the communications network that links the commander, sensors, and shooters to form the "nervous system" of the machine commander. Many of the systems in the network are already fielded or in development and will function across the military services. For tactical systems, the Joint Tactical Information Distribution System provides jam-resistant communications, navigation, and identification to coordinate the surveillance, identification, and use of weapons in military operations.[23] At the theater level, the Global Command and Control System provides an integrated picture of imagery, intelligence, military forces, and planning information.[24] When combined, these systems will give the human or machine commander a remarkably detailed, real-time picture of military operations on the battlefield.

For the machine commander to perform effectively, its decisions must be made rapidly, must be based on timely and complete information, and must be communicated with sufficient speed and detail to maintain the initiative during fast-paced operations. The U.S. military is increasing its dependence on satellites as a way to provide "communications on the move" to commanders. One problem with using satellites to communicate these decisions, however, is the information delay, termed *latency,* that is a function of the distance between transmitter and receiver. For communication satellites in geosynchronous orbits (popular because of their "fixed" appearance relative to the ground), round-trip signal times are about 240 milliseconds, whereas satellites in low-earth orbit (advantageous for lower transmission power) produce delays of about 5 milliseconds.[25] The magnitude of this delay directly impacts the rate at which information can be passed. A Navy study found that combat ships need a minimum data transmission rate of 128 kilobits per second to satisfy this requirement.[26] Current systems provide half this rate, whereas the Global Broadcast System will operate two hundred times faster. The challenge is to increase the quantity of information available to commanders during a military operation while minimizing the time delay, which is essential if commanders are to have timely access to information about conditions on the battlefield.

Existing Computer Commanders

The reality is that computers have acted in a command advisory role for some time. During the mid-1980s, DARPA sponsored programs that applied artificial intelligence to command and control functions. The Navy's machine intelligence program, as the Naval Battle Management Applications Program, was designed to compress the time for making decisions.[27] A program for the Air Force used artificial intelligence at the tactical level through a "pilot's associate" to give fighter pilots better situational awareness and to manage the pilots' workloads.[28]

There are several examples of fielded or soon-to-be fielded weapon systems that exhibit the automatic control functions or precursor capabilities associated with the machine commander. The Navy deployed the Phalanx Close-In Weapon System in 1979 to defend against antiship missiles. The Phalanx is a self-contained package that "automatically carries out search, detection, target threat evaluation, tracking, firing and kill assessment."[29] It generally uses the anti–air warfare automode when a ship is at general quarters.[30] Although human operators can override this mode, the Phalanx reacts so quickly that human intervention is meaningless in most tactical situations and could worsen the outcome.

The Army's Patriot air-defense guided-missile system is a self-contained sensor-to-shooter system that depends on an automatic, computer-controlled operation. Patriot was given this capability to enable it to handle the high-density threat that was anticipated on the Western European battlefield of the 1980s. Even today, Army doctrine calls for using the automatic mode in theater missile defense.[31]

The Air Force's airborne laser, which will use a high-energy laser to destroy theater ballistic missiles in the boost phase, will rely on computers to handle missile intercepts. Human intervention will occur only in exceptional cases. This level of automation is necessary because the system must sort and kill ballistic missiles within seconds, particularly if missiles are launched in tightly spaced salvos. Humans simply cannot make decisions fast enough to control this process.

Control of Machine Commanders

The challenge for machine commanders is to make and execute good decisions about the use of lethal force. To accomplish this function, the machine will be controlled by two sources. The first source is an internal governor that will keep the machine commander from consuming excessive resources, corrupting communications and degrading networks, or creating unnecessary vulnerabilities. To help automated command and control "agents" support the human commander, DARPA is researching an agent-based system control that could form the basis for the machine commander's "inner ear" to ensure that it maintains a sense of equilibrium.[32]

The second, and ultimate, source of control is a human supervisor who operates the kill switch. Inevitably, there will be times when humans will want to interrupt the machine commander and take control before the system reaches the "point of no return" in executing bad decisions. Although keeping humans in the loop makes the machine commander more vulnerable to enemy attack, preserving final human authority is essential if a machine commander is to gain wide acceptance in American society, as well as among political and military leaders.

The value of machine commanders is recognized in U.S. joint military doctrine.[33] Beyond integrating the reams of information that will be available in the modern battlefield without sacrificing control of the speed of military operations, the machine commander offers at least two other advantages over the human commander. First, because the components of the machine commander are built to design, it is reproducible, which means that the machine commander could be cloned. Second, because senior military officers would repeatedly exercise and evaluate the machine commander through war games and simulations, humans could retrain its "mind" to account for emerging technologies and doctrines in warfare.

Synthesis of Man and Machine

A radical alternative to alleviating the information and decision-making overload on human commanders is to merge man and machine. According to an Air Force study, a machine commander would help the commander to understand the nature of the military action, calculate the probabilities of success for various lethal or nonlethal options, recommend the best course of action, execute that option, and provide timely feedback on its results. Extending this concept further might mean implanting a microchip in the human commander to feed computer-generated mental images directly into the brain.[34] There are, however, profound social and ethical implications of technologies that synthesize humans and machines.

Limitations and Potential Problems

The history of military technology is littered with examples in which technology failed to deliver the capabilities that would penetrate Clausewitz's fog of war.[35] Although technological advances could make the concept of a machine commander a reality, this machine will have at least three technological limitations.

First, there are questions of whether it is possible to build the software that allows the machine commander to make rational decisions consistently during complex and fast-paced military operations. Humans do not fundamentally understand how they make decisions or how to escape the limitations of combat models that are governed by "linear" or "Newtonian" laws of war. These models do not capture warfare's nonlinear and chaotic nature. Second, it is difficult to estimate the problems that noise, jamming, delays, and saturation associated with the supporting communications system might have for the machine commander. Third, there is the problem of developing systems that will ensure that U.S. military forces can operate with coalition partners, particularly when American technology continues to outpace that of its allies. These technological issues represent significant concerns, but they do not constitute fundamental barriers to the development of the computer technologies that can help humans to make critical decisions in war.

Organizations, Information Overload, and Tempo

The current approach to adapting technologies to modern warfare is to change the existing staff model, which involves shifting from traditional and hierarchical military command structures to less hierarchical organizations.[36] It stresses the philosophy of command by influence, which means that some critical battlefield information cannot be communicated to and acted upon by the higher levels of command because of the rapid and urgent character of events.

The fundamental goal of a technological organization is to transmit information as rapidly as possible to those who need it, which, in combat, are tactical units on the battlefield. The ability to link military units with commanders and each other through a massively parallel organization would accelerate command by eliminating intermediate levels of command and reducing the size of staffs.[37] Another alternative is to develop an organization that has two concurrent, layered decision cycles, in which one focuses on planning while the other concentrates on execution. In this model, the commander controls the slower planning loop.[38]

The close coordination of military operations, which was previously achieved through a rigid, centralized command and control system, now occurs when adaptive and innovative commanders understand the theater commander's intent.[39] These commanders form a collective system that uses the speed of machines with human ingenuity to produce victory in war. The problem, however, is that this organization sacrifices unity of command and economy of force, which are critical when combat resources are scarce. For example, experiments with flat command structures have shown that troops are more likely to expend valuable resources, such as precision-guided munitions, at excessive rates when higher levels of command did not closely manage their assets. The fact is that using technology to improve troop awareness of events on the battlefield might not necessarily produce an optimal strategy.[40]

Human Elements of Command

Ultimately, a machine commander would challenge the role and nature of human command in war. This underlying principle is reflected in the *U.S. Army Field Manual 100-5, Operations,* which says that "command remains an expression of human will embodied in the commander charged to accomplish the mission."[41] The unique human roles and responsibilities of the military commander would be challenged on several levels by the development of machines that control military operations.

Responsibility

Although it is technically feasible to transfer authority to machines, this concept is distinct from machines assuming responsibility for their actions, most particularly the loss of human lives. For now, it is unlikely that the American people or the political leadership would willingly accept casualties that are the product of decisions made by a machine commander, even if those decisions were correct or if human commanders would have made the same, or possibly worse, decisions. This intractable problem has profound implications as American society begins to debate the wisdom of allowing machines to make life-and-death decisions in war.

Legal Authority

A related problem is the legal basis on which the military commander exercises authority.[42] By law, the combatant commander "is responsible to the President and to the Secretary of Defense for the performance of missions assigned to that command by the President or by the Secretary with the approval of the President, employing forces within that command as he considers necessary to carry out missions assigned to the command; (and) assigning command functions to subordinate commanders."[43] Below the combatant commanders, command authority passes to the lower echelon that "normally provides full authority to organize commands and forces and to employ those forces as the commander in control considers necessary to accomplish assigned missions."[44] Despite these legal definitions, no serious thought has been devoted to the legal implications if commandlike functions are exercised by machines. Considerable attention to these implications would be required, however, before machines could be given even limited control over combat operations.

Creativity

Creativity distinguishes humans from the rest of the animal kingdom and machines because humans can deal with events for which there is no previous experience. They extend their expertise by learning, by using analogies to similar problems, or, when the situation warrants it and the resources are available, by seeking assistance from experts.[45] The advantage of human creativity is that the commander can adapt to new and unexpected events on the battlefield.

By its nature, creativity is directly tied to human physiology because humans subconsciously understand what their senses tell them about the environment and know how to use these senses to interpret and interact with reality. Although military technology uses mechanical devices to augment human senses, the ability of humans to integrate information fully in creative ways is limited. If humans cannot explain precisely how sensory data are interpreted and fused into creative human decisions, it will be difficult for them to build machines that can mimic these processes.[46]

Empathy

A fundamental characteristic of human commanders is their ability to forge relationships with soldiers. For example, the Army views command as the product of decision making and leadership, which include loyalty to the troops and building the esprit de corps that transforms a group of individuals into a team focused on achieving success despite profound physical and emotional challenges. Leadership is the ability to take charge, to set an example, and to provide a clear vision that others will follow to the point of defending it with their lives. Because many of these leadership precepts require an understanding of the nebulous quantity known as *human nature,* command is more equivalent to an art than to science.[47]

Command requires the ability to understand the physical and emotional conditions of the troops and to deduce from their voices and eyes the difference between confidence and bravado or fear and fatigue. Fully understanding the conditions in combat, including the readiness of the troops and their lower-echelon commanders, requires much more than written reports or video teleconferences.[48] The fundamental challenge is whether machines, which currently are challenged by voice-recognition tasks in the office, could assess the nuances of human communication that help commanders to understand the battlespace and to fight effectively within it.

Although personal contact is essential to the current generation of military commanders, technology could conceivably change the expectations of future generations of military commanders who might be more comfortable with technology than were their predecessors. The trust and faith fostered in the past through the human commander's rapport with the troops and forged from shared experiences might be replaced with a trust in the ability of machines to make good decisions that is based on a lifetime of interaction with machines.

This discussion should not lead to the conclusion that human military commanders are without limitations. The most important human limitations are the physiological constraints that affect the response time of humans, especially when they are under stress. Although these limitations can be minimized through physical and emotional conditioning, human endurance will continue to have limits. In addition, human commanders are governed by cycles ranging from the hours or days that match the body's need for rest to the months or years associated with tours of command. If physical and emotional conditions are not monitored, human commanders are vulnerable to making bad decisions, especially in times of great stress.

The Necessity for Machines

If military command and control are viewed in terms of decision cycles, it could be progressively more difficult for human commanders to make decisions in the increasingly chaotic, fast-paced, and nonlinear conditions of future war. The abundant information and greater number of options that are available to commanders, such as weapon options alone, could lengthen the time that it takes them to make decisions and to achieve military objectives. For this reason, a decision-cycle model helps military commanders and political officials to understand how automated decision making might be the logical step in the evolution of military command.

This concept of automated command has implications for understanding the role of chaos in war. Chaos is *not* synonymous with chance or randomness. Chaotic systems are bounded and ordered, and their complexity can be understood in terms of many possible outcomes. With more decision points, the number of possible futures increases. The commander must recognize, understand, and take advantage of these possibilities in order to select the course of action that can best achieve the objective. The great military commanders of history, including Napoleon Bonaparte, German Gen. Erwin Rommel, and U.S. Gen.

George S. Patton, exemplify those who could perform this function better than their contemporary opponents.[49]

In contrast with chaos, randomness is a measure of disorder whose effects are expressed and measured by the laws of probability and statistics. Together with chaos, chance reduces the commander's certainty that actions taken to achieve the military objective will succeed. Unlike the order hidden in chaos, however, chance does not permit the commander to understand what is happening on the battlefield.

A critical influence on to military operations is the rate at which commanders make decisions. This decision cycle consists of the activities by which the commander senses, decides, and acts. An important aspect is the time that it takes to complete this cycle, which is known as the commander's characteristic time. (This time also can be thought of as a response or reaction time.) The impact of this time on battlefield outcome depends on its relative length compared with the characteristic times of other events and individuals who can influence the battlespace. Characteristic times can be explicit quantities, such as the time required for a commander to develop a thought, or derived quantities, such as the time that it takes smoke to cross a battlefield. A commander whose characteristic time is less than the opponent's has the ability to react more rapidly than the opponent and thus improve the chances of controlling events on the battlefield.

The span of responsibility made possible by long-range sensors and weapons increases the amount of time required to collect, review, and process the available information, which increases a commander's characteristic time. The challenges of absorbing and making sense of this information are exacerbated by stress or fatigue, which impairs the commander's performance and further increases the commander's characteristic time.

The challenge for computer technology is to reduce the commander's characteristic time even in the face of unsurpassable minimum values. For example, psychological studies show that it takes humans a minimum time to make decisions. In addition to human characteristic times for decisions, there is a battlefield characteristic time, which is a function of interactions between military forces. Several examples help to illustrate this characteristic time. One example at the tactical level is the time waiting for radio messages or the time for a platoon to cross territory, and operational examples are the orbit of communications or reconnaissance satellites or the effects of a weather front. Strategically, the battlefield characteristic time can be influenced by seasonal weather conditions and religious holidays, both of which influenced events during the Persian Gulf War.

Recent thinking about this problem suggests that the commander with the smaller characteristic time can work within the opponent's decision cycle and thereby gain a distinct advantage in combat.[50] A commander whose characteristic time is smaller than that of the opposing commander and of the battlespace has a definite advantage. By contrast, when the commander's characteristic time is larger than that of the opponent, warfare will appear to be chaotic. The reason is that when the gap between characteristic times grows sufficiently large, there might appear to be no clear relationship between cause and effect because the commander with the larger characteristic time will find that no action can achieve the desired outcome. This commander will be perplexed and frustrated by an opponent who can act with impunity to achieve the military objectives.

The increased speed of weapons during the last half of the twentieth century, coupled with increased troop and target mobility, has decreased the battlefield characteristic time by several orders of magnitude. Current doctrine and technology produce a battlefield characteristic time of approximately one hour.[51] The implication is that the characteristic times of the commander, opposing commander, and battlefield all interact in ways that influence how quickly decisions are made and ultimately influence the outcome of war.[52]

The key to gaining control at a time when the battlefield characteristic time is decreasing is to counterbalance the inherent limitations of human commanders. One solution might be to increase the role of automation, which introduces a new characteristic time for automatic decisions. The motivation for compressing the time necessary for decisions is to reduce the underlying chaos of war and to increase the ability of the commander to understand the underlying order. If humans cannot understand that order, then they cannot make a "best" decision. The first commander to recognize that order will gain an extraordinary advantage on the battlefield. For machines to make useful decisions in combat, they must be designed to recognize the underlying order in war before humans can do so.

Warfare can be viewed as interactions between entities in the battlespace. Even though these interactions, observed on time scales greater than the characteristic time of the battlefield, appear unrelated or quantitatively unpredictable over short periods of time, entities (including weapons, people, obscurants, electromagnetic pulses, etc.) follow generally understood and generally linear predictable behaviors. It is critical to design the characteristic time of the automated command process to be smaller than these "short periods" and thus to create linear conditions in the battlespace.

Another motivation for compressing the decision cycle time deals with the chaos of warfare and the responsibility of the commander to deduce its underlying order. If there is no perception of order, there can be no "best" decision.

If, on the other hand, there is order, there are significant operational advantages associated with being the first commander to recognize it. The questions are how much data and how much time are required to make such a recognition, and can a machine recognize that order before a human can?

Conclusion

As a result of technological innovation, military units are on the threshold of a revolution in the ability to wage war. If the United States neglects opportunities offered by revolutions in command and control technology, its military could become so confident that it will be blind to radically new approaches to military operations. An important example is the value of automated command.[53] The concept of a machine commander is not new. As early as 1987, during a forum on command and control technology, the U.S. military called for a debate on the role of a machine commander, but more needs to be done.

For now, U.S. command by intent increases the risk that the fast-paced battlefield of the future will be constrained by the capabilities of the human commander. Although humans are prone to information overload in modern war, the load on senior commanders can be mitigated by distributing information, military capabilities, and decision-making authority to junior commanders on the front line. Current U.S. military doctrine reinforces the primacy of the human element in war, but it also suggests that automation can help to manage the accelerating tempo of battle. If this means placing machines in command of weapons or humans, even though we have done so in the past, there will be significant reservations about taking the technological step of giving computers greater authority to make and execute decisions in war. Given these conflicting ideas, the military has three alternatives.

The first alternative is to continue to resist changes in command in the belief that its ability to take advantage of the full benefits of information superiority will be limited. If senior military leaders accept an upper limit on the tempo at which human commanders can operate, they relinquish the initiative to enemy commanders who are willing to accept the risks. The second alternative is to claim that humans always will be in command, while relegating theater-wide planning and execution responsibilities to computers. This approach might appear to resolve the problem, but it would generate numerous doctrinal and operational problems. Third, there could be cases when a machine commander offers the best way to defeat the enemy. The unresolved question is whether machines can receive, interpret, and act on the massive quantities of data generated on the modern battlefield and thereby use military forces in the most effective manner.

The technological foundation for a machine commander exists and is being improved through U.S. investments in information superiority. It is essential for the leaders of the American defense establishment to examine the role and implications of machines in making fundamental decisions about war because the United States is closer to that reality than Americans might realize.

Notes

1. Joint Chiefs of Staff, *Concept for Future Joint Operations,* May 1997, 63–64; Joint Chiefs of Staff, *Joint Doctrine Capstone and Keystone Primer,* July 15, 1997, 33.
2. Joint Chiefs of Staff, *Joint Vision 2010,* 1996, 15. *Joint Vision 2010* is the American military "conceptual template" by which each of the services develops and fields people and technology to produce the world's best joint warfighting force.
3. Andrew F. Krepinevich, "Cavalry to Computer: The Pattern of Military Revolutions," *The National Interest* (fall 1994), 36.
4. Joseph G. Wohl, "Force Management Decision Requirements for Air Force Tactical Command and Control," in *Information and Technology for Command and Control,* eds. Stephen J. Andriole and Stanley M. Halpin (New York: IEEE Press, 1991), 12; Martin van Creveld, *Command in War* (Cambridge, Mass.: Harvard University Press, 1985), 2.
5. George A. Miller, "The Magical Number Seven, Plus or Minus Two: Some Limits on Our Capacity for Processing Information," *The Psychological Review* 63, no. 7 (March 1956), 95. See also Edward O. Wilson, *Consilience: The Unity of Knowledge* (New York; Alfred A. Knopf, 1998), 110–11.
6. A military commander's decision cycle, referred to as an OODA, is frequently attributed to the late Col. John Boyd, USAF. The definitions for each activity, as they appear in the *Joint Doctrine Encyclopedia* (Washington, D.C.: Joint Chiefs of Staff, 1997) are:

   Observe—gather information from the reconnaissance, surveillance, and target acquisition apparatus and from status reports of friendly forces.

   Orient—convert observed information into knowledge of "reality." The "reality" of the operational area is the actual situation in the operational area including, but not limited to, the disposition of forces on both sides, casualties to personnel and equipment suffered by both sides, the weather in the area, and morale on both sides. Since sources of input are imperfect and subject to manipulation by the opposing side, the commander's assessment of "reality" will invariably be something other than the actual "reality" of the operational area.

   Decide—make military decisions based on the assessment of the "reality" of the operational area, and communicate these decisions to subordinate commanders as orders via various communications methods.

Act—through the control of the subordinate commanders, convert these decisions into deeds.

7. One concept is "an intelligent, autonomous, self-aware being that will one day emerge partly out of the efforts of AI works and partly as an evolutionary imperative. . . . A machine with a mind of its own." See Denis Susac, "The Matter of Mind (1)," Dec. 7, 1998, available at http://ai.miningco.com/library/wekly/aa113097.hym.

8. An application of this structure is found in Col. A. Behagg, MBE, "Increasing Tempo on the Modern Battlefield," in *The Science of War: Back to First Principles,* ed. Brian Holden Reid (New York: Routledge, 1993), 110–30.

9. See *Joint Publication 1-02: Department of Defense Dictionary of Military and Associated Terms* (Washington, D.C.: Joint Chiefs of Staff, Mar. 23, 1994), 84.

10. Ideas on command types from Thomas J. Czerwinski, "Command and Control at the Crossroads," *Parameters* (autumn 1996), Oct. 29, 1998, available at http://carlisle-www.army.mil/usawc/Parameters/96autumn/czerwins.htrm. See also van Creveld, *Command in War.*

11. Karl W. Deutsch, *The Nerves of Government* (London: Free Press of Glencoe, 1963), 101–2.

12. Carl von Clausewitz, *On War,* ed. Michael Howard and Peter Paret (Princeton, N.J.; Princeton University Press, 1984), 102.

13. Neil Munro, *The Quick and the Dead* (New York: St. Martin's Press, 1991), 74, states: "By decentralizing battlefield leadership to their trusted stormtroop company, platoon, and squad leaders, the Germans constructed a military organization that achieved battlefield success, and they did so without any significant communications technology."

14. Joint Chiefs of Staff, *Joint Vision 2010,* 8, state: "The American people will continue to expect us to win in any engagement, but they will also expect us to be more efficient in protecting lives and resources while accomplishing the mission successfully. . . . Simply to retain our effectiveness with less redundancy, we will need to wring every ounce of capability from every available source."

15. Raymond C. Bjorklund, *The Dollars and Sense of Command and Control* (Washington, D.C.: National Defense University Press, 1995), 168, notes that "under increased risk, the commander will probably become more willing to trade off lack of assets (a reduction in the number of force assets from where the commander thinks the level should be) for an increased level of C2 [command and control] assets. If the commander has lost force assets in battle or otherwise doesn't have force assets readily available, a greater preference for C2 assets, rather than force assets, is likely, in order to make the best of what is left in the face of adversity."

16. Wilson, *Consilience,* 270, writes that "the more knowledge people acquire, the more they are able to increase their numbers and to alter the environment, whereupon the more they need new knowledge just to stay alive. In a human-dominated world, the natural environment steadily shrinks, offering correspondingly less and

less per capita return in energy and resource. Advanced technology has become the ultimate prosthesis."

17. Carl H. Builder, "Five Faces of the Service Personalities," in Carl H. Builder, *The Masks of War: American Military Styles in Strategy and Analysis* (Baltimore: Johns Hopkins University Press, 1989). According to the U.S. Air Force, "Air power is the result of technology. Man has been able to fight with his hands or simple implements and sail on water using wind or muscle power for millennia, but flight required advanced technology. As a consequence of this immutable fact, air power has enjoyed a synergistic relationship with technology not common to surface forces, and this is part of the airman's culture." See also Phillip S. Meilinger, *10 Propositions Regarding Air Power,* Air Force History and Museums Program, Maxwell Air Force Base, Montgomery, Ala., 1995, 57.

18. Arthur K. Cebrowski and John J. Garstka, "Network-Centric Warfare: Its Origin and Future," *United States Naval Institute Proceedings,* Nov. 24, 1998, available at http://copernicus.hq.navy.mil/divisions/n6/n60/it21/cebrowski.htm.

19. Steven Komarow, "Army Forces to See Major Restructuring," *USA Today,* Feb. 16, 1999, A1.

20. International Business Machines, "ASCI Blue Pacific Fact Sheet," Nov. 11, 1998, available at http://www.rs6000.ibm.com/resource/features/1998/asci_oct /asci_fact.html; "Energy Department, Silicon Graphics Unveil Record-Breaking Supercomputer," Nov. 11, 1998, available at http://www.sgi.com/newsroom/ press_releases/1998/ blue_mountain.html.

21. Department of Defense, "DoD High Level Architecture (HLA)," Feb. 24, 1999, available at http://hla.dmso.mil/hla/.

22. See Thomas A. Dempsey, "Riding the Tiger: Exploiting the Revolution in Military Affairs to Transform the Battlefield," U.S. Army War College, Carlisle Barracks, Pa., 1996, 12, for a discussion of the Prairie Warrior Advanced Warfighting Experiment.

23. Office of the Secretary of Defense, "Joint Tactical Information Distribution System (JTIDS), FY97 Annual Report," Nov. 12, 1998, available at http:// www.dote.osd.mil/reports/FY97/airforce/97jtids.html.

24. Office of the Secretary of Defense, "Global Command and Control System (GCCS), FY97 Annual Report," Nov. 12, 1998, available at http:// www.dote.osd.mil/reports/FY97/other/97/gccs.html.

25. Archie Clemins, "SATCOM Bandwidth Transmission Latency," MILCOM 97 Conference,]Jan. 30, 1999, available at http://www.cpf.navy.mil/pages/cpfspeak/ milcom97/sld030.htm.

26. Archie Clemins, "Mission Bandwidth Requirements (SATCOM), Seven Habits of a Highly Effective Information Technology System," Jan. 30, 1999, available at http://www.cpf.navy.mil/pages/cpfspeak/afcea980114/sld010.htm.

27. John P. Flynn and Ted E. Senator, "DARPA Naval Battle Management Applications," in *Artificial Intelligence and National Defense: Applications to C3I and Beyond,* ed. Stephen J. Andriole (Washington, D.C., AFCEA International Press,

1987), 66. Specifically, this study sought to "collapse the time required for plan-ning and monitoring operation, to identify sensitivities in key strategic and tacti-cal decisions, and to demonstrate the implications of complex combinations of events and decisions."

28. John P. Retelle Jr. and Michael Kaul, "The Pilot's Associate—Aerospace Applica-tion of Artificial Intelligence," in *Artificial Intelligence and National Defense*, 110.

29. Raytheon, "Phalanx," Feb. 24, 1999, available at http://www.raytheon.com/rsc/dss/dpr/dpr_msys/dpr_phlx.htm.

30. General quarters refers to "a condition of readiness when naval action is immi-nent. All battle stations are fully manned and alert; ammunition is ready for in-stant loading; guns and guided missile launchers may be loaded." Definition from *Joint Publication 1-02, Department of Defense Dictionary of Military and Associ-ated Terms*, 178.

31. Army Field Manual 44-85, "Operations," *Patriot Battalion and Battery Opera-tions*, February 21, 1997, January 30, 1999, available at http://www.fas.org/spp/starwars/docops/fm44-85/ch5.htm#top.

32. Information Systems Office World Programs, "Control of Agent-Based Systems," Nov. 5, 1998, available at http://dtsn.darpa.mil/iso.

33. See Joint Chiefs of Staff, *Concept for Future Joint Operations*, 25–26, which notes that, as a result of the "trend toward quantum increases in computer storage capacity and greater automation of warfare, the microprocessor will be deployed on smarter weapons. Computers will continue to augment, and in some cases may replace, human intervention, and automated decision making or aids to decision makers will increase. Microprocessors will be ubiquitous in the battlespace of the future. Advances in computer architecture and machine intelligence will have reached the point where weapons systems can analyze the environment and cur-rent battle situation, search likely target areas, detect and analyze targets, make at-tack decisions, select and dispense munitions, and report results. With each incre-mental improvement, the battlespace will become more lethal."

34. William B. Osborne, Scott A. Bethel, Nolan R. Chew et al., "Information Opera-tions: A New War-Fighting Capability," in *Air Force 2025* (Maxwell Air Force Base, Ala.: Air University, 1996), ix.

35. See, particularly, van Creveld, *Command in War.*

36. See, for example, Michael G. Mayer, "The Influence of Future Command, Con-trol, Communications, and Computers on Doctrine and the Operational Comman-der's Decision-Making Process," Naval War College, Newport, R.I., March 1996, or Gregory A. Roman, "The Command or Control Dilemma: When Technology and Organizational Orientation Collide," Air University Press, Maxwell Air Force Base, Ala., February 1997).

37. Gary A. Vincent, "A New Approach to Command and Control: The Cybernetic Design," *Airpower Journal* (summer 1993), available at http://www.airpower.maxwell.af.mil/airchronicles/apj/vincent.html.

38. Charles A. Bass Jr., "Decision Loops: The Cybernetic Dimension of Battle Com-

mand," School of Advanced Military Studies, Fort Leavenworth, Kans., December, 1996.

39. This is a key, and sometimes overlooked, element of command-by-intent systems. Successful application of this process presumes that young commissioned and noncommissioned officers have honed not only their technical and tactical skills but are able to understand and to make consistently correct decisions at the strategic level of warfare.

40. Not surprisingly, U.S. joint military doctrine has addressed these concerns. See Joint Chiefs of Staff, *Concept for Future Joint Operations,* 68. As a military unit achieves information superiority, the commander could vary the degree of control based on the current situation (e.g., rules of engagement, political constraints). Although the potential will exist to centralize the execution of future joint operations, appropriate decentralization will more fully exploit the capabilities of agile organizations and the initiative and leadership of individuals at every level. The future commander must resist the temptation to centralize execution authority when it is not warranted.

41. *U.S. Army Field Manual 100-5, Operations,* June 14, 1993, available at http://155.217.58.58/cgi-bin/atdl.dll/fm/100-5/100-5c2c.htm#COMBAT.

42. For an illuminating discussion of legal issues surrounding military command, see notes accompanying John R. Brancato, "In Search of Command and Staff Doctrine," *The Air Force Law Review* 28 (1988), 1–63.

43. Title 10 ("Armed Forces"), United States Code, Article 164.

44. U.S. Air Force, *Air Force Basic Doctrine, Air Force Doctrine Document 1,* September 1997, 64.

45. Michelle Youngers, Jude Franklin, Corey Lackey et al., "Improving C3: The Potential of Artificial Intelligence," in *Artificial Intelligence and National Defense,* 39.

46. Paul T. Harig, "The Digital General: Reflections on Leadership in the Post-Information Age," *Parameters* (autumn 1996), 139.

47. *U.S. Army Field Manual 100-5, Operations,* 2-14–2-15.

48. Garry W. Barringer, Technical Director, Aerospace C2 Agency, interview by author, Dec. 1, 1998.

49. Tom Czerwinski, *Coping with the Bounds* (Washington, D.C.: National Defense University, 1998), 45.

50. *Joint Doctrine Encyclopedia,* 222.

51. Gordon R. Sullivan and James M. Dubik, *War in the Information Age* (Carlisle Barracks, Pa.: U.S. Army War College, 1994), 5.

52. See Wayne P. Hughes Jr., *Fleet Tactics: Theory and Practice* (Annapolis, Md.: Naval Institute Press, 1986), 187.

53. Wu Guoqing, "Future Trends of Modern Operations," in *Chinese Views of Future Warfare,* ed. Michael Pillsbury (Washington, D.C.; National Defense University Press, 1996), 351.

12.   Information Warfare and Deterrence

Richard J. Harknett

As a result of technological innovation in computers and communications, states in the twenty-first century now have the ability, termed *information warfare,* to attack a society's fundamental electronic infrastructure, including vulnerable telecommunications, banking, and power systems. Because governmental, military, and intelligence organizations could launch attacks that would cripple societies but not cause the physical destruction often associated with war, deterring war is difficult. This chapter examines how information networks might be the critical target in future wars, evaluates how this new form of warfare could affect the ability to deter conflicts in the short term, and concludes that it would be extremely difficult to deter information warfare and that deterrence is not the best model for understanding this new form of war. Thus, this chapter examines how the revolutionary aspects of information technologies might affect contemporary thinking about war.

Introduction

The splitting of the atom led not only to a new military force structure but to a new way of thinking about military force. The nuclear revolution shaped how certain states interacted over security and how the security establishment thought about those interactions. The prospect of an information revolution includes discussions about how a unique form of warfare might be emerging.

The U.S. Department of Defense's definition of information warfare is remarkable for its lack of distinctiveness. *Information warfare* is described as "action taken to achieve information superiority in support of national military strategy by affecting an adversary's information and information systems, while leveraging and protecting our own information and information systems."[1] Although it is assumed that information warfare (infowar) involves the employment of advanced technology, the Department of Defense (DOD) definition does not require it. Information warfare is an intriguing concept, but whether it is analytically useful, in that it describes dynamics that differ from other forms of war, remains open to debate.[2]

This chapter also examines the unique features of the Information Age that can affect war and discusses the specific dynamics associated with deterring infowar. Before discussing the strategy of information warfare deterrence, however, we must clearly understand this new form of war. This chapter is divided into three sections. The first outlines the implications of information technology for future wars and concludes that connections among information networks could be a key target. The second discusses the distinctions among military connectivity (referring to the ability of computers to be connected), societal connectivity, and the forms of warfare that might involve each type. The third section examines the implications of these two forms of information warfare for deterrence. The two broad conclusions of this chapter are it would be extremely difficult to deter information warfare, and deterrence models should not guide strategic thinking about this new form of war.

The Information Age

Because the force behind many fundamental transformations has been advancements in technology, it should not be surprising that the emergence of networked computing and related technologies has led many writers to describe the mid-1990s as the beginning of a new historical era—the Information Age. War is one of the central human activities affected by technological transitions; therefore, it is equally unsurprising that the growing ubiquity of personal computers and other information technologies can establish the foundation for a new form of warfare.[3]

Before one can realize the impact of information technologies on warfare, it is essential to understand this technological transformation. The distinction of the late twentieth century as the Information Age rests on the fact that the computer chip has created a new level of computational and communicative power in the form of the networked computer. Computer networks support everything from local, regional, and national banking systems to telephones and transportation structures. Information technology also includes fax machines, cellular phones, and satellite television. Although these technologies are important, the Information Age could be governed by the growing significance and presence of the networked computer. For example, the explosive growth of the Internet, initially conceived to be part of an American defense plan to improve communications during a nuclear attack, has transformed computer usage.[4]

Although creation, accumulation, and manipulation of information always has been central to human activity, including warfare,[5] the networked computer has five distinctive features that have resulted in a restructure of human activity. The Information Age rests on accessibility, availability, speed, affordability, and recursive simplicity.

Accessibility
First, the networking of personal computers has led to the networking of individual networks. The universe of these networks, commonly termed *cyberspace,* carries information in all of its forms.[6] Through the use of modems, individuals at home can now connect into cyberspace to access depositories of information on a worldwide basis. A tremendous advance in information access exists when the retrieval of information does not depend on geographic proximity to the information storage facility itself.

Availability
Cyberspace significantly advances the availability of information, the second feature, because it creates opportunities for many individuals simultaneously to retrieve the same information. The limitation on availability is no longer how many copies of a particular instrument exist but the number of users who can access the site. In fact, one of the growing problems with the Information Age is how to manage too much available information.

Speed
The third feature of the Information Age is the enormous increase in the speed of computation and communication. As the computational speed of computers and networks grows exponentially, vast sums of accessible information can be disseminated in seconds. The fact that individuals can have real-time knowledge of events has significant implications for how individuals and organizations make decisions. The time that it takes to collect initial information, to analyze and process that information, to make a decision, and to implement it has been tremendously compressed. A large amount of information from multiple sources now can be retrieved without stressing the overall decision-making cycle.

Affordability

The fourth distinctive feature is the relatively low and steadily declining cost of the technology. As the average price for computing power decreases and software makes working with computers easier, the barriers to general access diminish. Information Age technology is affordable in the broad sense of the term.

Recursive Simplicity

The fifth feature of the Information Age is the recursive nature of computer technology, which means self-similarity in structure or, in essence, patterns that are inside patterns.[7] A recursive structure is one in which the whole is structurally identical to its parts. The early developers of computer software constructed large programs out of existing smaller ones. The recursive nature of software tremendously simplifies its development. Instead of separately regarding each independent part of a design, one can reuse them in similar but broader commands again and again. Given this feature, the trends in accessibility, availability, speed, and affordability, as identified above, are likely to continue.

Implications

The Information Age could affect human relations in significant ways, and a growing literature, particularly as it affects war, argues that the new technology represents revolutionary change.[8] Two implications, individual empowerment and organizational revolution, have significant consequences.[9]

Individual Empowerment

The ability to gain access to enormous amounts of information at a reasonable cost empowers individuals.[10] With existing information technologies, an individual can collect, organize, analyze, and disseminate the same amount of information that even decades ago would have required teams of technicians and researchers. The computational power in the personal computer is equivalent to the power that would have been found in large government or university computer centers just a few decades ago.[11] The networked computer empowers individuals, rather than the state, principally because of how the internet and cyberspace were developed.

Both are relatives of the U.S. Department of Defense plan in the 1960s to develop a communication system that could survive a Soviet nuclear attack. It was determined that the best communication system would be a distributed network of computers, whose redundancy would not allow the loss of links to disrupt the entire system. The network, therefore, would be more survivable without a central control, and could it reconfigure information even if significant parts of the communication system were destroyed.[12]

This approach eventually served as the foundation for a network of university and government small computer networks that was created by the Advanced Projects Research Agency of the U.S. Defense Department. This network of networks, known as the ARPANET (Advanced Research Projects Agency Network) consisted of four nodes in 1969, thirty-seven in 1973, and sixty thousand in 1989, when it was disbanded in favor of the Internet.[13] Importantly, the defense requirements of survivability led to a system in which the lack of centralized control was regarded as a structural prerequisite.

Because information technology empowers individuals in the political, economic, and social realms, it is essential to assess how the Information Age might affect the relationship between individuals and their governments, how business practices are shifting in modern democracies, and how "virtual reality" might redefine human contact.[14]

Organizational Revolution
The critical consequence of the information revolution is the potential for restructuring organizations. As individuals within an organization become more effective because they have access to more information, the organizational structure that shapes interactions between individuals could change. Just as bureaucratic hierarchy supported the Industrial Revolution, the information technology network could redefine organizational support for the Information Age.[15] The true revolution rests not in the technology itself, but in how changes in organizational form shape human activity.

That change influences the relationship between the individual and the information within an organization. In a bureaucratic hierarchy, information is linked to function. An individual's function places him or her within the bureaucracy and the information that flows to that individual is determined by function. Thus, the dockworker and the chief executive officer not only have different jobs but different access to different information. Although the bureaucratic form is more efficient than it has been in the past, it suffers from compartmentalization of information, which can lead to the left hand often not knowing what the right hand is doing.

The information technology network promises to sever the link between function and information so that all members in an organization have a shared situational awareness. Individuals with a more complete picture of where they fit into an organization or, in a broader sense, within society itself should become more effective participants. Human activity structured along these lines would become dependent on the information flow of the network, while the connection (both actual and psychological) to the network becomes the key to efficiency. The unanswered question is whether the network will become the superior form of organization for the Information Age.

The empowerment of individuals and the emergence of the networked organization are at the heart of the information revolution. A revolution in military affairs could lead to the emergence of a new military organization. Movement from a hierarchical bureaucratic military to a networked command and force structure would indeed have revolutionary consequences.[16] But what does the network mean for warfare? What does thinking in terms of networks do for threat perception and analysis? And what are the targets when networks dominate?

Information Warfare

There is no consensus about the term *information warfare*. In March 1993, U.S. Chairman of the Joint Chiefs of Staff Memorandum of Policy Number 30 (MOP 30) identified seven concepts to be grouped under the umbrella of information warfare, of which some, such as command and control warfare (C2W), intelligence-based warfare, and psychological operations, do not necessarily involve information technology. As one defense scholar concluded, the term is "an unfortunate catch-all phrase."[17]

Earlier discussion in Chapters 10 and 11 focuses on the distinctive aspect of information technologies. If it is not the technologies themselves that are significant, but how they empower individuals and create a new organizational form, then the question is the fundamental force for empowerment and organizational restructuring. This is the connectivity of the network.

The network functions on the basis of connections between nodes, which can be individuals at computers, several workstations, or small networks themselves. The strength of the network, which rests not on its individual nodes but on its degree of connectivity, is both a foundation and a critical target in information warfare.

Although a clear definition of information warfare has yet to be fully accepted, the consensus is that there is a division between combat involving strictly military forces and conflict that is directed at society at large.[18] It is essential to distinguish between military and societal information warfare as an important starting point.[19]

Societal Infowar

The term *societal infowar* can be understood as information-related conflict that seeks to destroy the enemy's societal connectivity while protecting one's own societal connectivity. The objective is to target a society's communication, financial transaction, transportation, and energy resource network links, termed *critical infrastructure*, as well as to defend the linkages that constitute the essence of a modern technological society.

The idea of societal infowar is useful only if it describes a new form of warfare. If societal connectivity is a critical target, however, the society must be so dependent on these networks that their loss would be painful. Thus, nomadic, feudal, or even moderately industrial societies that show little signs of network characteristics are not likely targets for offensive societal infowar operations. Knowledge about how networked organizations and network dynamics develop is critical to understanding the information revolution. In cases when societal connectivity is low because the information revolution has not taken hold, societal infowar might not be a useful concept.

Although computer communications are not the only measure of societal connectivity, they are critically important. For example, the ability to capture or destroy the single radio or television station in a state can have profound effects. Where hierarchies still dominate, decapitation (destroying the head of a government or military) is possible and traditional forms of propaganda and psychological operations are sufficient. In these cases, there is no need to conceive or prepare for a new dimension of conflict.

In a networked society, such as the United States, where the communications system is not centralized and there is no center, the defense establishment needs to contemplate new forms of warfare. Society's dependence on and connection to the network become the focus. The same holds for other societal resources. The disruption or defense of delivering energy from a centralized power grid system or supporting financial transactions from a centralized banking system involves a different type of analysis than in the case of highly networked systems. Thinking in terms of societal infowar could be useful when one recognizes that new forms of human organization could require new ways of thinking about conflict. As societies become more networked, new vulnerabilities and strengths might emerge.

Military Infowar

With the network's increasing presence in society, societal connectivity could emerge as a critical national asset. This logic holds for the networked military as well, where military connectivity will have considerable significance. The term *military infowar* refers to conducting and preparing to conduct military operations against or in defense of military connectivity, which is broader than the narrow focus on command and control warfare. As military organizations become less centralized and hierarchical and more networked, the overall flow and quality of information and knowledge, rather than specific control over information, must be contested.

Societal and Military Infowar and Deterrence

As information warfare becomes an instrument of national power, a critical question is whether the threat of information attacks is sufficient to deter foreign states from threatening the United States. In essence, deterrence means that any action of the United States influences the moves made by an adversary.[20] With offensive strategy, the challenger that wants the greatest freedom of action could use technical, tactical, and operational innovations to reduce (or, ideally, eliminate) the costs threatened by the state that wants to deter. The United States must weaken the challenger's ability to find acceptable alternatives by guaranteeing that unacceptable costs will be inflicted if there is an offensive challenge. This strategic dynamic, which is at the heart of deterrence, focuses on shared information and rationality.[21]

Shared Information

For deterrence to function, both the challenger and the deterring entity must understand each other's national objectives; its commitment to the issue in dispute; and the relative military, political, and economic resources that are available.[22] Incomplete or incorrect information about the challenger can weaken deterrence because either the challenger does not consider the costs prohibitive or the costs do not cover the entire spectrum of military options that are open to the challenger. If the deterring entity lacks clear information about the challenger's capabilities and tactics, the deterrence strategy would be vulnerable to countermeasures, such as weapons, tactics, or strategy.

Rationality

Deterrence can fail because either the deterring entity's strategy does not make the costs greater than the benefits gained by military action or the deterring entity's strategy threatens sufficient costs, but the challenger miscalculates. If a country does not base its deterrence strategy on bluff, a deterrent threat should encourage the challenger to calculate rationally all of its possible options. The deterring entity wants a potential challenger to assess deterrent threats intelligently and consistently. Ideally, the challenger might calculate that the expected benefits of using force are less than the costs inflicted by the deterring entity's response.

For deterrence to work, states must make decisions rationally, but, in practice, rational decision making is threatened by the conditions that exist in most deterrence situations. Both the deterring entity and the challenger must make decisions in the presence of the uncertainty, tension, time constraints, and stress that degrade rational decision making.[23] With respect to information warfare, the questions are: how is deterrence affected by a shift toward connectivity, how do societal and military infowar affect the pursuit of deterrence, and to what degree are threats to connectivity contestable?[24]

With societal and military infowar as the two general forms of information warfare, connectivity is the organizing principle for understanding offensive and defensive strategies in infowar. Because military organizations are developing strategies for conducting operations across command and control, electronic, intelligence-based, psychological, economic information, and computer systems, information warfare is being discussed in terms of deterrence as well.[25]

Deterrence and Military Infowar

Conducting military operations against systems that maintain connectivity in military organizations has significant implications for national security. The ability to threaten the connectivity of an opposing military force can be critical, particularly if that force is highly dependent on those connections, and raises two related problems. First, disrupting the military network must have substantial consequences if a state is to fear this attack. Because destroying only a segment of the network might not prevent the rest of the military force from achieving its offensive goals, attacking connectivity might not be seen as a prohibitive deterrent. Second, if a major objective of a networked military is to provide greater redundancy and the most efficient use of force, attacking connectivity might not be a reliable deterrent. If the state can withstand attacks against its connectivity, it could conclude that the deterrent effect of threatening connectivity could be manipulated, that is, contested.

Military infowar could be dominated by a contest for supremacy over the electromagnetic spectrum, and the side that achieves supremacy could see, decide, and move at a pace that overwhelms adversaries.[26] Because networked military forces depend on connectivity to operate, military operations against them must necessarily attack that connectivity.

The consequence of greater military connectivity is greater lethality if one has a better idea of where the opponent is and the capability of a precise hit against the opponent before it moves. The digital battlefield, with its shared situational awareness, promises to solve the traditional problem that "operational mobility has never matched the capability of intelligence to tell us what the enemy is trying to do."[27] By creating an integrated sensor-to-shooter capability, the digital battlefield could produce detection and reaction times that outmatch the enemy's ability to move.[28] This effect is amplified when one begins to consider the strengths of the networked military.

Traditionally, securing flanks or reserves and protecting the forces required the deployment of combat troops. If the electromagnetic spectrum can be seized and one can view the entire battlespace, however, combat troops would not have to be dedicated to protect the flanks and rear areas that are not under potential pressure from the enemy.[29] Instead, these combat forces could now be used in offensive operations, which implies that connectivity not only creates greater lethality but increases the number of lethal forces available to commanders.

Dominance in military infowar could make the prospect of challenging a state prohibitively costly, which might enhance its overall ability to deter attacks against vital national interests. The problem is that such dominance can be contested, challenged, or disputed by the opponent both before and after war begins. Command and control systems can be disrupted with computer viruses, electronic disinformation, or the direct destruction of sensing equipment, all of which could become more prevalent as the connectivity of military forces increases.[30]

Military infowar cannot be understood as a static condition. Future opponents of high-technology, networked militaries are unlikely to repeat Iraq's mistake by giving the United States a "free ride" with its communications network.[31] The ability to conduct and dominate in military infowar should be used to deter attacks against vital interests, but deterrence is unlikely to prevail if an opponent views the costs of a deterrent threat as contestable or disputable. One conclusion is that more time should be directed toward developing both offensive and defensive military infowar capabilities, tactics, and strategies, rather than believing that infowar capabilities deter their use.

Deterrence and Societal Infowar

Because military infowar differs little from traditional conventional warfare in a deterrence sense, deterrence, to the extent that it exists, is fluid, requires maintenance, and is prone to breakdown.[32] When applied to societal infowar, deterrence has limited utility. Societal infowar focuses on societal connectivity that, from an offensive perspective, can be attacked, disrupted, or destroyed on three different levels: the personal, the institutional, and the national.[33]

For example, targeting individual's electronic records could undermine societal connectivity. The act of changing or destroying those records alters the perception in society of who an individual is and how that individual interacts with others. Manipulating these records, which include credit reports, medical histories, school transcripts, financial portfolios and bank accounts, and law enforcement files, among others, could effectively change one's wealth or identity. The seriousness of this threat is compounded by the general public's tendency to view computer information as truth. In most instances, the difference between the reality described by the computer and the one to which an individual attests can be explained by data entry error, but large-scale, sophisticated, and purposeful manipulation of digital records could significantly disrupt a society.

The information on which societies are based and on which they depend is vulnerable. For example, because the financial strength of the modern corporation is increasingly tied to its ability to manage information more effectively than its competitors, information systems can become new arenas for economic conflict. Rather than send a naval fleet, an adversary could threaten the network systems that support economic activity. Why compete in expensive marketing contests when research and development projects could be disrupted with a well-placed computer virus even before production begins?[34] Instability in major corporations could create wide-ranging problems in society.

The consequences of societal infowar, which is the disruption or destruction of societal connectivity, might involve not only specific attacks on personal electronic or institutional records but occur on a broader scale, where electronic connectivity is indiscriminately targeted. Because networks rely on electronic circuitry that is extremely vulnerable to disruption by other magnetic fields, very little technical expertise is needed to use a magnetic field to disrupt the circuitry in computers or networks. As described in Chapter 5, high-energy radio frequency and electromagnetic pulse weapons, which are well within the state of the art, could disrupt the entire transportation, communication, and financial systems of a city.[35]

These three levels of societal infowar do not fit well with deterrence because deterrence rests ultimately on the principle of retaliation, in which the costs inflicted in retaliation exceed the costs of the offensive attack. If an attack does not destroy buildings or kill people directly but only destroys information, how should a state respond, and should it respond at all? Although information is intangible, its loss can have tangible costs for individuals, institutions, and societies. The problem is to know what can be credibly held at risk to dissuade a state from launching an information attack.

One answer is connectivity, but it raises two problems. First, it presumes that the attacking state depends on and values societal connectivity as much as the deterring state. In the Information Age, however, states have access to information warfare capabilities even if they are not highly networked societies. The United States produced the Global Positioning Satellite (GPS) system, which anyone can use by purchasing a GPS monitor at Radio Shack.[36] Retaliation against military or societal connectivity would not be necessarily viewed as prohibitive for low-tech societies. The problem is whether to threaten the physical destruction of national assets in response to information attacks or to treat attacks on societal connectivity as acts of conventional war.

The second problem with retaliating against attacks on connectivity is its consequences for the deterring entity. So far, connectivity has been treated as a national asset, but the nature of networks is that they weaken the value of using geographic or territorial boundaries as the unit of analysis. The connectivity of a "nationally" defined networked society transcends geographic conventions and makes it difficult to separate national and global disruptions in connectivity. Although this sort of electronic interdependence should dissuade states from conducting offensive attacks in the first place, the subjective nature of their effects complicates whether states will use this technology for destructive attacks.

A third problem with "retaliation in kind" deterrence is that an info attack can emanate not only from a state but also from a small group of terrorists, organized crime, or hackers. For deterrence to work, the state must identify the opponent. States can threaten to seek out "netwarriors" and promise retribution, but there is a difference between threatening to do so and actually finding the perpetuator. The ultimate way to raise doubts about the costs of retaliation is for the attacker to conceal its identity, which ultimately could diminish fears that it will be discovered as the source of the attack. One might conclude that societal infowar is no different from a traditional military attack against the homeland and that the state should threaten an appropriate military response, but ambiguity about who launched the attack could undermine the credibility of deterrence for determined adversaries.

Conclusion

Because the contemporary theory of deterrence is derived from the strategic models of the early twentieth century when offense-defense strategies were the dominant idea until deterrence became the strategic paradigm after 1945, it is natural for the defense establishment and scholars to use deterrence for a better understanding of information warfare. For reasons discussed in this chapter, however, deterrence does not provide a useful framework for understanding information warfare. The fundamental problem is that the ability to deter a state or group from launching an attack is highly contestable because the results of that attack could be challenged or disputed by the opponent. The consequence is that the information revolution and the ability to conduct information attacks against other societies and their military forces could create unique and misunderstood challenges for the U.S. military during the twenty-first century.

Notes

1. Cited in Wayne Rowe, *Information Warfare: A Primer for Navy Personnel* (Newport, R.I.: Naval War College Center for Naval Warfare Studies, 1995), 3.
2. John Arquilla and David Ronfeldt, "Cyberwar Is Coming!" *Comparative Strategy* 12, no. 2 (spring 1993), 141–65, point to the Mongols as a perfect example of a military force that exploited information superiority. A similar point is made in Norman Davis, "An Information-Based Revolution in Military Affairs," *Strategic Review* 24, no. 1 (winter 1996), 43–53.
3. William McNeill, *The Pursuit of Power: Technology, Armed Force and Society* (Chicago: University of Chicago Press, 1982); Martin van Creveld, *The Transformation of War* (New York: Free Press, 1991); Geoffrey Parker, *The Military Revolution: Military Innovation and the Rise of the West, 1500–1800* (New York: Cambridge University Press, 1988); Martin van Creveld, *Technology and War* (New York: Free Press, 1989); Stephen Rosen, "New Ways of War: Understanding Military Innovation," *International Security* 13, no. 1 (summer 1988), 134–68.
4. The links among innovation, warfare, and societal organization seem apparent. The original U.S. Defense Department plan created what was known as the ARPANET, without which the modern day internet would not have been developed. For background, see Katie Hafner and John Markoff, *CyberPunk: Outlaws and Hackers on the Computer Frontier* (New York: Simon and Schuster, 1991), 263–82.
5. The idea that information warfare is fundamentally new is resisted by those historians and military analysts who argue that emphasis always has been placed on knowing where the enemy is, what his plans are, and the capabilities that support his plans, as well as the importance of denying the same information to the enemy. Authors have pointed to the writings of Sun Tzu as an example. Arquilla and Ronfeldt, "Cyberwar Is Coming," 141–45, use the Mongol approach to war as another example.
6. The computer supports text, pictorial, and verbal, as well as real-time and taped full-motion video, forms of information. The ubiquity of computers by the late twentieth century in most of the developed world was such that most people had little recognition that they were interacting with these machines.
7. James Gleck, *Chaos: Making a New Science* (New York: Penguin Books, 1987), 98–103; David Gelernter, *Mirror Worlds: Or the Day Software Puts the Universe in a Shoebox . . . How It Will Happen and What It Will Mean* (New York: Oxford University Press, 1991), 54.
8. Davis, "Information-Based Revolution"; Patrick Cooper, "Information Warfare Sparks Security Affairs Revolution," *Defense News,* June 12–18, 1995, 8; Andrew F. Krepinevich, "Cavalry to Computer: The Pattern of Military Revolutions," *The National Interest* 37 (fall 1994), 30–42; William Odom, *America's Military Revolution: Strategy and Structure after the Cold War* (Washington, D.C.: American University Press, 1993).

9. The author ascribes to Kuhn's sense of revolution as a conceptual shift that requires the "reconstruction of prior theory and the re-evaluation of prior fact." Thomas Kuhn, *The Structure of Scientific Revolutions,* 2d ed. (Chicago: University of Chicago Press, 1970), 7.

10. For an overview of the impact of information technology on individuals, see Lee Sproull and Sara Kiesler, *Connections: New Ways of Working in the Networked Organization* (Cambridge, Mass.: MIT Press, 1991).

11. Even earlier, the electronic numerical integrator and computer (ENIAC), first demonstrated in 1946, required 1,500 square feet of space and 17,468 vacuum tubes to operate. It could make 5,000 additions per second. See Mary Kathleen Flynn, "Taming the Internet," *U.S. News and World Report,* Apr. 29, 1996, 22.

12. For greater detail, see Peter J. Denning, "The ARPANET after Twenty Years," in P. Denning, ed., *Computers under Attack: Intruders, Worms, and Viruses* (Reading, Mass.: Addison-Wesley, 1990), 11–19.

13. Ibid., 11.

14. See Sproull and Kiesler, *Connections*; Robert Anderson, Tora Bikson, Sally Law, Bridger Mitchell, *Universal Access to Email: Feasibility and Societal Implications* (Santa Monica, Calif.: RAND Center for Information Revolution Analyses, 1995), 119–21. On this point, see also J. D. Eveland and T. K. Bikson, "Evolving Electronic Communication Networks," *Office: Technology and People* 3 (1987), 103–28.

15. The classic work on the connection between the modern state (industrial) and the bureaucratic organizational form comes from Max Weber. See H. H. Gerth and C. Wright Mills, eds., *From Max Weber: Essays in Sociology* (New York: Oxford University Press, 1946).

16. Richard J. Harknett and JCISS Study Group, "The Risks of a Networked Military," *Orbis* 44 (winter 1999/2000), 127–43.

17. Martin C. Libicki, "What Is Information Warfare?," *Strategic Forum,* newsletter no. 28, National Defense University, Institute for National Strategic Studies, Washington, D.C., May 1995. Adm. Arthur Cebrowski, when he was Director for Command, Control, Communications, and Computers for the American Joint Staff, argued that, because "the implications are so new, it is best that no central authority control its [the concept of infowar] development," quoted in Cooper, "Information Warfare," 1.

18. Martin Libicki and John Arquilla are the most oft-cited authors on the subject of base terminology, and both of them make this distinction.

19. Aquilla and Ronfeldt, "Cyberwar Is Coming!" 144, 146–47, use the terms *cyberwar* and *netwar,* but the terms do not clearly convey what is unique about these forms of war. *Netwar* has been defined as "information-related conflict at a grand level between nations or societies. It means trying to disrupt, damage, or modify what a target population knows or thinks about itself and the world around it." By contrast, *cyberwar* "refers to conducting, and preparing to conduct, military operations according to information-related principles. . . . It means turning the 'bal-

ance of information and knowledge' in one's favor." It signifies a "transformation in the nature of war, [but] . . . does not necessarily require the presence of advanced technology." These terms capture the distinction but do not meet the test of explaining a new dynamic or dimension. The suggestion that cyberwar does not require advanced technology introduces definitional confusion. A focus on network connectivity provides a stronger analytical distinction.

20. Thomas Schelling, *The Strategy of Conflict* (New York: Oxford University Press, 1960).

21. Richard J. Harknett, "The Logic of Conventional Deterrence and the End of the Cold War," *Security Studies* 4, no.1 (autumn 1994), 86–114.

22. Jonathan Shimshoni, *Israel and Conventional Deterrence* (Ithaca, N.Y.: Cornell University Press, 1988), 10–16; Philip Green, *Deadly Logic: The Theory of Nuclear Deterrence* (Columbus: Ohio State University Press, 1966), 185–88.

23. The implication is that reducing uncertainty is fundamentally related to the requirement for and problems of shared information; however, greater certainty also carries a price. A country that specifies in detail its deterrence commitments is vulnerable to unexpected contingencies because the challenger might be able to employ "salami tactics" that avoid the brunt of the deterrence strategy by gaining objectives in a piecemeal fashion.

24. If a challenger can manipulate the strategic environment so that the costs threatened by the deterring entity can be significantly undermined, deterrence is likely to fail. To the extent that deterrent costs are viewed as contestable, deterrence strategy is weakened. Colin Gray uses the phrase *reliability of effect* in discussing the logic of contestability. See Gray, "Nuclear Weapons and the Revolution in Information Warfare," in T. V. Paul, Richard J. Harknett, and James J. Wirtz, eds., *The Absolute Weapon Revisited: Nuclear Arms and the Emerging International Order* (Ann Arbor: University of Michigan Press, 2000), 99–137. For more on the incontestability of nuclear deterrents see Harknett, "State Preferences, Systemic Constraints, and the Absolute Weapon," in ibid., 47–72.

25. William Perry, "Desert Storm and Deterrence," *Foreign Affairs* 70, no. 4 (fall 1991), 66–82.

26. Morris Boyd and Michael Woodgerd, "Force XXI Operations," *Military Review,* November 1994, 16–28.

27. Arthur DeGroat and David Nelson, "Information and Combat Power on the Force XXI Battlefield," *Military Review* (November–December 1995), 56–62.

28. Randall Bowdish, "The Revolution in Military Affairs: The Sixth Generation," *Military Review* (November–December 1995), 26–33, available at http://www.cgsc.army.mil/cgsc/milrev/95novdec/bow.htm; Boyd and Woodgerd, "Force XXI Operations," 18; DeGroat and Nelson, "Information and Combat Power," 59–60.

29. David Gelernter develops the concept of topsight, which captures the essence of dominant battlespace awareness—the current DOD term. See Gelernter, *Mirror Worlds,* 52.

30. Eliot Cohen, "The Mystique of U.S. Airpower," *Foreign Affairs* 73, no. 1 (January–February 1994), 109–25. As noted in the "Gulf War Airpower Summary Report," Department of Defense, Washington, D.C., 1992, "the more sophisticated and expansive the information gathering system, the greater the premium opponents will put on disabling it. . . . The pay-off for shooting down a state-of-the-art radar surveillance aircraft, for example, will surely attract efforts to do so."

31. Perry, "Desert Storm and Deterrence," acknowledges that "many of the C3I systems used in Desert Storm could be degraded by foreseeable countermeasures." Cohen, "Mystique of U.S. Airpower," makes a similar point.

32. Many conventional deterrence strategists assume that deterrence failure is ultimately necessary to strengthen deterrence. For an overview of this argument, see Charles Allen, "Extended Conventional Deterrence: In from the Cold and Out of the Nuclear Fire?" *Washington Quarterly* 17, no. 3 (summer 1994), 203–33.

33. This builds upon and modifies an argument put forward by Winn Schwartau, who discusses information warfare broadly defined as being conducting on the personal information, corporate information and global information levels. See Schwartau, *Information Warfare: Chaos on the Electronic Superhighway* (New York: Thunder's Mouth Press, 1995).

34. For an overview of such potentialities, see Peter Denning, ed., *Computers under Attack: Intruders, Worms, and Viruses* (New York: Addison-Wesley, 1990).

35. For more on these weapons and their effects, see Schwartau, *Information Warfare,* 177–85. He refers to some early possible uses during the Gulf War, as well as some instances in which the phenomenon of magnetic field disruption has disrupted or destroyed commercial and military systems.

36. See, for example, Paul M. Eng and Amy Borrus, "Who Knows Where You Are? The Satellite Knows," *Business Week,* Feb. 10, 1992, 120–21.

Conclusion
Technological Foundations of Military Power
William C. Martel

As a result of significant investments in technology, the capabilities of the U.S. military are without equal. The consensus is that no state has the military power to prevent the United States from achieving its military objectives. Despite its emphasis on technology, however, the United States might not be prepared for the lesser crises that could dominate this century. The conflicts in Somalia, Haiti, Bosnia, Serbia, and other countries did not fit the mold established by the twentieth century. Although the Persian Gulf War illustrated the importance of high-technology weapons, conflicts in this century could be quite different from the wars of the twentieth century. The problem is that the U.S. investment in advanced technologies virtually guarantees victory in major wars, but those same technologies might not be as useful in smaller-scale conflicts among ethnic, religious, or national groups within states.

A fundamental problem is the perception that the U.S. military was run down in the 1990s by inadequate investment and more overseas deployments. Reports that the armed services are plagued by low morale, shortages of weapons and fuel for training, and political decisions to use the military more frequently have combined to raise concerns that the U.S. military needs to be *recapitalized,* which is the term in Washington for investing billions of dollars to rebuild the force. Defense officials have called for significant increases in U.S. defense spending so that the Pentagon can modernize its forces for this century.[1] Although U.S. military forces are about one-third smaller than they were in the early 1990s, the demands placed on them in overseas peacekeeping and humanitarian missions and in combat operations increased radically during the

1990s. Thus, a strange picture emerges. On the one hand, the U.S. military is investing enormous resources in advanced technology weapons and systems, whereas, on the other hand, the forces are deteriorating because of inadequate funding for the level of commitments that American society places on the military. In the long term, U.S. military capabilities depend on maintaining technologies that are without equal in terms of both the breadth and the depth of technologies being developed.

To evaluate the foundations of U.S. technological power and its implications for American security and international security during this century, it is essential to examine the critical defense technologies in which the United States has invested for decades. In view of its investments in technology, the United States has achieved a level of military power that can be maintained as long as it continues to invest. As Washington acquires the technological tools that are commensurate with great military power, it will discover that directed-energy technologies, new weapons for targeting, and advanced computer and information technologies could change the nature of war and security.[2] Indeed, the technologies discussed in this book represent a comprehensive review of those that are most likely to affect U.S. military and hence political power in this century.

The underlying question throughout this discussion remains how technological progress could reshape military power. Not surprisingly, the United States faces complex choices as to which technologies should be developed, how other states might respond to those capabilities, and the consequences for international security if U.S. military capabilities are beyond the reach of other states.

Foundations of Military Power

As it evolved throughout American military history, the technological foundation of U.S. military power was based on the desire to use economic power to invest in technology for the purpose of saving American lives. During World War II, the United States harnessed only 30 percent of its immense technological, economic, and industrial power for military purposes, yet, by the end of the war, it was able to produce more weapons than Germany and Japan could destroy.

For generations, U.S. military strategy has rested on the development of military forces that are technologically superior to that of the adversary. This national style for military preparation was in full play during the Cold War when the U.S. military deliberately produced smaller numbers of more technologically advanced weapons than its adversary, the Soviet Union. To succeed, the United States invested trillions of dollars in defense while vastly outspending the economically inefficient Soviet defense complex.

For decades, American policymakers and government officials have argued that the United States will be able to defend the nation's interests successfully because it has military forces that are second to none. The Department of Defense, in the *1997 Quadrennial Defense Review,* reaffirmed that "it is imperative that the United States maintain its military superiority. . . ." During that same year, the National Defense Panel reported that if the United States does "not lead the technological revolution we will be vulnerable to it."[3] And, in the Senate Armed Services Committee Report, the committee wrote that its priority is "to maintain a strong, stable investment in science and technology in order to develop superior technology that will permit the United States to maintain its current military advantages . . . and hedge against technological surprise."[4]

In the military sphere the United States is often perceived as the preeminent technological state. By virtue of its significant resources invested in technology, as well as the breadth and depth of its technologies, other states cannot compete militarily with the United States and are likely to fail when they try for two reasons. First, the span of technologies being developed by private firms, defense contractors, universities, and government laboratories in the United States exceeds that of other states, and, second, the depth of technological knowledge in the public and private sectors is also without precedent. With its gross national product at approximately nine trillion dollars, the United States uses its economic power to invest billions of dollars in military and commercial research and development programs.[5] Although the absolute level of U.S. investment has declined as other economies have expanded in recent decades, it is nonetheless true that the United States retains its preeminence.

The reality is that these investments in technology established the basis for U.S. military power during the last century that even other great military powers cannot challenge. The best example is the former Soviet Union, which built a military machine that was considered roughly equal to U.S. military power. But, the United States had greater economic power, whereas Russia today is bankrupt; is barely able to feed, clothe, and house its military, and invests relatively little money in defense technologies.[6] For the foreseeable future, Russia's military forces are likely to remain moribund and unable to represent a serious threat to the United States. The other great military power, China, has an aggressive program to expand and modernize its military forces. During the 1990s, China purchased submarines, aircraft, and other advanced military technologies from Russia, which provides limited support to China's military. Although these actions increased its military capabilities, China remains a regional military power that cannot seriously threaten the United States.[7]

Critical Military Capabilities

The technologies being developed for the U.S. military, particularly in the fields of directed energy, targeting, and command and control, are likely to widen the technological gap between the United States and other states. As the U.S. military continues to invest in these technologies, its capabilities predictably will remain significantly greater than that of other states. This is especially true for the rogue states, such as Iran, Iraq, and North Korea, that have dominated U.S. military planning since the Persian Gulf War. Why, then, does the United States invest in these technologies?

The fundamental reason is that investing, first, in directed-energy technologies is to defend the United States and its military forces from an attack with ballistic missiles, which reflects the emerging consensus that Iran, Iraq, or North Korea could possess ballistic missiles within the first decade of this century.[8] In addition to missile defense, directed-energy technologies are useful for detecting and destroying, in real time, military targets anywhere in the world. As the United States gains the ability to observe and attack targets at will, the investments in directed-energy technologies will translate into the ability to use force with greater precision and effectiveness.

A second area of development is the targeting technologies that also will significantly expand U.S. military power. If, for example, military vehicles, including cruise missiles, that are "piloted" or controlled by computers and sensors, rather than humans, destroy targets as precisely as piloted vehicles, there are profound questions about whether humans should be exposed in war. Future generations of U.S. cruise missiles will be able to destroy targets with the same degree of precision as piloted aircraft, especially as improvements in sensor and artificial intelligence technologies could hit targets with accuracy measured in feet, search the battlefield for specific targets, destroy targets at a predetermined moment, and continue the search for more targets. It is inevitable that manned aircraft could become the technological equivalent of dinosaurs because their performance is limited by the ability of a human in the cockpit to withstand the physical stresses.[9]

At the same time, U.S. military power is being enhanced by the development of nonlethal technologies because it could fight without the killing and destruction that have defined war for millennia. The ability to minimize human casualties has emerged as one of the guiding principles in the U.S. strategy for war in this century. Further, U.S. military power is being enhanced by the development of computer, communication, and information technologies. Even now, computers are making life-and-death decisions in war that historically were reserved to humans. For example, computer and fire control systems on Aegis cruisers coordinate the radars and missiles that track hundreds of targets.

In the automatic mode, they can defend against enemy aircraft or missiles by firing missiles or guns without human commands. When the U.S. Air Force deploys the airborne laser during the first decade of this century, its computers will determine when to fire the laser at missiles because humans cannot make those decisions quickly enough.

With the development of information technologies, the United States will be able to focus its attacks against computers and communications networks rather than military targets, which are often located in cities. Once mature, information war could become the modern equivalent of nuclear weapons except that it disrupts societies without destroying the communications, power, and banking systems.

Investment in the Right Technologies

For the United States to maintain its military power, it is imperative for officials in private industry and in the government to develop the right technologies. As the U.S. defense establishment invests the nation's limited resources in technologies, the central question is whether to invest in modernizing military forces or maintaining the readiness of the military.[10] This is not an academic exercise because investing in the right technologies could determine whether the United States maintains its technological advantage. To cite one prominent example, the failure to develop ballistic missiles during the 1940s and 1950s would have seriously weakened U.S. military capabilities against the Soviet Union.

The choices made today by government and private sector officials will affect U.S. military capabilities for decades, but there is no formula for determining which technologies should be developed. To maintain its technological edge, the U.S. defense establishment considers two primary factors.

The first is the nature of the military threat to the United States. The realization that Nazi Germany might have been developing the atomic bomb influenced President Roosevelt's decision to spend billions of dollars during World War II on the Manhattan Project, the U.S. atomic bomb program. Another example was the decision to invest in missile defense technologies following the Persian Gulf War because of Iraq's programs for developing ballistic missiles and weapons of mass destruction.[11] In practice, military threats galvanize action within the U.S. technological community, as seen when the Soviet Union's active program for developing long-range ballistic missiles accelerated the U.S. missile program.

The second factor is investment in technologies that raise the possibility of creating a significant technological advance. Because the development of the GPS has radically increased the accuracy of aircraft, ships, and missiles, the U.S.

military has invested billions of dollars in equipping virtually all modern weapons with GPS-guidance systems. Although the strategic significance of GPS was not well understood originally, GPS satellites vastly increased U.S. military power.

The threat that ballistic missiles pose to the United States is now part of the public debate, which provides insights into how the defense establishment invests in technologies. As the debate about national missile defense became more intense, the Congress passed the 1999 National Missile Defense Act. Meanwhile, reports about the policymaking process inside the White House suggest that senior officials based their decisions on missile defense on four factors— cost, technological opportunity, effects on other countries, and urgency of the threat.[12] In addition to these criteria, domestic politics and other factors play a significant role in decisions about developing these technologies.

Although the criteria might be correct, there is no guarantee that private firms or government agencies in the United States will make the right technological choices. Predictably, the technological community might not invest in the right technologies given the difficulties of choosing among competing technologies during a time of great technological progress. The extraordinary rates of progress in computer, sensor, and communications network technologies highlight the problems of balancing investments in all military systems, especially when these choices involve billions of dollars. To cite one example, the development of lasers for missile defenses represents expenditures of hundreds of billions of dollars, but development of these weapons represents only one of thousands of programs currently being funded by the Department of Defense.

Harvesting Mature Technologies

To maintain its military power, the U.S. defense establishment must continue to invest in technologies that are in various stages of development or maturity. The same is true for the technologies that are discussed in this book.

The first level consists of the technologies that are mature, which means that these are likely to be immediately relevant for U.S. defense and foreign policy. Such technologies are well along in their development, are ready or nearly ready for use in the arsenal, or will be soon integrated into U.S. military forces. Of the technologies discussed in this book, the mature ones include the airborne laser, cruise missiles, nonlethal technologies, unmanned aerial vehicles, reachback operations, the role of computers in military decisions, and information war. This represents a comprehensive list of the most critical technologies that are being pursued in the U.S. research and development community. For example, the ABL that will be deployed by the year 2005 or 2006 will immediately create the ability to destroy ballistic missiles and thereby significantly improve U.S. military capabilities. At the same time, the development of cruise missiles, nonlethal technologies for minimizing human casualties among soldiers and civilians, and advanced communications and computers for planning and executing military operations from the relative safety of the United States all represent relatively mature technologies.

The second level includes technologies that are promising but that will not improve U.S. military capabilities for another decade or more. This category includes reusable launch vehicles; many of the potential applications for lasers, including SBL and GBL for missile defense and maritime operations; and high-powered microwave technologies. Although these technologies could radically increase military capabilities, the operational military forces will not have them available as weapons until the year 2010 or later.

The third level of technologies shows promise but will not be mature for decades. One example is the laser applications that will permit the United States to conduct surveillance of the entire world from space. An even more significant technological development will be the ability to integrate totally all sensors, weapons, and communications technologies into a seamless military system, but this will not occur for several decades.

There is no fundamental mystery to developing advanced technologies and ensuring that they become mature. The reality is that the dollars invested in these programs are a direct measure of their importance to the U.S. defense establishment. Although the SBL will not be technologically mature and operational for ten years or more, it is true that vastly increasing its funding will accelerate the schedule. In view of growing evidence that Iraq, Iran, and North Korea could possess long-range missiles with nuclear warheads, the U.S. Senate added $100 million the SBL budget in 1998 and $10 million in 2000.[13] Also worth noting is that the SBL represents only one of many technologies being developed by the United States, which gives some measure of the depth and breadth of U.S. technology.

Response of Other States to U.S. Military Power

The U.S. military is so technologically advanced that other states cannot realistically prevent the United States from achieving its military objectives. Although a state might be able to inflict a temporary setback or cause a tactical defeat, for example, by using nuclear weapons against U.S. military forces, U.S. military power cannot be directly challenged. In view of this constraint, the best option for states that want to challenge the United States is to attack the U.S. political will in order to deter American involvement.

The extent of U.S. military power, which is based on technology, is forcing states to turn to what are termed *asymmetric* strategies, in which states focus their technologies and weapons on U.S. vulnerabilities. A common example of an asymmetric strategy is to develop weapons that temporarily paralyze or disrupt U.S. military operations. A frequently cited example would have been Iraq's decision to attack U.S. military bases in Saudi Arabia with nuclear weapons. The objective of an asymmetric strategy is not to defeat the United States militarily, but to suggest to the American people that their vulnerabilities will make war very painful and costly, even if the United States ultimately wins. This strategy has great allure for states that are unwilling to surrender to U.S. military power.

Despite its extraordinary investments in technology, asymmetric strategies represent a critical weakness in the U.S. strategy for relying on advanced technology to win war. Although the high-technology strategy was successful during the twentieth century, there are signs that the technological option may not be as useful in future conflicts. During both World Wars and the Cold War, the U.S. military invested in technologies that were optimal for fighting against organized armies, navies, and air forces. There are doubts, however, whether the emphasis on technology will be successful during this century when conflicts are the product of struggles among religious, ethnic, and national groups, rather than classic wars between modern states. To complicate its strategy for investing in technology, the Department of Defense wants to be able to win another major theater war, such as the Persian Gulf War, and to prevail in conflicts against less capable adversaries.

A strategic weakness of the U.S. defense program is its focus on the development of advanced technologies for waging major wars. Undoubtedly, the U.S. military gains enormous advantage from weapons with longer ranges, as well as greater accuracy and lethality, but what if these technological advantages mean less in future wars? A fundamental conclusion is that U.S. military power will depend on developing technologies that are equally adept at winning major wars and defeating asymmetric strategies. For example, it is likely that China would rely heavily on mines to interfere with U.S. naval operations in the Straits of Taiwan during a conflict with the United States, but the United States has not invested significant resources in developing technologies for countering mine warfare.

The problem for the U.S. military is that states are investing in technologies that deter its involvement and prevent the use of its overwhelming superiority in conventional weapons. The strategy is to undermine the U.S. political will to fight, rather than to defeat the United States militarily, which often depends on threatening to kill Americans. For example, during U.S. military intervention in Serbia in 1999, U.S. political and military officials were sure that they were willing to fight but unsure how many U.S. soldiers they were willing to lose in that war. Historically, the foundation for a strategy that attacks American political will is the Vietnam War, whose legacy was that the United States could not be defeated by North Vietnam but did not have the political will to win that war.[14]

In the language of modern strategy, the United States is investing in a "denial" strategy, which prevents states from deterring the United States. Its military power is vulnerable if states can deter the United States by undermining its will to fight because it fears casualties or entangling military quagmires. As states develop technologies that allow them to attack U.S. military power, the United States will develop technologies that insulate the country from threats that might undermine its will to fight. The two prominent examples are the development of defenses against ballistic missiles, known as national missile defense, and cruise missile defenses, on which the United States is investing billions of dollars. If these technology programs allow United States to prevent states from deterring it by threats to attack the homeland or troops overseas, the asymmetric strategy will fail because the United States uses its technological abilities to insulate itself from attack.

The broader conclusion is that the United States is engaged, wittingly or not, in a technological arms race. Whether the United States prevails will depend on whether its technological base is sufficiently advanced to counter the efforts of states that are determined to prevent it from maintaining the ability to defeat other states in wars.

Technology and National Security

The purpose of technology in national defense is to be able to achieve the state's military objectives when its interests are threatened. But, military power matters little unless the United States is willing to use it. There are times when the United States lacks the political will to use its military power to prevail. In defense of the unwillingness to use American military power decisively, observers have argued that U.S. military power was disproportionate to the crisis, that U.S. intervention would unnecessarily kill innocent civilians and destroy the state that intervention was designed to save (such as Serbia), and that the United States must articulate a new strategy for guiding the use of military force in this century.

In view of the economic, military, and technological power of the United

States, it is no wonder that other states cannot match the depth and breadth of U.S. military power, which is illustrated by the case of cruise missiles. Cruise missiles are extremely precise weapons, but their effective use requires an immense infrastructure for collecting detailed information about potential targets, notably their exact location, elevation, physical layout, and vulnerabilities. Only the United States has the technological apparatus that can collect such information, for, in its absence, cruise missiles are highly accurate but militarily ineffective weapons. Other states will invest in advanced cruise missiles, but, without the technological capabilities to use these weapons effectively, they will be wasting their resources. More important, cruise missiles represent only one example of the totality of U.S. military power, but this technological edge will last only as long as the United States continues to invest significant resources in defense.

The early twenty-first century is a time of extraordinary technological progress in many areas, including the directed-energy, targeting, and information technologies examined in this book. Because the human condition is to explore and investigate the technological options that present themselves, states are bound to explore defense technologies to the limits of their abilities. Although the United States is developing other defense technologies that could influence U.S. military power, the technologies examined in this book are bound to have a decisive effect on war. Because all technological advancement has unintended risks, as illustrated by the risks associated with the development of nuclear weapons, there will be great pressure on officials in the private and public sector to weigh carefully the risks and benefits of investing in technology. For the United States, the strategy has been to invest broadly in all technologies in order to minimize the chances of surprise.

Despite the great technological power of the United States, it is difficult to explain the failures that have plagued its military operations in recent years. The high-technology military did not fare terribly well in Somalia, Haiti, or Serbia, in which the United States was deterred from using its military power in a decisive fashion out of fear of killing innocent civilians or destroying a country. Interestingly, the Serbian military shot down an F-117 stealth fighter on the fourth day of the NATO military operation.[15] What if the United States has designed its military to be so dependent on technology that it is irrelevant to the crises of this century? Alternatively, did the United States allow its defense spending to erode seriously during the 1990s? Regardless of the answer to these questions, the prudent option is to invest U.S. economic resources in military capabilities that other states cannot challenge, but this strategy is likely to perpetuate competition in technologies and responses by other states to those technologies.

On a positive note, the United States has the economic wealth to win this race, but one characteristic of this strategy is the enormous cost of modern weapons. One problem with the U.S. approach to military technology is that weapons are so expensive that the ability of the United States to buy the numbers of weapons that its military services say they need is increasingly limited, even though significant increases in defense spending are contemplated. Given that F-22 fighter aircraft will cost about $150 million each; B-2 bombers about $2 billion each; and aircraft carriers about $5 billion each, not including their aircraft and helicopters, an annual increase of $50–$100 billion dollars in defense spending is not unrealistic.[16] The current plan to modernize U.S. fighter aircraft has a price tag of $400 billion, and the development of lasers for missile defense is likely to cost hundreds of billions of dollars. Although the United States has great economic power and can afford to develop these weapons, it is worth reflecting on the fact that the United States spends twice the total amount spent by Russia, China, Iran, Syria, Iraq, Libya, North Korea, Serbia, Cuba, and Sudan combined for defense.[17]

Technological power is no substitute for the political will to use such power wisely. The book's contributors are unified by the belief that the United States is likely to use its military power constructively to promote international peace and prosperity. The wise strategy is to invest steadily in technologies to ensure that the United States preserves its ability to defend the nation's vital interests in times of crisis. The contributors agree, however, that U.S. political and military leaders should resist the temptation to believe that whatever technological edge in military security that the United States possesses in this century is permanent. As with most advantages, those resulting from technology can be the most fleeting.

Notes

1. "Defense Budget Boost to 4 Percent of GDP Would Pose Dramatic Shift," *Inside the Pentagon,* Aug. 31, 2000, 3.

2. See Joseph E. Eash III, "Joint Vision 2010 Technology," *Joint Forces Quarterly* (autumn/winter 1999–2000), 43–46.

3. William C. Cohen, *Report of the Quadrennial Defense Review* (Washington, D.C.: Government Printing Office, 1997), 14, who says that this "means harnessing new technologies to give U.S. forces greater military capabilities. . . ." See also *Transforming Defense: National Security in the 21st Century, Report of the National Defense Panel* (Arlington, Va.: National Defense Panel, 1997), 8; and *A National Security Strategy for a New Century* (Washington, D.C.: The White House, 1999), 11, in which U.S. Armed Forces must be able "to deter and, if necessary, to fight and win conflicts in which our vital interests are threatened."

4. National Defense Authorization Act for Fiscal Year 2001 Report 106-292, 106th Congress, 2nd Session (Washington, D.C.: U.S. Government Printing Office, 2000), 9.

5. *The Military Balance, 1999–2000* (London: Oxford University Press for the International Institute for Strategic Studies, 1999), 20.

6. Ibid., 105.

7. "Trip by Chinese to Military Site Raises Concern," *Washington Times,* Aug. 25, 2000, 1, for reports that "Chinese military officials were briefed yesterday on how the United States develops joint training for its forces at a sensitive U.S. military facility in southern Virginia."

8. John Donnelly, "ICBM Threat by U.S. by Next Year, General Predicts," *Defense Week,* Mar. 1, 1999, 16. See Commission to Assess the Ballistic Missile Threat to the United States, Washington, D.C., July 15, 1998.

9. See "High-Tech Suits Help Pilots Avoid Gravity's Perils," *The New York Times,* Aug. 22, 2000, D1, which notes that "today's military aircraft accelerate so quickly and turn so rapidly that they meet or exceed the physical limits of their pilots."

10. "Clinton to Boost the Defense Budget for Fiscal 2002, Blunting Bush Attack," *The Wall Street Journal,* Aug. 22, 2000, A1. See John Hillen, "Defense Death's Spiral: The Increasing Irrelevance of More Spending," *Foreign Affairs* (July/August 1999), 2–7.

11. See *Conduct of the Persian Gulf War: Final Report to Congress* (Washington, D.C.: Department of Defense, 1992).

12. See "U.S. Study Reopens Division over Nuclear Missile Threat," *The New York Times,* July 5, 2000, A1–A6, which discusses the factors that reportedly influenced President William J. Clinton's deliberations on whether to develop national missile defenses.

13. "Appropriators Boost FY01 Space-Based Laser Funding by $10 Million," *Inside the Air Force,* July 21, 2000, 10–11. The purpose of this additional funding is to accelerate the SBL demonstration, known as the Integrated Flight Experiment (IFX).

14. Guenter Lewy, *America in Vietnam* (London: Oxford University Press, 1978).

15. "U.S. Rescues Pilot as NATO Widens Attack; Stealth Fighter Down in Serbia, Reports of Atrocities Mounting," *The Washington Post,* Mar. 28, 1999, A1.

16. "Defense Budget Boost to 4 Percent of GDP [Gross Domestic Product] Would Pose Dramatic Shift," *Inside the Pentagon,* Aug. 31, 2000, 3.

17. Ibid.

Contributors

William C. Martel, Professor of National Security Affairs at the Naval War College in Newport, Rhode Island, was previously Associate Professor of International Relations and Russian Studies and founder and Director, Center for Strategy and Technology, at the Air War College. He received his doctorate in international relations from the University of Massachusetts (Amherst) and was a Post-Doctoral Research Fellow and MacArthur Scholar at Harvard University's Center for Science and International Affairs in the Kennedy School of Government. Martel served as a member of the professional staff of The RAND Corporation in Washington, D.C., where he directed studies on various national security problems, including the United States governmental process for managing proliferation. The author of several books and book chapters, Martel also has published scholarly articles in *Orbis, Defense Analysis,* and *Strategic Review* and has written articles for the *Wall Street Journal* and the *Christian Science Monitor*. He has been involved with the U.S. Air Force Scientific Advisory Board, has chaired the strategy panel for the Air Force's Lasers and Space Optical Systems Study, and currently directs studies on technological programs (space, precision targeting, and command and control) sponsored by the Defense Advanced Research Projects Agency. He is a member of the International Institute for Strategic Studies.

Col. Kenneth W. Barker, U.S. Air Force, is assigned to the C-17 program and aircraft training simulators at Wright-Patterson Air Force Base, Dayton, Ohio. He has been involved in research and development for high-technology systems throughout his Air Force career. He was assigned to the U.S. Air Force Academy, where he served as Chief of Honor and Honor Education and Chief, Astrodynamics Division, in the Department of Astronautics. Earlier, Colonel Barker had served as program manager, chief engineer, systems engineer, and test engineer for satellite, directed energy, and conventional munitions systems. As program manager and chief engineer for Phillip's Laboratory's High Altitude Balloon Experiment, he was responsible for this experiment conducted for the Ballistic Missile Defense Organization in the Pentagon. At the U.S. Air Force Phillip's Laboratory, Kirtland Air Force Base, in Albuquerque, New Mexico, he was responsible for satellite payloads. At the Strategic Defense Initiative Organization, he was a laser beam control performance analyst for the Air Force Weapons Laboratory's Airborne Laser Laboratory and managed the gyroscope test program that involved testing nine gyroscopes from six international companies. A distinguished graduate of the Air Force Academy, Colonel Barker earned his Master of Science degree in aerospace engineering from Massachusetts Institute of Technology in 1982 and his doctorate in aerospace engineering from the University of Washington in 1991.

Col. Scott M. Britten, U.S. Air Force, is director of the F-15 System Program at Robins Air Force Base, Georgia. A member of the Air Force's acquisition corps, he has held acquisition management and flight test positions. He served as program director for special projects at the Electronic Systems Center, Hanscom Air Force Base, Massachusetts, where he managed the development, test, and deployment of classified electronic weapon systems. Other assignments included a tour on the staff of the Assistant Secretary of the Air Force for Acquisition; Chief, Maintenance and Engineering, for the U-2 aircraft fleet, sensors, and ground stations; director of a joint test force for a classified aircraft; manager of all armament testing for the Air Force Flight Test Center; Deputy for Engineering, Antisatellite Combined Task Force; and manager of a data processing system development for a surveillance satellite. A distinguished graduate of the Air Force Academy and the U.S. Air Force Test Pilot School, Colonel Britten was also a National Science Foundation Fellow at the Massachusetts Institute of Technology, where he earned a master of science degree in aeronautical and astronautical engineering in 1977. He is a 1997 graduate of the Air War College.

Lt. Col. David B. Glade, U.S. Air Force, is Acting Chief, Air Superiority Mission Area Team, in the Requirements Directorate of the Headquarters of the Air Combat Command at Langley Air Force Base, Virginia. A flight test pilot, he was the deputy chief of test and evaluation for the F-22 System Program Office at Wright Patterson Air Force Base, Dayton, Ohio, where he was responsible for planning the ground and flight test program for the Air Force's F-22 fighter. He served as an experimental test pilot at Edwards Air Force Base, where he flight tested all models of the F-15, including certifying the F-15E for terrain-following operation in weather; tested a ground collision warning system; and conducted numerous radar, flight control, weapons, and engine tests. Colonel Glade also served as the chief F-15 instructor at the U.S. Air Force Test Pilot School. His operational assignments include a tour at Mountain Home Air Force Base, Idaho, as a flight examiner in the EF-111A and a tour at Royal Air Force Base Lakenheath, United Kingdom, as chief of aircrew training in the F-111F. He is a member of the Society of Experimental Test Pilots and a member of the Air Force's acquisition corps. He is a distinguished graduate of the Air Force Academy, Undergraduate Pilot Training, and the U.S. Air Force Test Pilot School and graduated with distinction from the College of Naval Command and Staff. He earned a bachelor of science degree from the Air Force Academy, a master of science degree from the Department of Mechanical and Aerospace Engineering at Princeton University, and a master of arts degree from the U.S. Naval War College.

Richard J. Harknett is associate professor of international relations in the Department of Political Science at the University of Cincinnati. He received his doctorate from The Johns Hopkins University, Baltimore, Maryland. Dr. Harknett is coeditor of *The Absolute Weapon Revisited: Nuclear Arms and the Emerging International Order* (University of Michigan Press, 1998) and has published scholarly articles in *Security Studies, Orbis, Congress and the Presidency,* and *Parameters,* as well as numerous book chapters. In 1997, he was presented the Edith C. Alexander Distinguished Teaching Award at the University of Cincinnati.

Capt. William J. McCarthy, U.S. Navy, is commanding officer of the aircraft carrier USS *George Washington* (CVN 73). A 1976 graduate of the College of the Holy Cross, he was designated a naval flight officer and flew E-2C Hawkeyes during the majority of his career. Operational flying tours included VAW-125, VAW-121, and VAW-126. While serving as executive officer of VAW-126, he participated in Operation Desert Shield and Operation Desert Storm and flew more than thirty combat missions. He assumed command of VAW-126 in December 1991. Under his command, the Seahawks deployed on the USS *John F. Kennedy* in support of Operation Provide Promise and operations in the Adriatic Sea. Following command, Captain McCarthy served on the staff of Commander, Carrier Group Four. In July 1993, he was selected for Navy nuclear power training and reported as prospective executive officer to the USS *John C. Stennis* in October 1995. Following the ship's commissioning, he served as executive officer until December 1996 and, in January 1997, assumed command of the fast combat support ship, USS *Detroit,* with successful Mediterranean and Arabian Gulf deployments. A distinguished graduate of the U.S. Naval Test Pilot School (USNTPS), Captain McCarthy's shore duty assignments included the Naval Air Test Center, where he served as the project officer for the E-2C APS-138 Radar and Update Development Programs, and he later joined the USNTPS faculty as the senior airborne systems instructor. Assigned to Naval Air Systems Command Headquarters, he served as the E-2C Avionics Systems project officer. Captain McCarthy has flown more than thirty types of military aircraft, accumulated more than four thousand hours of flight time, and made seven hundred arrested landings.

Lt. Col. William B. McClure, U.S. Air Force, is Chief, Deployed Division, at the Defense Information Systems Network in Washington, D.C., with responsibilities for improving communications for deployed forces. He is a developmental engineer with a background in weapon systems acquisition, system effectiveness analysis, and engineering instruction. He served as an aeronautical engineer in the Deputy for Engineering, Aeronautical Systems Center, where he worked on various technical issues, including integration of LANTIRN on the F-16 aircraft, dual role fighter assessments, and B-1B performance. Colonel McClure was assigned as the lead external aerodynamics engineer for the B-1B Systems Program Office, where he was responsible for working weapon separation and wind tunnel testing. He served two tours in the Department of Aeronautics at the Air Force Academy, where he developed and taught the supersonic aerodynamics portion of the U.S. Air Force Test Pilot School's academic program. As Chief, Air Superiority Branch of the Air Force Studies and Analyses Agency in the Pentagon, Colonel McClure directed military assessments of future Air Force air superiority systems. A distinguished graduate of the Air Force Academy, he earned a bachelor's degree in aeronautical engineering and master's and doctorate degrees in aerospace engineering.

Lt. Col. David J. Nicholls, U.S. Air Force, is serving in the Special Programs Directorate in the Office of the Assistant Secretary of the Air Force for Acquisition in the Pentagon. A materials engineer with experience in resource analysis, he worked as an operations analyst for the Program Analysis and Evaluation Directorate within the Office of the Secretary of Defense, where he performed statutorily required cost estimates for major weapon systems, including the New Attack Submarine, the AIM-9X (Sidewinder) missile, the Joint

Air to Surface Stand-off Missile (JASSM), and the Tomahawk cruise missile. He also performed economic and technical analyses supporting Secretary of Defense decisions for the Seawolf submarine, the Crusader howitzer, advanced munitions, the Defense Nuclear Agency, and public shipyards used by the U.S. Navy. Colonel Nicholls served at the Air Force Academy as an associate professor and Director, Applied Mechanics Laboratory, where he directed and taught courses in composite materials, metallurgy, failure analysis, strength of materials, and systems engineering design. He also worked as a development engineer at the Air Force Materials Laboratory, where he established in-house capabilities to fabricate specialized composite matrix materials. Colonel Nicholls also conceived and managed research contracts for thermoplastic composites extensively used on the B-2 bomber and for composite fabrication methods. He earned his bachelor of science degree from Rensselaer Polytechnic Institute, a master of science degree from the University of Dayton, and a doctorate in philosophy from the University of Oxford and has published papers on defense topics.

Col. William H. Possel, U.S. Air Force, is Deputy Director, Space Based Laser Project Office, at Los Angeles Air Force Base, California. Involved in space systems acquisition management and space operations throughout his career, he was Director of Production for the Titan IV and Titan II space boosters at the Space and Missile Center at Los Angeles Air Force Base. Other assignments included director of systems engineering and mission director for various classified satellite programs and Chief, Advanced Research for Special Projects, Office of the Secretary of the Air Force. Colonel Possel also served as a project officer for laser experiments, both ground based and on the space shuttle. He is a graduate of the University of Cincinnati with a bachelor's degree in physics and has a master's degree in engineering physics from the Air Force Institute of Technology, Dayton, Ohio.

Col. Mark E. Rogers, U.S. Air Force, is Director, Forward Tier Defense Program Support Team in the Ballistic Missile Defense Office in the Pentagon. A 1976 physics graduate of the U.S. Air Force Academy, he has been involved in defense-oriented research and development for the past twenty years, with a primary focus on applications of lasers for military systems. His background includes test-range support for future space programs and analyses of capabilities for optical tracking systems at Vandenberg Air Force Base, California. After completing his master's and doctoral degrees in laser physics, Colonel Rogers managed research at the U.S. Air Force Weapons Laboratory for various high-energy laser weapons, which included technology for space-based lasers as part of the Strategic Defense Initiative. In addition to teaching undergraduate physics at the U.S. Air Force Academy and directing a research team for laser devices, he headed a laser biophysics team at the U.S. Air Force Armstrong Laboratory that established new safety thresholds for lasers and studied various nonlethal technologies based on optical systems. He also served as the deputy chief scientist for Armstrong Laboratory with responsibility for its information warfare program and, in that capacity, supervised basic research and scientific personnel programs.

Col. Joseph W. Siniscalchi, U.S. Air Force, is Chief, Reconnaissance Operations Division, in the Joint Chiefs of Staff in the Pentagon. He entered the Air Force in 1975 as a graduate of the Air Force Academy. He has been involved in Air Force reconnaissance operations and program management. As an instructor and evaluation pilot, he has flown more than 4,500 hours primarily in RC-135 reconnaissance aircraft supporting worldwide peacetime intelligence collection and contingency operations. He was assigned to staff positions at Headquarters Strategic Air Command and the Air Staff, where he managed all Air Force strategic reconnaissance platforms, tactics development, and programs. During his assignment at the Air Staff, Colonel Siniscalchi also served as the Joint Staff representative to the United States Open Skies Delegation. In addition, he was instrumental in developing the intelligence broadcast architectures for Operation Desert Storm. Following his assignment at the Air Staff, he commanded an overseas operational detachment and the Air Force's RC-135 Rivet Joint squadron at Offutt Air Force Base, Nebraska, where he established a new operating location at Souda Bay, Greece, and supported major contingency operations. He served as a deputy operations group commander responsible for more than three thousand personnel at U.S. and overseas operational squadrons. Colonel Siniscalchi earned a bachelor of science in civil engineering from the Air Force Academy and a master's degree in economics from the University of Oklahoma.

Col. Eileen M. Walling, U.S. Air Force, is Chief, Weapons Systems Sector, at Headquarters, Air Force Research Laboratories, in Dayton, Ohio. She has spent the last nineteen years in working with Air Force technology programs. She served as the director for the Air Force's High Power Microwave Program, where she was responsible for technical oversight and direction of all electromagnetic technologies and applications for military uses. Previously, Colonel Walling handled numerous jobs on the staff of the Air Force Acquisition Executive. She served as the program element monitor for Rome Laboratory, Armament Laboratory, and Civil Engineering Laboratory, with responsibility for oversight, direction, and advocacy of nine science and technology programs with $280 million in total annual funding. During her assignment at Headquarters, Air Force Systems Command, she managed all of the advanced weapons technologies and conventional armament programs. For several years, Colonel Walling directed technical efforts in adaptive optics and ground-based laser programs at the Air Force Weapons Laboratory. Early in her career, she was a technical systems manager for all U.S. Air Force ground communications terminals and a maintenance supervisor for a radar squadron in upstate New York. She has a master's degree in engineering physics from the Air Force Institute of Technology, a master's degree in systems management from the University of Southern California, and a bachelor of science degree in mathematics and physics from the College of William and Mary, and she has completed the program managers course at the Defense Systems Management College. Colonel Walling is a member of the Acquisition Corps and is certified at Level III in systems planning, research, development, and engineering.

Lt. Col. John E. Ward Jr., U.S. Air Force, is Chief, Space Support Division, in the Directorate of Operations at the Air Force Space Command in Colorado Springs, Colorado. He has been involved in space systems testing, development, acquisition, and operations throughout his career. He was commander of the Atlas Launch Squadron at Cape Canaveral Air Station, Florida. Other assignments include Minuteman and Peacekeeper missile launch controller, mission planner for the F-15–launched antisatellite program, program manager for Strategic Defense Initiative tracking demonstrations, special project officer for the Secretary of the Air Force (Space), and space-based surveillance project officer for the U.S. Space Command. A graduate of the Air Force Academy with a bachelor's degree in astronautical engineering (1980), Colonel Ward earned master's degrees in systems management (1982) and in astronautical engineering at the Air Force Institute of Technology (1984), completed his doctorate in business administration in 1992, and is a 1999 graduate of the Air War College.

Index

acquisition, tracking, pointing, and fire control system, 25, 28, 45
active imaging, 49
adaptive optics, 28–29, 46
Advanced Concept Technology Demonstration (ACTD), 97
Advanced Research Projects Agency (ARPA), 245. *See also* Defense Advanced Research Projects Agency (DARPA)
Advanced Research Projects Agency Network (ARPANET), 245
Aegis-guided missile cruiser, U.S. Navy, xviii
Afghanistan, xvii, 108, 112, 115, 183
airborne infantry, 12
airborne laser (ABL), xvi, 4, 5, 7, 21–22, 38–54, 99, 226, 228, 261–63
Airborne Laser Laboratory (ALL), 40
Airborne Optical Adjunct (AOA), 40
airborne warning and control system (AWACS), 14, 50, 100, 109, 186
air campaign planning, xviii, 199, 201
Air Command Combat, U.S. Air Force, 91. *See also* Langley Air Force Base
aircraft: A-10, 102; B-1, xiv; B-2, xiv, 163, 267; B-52, xiv; Backfire, 76; Badger, 76; 747, xvi, 40; C-130, 99; C-141, 203, 210; C-17, 99, 164; F-117, xiv, 179, 183, 267; F-15, 177, 178; F-15E, 163; F-16, 97, 114, 163; F-22, 226, 267; fly-by-wire, 42; high-value, 48; MiG-23, 177–78; P-51, 178;

SR-71, 226; U-2, 184–85, 208, 212; Wright Flyer, 226
aircraft carrier: 55–89, 70, 72, 74, 81, 163, 204, 226, 267; battle group operations, xvi; *Nimitz*-class, xvi; task force, 77
air defenses, 49, 51, 67, 108, 144, 163, 191; suppression of enemy, 174
Air Force, U.S., 13, 21, 26, 40, 56, 62, 67, 98, 111, 154, 159, 161–62, 189–90, 192, 200–1, 204, 211, 228, 261
Air Force Phillips Laboratory, 45, 156
Air Force Research Laboratory (AFRL), 93, 97
Air Force Scientific Advisory Board, 174, 182, 190–91
Air Force Space Command, 161, 165
airlift, 118–19, 123, 164. *See also* Sealift
air superiority, 51, 100, 115
air tasking order (ATO), 201–3
Alaska, 23
Albuquerque, New Mexico, 28
Al Firdos bunker, Baghdad, 211
amphibious forces, 77; amphibious ready group (ARG), 57
anthrax, 117
antiaircraft weapon, 16, 70–72, 174
Antiballistic Missile (ABM) Treaty, 21, 39. *See also* missile defense; national missile defense
antisatellite weapon: 14–16, 39, 49, 53, 80, 166; ground-based laser, 16, 29; kinetic energy missile, 14; space-based, 16

antiship missile defense, 67–70, 72
Arabian Gulf, 60, 73
Archimedes, 61
Argentina, 58
Arizona, 28
Army, U.S., 133, 185, 189, 225–28, 230–31
Army Air Force, U.S., 62
Army Field Manual 100-5, 230
Arnold, General Hap, 62
artificial intelligence, 180, 188
Ascender Project, 160
asymmetric strategy, 264
atmospheric compensation, 16, 43, 46, 52. *See also* adaptive optics; antisatellite weapon; laser, ground based
atmospheric effects, 6, 8, 14, 28, 39, 43, 63, 66
attrition, 115, 180
Auftragstaktik, 223
Australia, 160, 207
automatic target recognition, 185
automation, 178–79, 181
autonomous vehicle, 41, 99, 159, 175–76, 183, 187–88

Baghdad, Iraq, 40, 112
Ballistic Missile Defense Organization (BMDO), 14, 26
bandwidth, 92, 185–86
banking systems, information warfare, xiv–xix, 241
basing rights, 118
battle damage assessment (BDA), 9, 12, 17, 98. *See also* war effects confirmation
battlefield air interdiction, 102
battlefield illumination, 17. *See also* laser
battle management, 48
battleship, 107
beacon illuminator, laser, 47
Beale Air Force Base, 208
bifocal mirror, 28
Biological Weapons Convention, 139
"Black Hole," planning cell, 200. *See also* Persian Gulf War
Boeing Corporation, 40, 159
Bonaparte, Napoleon, 232
Bosnia, 129–30, 183, 207–8, 257, 265
Brazil, 58
Bush, President George H. W., 118

California, 28, 208
camouflage, 124
Canada, 60

casualties, xiv, xvii, 115, 117–18, 124, 129, 138, 140, 143, 175
center of gravity, 119, 144, 150, 203, 209
Certain Conventional Weapons Convention (CCWC), 139
chaos, in war, 232
characteristic times, 233
Charleston, South Carolina, 164
chemical, biological weapons, 9, 11–12, 20, 22–23, 59, 78, 98, 117, 120, 130, 132, 134, 174, 185, 188
chemical oxygen iodine laser (COIL), 28, 45
Chemical Weapons Convention, 140
Chile, 60
China: 23, 58–59, 61, 110–11, 113, 259, 264, 267; land-based missiles, 114; laser program, 81
close air support, 102
Coast Guard, U.S., 99
Cold War, xvii, 20, 24, 57, 64, 78, 108, 130, 174, 208, 225, 258, 264
collateral damage, 96, 123, 136–37, 145–46, 148, 182, 188. *See also* casualties
Colorado, 209
combat air patrol, 51, 122–23
Combined Air Operations Center, 208
command and control, xiv–xv, 9, 11, 50, 177, 199–256
command and technology, 220–40
command by influence plan, 224
commercial firms, xv, xvii, xx, 3, 7, 13–14, 20, 30, 40, 57, 62, 80, 92, 108, 113, 122–23, 125, 130, 143, 153, 164, 166–67, 200, 226–27, 241–42, 244–45, 259, 262, 264
commercial satellite imagery, 9, 61, 112, 162
commercial space systems, 165
communication: network, xix, 14; satellite, 3, 5–7, 17, 48, 199
computer: xix, 199, 220–40, 242–44, 258; networked, 243. *See also* information warfare
Congress, U.S., xix, 21, 41
Congressional Budget Office, 190
connectivity, 249, 251
Contingency Theater Automated Planning System (CTAPS), 200, 203–4, 227. *See also* reachback operations
Corbett, Sir Julian, 57, 77
cost-effectiveness, 113, 125, 155, 166–67, 176, 181, 192, 208
countermeasures, 5, 15, 17, 79–80, 97, 121, 125, 135, 137, 141

counterspace operations: 39, 49; defensive, 165. *See also* space control
countersurveillance, maritime, 73
counterterrorism, 73. *See also* terrorism
creativity, computers, 231
critical infrastructure, nodes, 136, 247
cruise missile, 9, 49, 55–89, 69, 81, 107–28, 143, 163, 166, 175, 180, 183, 187, 191, 209, 212, 260, 262–63, 266; Alfa, 110, 114; antiship, 56, 58, 67, 71, 77, 114; cost, 117; cruise missile defense, 108, 118, 120–25, 265; delay deployment, 117–18; employment, 115–20; Kingfish, 58; Koral antiship, 58; nonlethal technology, 137; offensive attack operations, 120–21; precision targeting, 109, 111; proliferation, 107, 109–13; range, 109; survivability, 109–11; tactical defeat, 119–20, Tomahawk, 58, 78, 111–12, 114, 163
Cuba, 267
Cuban Missile Crisis, 184
cyberspace, 243

databases, air campaign planning, 204
deception, 109, 124
decoys, 165
deep attack, 109
Defense Advanced Research Projects Agency (DARPA), 41, 62, 227–29
Defense Mapping Agency, 112
defense planning, 8, 11, 24, 50, 125
defense spending, xv, 20, 119, 165, 257, 267
Defense Support Program, 14
Denial strategy, 265
Department of Defense, xv, xx, 14, 20, 30, 40, 57, 62, 80, 92, 108, 122–23, 125, 130, 143, 153, 164, 166–67, 200, 226–27, 241–42, 244–45, 259, 262, 264
Department of Energy, 40, 226
deterrence: 57, 241–56; U.S. involvement, 116–17
Dhahran, Saudi Arabia, 40
diplomacy, 165
directed energy, xiv–xv, xx, 3–104
Directed Energy Applications for Tactical Airborne Combat (DE-ATAC), 67, 97
Directed Energy Directorate, Kirtland Air Force Base, 97
Director of Defense Research and Engineering, DOD, 174

Eaker, General Ira, 62

economic sanctions, 147
Egypt, 60
electrical power systems, xiv, xix, 241
electromagnetic pulse (EMP), 64, 91, 135–37, 140, 142, 144, 146–47, 212
electromagnetic spectrum, wavelength, xvi, 4, 12, 90–91
electronic circuits, 24
electro-optical (EO) sensor, 11, 73, 182
environmental sensing, 12, 17
Europe, 160
European Space Agency (ESA), 160
Evolved Expendable Launch Vehicle (EELV), 26, 154
expeditionary warfare, 57
expendable: launch systems, 166; weapons, 176

Falklands War, 61
fiber-optic communication network, 14
fire control system, 25, 47
fleet defense, 55–89
fog of war, von Clausewitz, 229
footprint, 95, 101, 203, 207
foreign policy, xix
Forward from the Sea, 57
France, 59–61, 110, 207
fratricide, 77, 95, 179
fuel tank, missile vulnerability, 24, 47

Germany, 58, 60–61, 164, 176, 225, 258, 261
Global Broadcast System (GBS), 209, 212, 228
Global Command and Control System, 227
Global Positioning System (GPS): xiv, 6, 8, 59, 91, 102, 112–13, 117, 124, 166, 180, 191, 251, 261–62; differential, 111
gravity bombs, 11
Great Britain: 58, 60–61, 160; air defenses, 124; Ministry of Defense, 73
gross national product, 259
Guam, 208
guerrilla attack, 209
guidance, terrain following, 112

Haiti, 129, 210, 257, 265
hardbody handover, 43, 47. *See also* missile defense
hardened targets, 98
Hawaii, 23
helicopter, Comanche, 190
high-altitude balloon experiment (HABE), 45
High Power Microwave Power Division, Kirtland Air Force Base, 100

Hippocrates, 61
homeland defense, 199
Hoover Dam, 97
Horner, Lt. General Charles A., 200, 213
Hubble space telescope, 25, 164
human: brain and military command, 221;
    control, 50, 183; pilots, xvii, 7, 173–95
hyperspectral imagery (HSI), 49

identify friend or foe (IFF), 48
India, 23, 58, 110
individual empowerment, information tech-
    nology, 244
Indonesia, 58
industrial revolution, 245
inertial guidance system, 111
information: age, 242; overload, 229; military,
    247–48; retaliation, 251; societal, 246, 248,
    250; superiority, 236; technology, 220; war-
    fare, xiii, xix, xviii, 61, 130–31, 241–56,
    263
infrared: emissions, 8; imagery, 214; sensor,
    9, 16
injuries, retinal, 7
intelligence community, 142, 162, 186
international agreements, 7, 132
international space station, 166
Internet, 241–52
Iran, xv, 20, 31, 58–60, 260, 263, 267
Iraq, xv, xvii, 10, 20, 22–23, 31, 58, 60, 98,
    107–8, 112, 115, 202, 210, 250, 260,
    263–64, 267; air defense sites, 10; ballistic
    missiles, 22–23, 40, 261. *See also* missiles;
    Persian Gulf War missiles
Iridium, satellite, 159
Israel, 22, 58, 60–61, 184
Italy, 58, 60, 208

jamming, 72, 92, 145, 165, 185–86, 212
Japan, 23, 58, 160, 208, 258
Johnston Island, 64
joint air tasking cycle, 201
Joint Air to Surface Standoff Missile (JASSM),
    114
Joint Chiefs of Staff, 123, 221, 246
Joint Direct Attack Munition, 115
Joint Force Air Component Commander
    (JFACC), 199–219. *See also* military com-
    mander
Joint Force Commander (JFC), 199–219
Joint Forces Air Component Command Pro-
    gram (DARPA), 227

Joint Surveillance and Target Attack Recon-
    naissance System (JSTARS), 50, 109, 202
Joint Tactical Information Distribution Sys-
    tem, 227
Joint Vision 2010, 57, 221

Kelly Space and Technology, 159
Kettering Bug, 180, 184
Khafji, Saudi Arabia, 202
kinetic energy weapons, 164
Kirtland Air Force Base, 9. *See also* Air Force
    Research Laboratory (AFRL)
Kistler Corporation, 159
Korean War, casualties, 118
Kosovo, xiv, 108, 112, 129, 166, 173, 192
Kuwait, 117

Langley Air Force Base, 200, 213
LANTIRN, 97
laser, xv, 3, 13, 14, 20–37, 40, 45, 55, 62–63,
    90, 97, 142; absorption, 63; adjunct mis-
    sions, 49; beacon illuminator, 47; beam
    control system, 25; beam director, 28, 45,
    47; chemical, 5, 16; communications and
    data relay, 14; continuous wave and pulsed,
    4, 17; exploitable characteristics, 4; flood-
    light, spotlight, 6, 7; ground-based (GBL),
    xv, 20–21, 26, 263; guided bomb, xiv, 4, 11,
    70; high-energy, 13, 15, 21, 25, 40, 47, 78;
    hydrogen fluoride, 5, 6, 15–16, 25–26, 45;
    illuminator, 47; low-energy, 13, 132; optics,
    24; pointing and tracking systems, 16, 25;
    power beaming, 4, 9; primary mirror, 28,
    44, 46; ranging, 7, 47; relay mirror, 30; re-
    mote sensing, 17; scattering, 63; semicon-
    ductor, 5, 10; space-based (SBL), xv–xvi,
    3–20, 24, 30, 38–54; target designator,
    space-based 8, 9; thermal blooming, 28, 63,
    67; track illuminator, 47
latency, satellite communication, 227
Lawrence Livermore National Laboratory, 160
leadership bunkers, 132
Lebanon, 185
legal authority, 230
leveragability, technological, 42
Libya, 60, 183, 267
littoral, 55
Lockheed-Martin Corporation, 40, 160
London, 167

Machina sapiens, 223. *See also* command and
    technology

machine commander, xviii, 220, 228
magnetically insulated linear oscillator
    (MILO), 64
Mahan, Alfred Thayer, 57
Manhattan Project, 42, 261
Marine Corps, U.S., 77, 131, 185, 204, 225
Marine Expeditionary Force (MEF), 57
maritime threats, 58–61
mass attacks, 122
master air attack plan (MAAP), 202
Mauvenet (Turkish destroyer), 72
McDonnell-Douglas Corporation, 14, 156
measurement and signature intelligence
    (MASINT), 12
meteorological effects, 12, 43
microwave, xiv–xv, 9, 55; area weapon, 99;
    back door, 65, 93; damage, 65, 94; degrade,
    94; deny, 94; destroy, 94; entry points, 93;
    front door, 65, 93; high power, xvi, 64,
    90–104, 146; latch-up, 65; lock-up, 65;
    power systems, 65–66; upset, 65; vulnera-
    bility, 95
Middle East, 23
mid-infrared advanced chemical laser
    (MIRACL), 17, 80
military commander, xviii, 8, 49–50, 53, 101,
    135, 137–38, 145–46, 162, 187, 190, 192,
    199, 206, 211
military doctrine, 103, 124, 144, 223
military operations, covert, 4, 95
military power, technological foundation,
    257–68
mines, 57, 60, 98, 147
mirror: bifocal, 28; deformable, 28, 46; laser,
    15–16, 20–21, 24–25, 28–30, 44, 46; orbit-
    ing relay, 16, 20–21, 28–30; primary, 28,
    44, 46
missile: air-to-air, 17, 98; antisatellite kinetic
    energy, 14; antiship cruise, xvi; ASMP, 58;
    ASURA, 58; ballistic, xvii, 3, 7, 13, 15,
    20–21, 23, 31, 40, 43, 44, 48, 78, 95, 107–8,
    115, 144, 191, 209–10, 212, 260–61; cruise,
    xiii–xiv, xvii, xviii, 9, 49, 175, 179–80, 183,
    187, 191, 209, 212; defense, theater ballis-
    tic, 39, 49; Exocet, 58; fuel, 47; Harpoon,
    58, 110, 114; Hsiung Feng II, 58, 114; inter-
    continental ballistic (ICBM), 24, 43, 155; in-
    termediate-range ballistic (IRBM), 23; Mav-
    erick, 190; Minuteman, 167; Patriot, 40, 51,
    119, 123, 228; Peacekeeper, 167; RIM-116A,
    68–69, 72, 74–75; SA-10, 99; SA-8, 98;
    Scud, 23, 40, 59, 109, 111–12, 177, 191–92;
Seasparrow, 72, 75–76; short-range ballistic
    (SRBM), 23; Sidewinder, 5; Silkworm, 58;
    Stinger, 98; Sunburn, 58; surface to air, xvi,
    53, 55, 68, 95, 98, 174, 180; Taep'o-dong
    II, 23; theater ballistic (TBM), 7, 13, 59; V-1,
    111, 121, 188; V-2, 43; vulnerability, 23–24;
    warning and attack assessment, 13
missile defense, xx, 14, 16, 20–37, 39; ancil-
    lary mission, 49; boost phase, 15, 23–24, 39
missile gap, 56
missile proliferation, 22
missile Technology Control Regime (MTCR),
    113–14
Mitchell, General William "Billy," 107
mobile (relocatable) target, 11, 100, 113,
    177–78, 187, 190
Motorola Corporation, 159
munition: conventional, 4, 8, 11–12, 95, 100–1;
    GBU-28, 98; precision guided, 5, 11, 230

National Aeronautics and Space Administra-
    tion (NASA), 13, 29, 157–58, 164
National Aerospace Plane, 156
national command authority, 50, 221
National Defense Panel, 259
national leadership, 144
national missile defense, xv–xvi, 20, 164, 265
National Missile Defense Act, 262
National Research Council, 56, 67
Naval Battle Management Applications Pro-
    gram, 228
naval operations, 55–89
navigation, 111
navy, Great Britain, 61, 73
navy, Soviet Union, 76
Navy, U.S., 55–89, 99, 123, 185, 189, 201,
    220, 226, 228
Nebraska, 209
network centric warfare, information warfare,
    226
networked military, 249
New Mexico, 9, 28
New York, 167
night vision device (NVD), 7, 10, 132
nonlethal technology: xiv, xvii, 72–74, 76,
    129–52, 165, 262, 263; acoustics, 133, 139;
    adventurism, 140–41; antimateriel effects,
    134–36; antipersonnel effects, 132–34;
    characteristics, 136; chemical agents, 132;
    crowd control, 132; deterrence, 140–41;
    doctrine, 148; emerging conflicts, 143;
    employment, 145–49; ethical, 138–40;

nonlethal technology *(continued)*
expectations, 138; just war doctrine, 139; legal, 138–40; major conflict, 144, 147; optical weapons, 132; precision effects, 136; proliferation, 140; repeatable effects, 136; sanctions enforcement, 146; selective effects, 137; supercaustic agents, 134; superlubricants, 134; utility, 137–42

North Atlantic Treaty Organization (NATO), xiii, 74, 108, 192

North Korea, xv, 20, 23, 31, 58, 60, 260, 263, 267

North Vietnam, 265

Norway, 58

Nuclear Nonproliferation Treaty (NPT), 23

Nuclear Suppliers Group, 23

nuclear weapon, xiii, 6, 20–24, 31, 80, 188, 263

Oahu, Hawaii, 64

observe, orient, decide, act (OODA) cycle, 222

Office of Naval Intelligence, 60–61

Office of Naval Research, 62

Offutt Air Force Base, 209

operational: compatibility, 38, 40, 49; strategy, 49; synergy, 49; tempo, xviii, 221, 229

Operation Barbarossa, 119

Operation Desert Storm, 145, 202, 208

Operation Eldorado Canyon, 183

optical: bombs, 133; communication, 4; radiation, 4; sensing, 7–8, 13

orbit: 7–8, 13, 17; geosynchronous, 8, 24, 28–29; low-earth, 28, 162

orbital debris, 13

Orbital Sciences Corporation, 158

organizations, information technology, 229, 245

organized crime, 252

overflight authorization, 118

Pakistan, 23, 60

passive defenses, 120, 123–25

patrol boat, coastal, xvi, 56, 67, 78

Patton, General George S., 233

peace enforcement operations, xvii, 129, 131

peacekeeping and humanitarian operations, xvii, xix, 129–31, 133, 143, 174, 192, 257

Pentagon, 26, 174, 209. *See also* Department of Defense

Persian Gulf War, xiii, 7, 10–11, 20, 23, 40, 91, 98, 109, 111, 115, 117–18, 121, 129, 133, 138, 142, 144, 180, 185, 190, 200–4, 207–8, 210–15, 233, 257, 260, 264

Phalanx Close-In Weapon System, 228

piloted vehicles, advantages, 175, 181–83

Pioneer Corporation, 159

polymer adhesives, 134

Powell, General Colin, 211

power projection, military, 57

precision guided munitions, 4, 11, 42, 97–98, 100–1, 162–3, 230

Project Defender, 62

Project Seaside, 62

proof: of concept, 44; of principle, 42

psychological operations, 10

public support, 118

Quadrennial Defense Review, 259

radar: xvi, 13, 16, 42, 73, 90, 100, 110, 121, 182; cross section, 110; differential absorption laser (DIAL), 9, 11; ground clutter, 110; signature, 61; space-based laser, 13; SPS-48E, 69; synthetic aperture, 214

radiation, 4, 24

radio frequency (RF) weapons, 61, 64–67

rail guns, 64

Ramstein Air Base, 164

rationality, 248

Rayleigh scattering, 63

reachback operations, xviii, 199–219, 263. *See also* Contingency Theater Automated Planning System (CTAPS)

Reagan, President Ronald, 15

rebel forces, 98

reconnaissance, xvii, 186

recursive simplicity, information technology, 244

reentry vehicle (RV), 7, 14–15, 17. *See also* laser; missile defense; national missile defense; nuclear weapon

refueling, spacecraft, 6

remotely operated vehicle, 183, 186

remotely piloted vehicle, 59, 186–87

remote sensing lasers, 3–5, 11–12. *See also* lasers

research laboratories, military, xvi. *See also* Air Force Research Laboratory (AFRL); Lawrence Livermore National Laboratory

responsibility, command, 230. *See also* command and technology; machine commander

retinal injuries, laser, 7. *See also* laser

reusable launch vehicle: xvii, 153–72, 263; commercial program, 159, 166; Common Aero Vehicle, 163; cost, 154, 164; Delta

reusable launch vehicle *(continued)*
Clipper Experimental Advanced (DC-XA),
156; Dynasoar (X-20), 156; Eclipse Astro-
liner, 159; Globalstar, 159; global strike, 162;
global transport, 164; HOPE-X, 160–61;
military uses, 161; National Aerospace
Plane, 156; Pathfinder, 159–60; reconnaissance, 161; Roton, 160; satellite servicing,
164; Skylon, 160; space control, 165;
Spacecab, 160; spacelift, 166–67; Space
Maneuver Vehicle, 159; Space Operations
Vehicle, 153–72; space tourism, 167; VentureStar, 160; X-33, 157–58, 160; X-34, 158
revolution in military affairs, xiii, 174, 220,
246. *See also* technological innovation
risk: reduction, 42, 44; technological, xv, 20, 43
rocket: Delta II, 159; H-IIA, 160; Titan IV,
25–26
rogue states, 21, 23
Rome, 62
Rommel, General Erwin, 232
Roosevelt, President Franklin Delano, 261
Rotary Corporation, 160
Russia, 21, 23, 39, 58–61, 110, 259, 267; mi-
crowaves, 66
Rwanda, 129
Ryan Lightening Bug, 190

Saddam Hussein, 118
sarin, 60, 117
satellite: xiv, xvii, 6–10, 12–13, 17, 26–28, 48,
51, 61, 102, 162, 233; commercial, 9; communications, 6, 48; early-warning, 14–15;
reconnaissance, 9–10, 48; weather, 9
Saudi Arabia, 22, 40, 60, 202, 264
scalability, technological, 42, 44
Schriever Air Force Base, 209
sea control, 57
sealift, 57, 118–19, 123. *See also* airlift
Sea Lite Beam Director, 71
secretary of defense, 230. *See also* Department of Defense
secure communication, 7
Senate, 80, 263
Senate Armed Services Committee Report, 259
sensing: environmental, 12; remote, xv, 17
sensors, 8, 16, 67, 174, 182, 184, 186, 221,
226, 233
Serbia, xiii, xiv, xvii, 107, 115, 183, 257,
265–66, 267. *See also* Kosovo, Yugoslavia
Ship Self-Defense System (SSDS), 69
simulation, 227. *See also* computer

Singapore, 58
situational awareness, 182, 186
solar panel, 7. *See also* satellite
Somalia, 129–30, 133, 257, 265
soman, 60
sortie, 114
South Africa, 58
South Korea, 23, 208
Soviet Union: 15, 20–22, 24, 40, 60, 64, 119,
184, 244; defense spending, 258–59. *See
also* Russia
space, tracking and identifying objects in, 49
space access, 155–56, 168
space-based: antisatellite weapon, 16; ballistic
missile defense, 15; battlefield illumination,
10; counterforce weapon, 14; Integrated
Flight Experiment (IFX), 26, 38; laser (SBL),
20, 24, 30, 38–54, 164, 263; laser radar, 13;
Laser Readiness Demonstrator, 26, 38; laser
surveillance system, 13; laser target designator (SB-LTD), 9, 11, 17; laser weapons, 5;
weapon, 14; Technical Requirements Document, 44
space control, 102, 165–66
space debris, 13
spacelift, 167
space operations vehicles (SOV), commercial
applications, 153–72. *See also* reusable
launch vehicle
space shuttle, 156–57, 167. *See also* reusable
launch vehicle
Space Surveillance Network (SSN), 13. *See
also* satellites
Space Systems/Loral, 159
space tourism, 167
Spain, 60
Special Operations and Low Intensity Conflict, 131
special operations team, 10
Starfire Optical Range, 9, 28, 45. *See also*
antisatellite weapon; laser, ground-based
stealth technology: 42, 56, 58, 60–61, 100,
108, 110, 125, 186; cruise missile, 113
stepping stone, technological, 42–43, 53
strategic bombing, 115. *See also* aircraft
Strategic Command, 91
Strategic Defense Initiative Organization, 41,
156. *See also* Ballistic Missile Defense Organization (BMDO)
stream raid, 69
submarine, 14, 56–57, 60, 73, 76, 78, 117,
226, 259

Sudan, xvii, 108, 112, 115, 267
surveillance, 8, 13, 48–49, 186
sustainment, 52
Sweden, 58, 60
synergism, technological, 42
Syracuse, 61
Syria, 59–60, 267
System of Systems, 123

Tactical Air Command, 200, 213. *See also*
    Langley Air Force Base; reachback opera-
    tions
Taiwan: 58–59; Straits of, 264
target: acquisition, 6, 25; designation, 3, 5, 11;
    high-value, 10; time-critical, 5, 175, 190
targeting: xiv–xvii, 9, 20, 107, 164, 258, 265;
    precision, 11
technological: compatibility, 38, 40–43; inno-
    vation, xiv, xvii–xix, 17, 109, 111–12, 150,
    200, 235, 267; investment, 261–62; matu-
    rity, 21, 262–63; obsolescence, 192
technology, national security, 257–68
technology push, 130
Tel Aviv, 40
telecommunications, xiv, xix, 241. *See also*
    communication
terrorism, 98, 141, 209, 252. *See also* counter-
    terrorism
Theater High-Altitude Area Defense, 51. *See*
    also missile defense; national missile defense
theater of operations, 24, 51–52, 206
thinking machine, 223
time, cruise missile attack, 122–23
time, military decision-making, 221
torpedoes, 60
traceability, technological, 42, 44
tracking system, 16, 25
transporter erector launcher (TEL), 3. *See also*
    missile
Tri-Service Standoff Attack Missile (TSSAM),
    114
TRW Corporation, 45

Ukraine, 58
United Nations Conventions on Prohibitions
    on Conventional Weapons, 73

unity of command, 230
unmanned aerial vehicle: xvii, 14, 79, 80,
    112, 137, 148, 173–95, 263; air-to-air com-
    bat, 191; attacks on mobile targets, 190;
    categories, 176; characteristics, 183; com-
    bat support missions, 191; Dark Star, 99;
    evaluation, 180; Global Hawk, 99, 176–78,
    183, 185, 189; Hunter, 99; intelligence, sur-
    veillance, and reconnaissance (ISR), 189;
    military roles, 189; Pioneer, 185; Predator,
    99, 183–84, 187, 189; transportation, 189
unmanned combat aerial vehicle, 67, 98, 101
USCINCSPACE, 50, 165

Verne, Jules, 62
Vietnam War, 7, 11, 61, 184, 265; casualties,
    118
Virginia, 200, 213
voice-recognition technology, 231
von Clausewitz, Karl, 224, 229. *See also* fog
    of war

war, major theater, 174, 192
war effects confirmation, 98. *See also* battle
    damage assessment
war plans, 199
wartime readiness, 7
Washington, D.C., 209
weaponization, of space, 163, 165
weapons of mass destruction: xv, 21, 56,
    59–60, 117, 122–24, 140, 147, 175, 190,
    210, 221, 261; proliferation, 21. *See also*
    chemical, biological weapon; nuclear
    weapon; missiles
weather monitoring, satellites, xv, 3, 9, 12, 17,
    27, 74, 95, 178, 186, 204
Wells, H. G., 62
wind sensing, 6, 12–13, 49. *See also* laser
World War I, 107, 180, 184, 225, 264
World War II, 76, 111, 121, 142, 178, 184,
    201, 258, 261, 264

Yemen, 109
Yom Kippur War, 184
Yugoslavia, 108. *See also* Kosovo; Serbia